NEW PERSPECTIVES ON INTERNATIONAL MARKETING

Marketing strategy is constantly adapting in the changing environment of International Business. To retain or extend a grasp of existing markets, organizations need to keep abreast of commercial innovation, social change, economic developments, and the ever-shifting political climate. Within this uncertain framework, marketing practices are tried and tested, and succeed or fail.

For this reason, the international marketeer has much to learn from the cutting-edge research presented in *New Perspectives on International Marketing*. Aimed at the reader with at least some prior knowledge of the field, it draws together an eminent and international body of researchers to analyse recent changes in world markets and marketing practices. It analyses, codifies, and challenges existing literature on the subject; it offers industry-specific studies of international marketing practices and their relative successes; and it presents valuable research findings on the increasingly important markets of China and Japan.

New Perspectives on International Marketing is thus a threefold contribution to the study and practice of International Marketing. Blending empirical studies with critical theory, the collection sheds new and much-desired light on this important and often-neglected area. Students, lecturers, and practitioners of International Business and Marketing will find it a very welcome summary of recent developments in their discipline.

Stanley J. Paliwoda is Professor of Marketing at the University of Calgary, Alberta, Canada. His previous publications include *International Marketing, Research in International Marketing* (with Peter Turnbull), and *The AMBA Guide to Business Schools* (with A.C. Harrison).

NEW PERSPECTIVES ON INTERNATIONAL MARKETING

EDITED BY
STANLEY J. PALIWODA

ROUTLEDGE
London and New York

First published 1991
by Routledge
11 New Fetter Lane, London EC4P 4EE

Simultaneously published in the USA and Canada
by Routledge
a division of Routledge, Chapman and Hall, Inc.
29 West 35th Street, New York, NY 10001

Typeset by J&L Composition, Filey, North Yorkshire
Printed and bound in Great Britain by
Mackays of Chatham PLC, Chatham, Kent

British Library Cataloguing in Publication Data
New Perspectives on international marketing.
1. International marketing
I. Paliwoda, Stanley J.
658.848
0–415–05344–7

Library of Congress Cataloging in Publication Data
New Perspectives in international marketing / edited by Stanley J. Paliwoda.
p. cm.
Includes bibliographical references and indexes.
ISBN 0–415–05344–7
1. Export marketing—case studies. 2. Marketing—China—Case studies. 3. Marketing—Japan—Case studies. 4. International business enterprises—Case studies. I. Paliwoda, Stanley J.
HF1416.A38 1991
658.8′48—dc20 90–37092
CIP

CONTENTS

Part II Marketing to China and Japan: research findings

Part III Empirical studies of international marketing that are industry-specific

Table 1.1 Facilitators and inhibitors to the export initiation decision

Decision-maker's characteristics	Level of foreign market orientation Type and level of education Ethnic origin Ability to speak foreign languages Management quality and dynamism Perception of risk in export markets Perception of profits in export markets Perception of costs in export markets
Firm's characteristics	Available staff time Paperwork and management of export operations Type of product line History of the firm Previous extra-regional expansion
Firm's environment characteristics	Rules and regulations of foreign governments Information needed to analyse foreign markets Size of the domestic market Various infrastructural and institutional factors

his/her management quality and dynamism (Groke and Kreidle 1967, Bilkey and Tesar 1977, Ogram 1982), his/her perception of profits (Simpson and Kujawa 1974, Roy and Simpson 1980, Ogram 1982), and his/her perception of costs (Simpson and Kujawa 1974, Roy and Simpson 1980, Brooks and Rosson 1982, Joynt 1982). More specifically, firms with decision-makers possessing foreign market orientation, better type and level of education, foreign country origin, foreign language proficiency, and high management quality and dynamism are more likely to become exporters. In addition, firms with a decision-maker perceiving risk in the export market as being lower versus risk in the domestic market, profits in the export market as being higher versus profits in the domestic market, and costs in the export market as being lower versus costs in the domestic market are more likely to become exporters.

Firm's characteristics which provide another form of facilitators and inhibitors in the export decision are the following: available staff time (Rabino 1980, Cavusgil and Nevin 1980, Cavusgil 1982, Kaynak and Kothari 1984b), the paperwork and management of export operations (Cavusgil and Nevin 1980, Cavusgil 1982, Ogram 1982, Albaum 1983, Kaynak and Kothari 1984b), type of product line (Wiedersheim-Paul *et al.* 1978), history of the firm (Wiedersheim-Paul *et al.* 1978), and previous extra-regional expansion (Wiedersheim-Paul *et al.* 1978, Garnier 1982). More specifically, firms with lack of staff time, preoccupying themselves with day-to-day affairs, perceiving foreign documentation as difficult and enormous, producing a bulky product, having a lack of realized goals, possessing unfavourable past behaviour and actions towards exporting, and undergoing no previous extra-regional expansion, suffer from inhibiting gaps, and are less likely to become exporters.

Facilitators and inhibitors in the firm's decision to go abroad stemming from its environment are the following: rules and regulations of foreign governments (Pavord and Bogart 1975, Bilkey and Tesar 1977, Rabino 1980, Albaum 1983, Kaynak and Kothari 1984b), information needed to analyse foreign markets (Pavord and Bogart 1975, Wiedersheim-Paul *et al.* 1978, Albaum 1983, Kaynak and Kothari 1984b), size of the domestic market (Rabino 1980, Kaynak and Kothari 1984b), and various infrastructural and institutional factors (Bilkey 1978). More precisely, firms producing products which have to be modified in order to conform with the rules and regulations of foreign governments, having lack of information needed to analyse foreign markets, operating in large domestic markets, and facing various infrastructural and institutional obstacles are less likely to become exporters. Table 1.1 summarizes these facilitators and inhibitors.

SHORTCOMINGS IN INITIATION STUDIES

Studies into the initiation of international marketing have served to shed some light on the firm's behaviour before its export debut. However, despite their merits, they suffer from serious deficiencies, particularly linguistic, conceptual, methodological, and statistical.

Linguistic problems appear because often the same variable is expressed in different ways. For instance, international outlook (Aharoni 1966), supranational outlook (Simmonds and Smith 1968), international orientation (Olson and Wiedersheim-Paul 1978), foreign marketing orientation (Reid 1980), and interest in foreign affairs and foreign ways of life (Garnier 1982) are used synonymously. The result of these linguistic problems is confusion and misunderstanding about the variables involved.

INTRODUCTION

This book is aimed at those with some prior knowledge of international marketing, but it arrives at a time when awareness of international marketing amongst people everywhere is greater than ever before. Developments in one country, whether they are commercial innovations, economic changes, or political demands, can spread more quickly than ever before, and to all parts of the world simultaneously, as a result of greatly improved communications. Whenever change takes place, information is sought to try and quantify that change so as to respond to it accordingly. In this book, the contributors have addressed themselves to the tasks of changing marketing practices and changed world markets. In so doing, they question the wisdom of established practice and existing literature.

The book is divided into three parts, entitled:

'Challenging the international marketing literature';
'Studies on marketing to China and Japan'; and
'Empirical studies of international marketing that are industry-specific'

Part I begins with a contribution from Ford and Leonidou, who provide an overview of the literature, interpreting it from a European standpoint. This is not only legitimate, but overdue. Before the foundation of the United States of America, it was the European states which provided the engine for international trade. Today, it remains true that for many European nations, international trade is the most important economic activity in the creation of national wealth. However, this is not the case with the USA, for which foreign trade may constitute only around 10 per cent of national income.

International marketing research within Europe has developed its own direction, where, in addition to studies on exporting and success in exporting, there are also studies which adopt a non-normative perspective. This leads on to the interaction studies of the International Marketing and Purchasing (IMP) Group, on which many of the contributions are based (see Chapter 5 and later). Ford and Leonidou, in reviewing the developments in the literature, discuss the facilitators and inhibitors to the export-initiation decision; the shortcomings of initiation studies; comparisons of export development models; and finally, performance problems and solutions when using overseas distributors.

In chapter 2, Gemünden presents a critical review of fifty empirical studies which have tried to identify critical success factors of export marketing. He describes their main findings, discusses the question whether and how generalizations can be derived from these studies, and proposes outlines for further research.

In chapter 3, Cannon, McKay, and McAuley focus on the international involvement of companies in the Unlisted Securities Market (USM). Background information is presented on the aims of the research study and the methodological approach adopted. They begin with an outline of the major theories of internationalization. The genesis and development of the USM is also summarized. The major focus of this chapter is on the characteristics of international companies in the USM. The findings are derived from an analysis of the annual reports of these companies.

In chapter 4, Burton and Hammoutene explore the notion, commonly held in the literature, that the management contract is or is likely to become an increasingly predominant form of industrial co-operation. They argue that the emphasis which has been placed on the management function *per se*, and on the operational aspects of the 'pure' management contract, has distracted attention away from their primary purpose as technology transfer modes.

In chapter 5, Wilson and Moller trace the development of different theoretical approaches to long-term relationships. Although the IMP concept of interaction has long been accepted as an approach to buyer–seller relationships in Europe, it has only recently attracted attention in North America. A number of North American scholars' work in developing theory in the area of long-term relationships is reviewed. The underlying theories that drive the work of Anderson and Narus, Dwyre, Schurr and Oh, Speckman, Fraser and Johnson, and Erin Anderson, are reviewed, along with the IMP Group work. Wilson and Möller conclude with some directions for future research.

In chapter 6, Hallen and Sandström focus on interaction processes between customers and suppliers in international markets. They argue that these are conditioned not only by the characteristics of the parties, the exchange, and the interaction environment, but also by the emotional setting and atmosphere in which the interaction takes place. The atmosphere is described in six dimensions, namely: power/dependence balance; co-operativeness/competitiveness; truth/opportunism; understanding; closeness/distance; and commitment. These dimensions can be used then to define atmosphere typologies.

In chapter 7, Tornroos also focuses on the concept of distance, defining different aspects of distance in international industrial marketing and evaluating physical, cultural, organizational, and personal distance in the interaction process. Tornroos includes a theoretical basis for further research in this field.

Heidi and Lawrence Wortzel report an empirical study of new product development in an industrializing country, Indonesia. They compare and contrast the new product development process in Indonesia with the process typically observed in an industrialized country, and suggest generalizations applicable to other industrializing countries. In Indonesia, the principal problem is not identifying a product that will sell, but manufacturing it. New products often require purchased parts and capital equipment. In many cases, purchasers expect sellers to help define, organize, and debug the manufacturing process for the new product, as well as to provide parts or machinery. Suppliers tend to be more powerful, and buyers less so, than in the industrialized countries. New product development in industrializing countries represents significant opportunities for supplier firms.

Part II on China and Japan begins with chapter 9, which is an empirical study by Cronin based on thirty-three company interviews in England, and thirty-four in Denmark, which form the basis of a framework of the possible pitfalls that may face an organization seeking to do business with the People's Republic of China (PRC). Likewise, in chapter 10, Schlegelmilch, Diamantopoulos, and Petersen present yet another empirical study, based on forty-nine company respondents. They examine the experience of small- and medium-sized Danish companies in dealing with the PRC. In chapter 11 Johnston examines three alternative approach strategies for buyer–seller relations with the PRC, including: the authorized buying group; the agency representational model; and joint ventures with licensing. Finally, in chapter 12 Holden uses the IMP interaction model and applies it to Japanese buyer–seller relationships to elucidate the distinctively Japanese features.

Part III presents empirical studies of international marketing that are industry-specific. It begins with a chapter by Cunningham and Culligan, who look at competitiveness through networks of relationships in information technology product markets. This examines competition and the competitive process within industrial markets, and seeks to answer the question 'How can firms both create and sustain a competitive advantage?'. The argument advanced is that the sophistication of IT, the increasing rate of change of that technology, and the shifting patterns of international trade and competition have strained the ability of traditional organizational forms to cope. As a result, the network form has arisen as an alternative, and, by implication, a superior mode of organization.

In chapter 14, Frear and Metcalf, drawing upon the IMP Interaction model, examine the marketing–purchasing interface between organizations in the US aircraft engine manufacturing industry. Their findings show that high levels of co-operation and information and social exchange exist between purchasing and marketing organizations. Both buyers and sellers alike perceived their counterparts to be equally willing to exchange information, and to be generally co-operative in their dealings with each other. Perceptions of mutual trust and understanding between purchasing and marketing organizations were found to be equivalent as well. On the other hand, there were significant differences in the perceptions of buyers and sellers with regard to the level of mutual adaptation present within the buyer–seller relationship. This difference in opinion may be due to the power/dependence relationship existing between buyers and sellers in this industry; disproportionate financial strength and knowledge power rests with the purchasing organizations.

In chapter 15, Scheinman examines the explosive growth in US retail car sales of captive imports produced by the foreign subsidiaries or affiliates of Chrysler, Ford, and General Motors. Given a scenario of sluggish growth, Mexico and South Korea will replace Japan as the leading suppliers of captive imports for the US market, producing small cars for Chrysler, Ford, and General Motors. Further increases from Japanese affiliates will be severely constrained by the appreciation of the yen, and by the Voluntary Restraint Agreements.

Chapter 16 describes research into user–producer intermediary interactions in the medical equipment industry. The locus of innovation in the medical equipment industry lies with the user, when state-of-the-art expertise is with the medical researchers/practitioners in their clinical and/or diagnostic expertise. The prime characteristic of the medical equipment innovation process identified by the study is that there are multiple and continuous interactions between users, intermediaries, and producers throughout the process.

Forsström combines the traditional distribution chain approach founded on direct and indirect distribution channels with a competitive framework integrating the Swedish 'market as network' approach. The empirical context is founded on supplier–buyer relationships in the UK magazine paper market, focusing on the changing roles of micro- and macro-positions in the distribution network. The competitive scene in the UK for Finnish suppliers is finally elaborated stressing the Porter line of a strategic short-term framework.

In the final chapter, Easton uses a case study of the Swedish computer imaging industry to describe changes in industrial networks as flow-through nodes.

Part One

CHALLENGING THE INTERNATIONAL MARKETING LITERATURE

Chapter One

RESEARCH DEVELOPMENTS IN INTERNATIONAL MARKETING

A European perspective

DAVID FORD AND LEO LEONIDOU

This paper attempts to examine some of the trends in the literature on international marketing, and, in particular, it concentrates on some of the conceptual and methodological developments in the area. A number of points can be made initially.

First, there is a strong tradition in Europe of research into the dynamics of large-scale international business and the processes of organizational and strategic development within transnationals. Nevertheless, many large European companies are *international* rather than *multinational* in orientation. The difference between these orientations is seen in European companies in (perhaps) an inclination towards stronger centralized control of overseas sales and manufacturing operations than is the case in many US multinationals. This may be the reason why much European research has concentrated on the issues of development from a single country base, and the relationships between headquarter country operations and overseas. This means that it is difficult to draw a clear distinction between some of the 'export literature' and the 'international marketing literature'.

Second, there are perhaps almost as many studies in Europe as in North America into 'Why do companies export?' and 'What makes for success in exports?', etc. However, there is considerable research in Europe which starts from a *non*-normative perspective, and which has used international marketing as a suitable research situation in order to examine the relationships between buying and selling organizations in different circumstances (Hakansson 1982).

Third, and perhaps most important, there is a significantly different conceptual approach to marketing research in Europe. This approach many years ago realized the limitations of the marketing mix view as a way of describing and understanding market activity. Instead of the view of an active seller and a relatively passive buyer implicit in the mix approach, much European research has examined the *interaction* between two active parties, a buyer and a seller. This research is, of course, built in the context of industrial markets, and it involves understanding of the nature of the *relationship* which develops between the parties through their interaction. This approach of examining interaction and relationships also marks a move away from concentrating on the analysis of single purchases, of which the classic 'industrial buyer behaviour model' is the best example. Instead, the research in Europe tends to see each purchase as an 'episode' in the close, or perhaps distant, relationship between the parties. Thus, the purchase can only be understood in the context of the previous and current relationship and the wider 'network' of relationships in which it is enmeshed (Cunningham 1980).

Fourth, the approach to marketing (and international marketing) which emphasizes the examination of relationships has led to a distinctive methodological approach. This approach has relied on large-scale, in-depth empirical studies. For example, the original IMP study in Europe was based on 1,300 interviews. Perhaps, more importantly, the approach has rested on empirical analysis in both the selling and buying parties, to ensure a view of the relationship is obtained as seen from both sides (Hakansson 1982).

Fifth, much of the European research has concentrated on international marketing within Europe and from Europe to US/Japan. However, more recently there has been a tendency to extend these studies. This has occurred in analysis of international marketing from Europe *to* the Third World, and most recently in examining international marketing *from* the Third World to the USA and Europe (Ford and Djeflat 1983 Ford *et al.* 1987).

A REVIEW OF DEVELOPMENTS IN THE LITERATURE

This review is based on the literature which sees international marketing as a process of initiation and development through a series of stages. This is the 'classic' approach to the area and provides a useful context for some of the more recent work on buyer–seller relationships in international markets.

THE INITIATION PROCESS

Much of the published work on international marketing limits itself to describing the firm's initial motives towards export, which are perhaps the most dynamic elements in the decision to 'go international'.

Export stimuli are often classified into those arising within the firm, that is, internal or proactive stimuli, and those exogenous to it, stemming from its environment, that is, external or reactive stimuli (Olson and Wiedersheim-Paul 1978, Wiedersheim-Paul *et al.* 1978, Cavusgil and Nevin 1980). According to Wiedersheim-Paul *et al.* (1978), the above classification of export stimuli is important because 'it provides a framework for examining whether a firm's export start was stimulated mainly by the internal qualities of the firm or due to factors operative in its environment'.

Internal export stimuli are any excess capacity in the firm's resources (for example management, marketing, production, and finance) and/or any unique competence, for instance product superiority (Olson and Wiedersheim-Paul 1978, Wiedersheim-Paul *et al.* 1978). On the other hand, external export stimuli are unsolicited orders from foreign customers, entry of domestic competitors into foreign markets, increase of competition in the domestic market caused by domestic or foreign competitors, government stimulation measures, and various market opportunities (Simpson and Kujawa 1974, Wiedersheim-Paul *et al.* 1978, Olson and Wiedersheim-Paul 1978).

The decision to export which has been stimulated by internal or proactive stimuli is characterized as rational, objective-oriented behaviour, and a problem-oriented adoption process, while the stimulation of the export decision by external or reactive stimuli is described as less rational, less objective-oriented behaviour, and innovation-oriented adoption process (Simpson and Kujawa 1974, Lee and Brasch 1978).

A large number of research studies have been conducted in order to find out the kind of stimuli which influence the firm's export decision (Simpson and Kujawa 1974, Tesar and Tarleton 1982, Joynt 1982, Brooks and Rosson 1982). A summary of their findings indicates that the company's export initiation is stimulated by both internal or proactive, and external or reactive factors, which appear with *different* rank order in each case. Of significance is the fact that among the external or reactive stimuli, the most popular was an unsolicited order from a foreign customer (Groke and Kreidle 1967, Simmonds and Smith 1968, Simpson and Kujawa 1974, Pavord and Bogart 1975, Tesar 1975, Welch and Wiedersheim-Paul 1980). This is the first indication in the literature of the recognition of the active customer.

Despite the importance of the export stimulus in the export decision, its existence or its emergence is a necessary but *not* sufficient condition for the firm's decision to look abroad (Aharoni 1966, Simpson and Kujawa 1974). Rather, 'it depends on various feelings and social and organizational structures, on previous events in the company's history and on other problem areas facing the company' at the time this stimulus has arisen (Aharoni 1966). In other words, only in conjunction with certain opinions and attitudes of the decision-makers concerned will these latent motives become effective. The decision-maker's opinion and attitude towards exporting is influenced by facilitating and inhibiting factors which are derived mainly from three major areas: the decision-maker's characteristics, the firm's characteristics, and the firm's environmental characteristics (Wiedersheim-Paul *et al.* 1978, Brooks and Rosson 1982, Garnier 1982). These are summarized in table 1.1.

A number of facilitators and inhibitors to the export decision can be seen in the literature. Examples are the decision-maker's foreign market orientation (Wiedersheim-Paul *et al.* 1978, Cavusgil and Nevin 1980), his/her type and level of education (Brooks and Rosson 1982, Garnier 1982), his/her ethnic origin (Simmonds and Smith 1968, Garnier 1982), his/her ability to speak foreign languages (Brooks and Rosson 1982, Joynt 1982),

Conceptual problems represent another form of confusion and inconsistency. For instance, what is defined as an external stimulus by Kaynak and Stevenson (1982), is considered as an internal stimulus by other researchers in the field (Aharoni 1966, Simpson and Kujawa 1974, Wiedersheim-Paul *et al.* 1978, Brooks and Rosson 1982).

Methodological problems appear in different forms in these studies. One form is their *ex post facto* character which is criticized by other researchers: 'The recall of experienced export managers concerning preceding events, attitudes, background, etc., which in their firms led up to an export decision, seems unsuitable not only on memory–psychological, but also on dissonance–theoretical grounds, as a basis for formulating constructs' (Dichtl *et al.* 1983).

Another methodological flaw of these studies stems from the lack of attempts to operationalize in an efficient and effective way the variables used by the researchers. In contrast, most of them prefer the quick and easy way, to use the same variable operationalization as previous studies did, which sometimes is too superficial and inadequate.

Other methodological problems are related to the different criteria used to classify firms according to their size, the absence of non-exporters from some studies, and the definitions given to an exporter and/or non-exporter.

Statistical problems arise from the different statistical methods employed and the size of the study sample. With regard to these issues, these studies have been improved over time. More precisely, the first studies on export initiation in the 1960s were unsophisticated, conveniently small sample studies, while the most recent ones are characterized by relatively large samples, tested by univariate or multivariate statistical techniques. However, the use of non-parametric statistical techniques was relatively limited in these studies, despite the fact that their research design had a qualitative nature (Albaum and Peterson 1984).

FACTORS AND OBSTACLES TO SUCCESS IN INTERNATIONAL SALES

Another major stream of the international marketing literature deals with the identification of the factors associated with success in exporting and the various obstacles which hinder it. Factors and obstacles to export success fall into one of the following categories: environmental, organizational, managerial, strategic, and functional. These are summarized in table 1.2.

Table 1.2 Factors and obstacles to export success

Environmental	Cultural differences
	Government barriers
	Infrastructural facilities
	Availability of export services
	Regularity of supplies
	Degree of competition
Organizational	Amount and quality of export staffing
	Size of the firm
Managerial	Level of management quality and determination
	Marketing vs. selling orientation in exporting
	Long-term vs. short-term commitment to exporting
	Frequency of personal visits to foreign markets
	Degree of management's international outlook
	Foreign language proficiency of export executives
	Frequency and clarity of communication with customers
Strategic	Degree of product and packaging adaptation
	Level of product quality and design
	Product delivery performance
	Pricing practices in foreign markets
	Extent of overseas promotion
	Degree of promotion adaptation
	Selection of the right overseas distribution channel
Functional	Level and use of export marketing research
	Existence and adequacy of export market plans
	Availability of sources to finance the export effort

Environmental factors and obstacles include cultural differences between home and export markets (Ricks *et al.* 1974, Douglas and Dubois 1977, Jackson 1981, Elbashier and Nicholls 1983, Hooley and Newcomb 1983, Johanson and Nonaka 1983), government barriers (Rabino 1980, Kaynak and Kothari 1984a), infrastructural facilities (Green 1982), availability of export services by various institutions, governmental or not (Tookey 1964, Cunningham and Spigel 1971, Johanson and Nonaka 1983), regularity of supplies (BETRO Trust Committee 1976, Jackson 1981), and degree of competition in foreign markets

(Alexandrides 1971, Kaynak and Kothari 1984a). More specifically, exporters which do not appreciate the existence of cultural differences in foreign markets, exporting to countries where there are tariff or non-tariff barriers for their products, and where there is a lack of infrastructural facilities (such as an efficient transportation and communication system), with limited access to and availability of export services in their country, with irregular supplies of raw materials, and with keen competition in foreign markets, reduce their chances for successful export operations.

Organizational factors and obstacles include the amount and quality of export staffing (Tookey *et al.* 1967, Hunt *et al.* 1970, Tookey 1975, BETRO Trust Committee 1976, Hooley and Newcomb 1983), and the size of the firm (Tookey 1964, Hunt *et al.* 1970). In other words, exporters with an adequate number and high quality of export sales staff and large firm size (which provides them with financial, manpower, marketing and production advantages) have more chances to be successful in exporting. This statement does not imply that small firms cannot be successful. In fact, some studies showed that export success is not limited to large firms, but it is extended to small- and medium-sized firms as well (Groke and Kreidle 1967, Bilkey and Tesar 1977).

Managerial factors and obstacles are perhaps the most crucial among the other groups, because of their immediate role in formulating the firm's policies and objectives. This category includes the following: the level of management quality and determination related with exporting (Hunt *et al.* 1970, Paulden 1976, Jackson 1981, Czinkota and Johnston 1983), the adoption of either marketing or selling orientation in exporting (Meidan 1975, Baker 1979, Hooley and Newcomb 1983, Johanson and Nonaka 1983, Kaynak and Kothari 1984a), the adoption of either long-term or short-term commitment to exporting (Tookey *et al.* 1967, Tookey 1975; Jackson 1981, Hooley and Newcomb 1983, Johanson and Nonaka 1983, Czinkota and Johnston 1983), the frequency of personal visits of company executives to their foreign markets (Root 1964, Cunningham and Spigel 1971, Tookey 1975, BETRO Trust Committee 1976, ITI Research 1979, Jackson 1981, Kaynak and Kothari 1984a), the adoption of an international outlook by the management

(Cunningham and Spigel 1971, Tookey 1975, Czinkota and Johnston 1983), the foreign language proficiency of the export staff (Cunningham and Spigel 1971, Suntook 1978, Mason 1980, Hooley and Newcomb 1983), and the frequency and clarity of the communication with foreign customers (Rabino 1980, Jackson 1981, Kaynak and Kothari 1984b). More specifically, exporters with high quality management and with the determination to succeed in international markets, possessing a marketing orientation in exporting, committing themselves to exporting with a long-term emphasis, frequently visiting their foreign markets, with internationally oriented management philosophy, with a high foreign language fluency by their export staff, and with frequent and clear communication with their foreign customers, are more likely to have a successful export business.

Strategic factors and obstacles to export success relate mainly to the elements of the export marketing mix, namely product, price, promotion, and distribution channels. This category includes the degree of product and packaging adaptation according to the requirements of foreign customers (Tookey 1964, Root 1964, Groke and Kreidle 1967, Kacker 1975, Alexandrides and Moschis 1977, Hooley and Newcomb 1983, Elbashier and Nicholls 1983, Kaynak and Kothari 1984a), the level of product quality and design (Tookey 1964, Cunningham and Spigel 1971, Piercy 1981, Kaynak and Kothari 1984, Johanson and Nonaka 1983), the product delivery performance (Thomas 1969, ITI Research 1979, Hooley and Newcomb 1983), the pricing practices followed in export markets (Root 1964, BETRO Trust Committee 1976, ITI Research 1979, Piercy 1981, Hooley and Newcomb 1983, Johanson and Nonaka 1983, Kaynak and Kothari 1984a), the extent of overseas promotion (Tookey 1964, Cunningham and Spigel 1971, Alexandrides and Moschis 1977, ITI Research 1979), the degree of promotion adaptation to foreign markets (Root 1964, Douglas and Dubois 1977, Elbashier and Nicholls 1983, Hooley and Newcomb 1983, Johanson and Nonaka 1983), and the selection of the right channel of distribution (Root 1964, Hunt *et al.* 1970, Cunningham and Spigel 1971, Tookey 1975, Alexandrides and Moschis 1977, Rabino 1980, Elbashier and Nicholls 1983, Kaynak and Kothari 1984a). More precisely, exporters with high product quality and design, with consistent product delivery to foreign customers with products, packaging, and promotion policies appropriately adapted to meet the specific needs of each foreign market, with pricing practices more suitable to the foreign market's situation, with extensive overseas promotion, and with reliable overseas distributors are more likely to have successful foreign activities.

Functional factors and obstacles to the firm's export success are: the level and use of marketing research in export markets (Root 1964, Hunt *et al.* 1970, Pointon 1978, ITI Research 1979, Jackson 1981, Hooley and Newcomb 1983), the existence and adequacy of export market plans (Root 1964, Hunt *et al.* 1970, Jackson 1981, Garnier 1982, Kaynak and Kothari 1984b), and the availability of sources to finance the export marketing effort (Tookey 1975, BETRO Trust Committee 1976, Kaynak and Kothari 1984b). In other words, exporters with a low level and use of export marketing research, with ineffective or non-existent export market plans, and with scarce sources to finance their export marketing effort are less likely to be successful in their foreign markets.

SHORTCOMINGS IN THE STUDIES OF FACTORS AND OBSTACLES IN EXPORT SUCCESS

The studies conducted to identify the factors and obstacles in export success suffer from certain shortcomings, which are mainly *methodological*.

The major shortcoming is the difficulty of defining whether an exporter is successful or not. The majority of the studies in the field measure success as the proportion of export sales to the firm's total sales, usually over a certain period of time (Tookey 1964, Hirsch 1971, Cunningham and Spigel 1971, McFarlane 1978). Despite the 'objective' character of this measure, 'it gives little or no clue as to whether a firm is grasping all the profitable opportunities open to it' (Hunt *et al.* 1970). Reid (1981) suggests that export performance measures should be a combination of growth, absolute level of exports, relative growth of export sales, rate of new market expansion, and rate of new product introduction into foreign markets. Besides, the measurement of export success involves not only objective, but subjective criteria as well.

Operationalization of the variables in these studies is another methodological flaw. In general, there was no serious attempt to operationalize effectively and efficiently the variables used, although there were some suggestions of how to achieve that. For instance, Meidan (1975) provides a tool – the export marketing matrix – for differentiating between firms which are marketing-oriented and those export- (sale-) oriented in their overseas markets activities; this tool has not been used so far. This indicates a lack of interest in making more sophisticated attempts to operationalize the variables used and to depart from the status quo of the simple approaches.

Another interesting point, concerning these studies, is the lack of attention among researchers on the findings of previous studies. According to Cavusgil and Nevin (1980) 'literally dozens of "studies" have been conducted on the obstacles encountered by firms in export marketing. Some even claim to be pioneering. A tradition of building upon the findings of previous research is not well established in international marketing.'

The classification of firms according to their size is another shortcoming of these studies. Some researchers classify the firms in their studies according to the number of employees (for example Tookey 1964), while others classify them according to their sales turnover (for example Cunningham and Spigel 1971). As a result, the terms small, medium, and large firms are very flexible.

Another methodological flaw stems from the 'checklist' approach in conducting research. More specifically, the prepared checklist of factors and obstacles in export success from which the respondent is asked to pick and choose, is a limiting factor of his/her views about the specific area.

The influence of uncontrollable variables on the research findings is another flaw. It has been postulated that the results of the empirical studies in export success might reflect the influence of various non-controllable factors, such as recession in the economy, exchange rate fluctuations, etc. (Amine and Cavusgil 1983).

Finally, the majority of these studies underestimate the significant role of the importer/overseas agent as one of the most crucial determinants of export success, which make it an 'incomplete analysis' (Cavusgil and Nevin 1980).

EXPORT DEVELOPMENT MODELS

In the last decade several attempts have been made in order to explain the firm's export development process. Most of these attempts have been confined to 'single activity models' dealing with the firm's export behaviour over a long time period (Bilkey 1978).

Up to now, there are four popular models explaining the export development process: those of Johanson and Wiedersheim-Paul (1975), Bilkey and Tesar (1977), Cavusgil (1980), and Czinkota (1982).

All four models adopt a 'stages approach', but are built on different criteria. Figure 1.1 illustrates the export development stages of each model. In addition, an attempt is made to find any corresponding stages among the models, bearing in mind the limitations imposed by the criteria set for each model. A comparison among the four models indicates that some of their stages are identical, others are completely different, while others overlap. These observations should be treated with caution, because the 'demarcation' line of each stage was determined by rough approximation.

Despite the different criteria employed in each of the four models, some commonalities are identifiable. These common grounds are the incremental character of the internationalization process, the concept of psychic distance, the commitment of resources, the ongoing export motivations and the ongoing obstacles to exporting.

INCREMENTAL CHARACTER OF THE INTERNATIONALIZATION PROCESS OF THE FIRM

The internationalization process of the firm is an incremental/sequential process, which means that the firm progresses along the export path on a step by step basis (Johanson and Wiedersheim-Paul 1975, Bilkey and Tesar 1977, Cavusgil and Nevin 1980, Cavusgil 1982). In the four models, the developmental character of the export process is conceptualized either as a *learning sequence*, that is, the firm moves forward only after a long process of learning about foreign markets and operations, or as *export stages*.

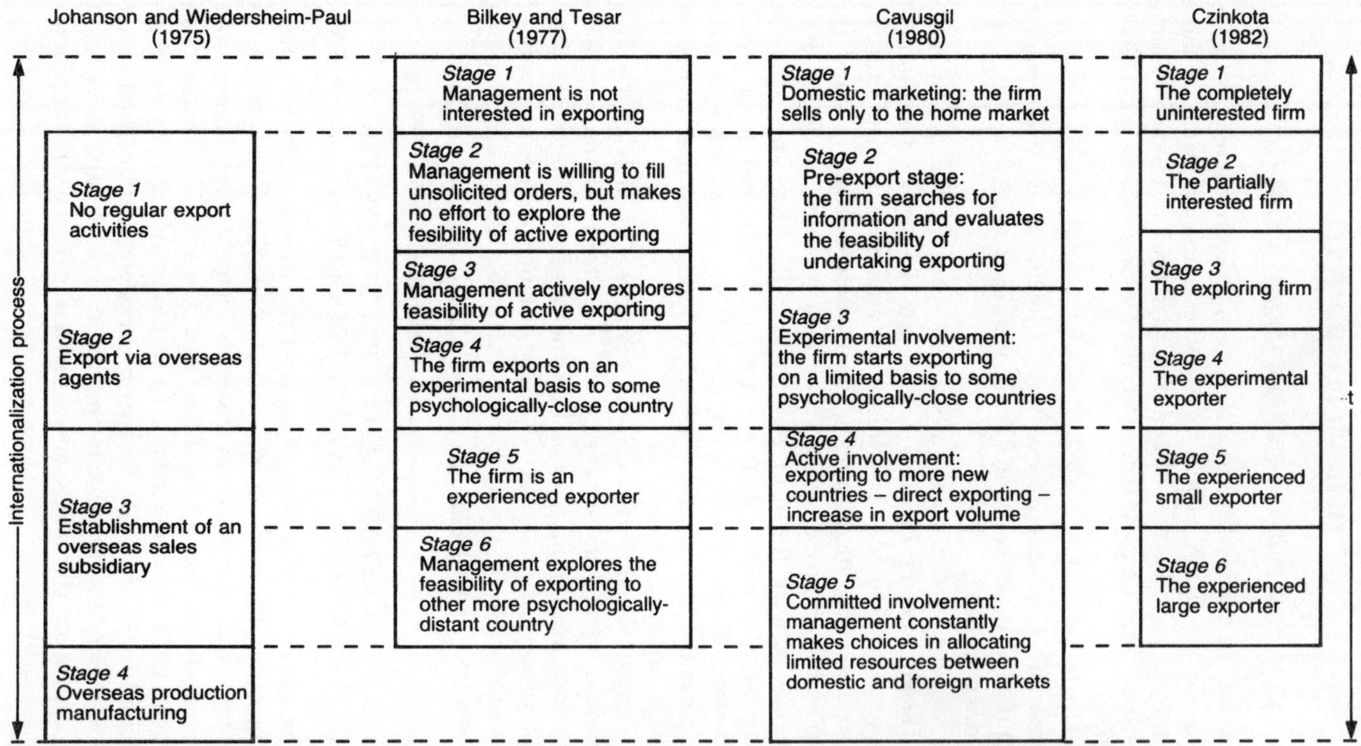

Figure 1.1 Comparison of the export development models

The gradual nature of the firm's internationalization process is attributed mainly to two reasons. First, it is the lack of and difficulty in gathering market information in international operations (Johanson and Vahlne 1977). The second reason concerns the lack of 'experiential knowledge' by the firm, which is the knowledge learned through experience in foreign activities (Johanson and Vahlne 1977, Cavusgil and Nevin 1980, Cavusgil 1982). As a result of both, there is an uncertainty associated with the international markets which 'is reduced through increases in interaction and integration with the market environment – steps such as increases in communication with customers, establishment of new service activities, or in the extreme case, the taking over of customers' (Johanson and Vahlne 1977: 29). Therefore, the existence of uncertainty which is inversely related with the availability of information and 'experiential knowledge' about foreign operations, is the determinant for incremental international decisions.

PSYCHIC DISTANCE

Closely related to the learning nature of the firm's internationalization process is the concept of 'psychic distance' which is defined as 'the sum of factors preventing the flows of information from and to the market, for example differences in language, education, business practices, culture, industrial development, etc.' (Johanson and Vahlne 1977: 24).

The relationship of psychic distance with the firm's learning process in international operations implies that firms at the early stages of their internationalization process concentrate their efforts on psychologically close countries, while firms at the later stages extend their activities to psychologically more distant countries.

RESOURCE COMMITMENT

Another commonality of the four models is the amount of resources which are committed to international operations over time. The models suggest that firms have a tendency to increase their resource commitment to foreign operations the further the firm moves along the export path.

Resource commitment to exporting comes in various forms, such as the management time devoted to exporting, the number of personnel engaged in exporting, the existence of separate departments for exporting, and the amount of funds allocated to exporting (Groke and Kreidle 1967, Johanson and Wiedersheim-Paul 1975, Cavusgil 1982).

The method of overseas distribution is perhaps one of the most crucial indicators of the firm's degree of commitment to exporting. It has been proposed that firms begin export operations via indirect distribution methods (an indication of low resource commitment) and switch to direct exporting methods (an indication of high resource commitment) over time (Johanson and Wiedersheim-Paul 1975, Cavusgil 1982). This proposition has been confirmed empirically in the study of Brady and Bearden (1979).

CONTINUING MOTIVATIONAL FACTORS

The type and significance of the firm's motives for export development change over time (Czinkota and Johnston 1981, Johnston and Czinkota 1982). In other words, the set of motivational factors at one export stage will be different from that of another stage of the firm's internationalization process.

Continuing motivational factors for exporting are usually classified into two broad categories: proactive and reactive. This typology corresponds to the internal/external typology used for the firm's export initiation stimuli.

Proactive motives include active or aggressive export behaviour based on the firm's internal situation. This category includes a list of on-going motivational factors such as exclusive information, managerial urge, unique products, profit advantage, marketing advantage, and technological advantage.

Reactive motives stem from a reactive firm's behaviour to environmental or outside change. Competitive pressures over production, declining domestic sales, excess capacity, and saturated domestic market are some on-going motivational factors which belong to this category.

CONTINUING OBSTACLES TO EXPORTING

The firm's internationalization process is hindered by certain barriers. Continuing obstacles to exporting tend to differ systematically by export stage (Bilkey and Tesar 1977, Cavusgil 1982, Czinkota 1982). More specifically, some of these obstacles increase their gravity over time, whereas others decrease their presence.

Most of the continuing obstacles to exporting have been mentioned before. A quick review of them produces the following list: difficulty in obtaining funds necessary to finance export sales (Bilkey and Tesar 1977, Ogram 1982), difficulty in obtaining adequate representation in foreign markets (Bilkey and Tesar 1977, Rabino 1980, Tesar and Tarleton 1982, Kaynak and Stevenson 1982, Kaynak and Kothari 1984b), difficulty in understanding foreign business practices (Groke and Kreidle 1967, Alexandrides 1971, Bilkey and Tesar 1977, Tesar and Tarleton 1982, Ogram 1982), foreign government restrictions (Groke and Kreidle 1967, Bilkey and Tesar 1977, Rabino 1980, Tesar and Tarleton 1982, Kaynak and Stevenson 1982, Kaynak and Kothari 1984b), troublesome export documentation and paperwork (Groke and Kreidle 1967, Alexandrides 1971, Ogram 1982), keen competition in foreign markets (Alexandrides 1971, Ogram 1982, Kaynak and Stevenson 1982, Kaynak and Kothari 1984b), difficulty in collecting money from foreign markets (Bilkey and Tesar 1977, Tesar and Tarleton 1982), and communication problems with foreign customers (Rabino 1980, Kaynak and Stevenson 1982, Kaynak and Kothari 1984b).

SHORTCOMINGS OF THE EXPORT DEVELOPMENT MODELS

The export development models presented have an immense value, not only because they shed light on the firm's internationalization process, but also because they provide useful information and guidelines to policy makers planning export promotion programmes at the national or regional level. Another positive aspect of these models is their successive improvement, which indicates an ability to build upon the findings of previous researchers. However, export development models suffer from certain theoretical and methodological flaws.

Some of the theoretical shortcomings stem from the 'stages approach' adopted by these models. More specifically, the latter describe the firm's characteristics and management's behaviour towards exporting at each stage, but they do *not* explain the dynamics of the firm's progression from one export stage to another (Ford *et al.* 1982). In addition, these models lack clearcut definitions of the boundaries of each stage in the internationalization process.

The stages models presented suffer also from causality problems. In other words, the direction of the cause-and-effect relationships of the variables used is not clearly defined.

Other shortcomings are related to the *empirical* testing of these models. In general, the empirical verification of the presented models is considered as too simplistic compared with their relatively complex character (Dichtl *et al.* 1983). One interesting point, concerning the empirical validation of the internationalization process models, is the absence of longitudinal studies. The latter are the most appropriate to dynamic and prolonged models such as the ones presented.

BUYER–SELLER RELATIONSHIPS IN EXPORT MARKETS

Behaviour research in the form of buyer–seller relationships in export markets has perhaps the most contemporary nature in the export marketing literature. The studies conducted in this area depart from the traditional way of examining exporting from the point of view of the exporting firm and/or would-be exporter only. Rather, they take into consideration both sides in the 'trading equation', that is, exporters and importers, and investigate their relationships based on such behavioural concepts as power, cooperation, conflict, satisfaction and performance.

Ahmed (1977) is considered as among the first to introduce the 'dyadic' buyer–seller analysis in international markets. In his study among foreign automobile manufacturers and their American distributors, he found that the manufacturer's success is related positively with the exercise of control over their respective dealers. Despite this, the pioneer character of Ahmed's study is considered as simplistic in both theoretical and methodological terms.

An early study in this area is provided by Hakansson and Wootz (1975) which examined some of the issues in the relationship between international buying and selling companies, from the perspective of the importer. Later, the IMP Group carried out a major study into buyer–seller relationships between five European countries (Hakansson 1982).

Subsequent analysis of this and other following studies have shown the importance in understanding international operations of analysis of market and customer commitment, adaptation, power, conflict, and expectations. Additionally, the work has led to analysis of the stages in the development of a relationship between a company and its markets and individual customers (Ford 1980, Ford and Rosson 1982). An overall review of the implications of this work for international marketing is provided by Cunningham (1985).

In the last five years, more sophisticated studies have been executed with regard to the manufacturer–import customer relationships. These studies are confined mainly to industrial product markets and they draw issues from inter-organizational theory, the new institutional economic theory, industrial buyer behaviour, and distribution channel behaviour. They adopt a dyadic interaction approach, and they are characterized as employing improvements in operationalizing the concepts used and in empirical testing.

Rosson and Ford (1980) investigated the issues of stake, conflict, and performance among Canadian export manufacturing firms and their overseas distributors in the United Kingdom. In their research, strong support was found for the hypothesis that low levels of conflict are associated with high performance, while moderate support was found for the notion that low levels of conflict are associated with high manufacturer dependency.

Rosson and Ford (1982) extended their investigations on manufacturer–overseas distributor relationships and their effect on export performance, with the construction of a model. The model has three components:

(a) the participant variables: stake, experience and uncertainty;
(b) the relationship dimensions: formalization, standardization, reciprocity, intensity and conflict: it has been stated that the intensity of the relationship and the formalization of the parties' responsibility to it are indicators of the *commitment* to the relationship; similarly, the *adaptability* of the two parties is expressed by the degree of standardization

in intercompany relations and of reciprocity in decision making;

(c) the single outcome component, which is the performance of the relationship.

Rosson and Ford found that successful manufacturer–overseas distributor dyads are those which exhibit the following relationship characteristics: more formalization, less standardization, more reciprocity, more contact and resource intensity, and less conflict. This in turn implies that the ingredients of successful relationships between manufacturers and their overseas distributors are high levels of adaptation and commitment and low levels of intercompany tension and disagreement.

It was also found that the *state* of the manufacturer–overseas distributor relationship development is seriously affected by the extent to which the other party will make commitments and adaptations. The study findings developed Ford's original model of buyer–seller relationship development. It indicates that five stages can be identified in the development of a relationship, that is, new, growing, troubled, static and inert.

Rosson (1984) classified the performance inhibitors in manufacturer–overseas distributor relationships into three broad categories: separate ownership, geographic and cultural separation and different rules of law. The individual problems of each category and the suggested remedies are presented in figure 1.2.

A study conducted by Ford and Djeflat (1983) examines the relationships between high technology sellers from developed countries and low technology buyers from developing countries in industrial markets. The study attempted to shed some light on the association of conflict and co-operation with success in the buyer–seller relationship, as this is perceived by both parties. The findings showed a negative correlation between conflict in the relationship and success, and a positive relationship between co-operation in the relationship and success (where success was measured by each member's satisfaction with the relationship). However, the hypotheses set by the authors had not been fully validated, revealing the complexities which arise in the associations between conflict, co-operation, and success.

High export performance inhibitors →	bring →	remedy lies in
Separate ownership	• divided loyalties • seller–buyer atmosphere • unclear future intentions	offering good incentives, helpful support schemes; discussing plans frankly and interacting in a mutually beneficial way
Geographic and cultural separation	• communication blocks • negative attitudes towards foreigners • physical distribution strains	making judicious use of two-way visits; establishing a well managed communication programme
Different rules of law	• vertical trading restrictions • dismissal difficulties	full compliance with the law; drafting a strong distributor agreement

Figure 1.2 Performance problems and remedies when using overseas distributors

More recently, the interaction approach has been extended to studies of buyer–seller relationships in international markets between vendors in the Third World and customers in the West (Ford *et al.* 1987).

SHORTCOMINGS IN BUYER–SELLER RELATIONSHIPS STUDIES

The buyer–seller relationships studies in export markets underline the crucial role of behavioural factors in affecting export performance. Despite their value, these studies suffer from certain shortcomings and limitations.

As far as the concepts used are concerned, these studies do not investigate the causality of the relationships between the variables. Rather, they assume a certain route of cause and effect, which sometimes can lead to misconceptions and inconsistencies. The problem of causality is not restricted only to these studies, but is also a common problem among the other areas of the export marketing literature, such as the export development models.

Another flaw stems from the lack of longitudinal research. In spite of the long lasting and dynamic phenomena that these studies investigate, so far there has been little attempt by researchers in this field to gather data on a longitudinal basis for empirical validation. This is mainly attributed to financial and time constraints, which confine the researcher to short-time length studies. An exception is provided by Rosson (1985).

The studies are also limited to the export marketing of industrial products. So far, few attempts have been made to examine the exporter–importer relationships in consumer markets, an area which is also crucial in international trade in general and LDCs' foreign trade in particular. One exception is provided by Leonidou (1987).

SOME CONCLUSIONS ON THE DIRECTION OF FUTURE RESEARCH

The preceding review of the literature emphasizes its growing, fragmentary, and unprogrammatic character. In addition, certain theoretical and methodological shortcomings have been identified which, as a result, have created incomplete and/or inconsistent insights in the field of exporting and international marketing development. We can now try to identify some of the gaps in the literature and indicate ways in which they might be filled.

The need to conduct more research at the micro-level

There is a need for research to be oriented at the micro-business level of exporting, because it 'offers the greatest attraction to decision makers and marketing specialists alike, since it is more accessible and certainly more relevant to the day-to-day policy decisions of exporters' (Amine and Cavusgil 1983).

The need for conceptual clarity

Concepts related to exporting should be stated in a clear and scientific way in order to facilitate communication among researchers and avoid misconceptions in the field. Attempts to use the same concepts in different meanings create more confusion in and delay the promotion of knowledge about exporting.

The need for common linguistic expression

It has been demonstrated that export literature suffers from linguistic problems, in the form that the same notion is expressed in various linguistic versions. As a result, more confusion and misunderstanding is created among export researchers. What is needed here is the uniform and precise expression of statements concerning exporting. In addition, a standardization of constructs and definitions in the field should be developed, which should be respected by all researchers.

The need to build upon the findings of others

Repetition and/or similarity of studies is very common in the export marketing field. This indicates that there is a lack of attempt to build upon the findings of others. What is needed is to promote the knowledge about exporting, through the execution of pioneer studies based on the findings of previous studies (Cavusgil and Nevin 1980).

The need to minimize the impact of the uncontrollable variables on the analysis

It has been postulated that the will to apply 'scientific method' to export marketing research is very often hindered by the sheer number of uncontrollable variables (Amine and Cavusgil 1983). What is needed is to minimize the impact of these variables on the research analysis by conducting, for example, laboratory studies (Thomas and Araujo 1985).

The need to develop more effective and efficient ways to operationalize the controllable variables

If the research findings of export studies were to reflect more realistic situations, the controllable variables should be operationalized in a more effective and efficient manner. New studies about exporting should employ better operationalization methods compared with those adopted by previous studies in the field (Dichtl *et al*, 1983). In addition, researchers should be encouraged to provide information about the operationalization of their research designs, in order to permit independent evaluation of research quality and facilitate extension of the research.

The need to specify the causality of the variables used

Causality problems represent a major drawback for some areas of the export marketing literature. Therefore, more attempts should be made by researchers in the field, in order to specify the direction of the cause-and-effect relations among the controllable variables used.

The need for longitudinal studies

Some parts of the export marketing literature deal with phenomena which have a dynamic and long lasting nature. However, there is a 'myopic' habit among the researchers in the field to use ephemeral studies in order to investigate these (Kaynak and Kothari 1984a). What is needed is the execution of longitudinal studies which could examine these phenomena over time (Cavusgil and Nevin 1980, Czinkota 1982, Thomas and Araujo 1985).

The need to treat with caution ex post facto *analysis on export behaviour studies*

Ex post facto analysis is very popular among researchers in empirical studies on export behaviour. There is a need to treat with caution *ex post facto* analysis on behaviour concepts in exporting. This kind of analysis is risky and inaccurate, mainly because the assessment of past behaviour is biased by present actions (Dichtl *et al.* 1983).

The need to employ appropriate statistical techniques

Some parts of the export marketing literature are characterized by a relatively high level of conceptual complexity and a corresponding relatively low level of statistical testing (Dichtl *et al.* 1983). It is necessary to bring to the same level the conceptual complexity suggested and the statistical techniques employed, in order to avoid misleading and/or unreliable research findings. For instance, greater use of non-parametric statistical techniques should be employed, especially in research studies with a qualitative character (Albaum and Peterson 1984).

The need to conduct export marketing studies in LDCs

The overwhelming majority of the export marketing studies were conducted in the developed economies of Europe and North America. Few attempts have been made so far to examine export marketing in the LDCs of the world, which is perhaps a very crucial and critical area due to their chronic deficits in their balance of payments and their striving for economic development. Therefore, more research effort should be directed to the world's developing economies, in order to provide guidelines for export promotion and success in these countries.

The need for more behavioural studies in the form of buyer–seller relationships in export markets

Behavioural research in export marketing, in the form of buyer–seller relationships in export markets, is relatively 'complete' in analysis comparing with other studies, because it takes into consideration both partners in the trading equation (Cavusgil and Nevin 1980). More research in this area will be of invaluable importance, particularly if the research effort is concentrated on the investigation of manufacturer–overseas distributor relationships in export consumer markets.

The need to develop export marketing thought from other disciplines

The field of export marketing is far behind the level of maturity in the development of a body of conceptual work. It has been postulated that 'export marketing' today is at the same stage of conceptual development as 'marketing' was in the 1930s (Ryans and Woudenberg 1977). What is needed is to develop export marketing thought via contributions from other business and social science disciplines, such as economic theory, development economics, organization theory, and marketing theory.

REFERENCES

Aharoni, Y. (1966) *The Foreign Investment Decision Process*, Cambridge, MA: Harvard University Press.

Ahmed, A. A. (1977) 'Channel control in international markets', *European Journal of Marketing* 11: 327–35.

Albaum, G. (1983) 'Effectiveness of government export assistance for US smaller-sized manufacturers: some further evidence', *International Marketing Review* 1: 68–75.

Albaum, G. and Peterson, R. (1984), 'Empirical research in international marketing, 1976–82', *Journal of International Business Studies* (Spring/Summer): 161–73.

Alexandrides, C. G. (1971) 'How the major obstacles to expansion can be overcome', *Atlantic Economic Review* (May): 12–15.

Alexandrides, C. G. and Moschis, G. P. (1977) *Export Marketing Management*, New York: Praeger.

Amine, L. S. and Cavusgil, S. T. (1983) 'Exploring strategic aspects of export marketing', *International Marketing Review* 1: 5–11.

Baker, M. J. (1979) 'Export myopia', *The Quarterly Review of Marketing* (Spring): 1–10.

BETRO Trust Committee (1976) *Concentration on Key Markets: A Development Plan for Exports*, London: Royal Society of Arts.

Bilkey, W. J. (1978) 'An attempted integration of the literature on the export behaviour of firms', *Journal of International Business Studies* (Spring/Summer): 33–46.

Bilkey, W. and Tesar, G. (1977), 'The export behaviour of smaller Wisconsin manufacturing firms', *Journal of International Business Studies* (Spring/Summer): 93–8.

Brady, D. L. and Bearden, W. O. (1979) 'The effect of managerial attitudes on alternative export methods', *Journal of International Business Studies* (Winter): 79–84.

Brooks, M. R. and Rosson, P. J. (1982) 'A study of export behaviour of small and medium-sized manufacturing firms in three Canadian provinces', in M. R. Czinkota and G. Tesar (eds) *Export Management: An International Context*, New York: Praeger.

Cavusgil, S. T. (1980) 'On the internationalization process of firms', *European Research* (November): 273–81.

Cavusgil, S. T. (1982) 'Some observations on the relevance of critical variables for internationalization stages', in M. R. Czinkota and G. Tesar (eds) *Export Management: An International Context*, New York: Praeger.

Cavusgil, S. T. and Nevin, J. R. (1980) 'A conceptualization of the initial involvement in international marketing', in C. W. Lamb, Jr. and P. M. Dunne (eds) *Theoretical Development in Marketing*, American Marketing Association.

Cunningham, M. T. (1980) 'International marketing and purchasing of industrial goods: features of a European research project', *European Journal of Marketing*, 14: 322–38.

Cunningham, M. T. (1985) 'An interaction approach to competitive strategy in European markets: a British perspective', paper presented at the 2nd Open International IMP Research Seminar on International Marketing, Uppsala.

Cunningham, M. T. and Spigel, R. I. (1971) 'A study of successful exporting', *British Journal of Marketing* (Spring): 2–11.

Czinkota, M. R. (1982) *Export Development Strategies: US Promotion Policy*,

Czinkota, M. R. and Johnston, W. J. (1981) 'Segmenting US firms for export development', *Journal of Business Research*, 9: 353–65.

Czinkota, M. R. and Johnston, W. J. (1983) 'Exporting: does sales volume make a difference?', *Journal of International Business Studies* (Spring/Summer): 147–53.

Dichtl, E. M. Leibold, Koglmayr, H-G. and Muller, S. (1983) 'The foreign orientation of management as a central construct in export-centred decision-making processes', *Research for Marketing* 10: 7–14.

Dichtl, E. M. Leibold, Koglmayr, H-G. and Muller, S. (1984) 'The export decision of small- and medium-sized firms: a review', *Management International Review* 24: 49–60.

Douglas, S. and Dubois, B. (1977) 'Looking at the cultural environment for international marketing opportunities', *Columbia Journal of World Business* (Winter): 102–9.

Elbashier, A. M. and Nicholls, J. R. (1983) 'Export marketing in the Middle East: the importance of cultural differences', *European Journal of Marketing* 17: 68–81.

Ford, I. D. (1980) 'The development of buyer–seller relationships in industrial markets', *European Journal of Marketing* 14: 339–53.

Ford, I. D. *et al.* (1987) 'Managing export development between industrialized and developing countries', in P. J. Rosson and S. D. Reid (eds) *Managing Export Entry and Expansion*, New York: Praeger, 71–90.

Ford, I. D. and Djeflat, A. (1983), 'Export marketing of industrial products: buyer–seller relationships between developed and developing countries', in M. R. Czinkota (ed.) *Export Promotion: The Public and Private Sector Interaction*, New York: Praeger.

Ford, I. D. and Rosson, P. J. (1982) 'The relationships between export manufacturers and their overseas distributors', in M. R. Czinkota and G. Tesar (eds) *Export Management: An International Context* New York: Praeger.

Ford, I. D., Lawson, A. and Nicholls, J. R. (1982) 'Developing international marketing through overseas sales subsidiaries', in M. R. Czinkota and G. Tesar (eds) *Export Management: An International Context*, New York: Praeger.

Garnier, G. (1982) 'Comparative export behaviour of small Canadian firms in the printing and electrical industries', in M. R. Czinkota and G. Tesar (eds), *Export Management: An International Context*, New York: Praeger.

Green, C. H. (1982) 'Effective marketing planning for exporting to the United States', in M. R. Czinkota and G. Tesar (eds) *Export Management: An International Context*, New York: Praeger.

Groke, P. O. and Kreidle, J. R. (1967) 'Export! Why or why not? Managerial attitude and action for small-sized business firms', *Business and Society*, 8: 7–12.

Hakansson, H. (ed.) (1982) *International Marketing and Purchasing of Industrial Goods*, New York: Wiley.

Hakansson, H. and Wootz, B. (1975) 'Changes in the propensity to import: an interaction model on the firm level', Department of Business Studies, University of Uppsala.

Hirsch, S. (1971) *The Export Performance of Six Manufacturing Industries: A Comparative Study of Denmark, Holland, and Israel*, New York: Praeger.

Hooley, G. J. and Newcomb, J. R. (1983) 'Ailing British exports: symptoms, causes, and cures', *The Quarterly Review of Marketing* (Summer): 15–22.

Hunt, H. G., Froggatt, J. D. and Hovell, P. J. (1970) 'The management of export marketing in engineering industries', *British Journal of Marketing* (Spring): 10–24.

ITI Research (1979) *The Barclays Bank Report on Export Development in France, Germany, and the United Kingdom: Factors for International Success*, London: Barclays Bank International Limited.

Jackson, G. I. (1981) 'Export from the importer's viewpoint', *European Journal of Marketing* 15: 3–25.

Johanson, J. and Nonaka, I. (1983) 'Japanese export marketing: structures, strategies, counter-strategies', *International Marketing Review*: 12–25.

Johanson, J. and Vahlne, J. (1977) 'The internationalization process of the firm: a model of knowledge development and increasing foreign commitments', *Journal of International Business Studies* (Spring–Summer): 23–32.

Johanson, J. and Wiedersheim-Paul, F. (1975) 'The internationalization of the firm: four Swedish case studies', *Journal of Management Studies* (October): 305–22.

Johnston, W. J. and Czinkota, M. R. (1982) 'Managerial motivations as determinants of industrial export behaviour', in M. R. Czinkota and G. Tesar (eds) *Export Management: An International Context*, New York: Praeger.

Joynt, P. (1982) 'An empirical study of Norwegian export behaviour', in M. R. Czinkota and G. Tesar (eds) *Export Management: An International Context*, New York: Praeger.

Kacker, M. P. (1975) 'Export-oriented product adaptation: its patterns and problems', *Management International Review* 15: 61–70.

Kaynak, E. and Kothari, V. (1984a) 'Export behaviour of small- and medium-sized manufacturers: some policy guidelines for international marketeers', *Management International Review* 24: 61–9.

Kaynak, E. and Kothari,V. (1984b) 'Export behaviour of small manufacturers: a comparative study of American and Canadian firms', *European Management Journal* 2: 41–7.

Kaynak, E. and Stevenson, L. (1982) 'Export orientation of Nova Scotia manufacturers', in M. R. Czinkota and G. Tesar (eds) *Export Management: An International Context*, New York: Praeger.

Lee, W. and Brasch, J. J. (1978) 'The adoption of export as an innovative strategy', *Journal of International Business Studies* (Spring–Summer): 85–93.

Leonidou, L. (1987) 'An analysis of the relationships between developing country-based exporters and developed country-based importers for manufactured consumer goods', unpublished PhD Thesis, University of Bath.

McFarlane, G. (1978) 'Scots Queen's Award winners don't excel', *Marketing (UK)* (April): 30–2.

Mason, M. (1980) 'Watch your export language', *Marketing (UK)* (July): 31.

Meidan, A. (1975) 'The export marketing matrix: a tool for investigating the marketing concept in exporting', *Management International Review* 15: 53–9.

Ogram, E. W. Jr, (1982), 'Exporters and non-exporters: a profile of small manufacturing firms in Georgia', in M. R. Czinkota and G. Tesar (eds) *Export Management: An International Context*, New York: Praeger.

Olson, H. C. and Wiedersheim-Paul, F. (1978) 'Factors affecting the pre-export behaviour of non-exporting firms', in J. Leontiades (ed.) *European Research in International Business*, Amsterdam: North Holland.

Paulden, S. (1976) 'The simple secret of export success', *Marketing (UK)* (October): 20–3.

Pavord, W. C. and Bogart, R. G. (1975) 'The dynamics of the decision to export', *Akron Business and Economic Review* (Spring): 6–11.

Piercy, N. (1981), 'British export market selection and pricing', *Industrial Marketing Management* 10: 287–97.

Pointon, T. (1978) 'The information needs of exporters', *Marketing (UK)* (July): 53–7.

Rabino, S. (1980) 'An examination of barriers to exporting encountered by small manufacturing companies', *Management International Review* 20: 67–73.

Reid, S. D. (1980) 'A behavioural approach to export decision-making, in R. B. Baggozzi, K. L. Bernhardt, P. B. Busch, D. W. Gravens, J. F. Hair, Jr, and C. A. Scott, (eds) *Marketing in the 80's: Changes and Challenges*, New York: American Marketing Association.

Reid, S. D. (1981) 'The decision-maker and export entry and expansion', *Journal of International Business Studies* (Fall): 101–12.

Ricks, D. M., Fu and Arpan J. (1974) *International Business Blunders*, Gruid.

Root, F. R. (1964) *Strategic Planning for Export Marketing*, Kobenhavn: Erhvervsokonomisk Forlag.

Rosson, P. J. (1984) 'Success factors in manufacturer–overseas distributor relationships in international marketing', in E. Kaynak, (ed.) *International Marketing Management*, New York: Praeger.

Rosson, P. J., (1985) 'Seven years on: revisits to buyer–seller relationships', paper presented at the 2nd Open International IMP Research Seminar on International Marketing, Uppsala.

Rosson, P. J. and Ford, I. D. (1980) 'Stake, conflict, and performance in export marketing channels', *Management International Review* 20: 31–7.

Rosson, P. J. and Ford, I. D. (1982) 'Manufacturer–overseas distributor relations and export performance', *Journal of International Business Studies* (Fall): 57–72.

Roy, D. A. and Simpson, C. L. (1980) 'Attitudes towards exporting in the smaller manufacturing firm: a survey of chief executive officers in 124 firms in the Southeastern United States', *Baylor Business Studies* 35–44.

Ryans, J. K., Jr and Woudenberg, H. W., Jr (1977) 'Marketing's role in international business theory development', *Foreign Trade Review* 12: 208–17.

Simmonds, K. and Smith, H. (1968) 'The first export order: a marketing innovation', *British Journal of Marketing* (Summer): 93–100.

Simpson, C. L., Jr and Kujawa, D. (1974) 'The export decision process: an empirical inquiry', *Journal of International Business Studies* (Spring): 107–17.

Suntook, F. (1978) 'How British industry exports', *Marketing (UK)* (June): 29–34.

Tesar, G. (1975) 'Empirical study of export operations among small- and medium-sized manufacturing firms', unpublished PhD dissertation, University of Wisconsin-Madison.

Tesar, G. and Tarleton, J. S. (1982) 'Comparison of Wisconsin and Virginian small- and medium-sized exporters: aggressive and passive exporters', in M. R. Czinkota and G. Tesar (eds) *Export Management: An International Context*, New York: Praeger.

Thomas, M. J. (1969) 'Product planning for export markets', in M. J. Thomas (ed.) *International Marketing Management: Readings in Systems and Methods*.

Thomas, M. J. and Araujo, L. (1985) 'Theories of export behaviour: a critical analysis', *European Journal of Marketing* 19: 42–52.

Tookey, D. A. (1964) 'Factors associated with success in exporting, *Journal of Management Studies* (March): 48–66.

Tookey, D. A. (1975) *Export Marketing Decisions*, Harmondsworth, Penguin.

Tookey, D., Lea, E., and McDougall, C. (1967) *The Exporters: A Study of Organization, Staffing, and Training*, Ashridge: Ashridge Management College.

Welch, L. S. and Wiedersheim-Paul, F. (1980) 'Initial exports: a marketing failure?', *The Journal of Management Studies* (October): 333–44.

Wiedersheim-Paul, F., Olson, H. C., and Welch, L. S. (1978) 'Pre-export activity: the first step in internationalization', *Journal of International Business Studies* (Spring–Summer): 47–58.

Chapter Two

SUCCESS FACTORS OF EXPORT MARKETING

A meta-analytic critique of the empirical studies

HANS GEORG GEMÜNDEN

This chapter has been inspired by Madsen's (1987) review of seventeen empirical export performance studies. I wanted to perform a quantitative meta-analysis of these studies in order to identify the key success factors of export marketing, and to assess their influence by means of objective statistical procedures. In attempting this I experienced the following problems.

First, a meta-analysis of success factors of export marketing is a very demanding and time-consuming task: there exist many more than seventeen studies. After an intensive search, fifty studies, published in more than seventy sources could be secured (see the references section). Further studies were unprocurable, in particular reports from export councils and unpublished dissertations (for example, the UMIST dissertations from Buatsi and Schlegelmilch).

Second, it is virtually impossible to perform a comprehensive quantitative meta-analysis of the complex influence net, because of the extreme diversity of the studies, the exploratory nature of data analysis, and the insufficient disclosure of measurement and data-analytic procedures.

The apparent discrepancy between the substantial effort necessary to review the forty-nine studies and the rather limited possibilities to exploit their findings for valid generalizations raises a central issue: what can be done to improve empirical research in order to establish a truly cumulative discipline?

In this chapter I intend to offer some answers to this challenging question.

By applying a *systematic review procedure* I want to show how the reliability and validity of generalizations can be improved. With this illustration I want to stimulate the discussion as to how review procedures could be adapted to ill-structured data. Quantitative meta-analytic procedures are appropriate for bivariate relationships, particularly those which have been tested experimentally. In business administration field studies are often performed. They analyse complex networks of relationships by means of multivariate statistics. Therefore a meta-analysis seems to be of limited usefulness. However, the limited opportunities to apply quantitative meta-analytic tools should not lead to the erroneous conclusion that a systematic approach would be useless at all.

In a *methodological assessment* the characteristics of the studies are compared with the requirements of a quantitative meta-analysis. With this comparison defects of current research are identified and *guidelines for better and more informative studies* are derived.

By describing the *main results* of current research I want to offer the reader an overview and an assistance in formulating his or her research framework.

THE REVIEW PROCEDURE

In principle the procedure of a meta-analysis is the same as that of a primary analysis: a frame of reference has to be developed; hypotheses have to be derived; data have to be gathered and analysed. Figure 2.1 shows the steps in more detail.

1 Theoretical framework
2 Derivation of hypotheses
3 Definition of parent population
4 Drawing of sample
5 Operationalization of variables
6 Evaluation of data quality
7 Analysis of relationships
8 Presentation of results

Figure 2.1 Steps towards a meta-analysis

The *theoretical framework* has a function of ordering. It helps to classify the studies and to illustrate fashioned and neglected research themes. The frame of reference should be conceived in a way broad enough to cover the research field of a large number of studies. It should have a clear and functional structure to permit an unambiguous classification of independent and dependent variables, and it should have a certain depth so that not only independent and dependent variables can be discerned, but also intervening and third variables, that is, complete chains of causality are taken into consideration. Such frameworks have been offered by Cavusgil and Naor (1987), Madsen (1987), Reffait (1984), Reid (1986, 1987), Roux (1979, 1983a, b, 1987), and others.

The *dependent variable* of my own framework (see figure 2.2) is '*export success*', a multi-dimensional construct which comprises export share of total sales, growth of export sales, and profitability of exporting. The *primary independent variables* are the *activities*, that is, the strategies and instruments of export marketing. These include export-related information activities, research and development, export-related actions and adaptations of products, communication, pricing, and distribution. *Managers* decide which activities are performed and how they are combined to strategies. Therefore characteristics of the managers are used as explanatory variables. Goals, expectations, and activities of the managers are influenced by the characteristics of the *contextual factors firm, export market,* and *home country*.

The second step is the *derivation of hypotheses*. It is necessary in order to decide which operationalizations of dependent and independent variables are appropriate to test a relationship. It depends on the *researcher* how general he/she wants to state his/her hypothesis. The problem of mixing 'apples' and 'pears' is *not* an inherent property of a quantative meta-analysis. One even can imagine a meta-research, exclusively oriented on theories which dispenses totally with considering methods and results, and which 'only' aims at backing up more precisely the terms and the theoretical arguments which substantiate their links. Such clarifications would be extremely useful in the field of export marketing, because there is a dearth of theories.

The result of the third step, the *definition of parent population*, is documented in figure 2.3. 'Profile' studies which only compare attitudes of exporters and non-exporters have been excluded: I don't analyse why a firm is *interested* in exporting; I want to know the reasons for its *success* on export markets. Studies which use

Table 2.1 Sample of present meta-analysis

No.	*Main source*	*Data age*	*Country*	*Number of cases*	*Unit of analysis*
1	Abdel-Malek 1974	1970	CDN	166	Firm
2	Airaksinen 1982	1980	SF	104	Plant
3	Bilkey 1982	1979	USA	168	Firm
4	Bilkey 1985	1984	USA	190	Firm
5	Brooks and Rosson 1982	1979	CDN	253	Firm
6	Burton and Schlegelmilch 1987	1982	GB, D	310	Firm
7	Cavusgil 1982	1982	USA	No Info	Firm
8	Cavusgil and Naor 1987	1985	USA	263	Firm
9	Cavusgil and Nevin 1981	1974	USA	473	Firm
10	Cooper *et al.* 1970	1967	GB	21	Firm
11	Cooper and Kleinschmidt 1985	1980	CDN	142	Firm
12	Crookell and Graham 1979	1976	CDN	136	Firm
13	Cunningham and Spigel 1971	1969	GB	48	Firm
14	Daniels and Goyboro 1976	1972	PE	190	Firm
15	Dichtl *et al.* 1984	1983	D	104	Firm
16	Fenwick and Amine 1979	1977	GB	48	Firm
17	Garnier 1982	1977	CDN	105	Firm
18	Glejser *et al.* 1980	1974	B	970	Firm
19	Hirsch 1971	1969	DK, NL, IL	497	Plant
20	Hirsch and Bijaoui 1985	1981	IL	111	Firm
21	Johnston and Czinkota 1982	1979	USA	181	Firm
22	Kaynak and Stevenson 1982	1981	CDN	183	Firm
23	Khan 1978	1976	S	155	Venture

aggregated data were excluded because of my limited research capacity; besides, it is difficult to combine their correlation coefficients with those of micro-economic investigations in order to estimate a 'common' effect size. Case studies and studies which disclose no quantative data have been excluded, because my intention was to perform a quantitative meta-analysis.

All published empirical studies on export marketing which satisfy the following conditions:

1 *export success* as the dependent variable: export share, growth, or profitability
not: intention to export, perceived barriers;
2 *micro-economic units of analysis:* firms, products, ventures, business relationships
not: countries, or industries;
3 export of *manufactured goods or services*
not: export of capital or property rights;
4 *quantitative statistical studies*
not: qualitative case studies.

Figure 2.3 Definition of parent population

The *drawing of the sample* is a crucial step in a meta-analysis. I have checked the bibliographical references given in the studies, scanned relevant journals and conference proceedings published in German and English, and consulted colleagues working on this field. As no on-line search has been performed, completeness cannot be guaranteed. However, I would be very pleased if readers would inform me about further studies, because this is a report of on-going research.

Table 2.1 shows the sample of our meta-analysis. The fifty studies reviewed here have analysed more than 700 indicators which were assumed to influence the performance of more than 9,000 exporting firms in eighteen different countries. This large empirical base should promise valid generalizations about the 'critical success factors' of export marketing.

The table shows that most studies were either performed in Europe (twenty-six samples) or North America (Canada: fifteen samples, USA: nine samples), only seven samples were gathered in other countries. (Numbers do not add to fifty, because in some studies samples were gathered from several countries.)

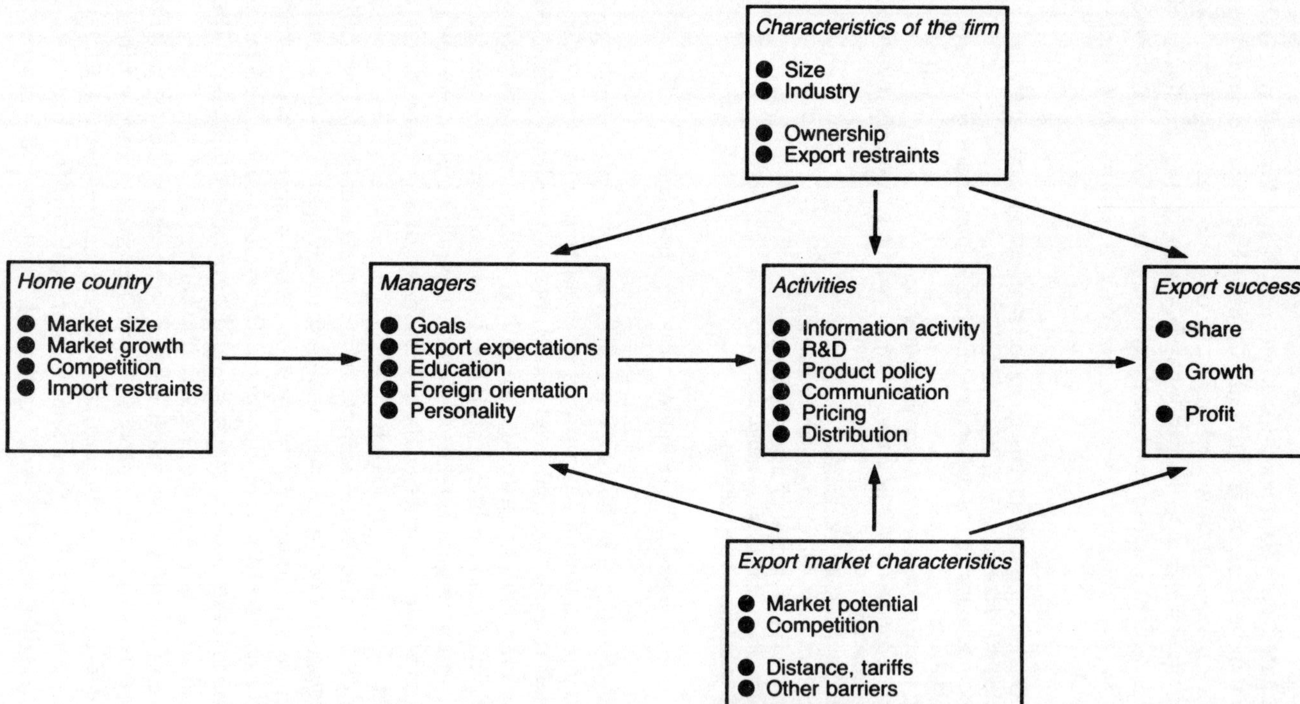

Figure 2.2 Theoretical framework

24	Kirpalani and Macintosh 1980	1978	CDN	34	Firm
25	Kleinschmidt and Cooper 1986	1986	CDN	203	Product
26	Lall and Kumar 1981	1979	IND	100	Firm
27	Langeard *et al.* 1976a, b	1975	F	130	Firm
28	Madsen 1987	1986	DK	134	Venture
29	McConnell 1970	1968	USA	148	Firm
30	McDougall and Stening 1975	1975	CDN, NZ, AUS	175	Firm
31	McFetridge and Weatherly 1975 1. Study	1973	CDN	127	Firm
32	McFetridge and Weatherly 1977 2. Study	1973	CDN	324	Firm
33	McGuinness 1983	1977	CDN	64	Product
34	McGuinness and Little 1981a, b	1971	CDN	82	Product
35	Moser and Topritzhofer 1979	1977	A	208	Firm
36	Ong and Pearson 1982	1978	GB	88	Firm
37	Reffait 1984	1979	F	138	Firm
38	Reffait and Roux 1981	1979	F	41	Firm
39	Reid 1986	1979	CDN	89	Firm
40	Reid 1987	1983	I	67	Firm
41	Rosson and Ford 1982	1978	CDN, GB	21	Dyad
42	Roux 1979	1979	F	19	Firm
43	Roux 1987	1984	F	520	Firm
44	Sarathy 1982	1979	J	459	Firm
45	Schlegelmilch 1986	1982	D	74	Firm
46	Schlegelmilch and Diamantopolous 1987	1982	GB	105	Firm
47	Simpson and Kujawa 1974	1972	USA	120	Firm
48	Tesar and Tarleton 1982 Virginia Study	1981	USA	190	Firm
49	Tookey 1964	1962	GB	52	Firm

Export profitability measures

Export intensity measures

Absolute volume scales

Johnston/Czinkota	Export Sales Volume	Ratio
McConnell	Export Sales Volume	Ratio
McFetridge/Weatherley	Export Sales Volume	Ratio
Reffait	Export Sales Volume	Ratio
Reid 1986	Export Sales Volume	Ratio
Rosson/Ford	Export Sales Volume	Ratio
Lall/Kumar	Average Export Sales Volume, 3 Years	Ratio
Fenwick/Amine	Average Export Sales Volume, 4 Years	Ratio

Dichotomous scales

Abdel-Malek	Exporting yes/no	Nominal
Brooks/Rosson	Exporting yes/no	Nominal
Cavusgil *et al.*	Exporting yes/no	Nominal
Cavusgil/Naor	Exporting yes/no	Nominal
Daniels/Goyboro	Exporting yes/no	Nominal
Garnier	Exporting yes/no	Nominal
Kaynak/Stevenson	Exporting yes/no	Nominal
McConnell	Exporting yes/no	Nominal
Roux 1987	Exporting yes/no	Nominal
Simpson/Kujawa	Exporting yes/no	Nominal
Reffait/Roux	Export Sales: Total Sales, above/below average	Nominal
Tesar/Tarleton	Export Sales: Total Sales less than/over 10%	Nominal
Burton/Schlegelmich	Export/Domestic Ratio – Ind. Avg. Ratio, dich.	Nominal
Moser/Topritzhofer	Export Sales: Total Sales, 3 Years, dich.	Nominal
Fenwick/Amine	Export Sales: Total Sales, 4 Years, dich.	Nominal

Relative scales

Langeard *et al.*	Export Sales: Total Sales, 1 Year, 3 Levels	Ordinal
Cavusgil/Nevin	Export Sales: Total Sales, 1 Year, 10 Levels	Ordinal
Madsen	Export Sales: Domestic Sales, Ratings, 7 Levels	Ordinal
Cooper *et al.*	Export Sales: Total Sales	Ratio
Reid 1986	Export Sales: Total Sales	Ratio
McDougall/Stening	Export Sales: Total Sales	Ratio
Schlegelmich	Export Sales: Total Sales	Ratio
Schlegelmich/Diamant	Export Sales: Total Sales	Ratio
Airaksinen	Export Sales: Total Sales, 1 Year	Ratio
Cooper/Kleinschmidt	Export Sales: Total Sales, 1 Year	Ratio
Crookell/Graham	Export Sales: Total Sales, 1 Year	Ratio
McGuinness	Export Sales: Total Sales, 1 Year	Ratio
McGuinness/Little	Export Sales: Total Sales, 1 Year	Ratio
Reffait	Export Sales: Total Sales, 1 Year	Ratio
Reid 1987	Export Sales: Total Sales, 1 Year	Ratio
Roux 1979	Export Sales: Total Sales, 1 Year	Ratio
Sarathy	Export Sales: Total Sales, 1 Year	Ratio
Tookey	Export Sales: Total Sales, 1 Year	Ratio
Lall/Kumar	Export Sales: Total Sales, Average 3 Years	Ratio
Hirach	Export Sales: Total Sales, Weight. Avg. 5 Years	Ratio
Glejser *et al.*	ln (Export Sales: Total Sales), 1 Year	Ratio

Export growth measures

Reffait/Roux	Export Sales Growth Rate, above/below Average	Ordinal
Abdel-Malek	Export Sales Growth Rate, 1965–1969, 3 Levels	Ordinal
Langeard *et al.*	Export Sales Growth Rate, 1969–1974, 3 Levels	Ordinal
Rosson/Ford	Export Sales Trend, 3 Years, Rating	Ordinal
Khan	Export Sales Growth 1970–75 yes/no, 13 Levels	Ordinal
Madsen	Export: Domestic Sales Growth, Rating 7 Levels	Ordinal
Airaksinen	Export Sales Growth 1976–1979	Ratio
Cooper *et al.*	Export Sales Change to Previous Year	Ratio
Reid 198e	Export Sales Growth	Ratio
Cooper/Kleinschmidt	Export Sales Growth Rate, 3 Years	Ratio
Kleinschmidt/Cooper	Export Sales Growth Rate, 3 Years	Ratio
Lall/Kumar	Export Sales Growth Rate, 3 Years	Ratio
Schlegelmich	Export Sales Growth Rate, 3 Years	Ratio
Schlegelm/Diamant	Export Sales Growth Rate, 3 Years	Ratio
Dichil *et al.*	Export Sales Growth Rate, 4 Years	Ratio
Raffail	Export Sales Growth Rate, 5 Years	Ratio
Hirsch/Bijaoui	Avg. Exp. Sales 1979–81: Avg. Exp. Sales 1975–77	Ratio

Export profitability Measures

Khan	Profit before Taxes 1970–1975: yes/no 13 Levels	Ordinal
Bilkey 1982	Profitability of Export vs. Home Market, Rating	Ordinal
Bilkey 1985	Profitability of Export vs. Home Market, Rating	Ordinal
Kleinschmidt/Cooper	Subjective Rating of Profitability	Ordinal
Madsen	Profitability of Export vs. Home Market, Rating	Ordinal
Airaksinen	(Sales – Variable Production Cost): Sales	Ratio

Mixed-measure-scales

Khan	Firm's Evaluation of Export Venture Success yes/no	Nominal
Kleinschmidt/Cooper	Firm's Evaluation of New Product Success yes/no	Nominal
Cunningham/Spigel	Queen's Award based on Export Intensity and Growth	Nominal
Raffait/Roux	Leadership: Export Share + Expert Rating	Nominal
Kirpalani/Macintosh	Factor Score, loads Export Growth and Intensity-Rating	Ordinal

Attitudinal measures

Cavusgil	Exporting High/Low/No but interested/No, not interested	Nominal
Daniels/Goyboro	Exporting yes/No but interested/No, not interested	Nominal
Dichtl *et al.*	System. Exp./Occasional Exp./Home Country Oriented	Nominal
Lee/Brasch	Problem vs. Innovation Oriented Exporters	Nominal
Pavord/Bogard	Seekers vs. Nonseekers	Nominal
Piercy	Active vs. Reactive Exporters.	Nominal
Tesar/Tarleton	Aggressive vs. Passive Exporters	Nominal
Bradley/Keogh	Export Motivation	Ordinal
Reid 1982	Intended Export Activties, Rating Scales	Ordinal
Johnston/Czinkota	Proactive vs. Reactive Exporters	Ordinal

Figure 2.4 Measurement of export success

Most studies use the firm as the unit of analysis and have a sample size between 100 and 200.

The next step of the review procedure addresses the *operationalization* of variables. We will first analyse how the dependent variable 'export success' has been operationalized. Figure 2.4 shows three prominent groups of 'success' measures: intensity measures, growth measures, and profitability measures. Besides, some studies construct composite scales which are based on two or more of these aspects. For the sake of completeness I have also included attitudinal measures of export behaviour, which are sometimes used as proxies for success measures. Measures which describe the concentration of export activity have been neglected.

It should be stressed that the majority of studies use rather crude nominal or ordinal scales, in particular dichotomous scales which classify the firms into exporters vs. non-exporters, low vs. high exporting firms, or declining/stagnating vs. growing firms. This means a considerable loss of information and inflates the type II error.

Some studies use absolute volume scales. We have discarded findings with these measures, because it is a trivial fact that – other things equal – larger firms have larger *absolute* export volumes than smaller firms. A noteworthy exception are studies which use absolute volume scales to *test* whether a non-linear relationship between size and export volume exists (for example McFetridge and Weatherly 1977).

The business economist is worried by the fact that most of the studies explain only the easily collectable export intensity, and not the well-known success measures return and profit which are important criteria for managerial decisions. Is a high share of export sales *per se* an indicator of efficiency?

Findings which have analysed the *relationships* between intensity, growth, and profit measures give rise to doubts. Figure 2.5 documents: *There is neither a positive relationship between intensity and growth, nor between intensity and profit.* This means export sales intensity is *no* good proxy for growth or profitability of exporting.

The findings from Khan (1978) and Madsen (1987) depart considerably from the other findings, and so deserve a comment. Both have used *export ventures* as the unit of analysis. They have asked the firms to select pairs of failed and successful ventures.

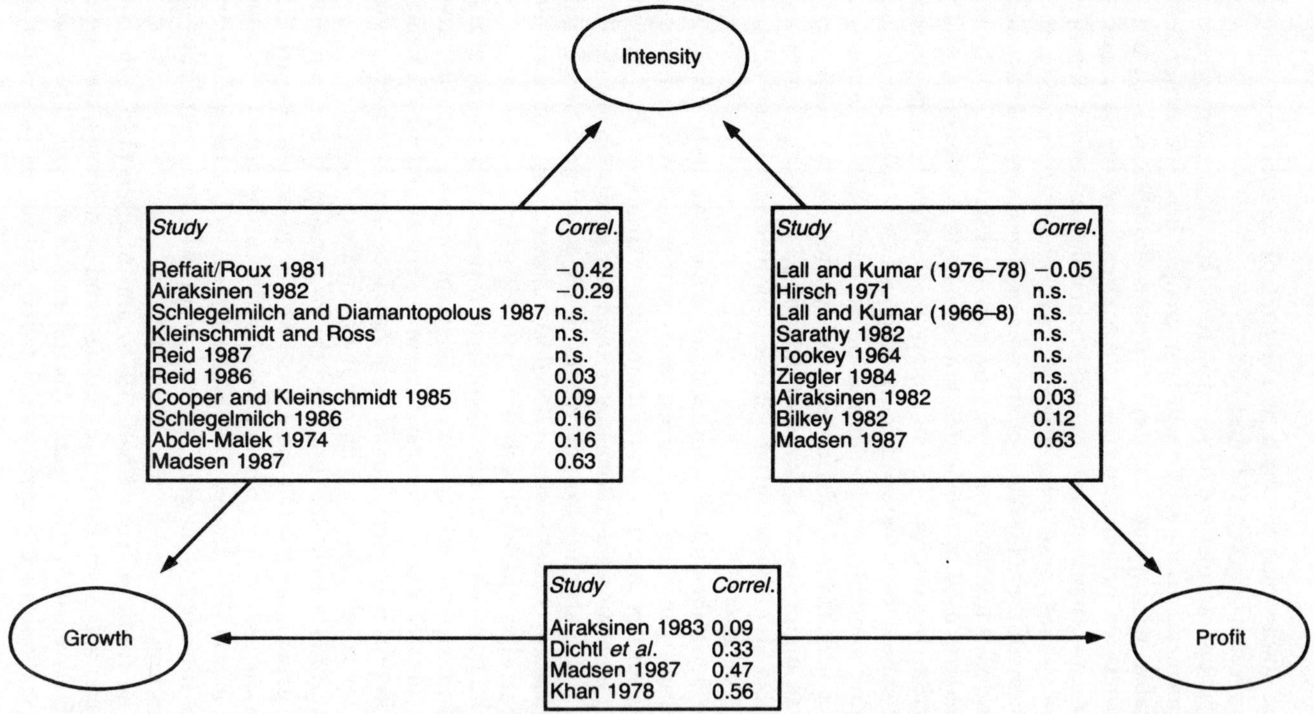

Figure 2.5 Relationship between success constructs

It might be that this selection procedure has influenced the relationship between the three success measures.

If we discard these two studies we have to acknowledge the following finding: at the firm level exists no strong relationship between intensity, growth, and profit measures of export activity.

This finding has important consequences. If these measures of export success are unrelated, then it makes no sense to develop only one model which explains all three variables. Rather, we have to develop different models for each dimension, and we have to perform different meta-analyses for the different types of relationships. (Findings from Schlegelmilch (1986), Burton and Schlegelmilch (1987), Kleinschmidt and Cooper (1986) and others confirm this hypothesis by showing that growth and intensity are indeed influenced by different factors.)

Under this perspective the empirical base to assess the relevance of 'success factors' is rather small. There are only five studies which have used profitability measures as the dependent variable, and four of these rely on crude subjective rating scales. This is clearly a field where further research is needed.

Problems which are connected with the *operationalization of the independent variables* will be discussed in the results section. We now come to step 6: *evaluation of data quality*. This step contains two sub-steps: evaluation of data-collection techniques, and assessment of data-analysis.

Table 2.2 documents the methodological characteristics of *data collection* and *measurement*. Our assessment shows that the typical study:

- uses a mailed questionnaire;
- shows a response rate below 30 per cent;
- does not report tests of reliability of measurement;
- does not report tests of validity of measurement;
- uses only one item to measure a construct;
- does not disclose its measures sufficiently, so that they can be reproduced.

With regard to the quality of the original data, the reliability and validity of the results have to be doubted.

How is the *data analysis* to be evaluated? Table 2.3 documents considerable defects in data analysis and documentation of results.

Many studies denounce formulating specific hypotheses from

Table 2.2 Data collection and measurement

Main source	*Data age*	*Country*	*Number of*	*Unit of analysis*	*Instrument*	*Response rate %*	*Reliability test*	*Validity test*	*Items per scale*	*Documentation of measure*
Langeard *et al.* 1976	1975	F	130	Firm	SecAnal.	no inf.	no	no	one	part.
Hirsch and Bijaoui 1985	1981	IL	111	Firm	SecAnal.	no inf.	no	no	one	yes
Lall and Kumar 1981	1979	IND	100	Firm	SecAnal.	no inf.	no	no	one	yes
McFetridge and Weatherly 1977 1st Study	1973	CDN	127	Firm	SecAnal.	no inf.	no	no	one	yes
McFetridge and Weatherly 1977 2nd Study	1973	CDN	324	Firm	SecAnal.	no inf.	no	no	one	yes
Sarathy 1982	1979	J	459	Firm	SecAnal.	no inf.	no	no	one	yes
Airaksinen 1982	1980	SF	104	Plant	Quest.	no inf.	no	no	one	yes
Cavusgil 1982	1982	USA	no inf.	Firm	Quest.	no inf.	no	no	one	part.
Daniels and Goyboro 1976	1972	PE	190	Firm	Quest.	no inf.	no	no	one	yes
Dichtl *et al.* 1984	1983	D	104	Firm	Quest.	no inf.	yes	yes	many	yes
Fenwick and Amine 1979	1977	GB	48	Firm	Quest.	no inf.	no	no	one	part.
Reffait 1984	1979	F	138	Firm	Quest.	no inf.	no	no	many	part.
Tesar and Tarleton 1982	1981	USA	190	Firm	Quest.	no inf.	no	no	one	part.
Tookey 1964	1962	GB	52	Firm	Quest.	no inf.	no	no	one	part.
Garnier 1982	1977	CDN	105	Firm	Quest.	11.1	no	no	one	no
Bilkey 1982	1979	USA	168	Firm	Quest.	12.1	no	no	one	yes
McConnell 1970	1978	USA	148	Firm	Quest.	13.0	no	no	many	part.
Schlegelmilch 1986	1982	D	74	Firm	Quest.	16.0	no	no	many	yes
Glejser *et al.* 1980	1974	B	970	Firm	Quest.	16.2	no	no	one	yes
Johnston and Czinkota 1982	1979	USA	181	Firm	Quest.	18.0	no	no	one	part.
Bilkey 1985	1984	USA	190	Firm	Quest.	18.5	no	no	one	yes
Burton and Schlegelmilch 1987	1982	GB, D	310	Firm	Quest.	20.7	no	no	one	no
Ong and Pearson 1982	1978	GB	88	Firm	Quest.	22.0	no	no	one	part.

McGuinness 1983	1977	CDN	64	Product	Quest.	22.5	no	no	many	part.
Reid 1987	1983	I	67	Firm	Quest.	24.3	no	no	one	part.
Schlegelmilch and Diamantopolous 1987	1982	GB	105	Firm	Quest.	26.0	no	no	one	yes
Reffait and Roux 1981	1979	F	41	Firm	Quest.	26.5	no	no	one	part.
Cavusgil and Naor 1987	1985	USA	263	Firm	Quest.	29.0	no	no	one	yes
Moser and Topritzhofer 1979	1977	A	208	Firm	Quest.	34.7	no	no	one	part.
Kaynak and Stevenson 1982	1981	CDN	183	Firm	Quest.	37.0	no	no	one	part.
Brooks and Rosson 1982	1979	CDN	253	Firm	Quest.	44.0	no	no	many	part.
Cunningham and Spigel 1971	1969	GB	48	Firm	Quest.	48.0	no	no	one	part.
Hirsch 1971	1969	DK, NL, IL	497	Plant	Quest.	48.7	no	no	one	yes
Reid 1986	1979	CDN	89	Firm	Quest.	50.5	no	no	one	part.
Madsen 1987	1986	DK	134	Venture	Quest.	52.0	yes	yes	many	yes
McGuinness and Little 1981	1971	CDN	82	Product	Quest.	53.9	no	no	one	part.
McDougall and Stening 1975	1975	CDN, NZ, AUS	175	Firm	Quest.	57.0	no	no	one	no
Cavusgil and Nevin 1981	1974	USA	473	Firm	Quest.	58.0	no	no	one	yes
Abdel-Malek 1974	1970	CDN	166	Firm	Quest.	88.0	no	no	one	yes
Cooper *et al.* 1970	1967	GB	21	Firm	Interv.	no inf.	no	no	one	yes
Crookell and Graham 1979	1976	CDN	136	Firm	Interv.	no inf.	no	no	one	part.
Kirpalani and Macintosh 1980	1978	CDN	34	Firm	Interv.	no inf.	no	no	many	part.
Rosson and Ford 1982	1978	CDN, GB	21	Dyad	Interv.	no inf.	no	no	one	yes
Roux 1979	1979	F	19	Firm	Interv.	no inf.	no	no	one	part
Simpson and Kujawa 1974	1972	USA	120	Firm	Interv.	no inf.	no	no	one	part.
Cooper and Kleinschmidt 1985	1980	CDN	142	Firm	Interv.	43.0	yes	no	one	part.
Kleinschmidt and Cooper 1986	1986	CDN	203	Product	Interv.	63.0	no	no	one	part.
Khan 1978	1976	S	155	Venture	Interv.	79.0	no	no	one	yes
Roux 1987	1984	F	520	Firm	Interv.	82.1	no	no	one	part.

Table 2.3 Data analysis and results

Main source	*Derivation hypothesis*	*Method. approach*	*Statistical approach*	*Statistical validity*	*Prognostic validity*	*Doc. of bivar.*	*Results multiv.*
			Exploratory studies				
Cunningham and Spigel 1971	no	expl.	univariate	no	no	–	–
Garnier 1982	no	expl.	bivariate	no	no	part.	–
Bilkey 1985	no	expl.	bivariate	no	no	yes	–
Crookell and Graham 1979	no	expl.	bivariate	no	no	yes	–
Kaynak and Stevenson 1982	no	expl.	bivariate	no	no	yes	–
Langeard *et al.* 1976	no	expl.	bivariate	no	no	yes	–
McDougall and Stening 1975	no	expl.	bivariate	no	no	no	no
Tookey 1964	no	expl.	bivariate	no	no	yes	–
Daniels and Goyboro 1976	no	expl.	bivariate	no	no	yes	–
Reffait and Roux 1987	no	expl.	bivariate	no	no	yes	–
Roux 1979	no	expl.	bivariate	no	no	yes	–
Burton and Schlegelmilch 1987	no	expl.	stepwise	no	no	no	part.
Khan 1978	no	expl.	stepwise	no	no	yes	yes
Moser and Topritzhofer 1979	no	expl.	stepwise	no	no	no	yes
Roux 1983	no	expl.	stepwise	no	no	no	yes
Sarathy 1982	no	expl.	stepwise	no	no	no	yes
Cavusgil and Naor 1987	no	expl.	stepwise	part.	no	yes	yes
Bilkey 1982	no	expl.	blockwise	no	no	no	yes
Kirpalani and Macintosh 1980	no	expl.	blockwise	no	no	yes	yes
			Hypothesis-oriented studies				
Cavusgil 1982	yes: firm/man./activ.	expl.	bivariate	no	no	yes	–
Johnston and Czinkota 1982	yes: manager	expl.	bivariate	no	no	yes	–

Kleinschmidt and Cooper 1986	yes: activities	expl.	bivariate	no	no	yes	–
Tesar and Tarleton 1982	yes: firm/manager	expl.	bivariate	no	no	yes	–
Simpson and Kujawa 1974	yes: manager	expl.	bivariate	no	no	yes	–
Cavusgil and Nevin 1981	yes: firm/manager	expl.	stepwise	no	no	no	yes
McGuinness 1983	yes: firm/activities	expl.	stepwise	no	no	yes	yes
Ong and Pearson 1982	yes: activities	expl.	stepwise	no	no	yes	part.
Reffait 1984	yes: firm/man./activ.	expl.	stepwise	no	no	yes	yes
Reid 1987	yes: firm/activities	expl.	stepwise	no	no	yes	yes
Roux 1987	yes: manager	expl.	stepwise	no	no	yes	yes
Schlegelmilch and Diamantopulous 1987	yes: activities	expl.	stepwise	no	no	no	yes
Schlegelmilch 1986	yes: activities	expl.	stepwise	no	no	no	yes
Dichtl *et al.* 1984	yes: manager	expl.	stepwise	no	yes	yes	yes
Reid 1986	yes: firm/activities	expl.	blockwise	no	no	no	yes
Madsen 1987	yes: firm/man./activ.	expl.	blockwise	part.	no	yes	yes
		Hypothesis-testing studies					
Abdel-Malek 1974	yes: firm/manager	prob.	bivariate	no	no	yes	–
Brooks and Rosson 1982	yes: man./activities	prob.	bivariate	no	no	yes	–
Rosson and Ford 1982	yes: activities	prob.	bivariate	no	no	yes	–
Hirsch 1971	yes: firm	prob.	bivariate	no	no	yes	–
Cooper and Kleinschmidt 1985	yes: activities	prob.	blockwise	no	no	yes	yes
Lall and Kumar 1981	yes: firm	prob.	blockwise	no	no	no	yes
Airaksinen 1982	yes: firm	prob.	simultan.	no	no	no	yes
Cooper *et al.* 1970	yes: market	prob.	simultan.	no	no	no	yes
Glejser *et al.* 1980	yes: firm	prob.	simultan.	no	no	no	yes
McFetridge and Weatherly 1977	yes: firm	prob.	simultan.	no	no	no	yes
Fenwick and Amine 1979	yes: firm/activities	prob.	simultan.	yes	no	no	yes
McGuinness and Little 1981	yes: firm/man./activ.	prob.	simultan.	no	no	no	yes
Hirsch and Bijaoui 1985	yes: activities	prob.	simultan.	no	yes	yes	yes

the beginning. They simply want to explore how export success is related to certain variables. Typically such studies want to explore how exporters and non-exporters 'differ'.

Another group of studies outlines some frames of reference and formulates some hypotheses which are usually based on selective perceptions of previous findings, and sometimes also on discussions of theoretical arguments. However, these studies do not perform strict tests of their hypotheses. Rather, they typically use stepwise multivariate tools (regression or discriminant analysis) to find out the combination of influence factors which best fit their specific data set.

Only a small group of studies derive hypotheses which are tested in a fixed procedure during which all parameters are estimated simultaneously in one pre-specified model, or blockwise in a pre-specified sequence of different models.

We have to admit that the borderlines between these three types of studies are fluent and difficult to draw. The phenomenon that different publications using the same data source exhibit different metholodogical approaches makes the distinction even more difficult.

But, this is not the real problem. What I want to show is that *most* studies follow an exploratory approach. This adds considerable heterogeneity to the empirical findings, and makes it even harder to compare and integrate the empirical results. Even if all the studies were to use the same unit of analysis, the same set of independent and dependent constructs, and the same (valid and reliable) operationalizations, we could not compare and integrate their reported *partial* effects, because these effects depend on the *other* variables which are included or excluded in the data-specific models.

Given our rather incomplete knowledge of the 'real' influence factors of export success, it seems to be useful to follow an exploratory approach, at least in the early stages of research. This seems useful, because relying only on tests of pre-specified models would probably lead to *model-specification errors* (see Madsen's (1987) review for this problem). However, this does not imply that the one model which a researcher has constructed for one data-set with a given theoretical knowledge and given data-analytic tools could not be improved in the light of new experience gained by him or herself or other researchers.

Therefore I want to make a strong plea not to document only the results of one (stepwise) multivariate analysis. Rather, I propose to publish also the matrix of bivariate relationships, so that a later re-analysis or meta-analysis becomes possible.

A well-known problem of stepwise procedures is the risk of capitalization on chance. Given this problem one is worried by the fact that few studies report how they have tested the assumptions of the statistical tools used. This casts severe doubts on the statistical validity of many analyses. Only two studies (Dichtl *et al.* 1984, Hirsch and Bijaoui 1985) use *new* data to test the prognostic validity of their models. (Fenwick and Amine 1979 use hold-outs and jack-knife estimation technique to validate their finding.) I have to add that many studies in the first group ('exploratory studies') do not even use a statistical test.

The next step in a meta-analysis is the *analysis of relationships*. For this step, four different strategies have been developed:

1 pooling of raw-data;
2 estimation and analysis of effect sizes;
3 combination of significance levels;
4 classification of results ('vote-counting').

Since raw-data were not available, my preferred choice was the estimation and analysis of effect sizes. With these methods I wanted to exploit the large empirical data base.

However, five factors strongly restrict the potential of this data-base.

The extreme diversity of the studies

The studies use different *units of analysis* (firms, plants, products, export ventures), different *performance aspects* (export share, growth, profitability), different sets of *success factors*, different *operationalizations* of independent and dependent variables, and a variety of different *statistical procedures*. This makes it rather difficult to compare the results and to reconcile conflicting findings.

The low quality of the data gathered

Most studies rely on self-administered questionnaires, have a response rate under 30 per cent, use only one item to measure a success factor, and do not check reliability or validity.

The exploratory nature of data analysis

Many studies use stepwise data-analytic techniques to identify critical success factors instead of testing pre-specified models. This leads to a diversity of data-dependent models whose partial effects cannot be compared across studies.

The lack of theoretical arguments

The 'hypotheses' are formulated often very vaguely, (for example, exporters and non-exporters 'differ'), it is seldom explained why and how 'success factors' make a difference, contingencies are seldom postulated *before* the data-analysis, and there are no path-analytic models which separate direct and indirect effects. In addition, theoretical reasoning is required to clarify the causal *direction* of influences (for example, is a large firm or an intensive R&D activity a consequence of growing exports or a condition for successful exporting?).

Insufficient disclosure of measurement and data-analytic procedures

Many measurements cannot be reproduced, or even evaluated because the wordings of the questions are not given. The statistical validity of results cannot be assessed because the procedures are not explained. Only significant partial effects of the final multivariate analysis are reported, but the basic bivariate relationships which could be compared across studies are omitted. Therefore meta-analytic techniques cannot be applied.

Faced with these problems I have developed an ordinal scale to evaluate the findings. It has the following levels and meanings:

++ the study shows one or more results which confirm the hypothesis at a significance level of 5 per cent or better (one-sided test);

\+ the overall tendency of the study confirms the hypothesis, but a minority of results or, less appropriate indicators fail to confirm the hypothesis, or no significance tests have been performed,

0 the study does not support the hypothesis, but according to measurement problems or stepwise procedures the reported evidence is not strong enough to falsify the hypothesis,

– the study falsifies the hypothesis by a significant result whose direction is contrary to the hypothesis, and which cannot be explained by artifacts (for example, multicollinearity).

This scale deserves comment. First, it was constructed to show the *central tendency* of the findings. Misclassifications of single studies on single indicators cannot be excluded, particularly because of the insufficient disclosure of data collection, data analysis, and results, but several mechanisms were used to improve the reliability of the classification:

- all classifications were made by the same senior researcher;
- separate classifications were made for each success factor;
- for each independent variable a codebook was developed which describes the content of the construct, and contains a list of all operationalizations which were embraced to this construct, and of those which were excluded;
- results which were influenced by specific defects of a study were carefully documented.

The relationships are evaluated by a simple counting procedure: I count how often a category value occurs. The categories '0' and '–' have been collapsed because definite falsifications occurred too seldom. Such vote-counting procedures are well-known for their conservative behaviour. For small effect sizes and small sample sizes the probability of making a type II error is rather high. It will *increase* with an increasing number of counted studies and converge toward 1 if the number of studies goes toward infinity. However, our scale probably has a *positive* bias. I had to rely on the positive results which were reported. 'Non'-significant results are often omitted, and sometimes hard to interpret. For example, in the organizational theory size of a firm is well-known to influence functional specialization. Therefore one can expect that larger firms more often have a full-time manager for the export function than smaller firms. If the variable 'export department' has a significant positive partial influence in a stepwise analysis and the size-variable is not significant, then one cannot conclude that size has no influence on export intensity, because it *indirectly* influences export intensity via functional specialization. Therefore non-significant partial effects have usually been neglected. (Besides, if partial effects conflicted with bivariate effects the latter were given higher weight.)

To make comparisons between influence factors easier I have constructed a *confirmation ratio*. It is defined as:

$$\frac{3 * \text{number of '++'} + 2 * \text{number of '+'}}{3 * \text{number of '++'} + 2 * \text{number of '+'} + \text{number of '0' or '}-\text{'}}$$

The last step of our procedure is the *presentation of results*. Table 2.4 documents my findings. It shows that four prominent success factors have been researched rather frequently:

1 size of a firm (forty-three findings);
2 export-oriented information activities (thirty-four findings);
3 intensity of R&D (thirty-one findings);
4 export-oriented product adaptations and services (nineteen findings);

All four factors show a positive influence on export share of total sales, but only export-oriented information activity also shows a stronger positive influence on growth and profitability of export.

The other factors which have been evaluated document that (perceived) product strength, the importance of growth as a goal of the firm, exports perceived contribution to growth or profit goals, managers' foreign orientation, export restraints laid upon foreign owned firms, existence of an export department, and attractiveness of export market, and saturation of domestic market correlate positively with export intensity. Perceived product strength, expected profit or growth contribution of exporting, attractiveness of export market, and saturation of home market also show positive correlation with growth and profitability of exporting but these tendencies are based on a much smaller number of results. These findings deserve some comment.

The positive relationship between *size* of a firm and export

Table 2.4 A meta-analysis of empirical export studies

Concepts	*Study Number*	*Abdel* 1	*Air* 2	*Axinn* 3	*Bil82* 4	*Bil85* 5	*BrRo* 6	*BurS* 7	*Cavu* 8	*CaNa* 9	*CaNe* 10	*CoHH* 11	*CooK* 12	*CrGr* 13	*CunS* 14	*DanG* 15	*Diln* 16	*Dich* 17	*FenA* 18	*Gar* 19	*GJP* 20	*Hir* 21	*HirB* 22	*JoCz* 23	*KaSt* 24	*Khan* 25	*KirM* 26	*KleiC* 27	*LaDu* 28	*LaKu* 29	*LaRR* 30
1. Activities	*Eff.*																														
Export market-related	I	++					+	+	++	+	++				+	++			0								++		+		0
Information-activity	G												++		+											+	++				0
	P																									+		++			
Intensity of	I	++		0				+	+	0	++		++									+					0			–	
R&D	G												++										++			0	0			+	
	P																									0					
(Perceived) product	I									0	+		+																		
quality/strength	G												++													0					
	P																									+					
Export-related	I																0		0			++					+				
adaptations of	G																									0	+				
products & services	P																									0		++			
Export-related	I																										0				
adaptations of	G																										0				
advertising	P																														
Export-related	I																										++				
adaptations of	G																									0	++				
prices & contracts	P																									0					
Export-related	I																														
adaptations of	G																									0					
delivery times	P																									0					
Distribution	I																					+									
channel/entry	G																									0					
mode	P				+	+																				0					
2. Managers	*Eff.*																														
Importance of	I	0		0							++								++								+				
growth as a goal	G												++																		
	P																														
Expected profit or	I	++		++			0	+	–	0	++					++								+							
growth contribution	G												++					++													
of exports	P																											++			
Foreign orientation	I			++														++													
of managers	G																	++													
	P																														

Table 2.4 cont'd

Concepts	*Study Number*	*Abdel 1*	*Air 2*	*Axinn 3*	*Bil82 4*	*Bil85 5*	*BrRo 6*	*BurS 7*	*Cavu 8*	*CaNa 9*	*CaNe 10*	*CoHH 11*	*CooK 12*	*CrGr 13*	*CunS 14*	*DanG 15*	*Diln 16*	*Dich 17*	*FenA 18*	*Gar 19*	*GJP 20*	*Hir 21*	*HirB 22*	*JoCz 23*	*KaSt 24*	*Khan 25*	*KirM 26*	*KleiC 27*	*LaDu 28*	*LaKu 29*	*LaRR 30*
3. *Organization*	*Eff.*																														
Size of	I	++	+	0			++	++	0	++	++	+	++	+		++	0			+	++	+							+	0	
organization	G		–										++					+					++			0	0			0	
	P		0																							0	0				
Export restraints	I												++																		
for foreign-owned	G												++																		
organizations	P																														
Institutionalization	I																++		0			+					++				0
of export function	G																										++				
	P																														
4. *Export market*	*Eff.*																														
Physical distance	I										0										+				0						
to export market	G																									+					
	P																									+					
Trade barriers	I																														
	G																														
	P																														
Attractiveness	I												++																		
of export market	G											0	++													++					
	P				++	+																				++		0			
5. *Domestic market*	*Eff.*																														
Saturation of	I												++								++										
domestic market	G											0	++																		
	P																														

intensity needs to be clarified. First I have to add findings which document a positive relationship between *absolute* domestic sales volume and export sales volume (for example, Fenwick and Amine 1979, McFetridge and Weatherly 1977). These rather trivial findings have been neglected in table 2.4, because absolute volume sales were usually discarded. The economically interesting question is: Do larger firms also export a larger *share* of their sales? A positive answer to this question would support the assumption that larger firms have special *scale economies* which facilitate exporting. The evidence for this relationship is less conclusive. In table 2.5 I have divided the thirty findings into those which used metric export-share scales and studies which used dichotomies ('exporters vs. non-exporters') or crude ordinal scales. One can see that eight of the nine findings which failed to support the hypothesis were gained from studies with metric scales. (The one study with dichotomous scales which failed to confirm the hypothesis was Cavusgil 1982. He compared interested non-exporters with low-exporters [under 10 per cent export-share]. This is an atypical comparison.) The reader should notice that the dichotomous scales were often used in studies where smaller firms dominated. Thus we may conclude that up to a certain minimum size, the probability of exporting in industries with export potential rises with increasing size, but beyond this limit, there is only a weak association between size and exporting. These findings are confirmed by macro-analytic investigations which have tried to identify critical minimum sizes for exporting (Auquier). We cannot conclude from this finding that a higher concentration of firms is needed to stay competitive, because there do exist many more small firms than larger firms. Macro-analytic investigation shows that this effect often outweighs the threshold effect, so that in many industries the export share of *all* small firms is rather high and not necessarily declining.

Table 2.5 Relationship between size and export intensity

Export intensity measurement	*Empirical relationship* ++	+	*0/–*	*Sum*
Non-metric scale	9	2	1	12
Metric scale	5	5	8	18

Information search measures

Main source	Operationalization	Relation
General search measures		
Abdel-Malek	use of government services	++
Brooks/Rosson	use of external information sources	+
Cavusgil 1982	yse of external information sources	++
Cavusgil/Naor	regularly sought: US Dep. of Commerce	++
Cavusgil/Naor	regularly sought: state govmt. agencies	++
Cavusgil/Naor	regularly sought: executives other firms	++
Cavusgil/Naor	regularly sought: export agents	0
Cavusgil/Naor	regularly sought: industry associations	0
Cooper/Kleinschmidt	use of external information sources	+
Moser/Topritzhofer	participation at fairs, trade shows etc.	0
Reffait	information search in export market	++
Reffait/Roux	use of information sources	++
Roux 1987	media exposure	++
Market research measures		
Burton/Schlegelmilch	likelihood own market research	+
Cavusgil/Nevin	formal evaluation of export opport. yes/no	0
Cavusgil/Nevin	systematic exploration of export yes/no	++
Fenwick/Amine	alternative markets researched	0
Khan	expend. market research & sales prom.	+
Kleinschmidt/Cooper	market res. spent on foreign markets	++
Kleinschmidt/Cooper	customer testing done in foreign markets	++
Kleinschmidt/Cooper	trial selling/testing done in foreign markets	++
Langeard et al.	general/special market research studies	0
Langeard et al.	general/special market research studies	0
Madsen	a priori market research	0
McDougall/Stening	market research in-house	+
Tesar/Tarleton	systematic exploration of export yes/no	++

Information use measures

Main source	Operationalization	Relation
Planning measures		
Burton/Schlegelmilch	likelihood formal market plans	+
Cavusgil/Nevin	plans development of markets yes/no	++
Cooper/Kleinschmidt	export marketing planning	+
Kirpalani/Macintosh	quality of forecasting international markets	+
Kleinschmidt	export planning efforts	++
Reffait	intuitive long-range planning	++
Control measures		
Kirpalani/Macintosh	information for control (3-item-factor: reporting frequency & quality, closeness of monitoring)	++
Madsen	planning and control intensity (budgeting, monitoring, control)	++

Communication measures

Main source	Operationalization	Relation
Personal communication measures		
Brooks/Rosson	personal contacts with outside executives	++
Cunningham/Spigel	visits to overseas markets by executives	+
Daniels/Goyboro	prior visits to Andean Bloc Countries	++
Madsen	personal contacts with end users	++
McDougall/Stening	number of visits by senior executives	+
Moser/Topritzhofer	number of visits	+
Moser/Topritzhofer	duration of visits	0
Rosson/Pord	number of visits	+
Tesar/Tarleton	number of visits	++
Impersonal communication measures		
Rosson/Ford	number of letters	++

Figure 2.6 Measurement of information activity

Intensity of *R&D* shows a positive relationship with export intensity, but not with export growth. This is an interesting finding which should be analysed in-depth by future studies. A high R&D activity appears to be necessary to defend a competitive position in the world market, but seems to be not sufficient to expand export activity, at least in the shorter run.

It is surprising that information activity is positively related to all three measures of export success. It appears to be a variable which has been neglected in the export-marketing field as a critical success factor. This raises a question: How was information behaviour measured? Which phenomena are hidden behind this variable? Figure 2.6 shows three groups of measures: information search measures, information use measures, and communication measures. All three groups show positive influences, particularly planning and control measures. It seems very promising to study these factors in depth and build upon the rich empirical research traditions which have been developed in the decision-making and information behaviour field.

REFERENCES

Abdel-Malek, T. (1974) *Managerial Export-Orientation: A Canadian Study*, London, Ontario: School of Business Administration, University of Western Ontario.

Abdel-Malek, T. (1978) 'Export marketing orientation in small firms', *American Journal of Small Business* 3: 25–34.

Airaksinen, T. (1982) 'Export performance of the firms in the Finnish engineering industry', Helsinki School of Economics.

Bilkey, W. J. (1982) 'Variables associated with export profitability', *Journal of International Business Studies* 13: 39–55.

Bilkey, W. J. (1985) 'Development of export marketing guidelines', *International Marketing Review* 2: 31–40.

Bradley, M. F. and Keogh, P. (1981) 'Export management: motivated – open-minded', *Journal of Irish Business and Administrative Research* 3: 29–40.

Brooks, M. R. and Rosson, P. J. (1982) 'A study of export behaviour of small- and medium-sized manufacturing firms in three Canadian provinces', in M. Czinkota and G. Tesar (eds) *Export Management*, New York: Praeger, 39–54.

Burton, F. N. and Schlegelmilch, B. B. (1987) 'Profile analyses of non-exporters versus exporters grouped by export involvement', *Management International Review* 27: 38–49.

Cavusgil, S. T. (1976) 'Organizational determinants of firms' export behaviour: an empirical analysis', dissertation.

Cavusgil, S. T. (1982) 'Some observations on the relevance of critical variables for internationalization stages', in M. Czinkota and G. Tesar (eds) *Export Management*, New York: Praeger, 276–86.

Cavusgil, S. T. (1984) 'Organizational characteristics associated with export activity', *Journal of Management Studies* 21: 3–22.

Cavusgil, S. T. and Nevin, J. R. (1981) 'Internal determinants of export marketing behaviour: an empirical investigation', *Journal of Marketing Research* 18: 114–19.

Cavusgil, S. T. and Naor, J. (1987) 'Firm and management characteristics as discriminators of export marketing activity', *Journal of Business Research* 15: 221–35.

Cavusgil, S. T., Bilkey, W. J. and Tesar, G. (1979) 'A note on the export behaviour of firms: exporter profiles', *Journal of International Business Studies* 10: 91–7.

Cooper, R. A., Hartley, K. and Harvey, C. R. M. (1970) *Export Performance and the Pressure of Demand: A Study of Firms*, London: Allen & Unwin.

Cooper, R. G. and Kleinschmidt, E. J. (1985) 'The impact of export strategy on export sales performance', *Journal of International Business Studies* 16: 37–55.

Crookell, H. and Graham, I. (1979) 'International marketing and Canadian industrial strategy', *The Business Quarterly* 44: 28–34.

Cunningham, M. T. and Spigel, R. I. (1971) 'A study in successful exporting', *British Journal of Marketing* 5: 2–12.

Czinkota, M. R. and Johnston, W. J. (1983) 'Exporting: does sales volume make a difference?', *Journal of International Business Studies* 14: 147–53.

Daniels, J. D. and Goyboro, J. (1976) 'The exporter–non-exporter interface: a search for variables', *Foreign Trade Review* 11: 258–82.

Dichtl, E., Leibold, M., Köglmayr, H.-G. and Müller, S. (1983) 'The foreign orientation of management as a central construct in export-centred decision-making processes', *Research for Marketing* 10: 7–14.

Dichtl, E., Köglmayr, H.-G. and Müller, S. (1984) 'Die Auslandsorientierung von Führungskräften: Eine Schlüsselvariable für Exportförderung und Exporterfolg', in E. Dichtl and O. Issing (eds) *Exporte als Herausforderung für die deutsche Wirtschaft*, Berlin: Deutscher Instituts-Verlag, 429–62.

Dichtl, E., Köglmayr, H.-G. and Müller, S. (1986) 'Die Auslandsorientierung als Voraussetzung für Exporterfolge', *Zeitschrift für Betriebswirtschaft*, 56: 1064–76.

Fenwick, I. and Amine, L. (1979) 'Export performance and export policy: evidence from the UK clothing industry', *Journal of the Operational Research Society* 30: 747–54.

Ford, I. D. and Rosson, P. J. (1982) 'The relationships between export manufacturers and their overseas distributors', in M. Czinkota and G. Tesar (eds) *Export Management*, New York: Praeger, 257–75.

Garnier, G. (1982) 'Comparative export behaviour of small Canadian firms in the printing and electrical industries', in M. Czinkota and G. Tesar (eds) *Export Management*, New York: Praeger, 113–131.
Glejser, H., Jacquemin, A. and Petit, J. (1980) 'Exports in an imperfect competition framework: an analysis of 1,446 exporters', *The Quarterly Journal of Economics* 94: 507–24.
Hirsch, S. (1971) *The Export Performance of Six Manufacturing Industries: A Comparative Study of Denmark, Holland, and Israel*, New York: Praeger.
Hirsch, S. and Adar, Z. (1974) 'Firm size and export performance', *World Development* 2: 41–6.
Hirsch, S. and Bijaoui, I. (1985) 'R&D intensity and export performance: a micro view', *Weltwirtschaftliches Archiv* 121: 238–51.
Hunt, H. G., Frogatt, J. D. and Hovell, P. J. (1967) 'The management of export marketing in engineering industries', *British Journal of Marketing*: 10–24.
Johnston, W. J. and Czinkota, M. R. (1982) 'Managerial motivations as determinants of industrial export behaviour', in M. Czinkota and G. Tesar (eds) *Export Management*, New York: Praeger, 3–17.
Kaynak, E. and Stevenson, L. (1982) 'Export orientation of Nova Scotia manufacturers', in M. Czinkota and G. Tesar (eds) *Export Management*, New York: Praeger, 132–45.
Khan, M. S. (1978) *A Study of Success and Failure in Exports*, Stockholm, Akademilitteratur.
Kirpalani, V. H. and Macintosh, N. B. (1980) 'International marketing effectiveness of technology-oriented small firms', *Journal of International Business Studies* 11: 81–90.
Kleinschmidt, E. J. (1986) *The Impact of Foreign Ownership on the Export Behaviour of Industrial Firms*, Canada, McMaster University.
Kleinschmidt, E. J. and Cooper, R. G. (1986) 'The performance impact of an international orientation on product innovation', Working Paper, Canada, McMaster University.
Kleinschmidt, E. J. and Ross, R. E. (1984) 'Export performance and foreign market information: relationships for small high-technology firms', *Journal of Small Business* 2: 8–23.
Lall, S. and Kumar, R. (1981) 'Firm-level export performance in an inward-looking economy: the Indian engineering industry', *World Development* 9: 453–63.
Langeard, E., Reffait, P. and Roux, E. (1976a) 'Les composantes de la performance commerciale des candidats aux oscars de l'exportation', Paris: Institut D'Administration des Entreprises.
Langeard, E., Reffait, P. and Roux, E. (1976b) 'Profil commercial de l'exportateur Français', *Revue Française de Gestion* (November–December) 91–109.
Lee, W.-L. and Brasch, J. J. (1978) 'The adoption of exports as an innovative strategy', *Journal of International Business Studies* 9: 85–93.
Madsen, T. K. (1987) 'Eksportsucces: Hvad og hvordan? En empirisk undersøgelse af nogle Danske fremdstillingsvirksomheders eksportaktiviteter', dissertation: Odense, Denmark.

McConnell, J. E. (1970) 'The export decision: an empirical study of firm behaviour', *Economic Geography* 55: 171–83.
McDougall, G. H. G. and Stening, B. W. (1975) 'Something to think about: identifying the high performance exporter', *Canada Commerce* (December): 12–15.
McFetridge, D. G. and Weatherly, L. J. (1977) 'Notes on the economics of large firm size', Minister of Supply and Services, Ottawa, Canada.
McGuinness, N. W. (1983) 'The influence of research and development on foreign sales performance', in A. M. Rugman (ed.) *Multinationals and Technology Transfer: The Canadian Experience*, 126–41.
McGuinness, N. W. and Little, B. (1981a) 'The influence of product characteristics on the export performance of new industrial products', *Journal of Marketing* 45: 110–22.
McGuinness, N. W. and Little, B. (1981b) 'The impact of R&D spending on the foreign sales of new Canadian industrial products', *Research Policy*, 10: 78–98.
Moser, R. and Topritzhofer, E. (1979) 'Exploratorische LOGIT-und PROBIT-Analysen zur empirischen Indentifikation von Determinanten der Exporttüchtigkeit von Unternehmen', *Zeitschrift für Betriebswirtschaft* 49: 873–90.
Müller, S. and Köglmayr, H.-G. (1986) 'Die psychische Distanz zu Auslandsmärkten: Ein verkanntes Exporthemmnis', *Schmalenbachs Zeitschrift für betriebswirt schaftliche Forschung* 38: 788–804.
Ong, C. H. and Pearson, A. W. (1982) 'The impact of technical characteristics on export activity: a study of small- and medium-sized UK electronic firms', *R&D Management* 12: 189–96.
Pavord, W. C. and Bogard, R. G. (1975) 'The dynamics of the decision to export', *Akron Business and Economic Review* (Spring): 6–11.
Piercy, N. (1981) 'Company internationalization: active and reactive exporting', *European Journal of Marketing* 15: 26–40.
Reffait, P. (1984) 'Corrélation entre le profil du responsable export et la réussite internationale de l'entreprise', *L'Exportation*, 72–94.
Reffait, P. and Roux, E. (1979) *Correlates of Small Business Export Performance*, Paris: Institut d'Administration des Entreprises, Aix-en-Provence, France.
Reffait, P. and Roux, E. (1981) 'Le profil idéal de la PMI exportatrice', *Revue Française de Gestion* (January–February): 88–96.
Reffait, P. and Roux, E. (1985) 'Marketing des produits agricoles: les voies du succès à l'exportation', *Revue Francaise du Marketing* 102: 95–107.
Reid, S. (1986) 'Is technology linked with export performance in small firms', in H. Hübner (ed.) *The Art and Science of Innovation Management*, Amsterdam: Elsevier, 273–83.
Reid, S. (1987) 'Export structures, strategy and performance: an empirical study of small Italian manufacturing firms', in P. Rosson and S. Reid (eds) *Managing Export Entry and Expansion: Concepts and Practice*, New York: Praeger, 335–57.
Rosson, P. J. and Ford, I. D. (1982) 'Manufacturer–overseas distributor

relations and export performance', *Journal of International Business Studies* 13: 57–72.

Roux, E. (1979) 'The export behaviour of small- and medium-size French firms: the role of the manager's profile', in L. G. Mattsson and F. Wiedersheim-Paul (eds) *Recent Research on the Internationalization of business. Proceedings from the Annual Meeting of the European International Business Association*, Stockholm: Almqvist & Wiksell, 88–101.

Roux, E. (1983a) 'Interaction effects of managerial and firm factors on export performance', CERRESSEC France, Corgy-Pontaise-Cedax.

Roux, E. (1983b) 'Firm and managerial determinants of small business export performance', Working Paper, Belgium, Brussel El ASM workshop.

Roux, E. (1987) 'Managers' attitudes toward risk among determinants of export entry of small- and medium-sized firms', in P. Rosson and S. Reid (eds) *Managing Export Entry and Expansion: Concepts and Practice*, New York: Praeger, 95–110.

Sarathy, R. (1982) 'The financial basis of export success: an analysis of Japan's major industrial exporters', in M. Czinkota and G. Tesar (eds) *Export Management*, New York: Praeger, 200–13.

Sarathy, R. (1985) 'Inter-industry differences in export activity among Japanese corporations', in H. Simon (ed.) *Proceedings of the Annual Conference of the European Marketing Academy*, 100–9.

Schlegelmilch, B. (1986) 'Controlling country-specific and industry-specific influences on export behaviour', *European Journal of Marketing* 20: 54–71.

Schlegelmilch, B. (1988) 'Der Zusammenhang zwischen Innovationsneigung und Exportleistung. Ergebnisse einer empirischen Untersuchung in der deutschen Maschinenbauindustrie', *Schmalenbachs Zeitschrift für betriebswirtschaftliche Forschung* 40: 227–42.

Schlegelmilch, B. and Crook, J. N. (1986) 'Firm level determinants of export intensity', Department of Business Studies, Edinburgh, Scotland.

Schlegelmilch, B. and Diamantopoulos, A. (1987) 'The impact of innovativeness on export performance: empirical evidence from the UK mechanical engineering industry', Department of Business Studies, Edinburgh, Scotland.

Simpson, C. L. and Kujawa, D. (1974) 'The export decision process: an empirical inquiry', *Journal of International Business Studies*, 5: 107–17.

Tesar, G. (1975) 'Empirical study of export operations among small- and medium-sized manufacturing firms', dissertation, Madison, U.S.A., University of Wisconsin.

Tesar, G. and Tarleton, J. S. (1982) 'Comparison of Wisconsin and Virginia small- and medium-sized exporters: aggressive and passive exporters', in M. Czinkota and G. Tesar (eds) *Export Management*, New York: Praeger, 85–112.

Tookey, D. A. (1964) 'Factors associated with success in exporting', *The Journal of Management Studies* 1: 48–66.
Ziegler, W. (1984) 'Die Unternehmerbeurteilung als Instrument zur Früherkennung von Kreditrisiken', dissertation Universität Hohenheim.

Chapter Three

THE INTERNATIONAL INVOLVEMENT OF FIRMS ON THE UNLISTED SECURITIES MARKET (USM)

T. CANNON, J. McKAY, AND A. McAULEY

The research upon which this chapter is based forms part of a two-year project funded by the Economic and Social Research Council of Great Britain. Structurally, the paper will divide into four broad sections. The first section aims to place the research in perspective, outlining the objectives of the study and the research strategy to be adopted. The second section will provide a brief review of the major theories of internationalization. In the third section the origins and workings of the Unlisted Securities Market (USM) in the UK will be outlined. This section will act as the bridge to the fourth section, the focal point of the paper, which reveals the characteristics of internationalized companies on the USM.

BACKGROUND TO THE STUDY

Research objectives and hypothesis

The purpose of the study is to examine the extent to which firms on the USM have adapted their domestic marketing techniques to the internationalization of their business. The research proposes to examine the use of marketing research within the domestic market and its contribution to the internationalization process; product, price and promotional policies at home and overseas; and, finally, the role of intermediaries and support networks in international ventures. The basic hypothesis of the research is that firms which:

- are strongly market-orientated domestically;

- apply the same disciplines, skills, and resources overseas;
- construct marketing strategies based on in-depth knowledge of the overseas market;
- base marketing decisions on local rather than domestic conditions;
- integrate this process through comprehensive marketing plans;

will be more successful in the international arena than firms which fail to adopt this approach.

Research strategy

Background research consisted of a review of literature on the internationalization of firms and on the operation of the USM. USM companies were selected as the sampling population because these businesses, which are in the process of expanding, will adopt internationalization as one possible strategy for growth. Annual reports were obtained from companies on the USM, providing a useful bank of secondary information on these businesses. A statistical analysis of the data on the international UK companies was undertaken subsequently. Primary data will be collected at a later stage from in-depth personal interviews with a sample of international companies on the USM. It is intended that the sample will comprise twenty companies which are successful overseas and ten companies which have failed in international ventures. Overseas turnover in excess of 50 per cent of total turnover is taken as an indicator of successful overseas involvement and an orientation towards the international marketplace. Conversely, unsuccessful involvement is signalled by withdrawal from export markets, or by an overseas turnover figure remaining at less than 10 per cent of total turnover in recent years. Interviews with the domestic and export marketing manager of these companies will yield valuable insights into the role of marketing at home and overseas. A comparative analysis of the marketing strategies of these thirty companies will be undertaken. This exercise will permit the development of case studies of best practices for the effective internationalization of high-growth UK companies.

THEORIES OF INTERNATIONALIZATION

The behavioural theory focuses on the role of management in guiding a firm towards internationalization. A positive correlation has been established between certain traits of management and involvement in international business activities. Simmonds and Smith (1968) found that an external stimulus was responsible for a firm's first export order. This, however, was assisted by the fact that top management adopted an aggressive and competitive stance, emphasized expansion and growth, and had a supra-national outlook. This finding is supported by the work of Langston and Teas (1976), who reported that people with an interest in and experience of international affairs were more inclined to initiate exporting activity.

A spate of authors are proponents of a stages approach to internationalization (Bilkey 1978, Denis and Depelteau 1980, Cavusgil and Nevin 1981, and Johanson and Wiedersheim-Paul 1978). Their studies conclude that the internationalization of a firm is a gradual process, taking place in incremental stages over a relatively long period of time.

Cavusgil (1980) pointed out that export marketing is usually considered to be a first step in the process of internationalization. From their empirical work in Sweden, Johanson and Wiedersheim-Paul (1978) identified the stages of development as: no regular export activities; export via independent representatives; the organization of sales subsidiaries; and, ultimately, the establishment of a production unit.

Cavusgil (1984) attributed the sequential nature of this process to the increased risk and greater uncertainty which is associated with conducting international business. Hence, with experience, management may develop a more confident approach to international business based on a learning and feedback process, which is evident in the stages approach. Internationalization is seen to begin in foreign markets which are most similar to those at home where the barriers to retrieval and interpretation of information are perceived to be less. However, evidence presented by Young (1980) indicates that the stages model is not applicable to every industry. A more revolutionary approach is taken by companies in the high-technology sector, which tend to engage in more rapid and distant international involvement.

THE UNLISTED SECURITIES MARKET

The establishment of the USM

The Unlisted Securities Market was established in November 1980 in direct response to criticism of the Official Stock Exchange List. During the 1970s it was becoming increasingly difficult for the smaller company to join the Official List because of the cost of compliance with the conditions and rules of entry. The Wilson Committee Report (1980) concluded that the growth and expansion prospects of the small firm sector were inhibited by a lack of long term equity finance. The Stock Exchange envisaged that the establishment of the USM would make a vital contribution to the growth of smaller companies by providing them with capital to finance expansion and by enhancing their trading status and corporate image.

Requirements for admission to the USM

The requirements for admission to the USM are, of necessity, less stringent than for a full listing on the Stock Exchange. A trading record of three years is required, as opposed to five years for the Official List. In exceptional circumstances, however, companies with a shorter track record may be eligible for entry to the USM. These start-up ventures must provide evidence that funds are required to finance a product or project which is fully researched and costed. The USM has no minimum size of market capitalization, whereas a minimum level of £700,000 is imposed for a company seeking admission to the senior market. USM companies must place at least 10 per cent of their equity capital in public hands, which is substantially less than the 25 per cent minimum requirement for the Official List. The costs of advertising are not prohibitive for newcomers to the USM. The regulation demands that details of sale be placed in one national newspaper. By contrast, companies seeking a listing on the senior market must publish their prospectus in full in two national newpapers.

Growth of the USM

For the smaller, expanding business, the USM, with its less stringent entry conditions, has proved a popular vehicle for quotation on the Stock Exchange. Since its inception in November 1980, the number of trading companies has continued to increase annually. Table 3.1 charts the development of this novel market from a membership roll of twenty-three trading companies in December 1980, to eighty-six after its first full year of operation, through to 370 at the close of 1987.

Table 3.1 Growth of the USM

Year end	*Number of trading companies*
1980	23
1981	86
1982	141
1983	204
1984	270
1985	337
1986	368
1987	370

Source: Stock Exchange Fact Service

In total, during this seven-year period of its existence, the USM attracted no fewer than 604 entrants. The pattern of exits from the USM serves as a useful measure of the progress of this market. The success of the USM is illustrated by the fact that 108 of the 234 departures represent transfers to the senior market. The USM is thus utilized by a number of high-growth companies as a springboard to officially listed status on the Stock Exchange. Acquisitions under offer account for eighty-eight of the exits from the USM. Ten companies which have reorganized their structure have been re-admitted to the USM in their new form. The number of failures on the USM has been markedly small, with the shares of twenty-eight companies being the subject of a suspension or cancellation at the end of 1987. Table 3.2 provides a summary of these statistics.

Table 3.2 USM summary

Total admitted	604
Transferred to Official List	108
Acquired under offer	88
Cancelled	15
Suspended	13
Reorganized	10
Total trading	370

Source: Stock Exchange Fact Service

RESEARCH FINDINGS

Introduction to findings

Desk research identified a total of 363 companies trading on the USM at the end of October 1987. Annual reports were received from 340 of these companies, yielding an overall response rate of 94 per cent. UK-based companies account for 318 of this total. Two hundred and nineteen of the UK companies (69 per cent) have some measure of involvement in international markets. However, data on overseas turnover was supplied by only 168 international companies, and it is on the characteristics of these companies that this chapter will focus.

Location and size of USM companies

The registered office address was taken as the base location of international USM companies. Although spread throughout the UK, two-thirds are concentrated in a cluster in the South East of England.

Employment figures and volume of turnover were adopted as indicators of the size of USM companies. The average size of labour force is 251, a figure which places USM companies within the medium-size range. The average figure does however mask enormous diversity in the size of USM companies – from a minimum of three, the employee total rises to a maximum of 2,237. The smallest company, Cityvision, is engaged in film and video distribution, while the largest, Millward Brown, operates as a market research agency, recruiting on average 1,931 freelance interviewers for fieldwork. A mere 8 per cent of international USM companies can boast a labour force in excess of 500.

The mean annual turnover for these internationalized businesses stood at £9.4m for the year 1984–5. For the year ended 1986, this figure had climbed to £10.5m, yielding an annual increase of 13 per cent. A comparison with the 1987 figure shows growth in average turnover to a level of £12.8m, a substantial increase of 22 per cent over the previous year. By volume of turnover, therefore, companies on the USM may be categorized as medium-sized concerns. The pronounced growth in average turnover is evidence that the USM is typically composed of vibrant and expanding businesses. At an individual level, for their last reporting year, 137 of the 168 companies (82 per cent) experienced a growth in turnover which levelled out at an average increase of 43 per cent. Ten international companies more than doubled their turnover in the last year for which data is available. The companies achieving phenomenal growth are concentrated predominantly in the electrical sector. Only a small proportion of companies, 18 per cent in fact, reported a decline in turnover. From these findings it is apparent that high growth is an identifying characteristic of international companies on the USM.

Organizational complexity

USM members are typically an amalgam of a number of individual companies. The average USM firm holds ownership of six subsidiaries of trading, holding or dormant status. Not surprisingly, the majority of USM members exist purely as holding companies engaged in the provision of management and financial services to subsidiaries of the group. Only 30 per cent of the internationalized companies have a trading status in their own right. USM companies in ownership of a large number of subsidiaries display most complexity in their organizational structure. These companies are organized into a series of tiers, comprising the parent company, intermediate holding companies, direct subsidiaries, and indirectly-held subsidiaries. Figure 3.1 illustrates the complex group structure of American Business Systems plc.

Only nine of the 168 companies studied are themselves

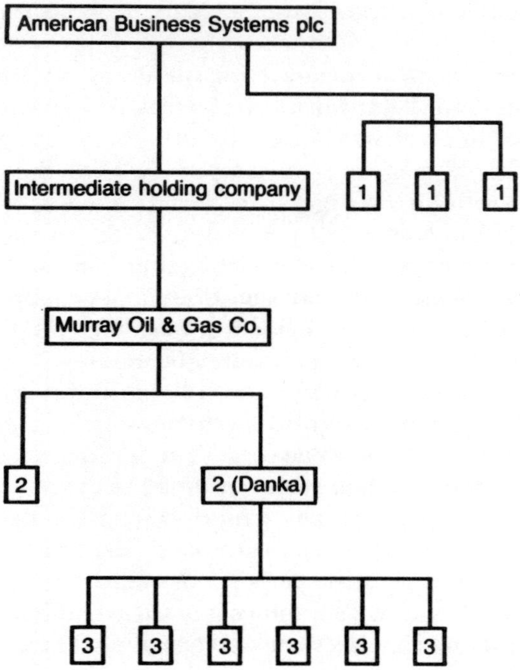

Key:
1 subsidiaries directly held by American Business Systems plc
2 subsidiaries held by Murray Oil & Gas Co.
3 subsidiaries held by Danka Industries Inc.

Figure 3.1 Structure of American business systems

subsidiaries of a larger organization which has ultimate control over the group's destiny.

Acquisition of new businesses

The acquisition of new businesses will undoubtedly contribute to the organizational complexity of USM members. The analysis shows that USM companies are on the acquisition trail, purchasing on average two companies per year. This figure includes direct and indirect acquisitions, and those businesses acquired through a subsidiary. It is apparent from this finding that USM members are pursuing acquisition as a route to growth and diversification. However, the search for acquisitions is by no means confined to the domestic market. In their last reporting year, ten companies cast their acquisition net into international waters, acquiring between them, directly or indirectly, a total of twenty-five foreign businesses.

International involvement of USM companies

The analysis revealed that over two-thirds (69 per cent) of the UK companies quoted on the USM engage in international business activities. Although this proportion is extremely high, the extent of internationalization of these companies is variable.

The overseas turnover of USM companies has increased from a mean figure of £1.8m for the year end 1985, to 2.7m in 1986, and to 3.5m in 1987. However, the virtual twofold increase in overseas turnover during this period is notably from a low base.

The extent of internationalization of USM companies is reflected in the percentage of annual turnover derived from markets overseas. For the period 1986–7 the average was 28 per cent, a figure which has shown no change since 1985. Thus, although the volume of overseas turnover is rising, overall, for USM companies, export markets are not gaining in importance. The 28 per cent mean for USM companies is marginally lower than the 30 per cent quoted for an average international company. The USM export ratio is biased moreover by the existence of six companies, all but one engaged principally in the oil industry, which derive their total turnover from markets overseas. Omitting these companies from the sample, overseas turnover would deflate to a level of 22 per cent of total turnover. The implication is that USM companies, at the present time, are not internationalized to a high degree. Indeed, 35 per cent of these companies have an overseas turnover measured at less than 10 per cent of total turnover. While some of these companies may be classified as new exporters, it is probable that a large number in this category are uncommitted exporters, regarding exporting as a marginal activity, as a mechanism for absorbing excess production. A sizeable majority of internationalized businesses on the USM (62 per cent) generate less than a quarter of their turnover in international markets. Export-orientated companies, defined as those deriving more than half of their turnover from overseas, account for only 21 per cent of the total. Table 3.3 indicates the extent of international involvement of USM companies.

Table 3.3 Overseas turnover of USM companies

Percentage of turnover overseas	*Number of companies*	*Percentage of companies*
1–9	58	35
10–24	45	27
25–49	29	17
50–74	21	12
75–100	15	9

International markets

Table 3.4 indicates the international markets served by companies on the USM. The percentage of companies with *known* interests in these geographical markets is noted.

Table 3.4 International markets of USM companies

Market	*Percentage of companies in market*
Europe	67
North America	56
Middle East	11
Africa	11
Australasia	11
South America	8
Far East	7
Asia	7
Undefined	65

These figures demonstrate that Europe is the most popular international destination for goods and services of USM companies. Sixty-seven per cent of companies are active in the European market, while a slightly lower proportion (56 per cent) derive turnover from North America. The reasons for this pattern are suggested by the concepts of geographic and psychic proximity. The closeness of Europe, however, is only a partial explanation for the high instance of involvement in this market. Membership of the EC, providing access to wealthy, tariff-free zones, has played a major role in stimulating the development of exports to Europe. Significantly, markets which are more remote in terms of geographic or cultural distance are much less attractive to USM companies. Only 7 per cent of companies have indicated involvement in Asia and the Far East, 8 per cent in South America, and 11 per cent in the Middle East, Africa and the distant continent of Australasia.

The most intensely developed markets are, not surprisingly, Europe and North America. For the 111 companies active in Europe, an average 55 per cent of their overseas turnover emanates from this market. The comparative figure for companies in North America is slightly lower, averaging at 51 per cent of overseas turnover.

Market withdrawal

Six USM companies, currently active in the international arena, have withdrawn from the following export markets: North America, Far East (2 companies), Africa, Asia, and other. It is noticeable that withdrawals are predominantly from markets which are geographically and culturally remote from the UK. Customers in these distant areas of the world may have needs and expectations which differ sharply from those held in the West. It is a reasonable assumption that a lack of cultural sensitivity on the part of these companies, a lack of product and marketing adaptation, contributed in many cases to failure in these markets.

Ownership of subsidiaries overseas

Half of the international companies under review own subsidiaries in export markets. However, at the level of the individual firm, the number of subsidiaries held is typically very low. Thirty-four of these eighty-four companies are in control of only one subsidiary, and seventeen hold two subsidiaries. Thus, the majority (61 per cent) hold ownership of only one or two subsidiaries in international markets.

In terms of location, 73 per cent of companies with overseas subsidiaries have a base in North America, 48 per cent have subsidiaries in Europe, and 18 per cent in other markets. The combined percentage total exceeds 100 as an individual company may have subsidiaries in more than one overseas market. Thus, although Europe is the most important international market, here, reliance on intermediaries is predominant.

The concept of psychological proximity may be used as one explanation for the tendency to locate in North America. In this English-speaking market, the legal, financial and administrative problems surrounding subsidiary formation may appear to be less. Geographical distance is perhaps another factor favouring direct representation in this important market. It is difficult (thought not impossible) for UK companies to maintain at such distance personal contact with and control over intermediaries in North America.

The stages model would appear to hold some validity for companies on the USM. Less experienced or less committed companies, deriving under a tenth of their turnover from overseas, tend to focus on exporting directly or through independent intermediaries. Only 17 per cent of companies in this category have a subsidiary organization trading in overseas markets. By comparison, two-thirds of companies with overseas turnover between 50 and 75 per cent have at least one subsidiary overseas. Service organizations, however, show a divergence from the sequential pattern of the stages model. The Pineapple Group, an operator of dance centres, established a subsidiary in New York to gain entry to the US market. Similarly, for Moorgate, a marketing consultancy firm, the formation of a Spanish subsidiary was the direct route to business development in Spain and Portugal. The stages model is thus limited in its ability to explain the internationalization of service industries which tend to bypass the exporting phase. It is generally not feasible for such firms to attract a volume of international business or serve world markets from the domestic base. For these businesses, the organization of subsidiaries overseas often constitutes the first and final stage of involvement in international markets.

Business activities

International companies on the USM were categorized by their principal class of activity. The primary sector accounts for 5 per cent of international USM companies, the secondary sector for

56 per cent, intermediate construction for 1 per cent, intermediate communication for 2 per cent, and the tertiary sector for 36 per cent. Thirty-seven companies (22 per cent) span two of these classifications, a finding which illustrates the diverse nature of international companies on the USM. The predominance of the manufacturing industry is not a striking finding. Service and construction industries, it must be realized, have less potential to internationalize.

International companies were further categorized by their field of business. Focusing on the principal activity of these companies, the electrical sector is the most important, accounting for 31 per cent of international companies. The industrials miscellaneous category is also well represented on this basis, with 20 per cent of international USM companies active in this sector. The diverse interests of USM companies are marked by the involvement of thirty-nine companies in two industrial sectors, four companies in three sectors, and by the participation of one company in four sectors of business. This company, Hughes Food Group, has interests spanning the food and grocery, industrials miscellaneous, property, and hire purchase and leasing sectors. Diversification of business interests is further exemplified by Rockwood Holdings. Originally with activities in electronic component distribution and security consultancy, the Group is now, following acquisitions, also engaged in tobacco and food distribution.

The USM provides examples of companies which have altered totally the major focus of their business. One such company, Hobson, was to the end of 1986 engaged principally in the development of the Hobson Process for the manufacture of extrusion dyes. Following acquisitions in 1986 and 1987, and the sale of this business, the Group now operates as exporters and commodity traders. To 1986 the sole activity of New Court Natural Resources was oil and gas exploration and production. The acquisition of Danka Industries in December 1986 directed the Group into its new, principal area of business – the supply and servicing of business equipment. The company name was changed to American Business Systems to reflect the new activity, and the majority of its oil and gas interests have now been sold. The examples cited above serve to indicate the opportunistic approach to business adopted by USM companies, which tend to move into new and uncomplementary areas of business as openings appear.

SUMMARY OF FINDINGS

The findings show that USM companies are adopting internationalization as one strategy for growth. The majority of these medium-sized companies are not, however, internationalized to a significant extent, deriving less than a quarter of their turnover from overseas. The favoured markets are North America and Europe, a choice which can be justified by their psychological or geographical proximity to the UK market. Subsidiary ownership is common in the North American market, whereas Europe, on the other hand, tends to be served by independent intermediaries. Acquisition is typically adopted by USM companies as a route to growth, but for a small number, acquiring overseas, it forms part of their strategy for overseas expansion. Diversification through acquisition is common among USM companies, many of whom operate in more than one field of business.

REFERENCES

Bilkey, W. J. (1978) 'An attempted integration of the literature on the export behaviour of firms', *Journal of International Business Studies* 9: 33–46.

Cavusgil, S. T. (1980) 'On the internationalization process of firms', *European Research* 8: 273–81.

Cavusgil, S. T. (1984) 'Differences among exporting firms based on their degree of internationalization', *Journal of Business Research* 12: 195–208.

Cavusgil, S. T. and Nevin, J. R. (1981) 'State-of-the-art in international marketing', in B. M. Enis and K. J. Roering (eds) *Review of Marketing*, Chicago: American Marketing Association, 195–216.

Denis, J. E. and Depelteau, D. (1980) 'Profile analysis of export activities of smaller-sized Quebec manufacturing firms', paper presented at the 1980 Canadian Regional Meeting of the Academy of International Business, 1980.

Johanson, J. and Wiedersheim-Paul, F. (1978) 'The internationalization of the firm: four Swedish cases', *The Journal of Management Studies* (October): 305–22.

Langston, C. M. and Teas, R. K. (1976) 'Export commitment and characteristics of management', paper presented at the Annual Meeting of the Midwest Business Association, St Louis, Missouri.

Simmonds, K. and Smith, H. (1968) 'The first export order: a marketing innovation', *British Journal of Marketing* (Summer): 93–100.
Wilson Committee Report (1980) *Committee to Review the Functioning of Financial Institutions*, Cmnd. 7937, London: HMSO.
Young, S. (1980) 'Scottish multinationals and the Scottish economy', paper presented at an IRM/SIBU conference in Glasgow.

Chapter Four

THE MANAGEMENT CONTRACT AS A MODE OF INDUSTRIAL CO-OPERATION

F. N. BURTON AND A. HAMMOUTENE

The primary purpose of this chapter is to encourage a re-appraisal and clarification of the role and potential of the management contract in international business. A management contract is defined in the literature as an arrangement under which an enterprise takes responsibility for the operational control of another for a given period of time in return for a fixed fee (Pugh 1961, Turner 1974) with possible variations based on performance indicators. While ownership is usually retained by the local partner (client), control is vested in the foreign vendor (contractor), with or without equity interest. This description refers particularly to the *explicit* (pure or basic) management contract, which separates the vendor's provision of capital from the supply of managerial functions. In contrast, an *implicit* contract represents an arrangement which combines the provision of managerial and technical functions with other contractual arrangements such as licensing, technical assistance, and turnkey projects. The essence of the argument in this paper is that undue emphasis has been placed on the explicit mode, with the consequence that the integrative role of the implicit management contract in facilitating technology transfer has been obscured in circumstances in which foreign ownership is denied.

The literature on the management contract as a distinct mode of international co-operation is limited and of recent origin. Early researchers (Gabriels 1967, Ellison 1972) explored the option of the management contract as an actual and potentially virile alternative to the wholly owned subsidiary of multinational firms in developing countries (LDCs).

Gabriel (1972) argued that the management contract has the potential to depose other international business modes, particularly foreign direct investment, by the end of the century because it dispenses with the issues of foreign ownership and entrepreneurial risk, which are substituted by rewards to foreign management for services rendered. Thus, the management contract was considered to be an appropriate arrangement between foreign firms and local industries and public enterprises in which FDI is excluded, or where legislation inhibits the performance and profitability of foreign subsidiaries.

It can be argued that the pioneering work of Gabriel, which emphasized the potential of the explicit management contract in an analysis restricted to four US firms, misdirected subsequent researchers in pursuit of specific examples of the management contract as an end in itself for the foreign firm (i.e., as a vehicle with which to exploit the monopoly rent-earning capacity of surplus corporate skills of multinational firms inside LDCs constrained by scarce management resources), particularly in countries which threatened foreign asset expropriation, or were expressing dissatisfaction with the contribution of FDI to the development process. Although Gabriel (1970) observed that the management contract was most prevalent in relatively high technology industries, that is to say, in industries which may require managerial and technical expertise appropriate to the successful absorption of technological inputs, his analysis sustained a conceptual weakness, repeated by others, which confused the management contract with co-production agreements, service contracts, and contractual joint ventures, without a clear appreciation that these represent quite distinct modes of technology transfer. In a single-minded search for explicit management contracts, there appears to have been a failure to concede that a typical arrangement, where the management contract is utilized, is for managerial and technical services to be formalized in a management contract, and for other elements of technology transfer to be formalized in (say) a licensing of joint venture agreement.

Ellison's (1972) analysis of the experience with management contracts of fourteen UK firms drew particular attention to potential areas of conflict between local and foreign partners over the technology transfer process and the provision of training, but the essence of the study, following Gabriel, was to describe the characteristics of the explicit management contract and to suggest guidelines for their implementation. The study of five Swedish firms by Sharma (1983) also centred on the merits of the management contract as an alternative to FDI, but emphasized more emphatically that the main purpose was to strengthen the foreign firm's control of manpower, technology and marketing.

It remained for Brooke (1985), in a study of firms' experiences in Africa, to clarify the fundamental nature of the management contract as a support for other types of contractual agreements, particularly turnkey projects and joint ventures. In other words, the management contract, typically an integral part of the technology transfer process, from the viewpoint of the contractor is an arrangement to guarantee that the managerial and training inputs will be sufficient to protect and exploit the sale of proprietary technology. However, despite reporting that there was no evidence of the explicit (basic) management contract in the manufacturing sector, and that it was quite rare elsewhere, for example in the hotel and agricultural sectors, this research persisted with the explicit mode as the analytical model.

In general, the direction of research to date has been to assess the feasibility of the management contract as a substitute for, rather than as a complement to, more traditional modes of international industrial co-operation, and the literature has tended to focus on the management contract as an end in itself (and with operational aspects) rather than with its implicit mode as a means to integrated organizational and technical skills with various technology transfer modes. Buckley (1983), for example, in demonstrating that emerging modes of industrial co-operation are integrative arrangements to facilitate technology transfer, draws on the literature describing the explicit model, but the role of the management contract, in any event, receives scant attention. To summarize, in a fruitless search for the explicit management contract, the prevalence of implicit management arrangements as a means to protect proprietary rights and technological inputs has probably been underestimated (Holly 1980), although their integrative significance in the technology transfer process has long been recognized by development economists (Cooper and Sercovitch 1970, Balasubramanyam 1983).

Despited their elusive nature, it was suggested by Brooke (1985) that the basic management contract may have considerable appeal to socialist states as a means to acquire managerial, specialist, and training skills from capitalist societies without compromising political ideology. The following section examines this notion by reporting on the attitudes of public sector administrators towards the concept of the management contract in Algeria, a centrally-planned economy.

CONTRACTUAL AGREEMENTS IN ALGERIA

Data on Algeria were derived from case studies, attitude measurement and interviews with ten public sector officials involved with contractual agreements with foreign firms. A semi-structured questionnaire, administered during March 1985, was used during interviews. The questionnaire consisted mostly of open-ended questions except for a section which contained ten statements of attitudes, measured on a Likert-type scale, to assess general attitudes and the perception of host government officials.

As part of a larger study of contractual agreements, four hypotheses were tested as follows:

1 the explicit management contract has limited validity;
2 the management contract is usually tied to technology transfer modes (apart from FDI), such as licensing agreements, technical assistance contracts, engineering contracts, turnkey projects, and product-in-hand contracts;
3 combined agreements are an increasingly-preferred technology transfer mode;
4 the demand for contractual agreements in LDCs arises from a lack of managerial and technical skills.

FDI was the predominant foreign investment mode in Algeria up to the early years of independence, when most foreign firms were either nationalized or had their activities restricted to non-strategic sectors (for example, consumer goods). Contractual agreements with foreign firms were initiated in the mid-1960s, and in the three-year development plan 1967–9, and sustained in succeeding plans which laid down ambitious industrialization programmes. Almost the total value of contracts in the manufacturing sector from 1962–77 was accounted for by six industry groups, as shown in table 4.1.

Table 4.1

Industry	*Total value of contracts (%)*
Steel	25.0
Metallic, mechanical	
Electrical construction	21.0
Construction materials	17.0
Chemicals	15.0
Food	10.0
Textiles	9.0
Total	97.0

Table 4.1 illustrates the pattern of change in contractual arrangements during this period. Two trends are apparent. First, there was a decline in the preference from one development phase to the next for engineering contracts, delivery and assembly, and 'other' projects, each of which represent multi-party contracts between two or more foreign firms and a local enterprise. Second, turnkey and product-in-hand contracts, which represent more integrated arrangements involving a single contractor from conception to the production stage, increased substantially throughout the period. The host government's preference for such agreements was related to Algeria's industrialization programme, the objectives of which were (i) greater integration of the domestic sector; (ii) technology transfer with indigenous participation in local R & D; (iii) 'Algerianization', and (iv) the local capability to manage and control simple technologies.

In 1985 there were about fifty contractual agreements in force throughout the economy, but there were no examples of the stand-alone management contract. The profile of these contracts can be generalized as follows:

Nature of agreements Singly, or in combination, these comprised technical assistance contracts, licensing agreements, maintenance contracts, and turnkey projects.

Company resources Inputs provided by contractors are largely technical, including technical skills, specifications, drawings, and production layout. Organizational and management control resides with the local partners, which have no access to the contractors' global marketing network.

Contract terms The duration of contracts vary from one to five years, usually with review and renewal agreements which are clearly specified at the negotiation stage.

Remuneration Firms are generally remunerated on a lump sum basis, with no allowance for separate payments for individual services (for example, general management, technical assistance, engineering, consultancy), although separate payments for training services are permissible (but would be difficult to process through the bureaucratic system).

Training Valued on a man-day basis, training is an important element in all contracts.

Control Contractors are restricted to day-to-day control, with the host government taking responsibility for investment decisions and bearing the entrepreneurial risk.

Performance Few contracts have escaped delays in their execution arising from bureaucratic and institutional bottlenecks, although cost effectiveness and completion deadlines are regarded by the client as critical elements in the performance criteria.

Host government perceptions of management contracts

The attitudes and perceptions of host government officials to the management contract concept were assessed according to their responses to ten attitudinal statements, measured on a Likert scale. This technique is relatively easy to construct and administer, is simpler and more reliable than other scaling methods, and individual statements can be analysed individually. This section reports their responses in decreasing order of agreement:

- a primary function of the management contract would be to secure greater compatibility between the respective objectives and priorities of the foreign firms and the host country;

- foreign management is likely to be more highly motivated than the client;
- the management contract is more likely to be linked with technology transfer modes;
- the rationale of the management contract is to acquire technological knowledge rather than management skills;
- interest in contractual agreements is due to a willingness to encourage foreign participation in local enterprises;
- a primary function of the management contract would be to reduce foreign control over technology inputs;
- foreign management, acquired via a management contract, is unlikely to induce a sufficient level of local expertise to justify such an arrangement;
- management contracts (basic) are unlikely ever to be employed in Algeria;
- foreign management does not have a superior ability to identify suitable markets for local production;
- since technical and management systems in industrialized countries are often unsuited to LDCs, they are unlikely to be acquired through management contracts alone.

DISCUSSION

The evidence supports *hypothesis 1*: 'The explicit management contract has limited validity'. Contractual agreements are perceived as technology modes rather than as management transfer modes.

Hypothesis 2: 'The management contract is usually tied to technology transfer modes . . .', also finds support. The reference here is clearly to the implicit management contract (to which the management and technical service contract has the strongest family resemblance). The host country's desire for technology inputs, as distinct from imported management skills, is the *raison d'être* for a variety of contractual agreements.

The evidence on foreign corporate involvement in Algeria emphasizes the predominance of a combination of contractual agreements, lending support to *hypothesis 3*: 'Combined contractual agreements are an increasingly preferred technology transfer mode'.

Hypothesis 4: 'The demand for contractual agreements in

LDCs arises from a lack of managerial and technical skills', is partly supported, but the constraints on development relate primarily to a lack of technological know-how rather than a lack of managerial capability. Perhaps we can dispense with the notion that western MNCs have superior firm-specific management skills which are in demand and can be readily transferred in a rent-earning capacity to LDCs.

In Algeria, a centrally-planned economy with considerable experience of contractual agreements, the *combined* contractual agreement is the most common means by which foreign firms operate. Arrangements permitting the mere sale of management know-how, for a fee, do not exist, nor are they likely to be given encouragement.

The literature presents a perspective of the management contract which neglects its primary characteristic as but one integrated aspect of complex business arrangements between contractor and client designed to match the legislative constraints in the host country with the protection and exploitation of proprietary rights in the conracting firm. Emphasis on the mythical explicit management contract distracts from closer analysis of the implicit contract as a technology transfer rather than as a management contract mode.

REFERENCES

Balasubramanyam, V. N. (1983) *International Transfer of Technology to India*, New York: Praeger.

Brooke, M. Z. (1985) *Selling Management Service Agreements in International Business*, London: Holt, Rinehart and Winston.

Buckley, P. J. (1983) 'New forms of international industrial co-operation', *Aussenwirtschaft* 38: 195–222.

Cooper, C. and Sercovitch, F. (1970) 'The mechanism for transfer of technology from advanced to developing countries', Science Policy Research Unit, University of Sussex.

Ellison, R. (1972) 'Management contracts', in M. Z. Brooke and H. L. Remmers (eds) *The International Firm*, London: Pitman.

Gabriel, P. P. (1967) *The International Transfer of Corporate Skills: Management Contracts in Less-Developed Countries*, Cambridge, MA: Harvard University Press.

Gabriel, P. P. (1970) 'New concepts in overseas investments', in R. Mann (ed.) *Art of Top Management*, New York: McGraw-Hill.

Gabriel, P. P. (1972) 'Multinational companies in the Third World: is conflict unavoidable?', *Harvard Business Review* 50.

Holly, J. (1980) 'Management contracts', *Planned Innovation* 3.
Pugh, R. C. (1961) *The Promotion of International Flow of Technology*, Report E/3492, New York: United Nations.
Sharma, D. D. (1983) *Swedish Firms and Management Contracts*, Negotiorum 16, Acta Univ. Uppsala.
Turner, L. (1974) *Multinational Companies and the Third World*, London: Allen Lane.

Chapter Five

BUYER–SELLER RELATIONSHIPS

Alternative conceptualizations

DAVID T. WILSON AND
K. E. KRISTAN MOLLER

The term relationships is very much in vogue as more buyers seek to gain what they see as the strategic advantage that results from a strong relationship with a selling firm. Questions as to how to develop and maintain relationships successfully abound. Academics, for a number of years, have been studying buyer–seller interactions, and should be able to make some contributions to the debate over the appropriate approach to long term relationships. This chapter attempts to assess the progress made in developing theories of interaction behaviour between buyers and sellers since the IMP Group first proposed the interaction model (Hakansson 1982). The major competing models of the interaction process that have been proposed over the past six years are reviewed. The theoretical underpinnings of these models are examined, and a comparison of the models is made. Proposed directions for future research conclude the paper.

INTERACTION MODELS

The IMP Group interaction model

The IMP Group developed their model through an inductive approach based upon the data from a large international study of buyers and sellers. Their theoretical underpinnings reflect inter-organizational theory and the new institutionalists as characterized by the Williamson approach to organization exchange. Their field studies contributed to the development of their model by suggesting the variables for inclusion in the model. Turnbull and Valla (1985) position the IMP model as 'a descriptive and explanatory framework of industrial market dynamics'. The model is described in figure 5.1.

The four major elements are:

- the interaction process;
- the buyers and sellers in the interaction process;
- the environment within which interaction takes place;
- the atmosphere of the relationship.

Products, information, financial and social exchange episodes define the interaction process. These exchange episodes can be viewed as the currency of the interaction between the buyer and the seller. The development of social relationships can, over time, become institutionalized such that neither party questions the morals and values that have developed to support the relationship.

Both individual and organizational variables are used to specify the characteristics of the buyer and seller interaction process. Although buyer and seller interaction is detailed in some depth in chapter 4 of the IMP book, the constructs are not well defined in terms of measurement and operationalization.

The atmosphere of the relationship encompasses such variables as power dependence, conflict, co-operation and social distance. The latter variable seems to be a combination of both physical and psychic distance between the buyer and seller. In discussing 'atmosphere', Hakansson states, 'These variables are not measured in a direct way in this study. Instead, the atmosphere is considered as a group of intervening variables, defined by various combinations of environmental, company specific, and interaction process characteristics. The atmosphere is a product of the relationship, and it also mediates the influence of the groups of variables' (Hakansson 1982: 21). It is obvious that atmosphere is a complex construct which has yet to be fully conceptualized and operationalized.

The environment, as presented in figure 5.1, is a broad set of economic and social variables which are conceived to act differently upon the buyer and seller. These macro variables are likely to be situation specific and open to definition within the situation.

Detailed descriptions of all of these variables are contained in Hakansson (1982) and Turnbull and Valla (1985).

The relationship of these IMP Group variables to dependent

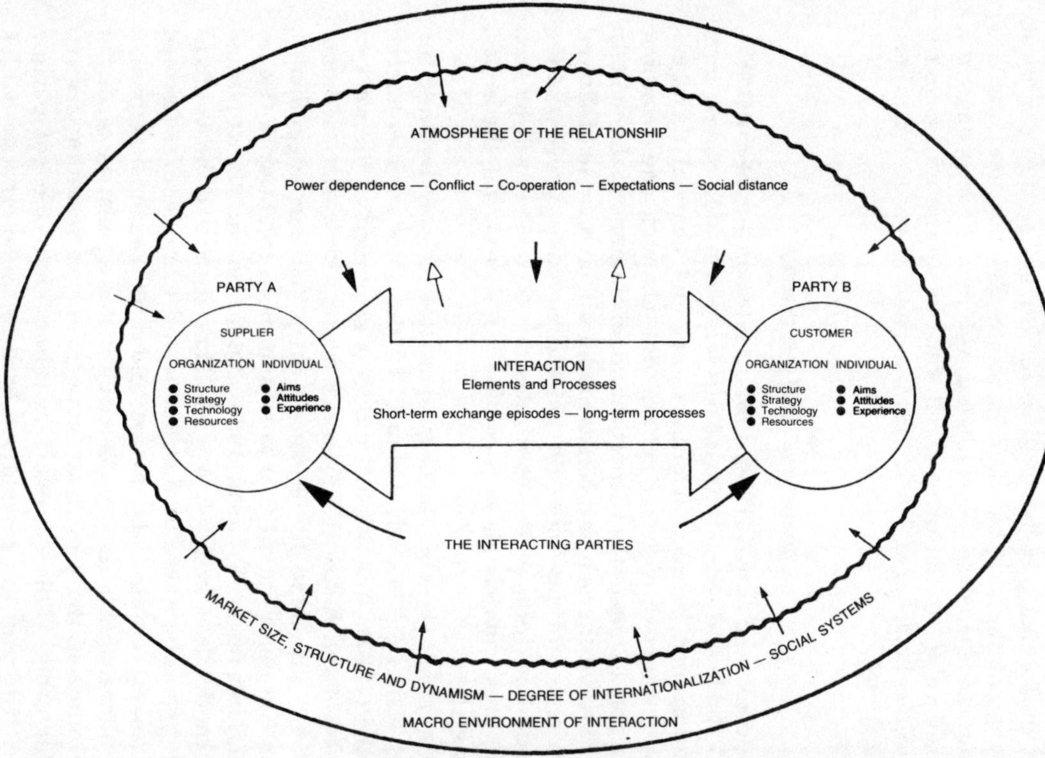

Figure 5.1 The Nature and Scope of Supplier-Customer Interaction
Source: Turnbull and Valla (1985)

measures of performance or relationship quality tends to be descriptive. A set of propositional statements – that is, the beginning of a testable theory – have not been developed and the model has not been subjected to a rigorous empirical testing, as the original data generally did not lend itself to quantitative analysis. Nevertheless, the model has generated a considerable stream of research since its appearance (see, for example, Haller *et al.* 1987, Johansson and Mattsson 1987, Ford *et al.* 1986).

Channel models of relationships

Anderson and Narus (1984, 1987), Anderson and Weitz (1987), and Heide and John (1988) have developed models of long-term relationships between manufacturers and channel members. The authors draw upon behavioural, channel, and economic concepts to create the theoretical underpinnings of the models. First, the Anderson and Narus model will be reviewed followed by a review of the Anderson and Weitz model. A review of the Heide and John model concludes this section. It will be seen that these models all have similar constructs and theoretical antecedents.

Figure 5.2 describes the original model developed by Anderson and Narus (1984), while figure 3.5 describes their enhanced model (1987). The original model is grounded in the work of Thibault and Kelley (1959), which, along with work by Homans (1958), has come to be known as social exchange theory. Drawing upon the original work and more recent work (Kelley and Thibault 1978, Kelley 1983), Anderson and Narus posited the model described in figure 5.2. They argue that the results of interaction between the distributor and manufacturer (termed outcomes) represent the rewards and cost for each participant in the interaction. These results are evaluated against the quality of the outcome the participant expects to receive within a given relationship. This construct is refined into the comparison level (CL) and the comparison level of the alternative (CL_{alt}). Anderson and Narus (1984: 63) define CL as 'a standard representing the quality of outcomes the distributor (manufacturer) has come to expect from a given relationship, based upon present and past experience with similar relationships, and knowledge of other distributors' (manufacturers') similar relationships'. CL_{alt} is defined as, 'the average quality of outcomes that are available from the best alternative exchange relationship. As such, CL_{alt} represents the lowest level of outcomes a manufacturer or distributor will generally accept and still remain in the relationship.'

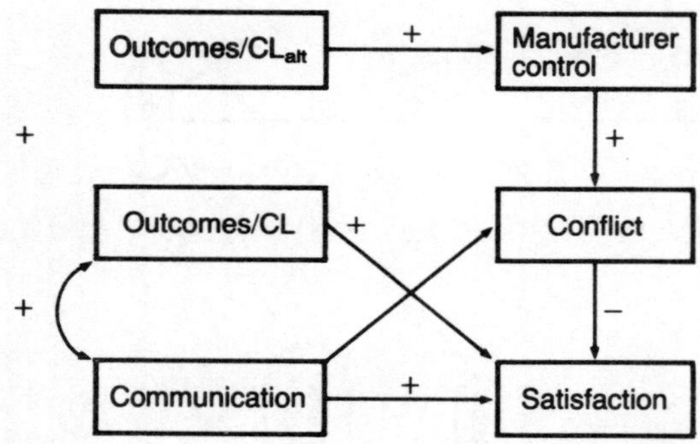

Figure 5.2 Distributor's perspective of the working relationship
Source: Anderson and Narus (1984)

In figure 5.2, outcomes/CL_{alt} represents the perceived dependence of the distributor upon the manufacturer, for as the outcomes increase in a positive direction given an alternative partner, the distribtuor becomes more dependent upon the manufacturer.

Outcomes/CL captures the extent that the outcome of a relationship exceeds or falls below the expectations for that relationship. As such, it is posited to be directly influential on the level of satisfaction.

Conflict is the frequency and degree of disagreements between the partners.

Satisfaction is the positive feeling that results from an evaluation of all of the aspects of the relationship.

Manufacturer control refers to the ability of the manufacturer to exert control over the distributor's actions, and, hence, have the ability to exert power over the distributor.

Communication is the formal and informal exchange of information and meaning between the partners.

Empirical testing of the model defined in figure 5.2 resulted in reasonable support for the social exchange constructs and

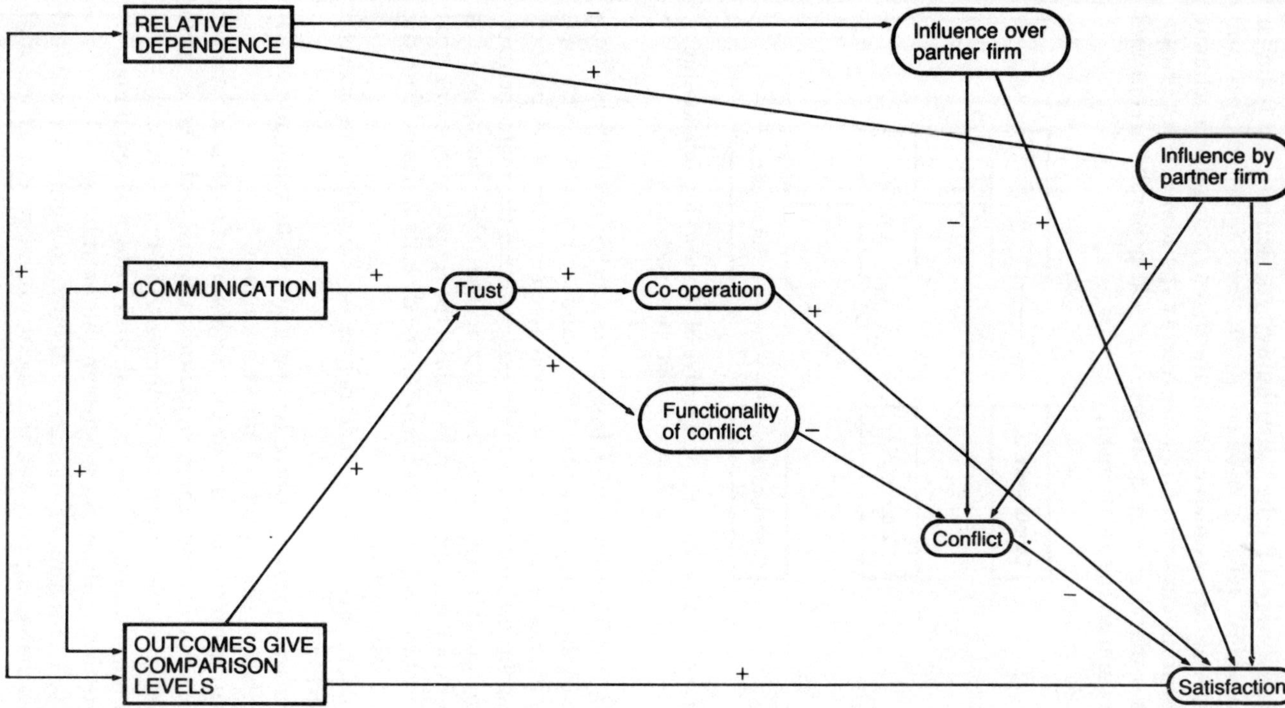

Figure 5.3 A model of manufacturer and distributor working partnerships
Source: Anderson and Narus (1987)

their relationship to the behavioural constructs. There were some measurement problems which limited the test of the model. Nevertheless, the authors were encouraged enough to follow up their initial work with a series of field interviews that lead to the refinement of the original model into the model shown in figure 5.3. The basic structure of figure 5.2 remains, but some of the constructs required refinement to reflect more adequately the intricateness of the exchange relationship.

They have modified or added the following constructs:

- relative dependence is the perceived difference between the firm's dependence and its partner's dependence on the relationship. It is conceptualized as outcome/CL_{alt} and represents the average quality of outcomes that are available for the best alternative relationship;
- influence over the partner firm and influence by the partner are constructs that reflect the reciprocal nature of a partnership and the need to have one's own partner take action to bring about positive outcomes for one's firm. They represent the ability to exert power to influence one's partner and, as such, capture the sense of the behavioural control construct implicit in the underlying theory (Anderson and Narus 1987, Kelley and Thibault 1978);
- trust is expecting one's partner to take actions that will result in positive outcomes for the firm and leads to trusting behaviour by each partner;
- co-operation refers to complementary action by the firms to achieve mutual benefits;
- functionality of conflict is the effective management of stress in an interdependent relationship.

The extended model of figure 5.3 is a much richer representation of the reality of working relationships and represents a natural extension of the earlier model. Anderson and Narus have blended theory and empirical results to build a theoretical representation of reality, which offers both explanation and prediction. Their models can be tested and revised to be more sensitive to the realities of the world.

In their empirical test of the second model, they tested one model from the manufacturers' perspective and another from the distributors' perspective. Results for both models were very encouraging in that the vast majority of the hypothesized relationships were supported and only a few of the nonspecified relationships between the constructs were found to have significant relationships.

The model developed by Anderson and Weitz (1987), described in figure 5.4, has many similarities to the Anderson and Narus model. Anderson and Weitz begin with the basic assumption that channel members assume continuity of relationships with their manufacturers. They state, 'At the most basic level, a manufacturer cannot hope to garner the benefits expected from a long term relationship unless the channel member is convinced the relationship is likely to last.' Using this assumption of continuity, they draw upon the work of Etgar (1979), Arndt (1979), Thorelli (1984), and Williamson (1985) to assert that channel members will engage in behaviour that supports the manufacturer's marketing efforts. The construct of continuity is one of the three major constructs of the model. The other two key constructs are trust and communications.

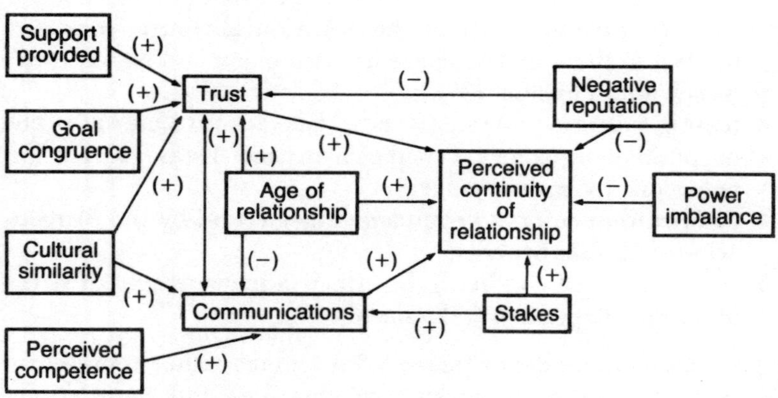

Figure 5.4 Hypothesized relationships
Source: Anderson and Weitz (1987)

They draw theory from social exchange, channel research (Robicheaux and El-Ansary 1975, Stern and Reve 1980), negotiation (Pruitt 1981), and structural economics (Williamson 1985), and the work of Dwyer *et al.* (1984), to define the main variables and constructs of their model. These variables and constructs are briefly defined below:

- trust is 'one party's belief that its needs will be fulfilled in the future by actions undertaken by the other party'. This view of trust is consistent with the earlier definition of trust;
- power imbalance is the ability of one party to get the other party to do something it would not normally do. It is directly related to the degree of dependence of one party on the other;
- communication is the two-way exchange of information, goals, plans, and expectations;
- stake is the importance of the outcomes of the interaction between the partners to at least one of the partners;
- age of the relationship refers to the length of time the relationship has existed.

All of the above are postulated as impacting the continuity of the relationship.

Trust is postulated to be dependent upon the following variables:

- Reputation is the market's view of the partnering behaviour of a firm.
- Support is the resources a manufacturer devotes to enhancing the efforts of the partners.
- Goal congruence is the degree to which the partners share goals.
- Cultural similarity refers to geographic and cultural distance between partners' values and methods.

Figure 5.4 describes how the above variables combine to form the main constructs of the model. Despite some measurement problems, the results of an empirical test of the model found 'the data largely in accord with the proposed model'. Trust was found to be of particular importance in maintaining stable dyads.

Heide and John (1988) draw upon dependence theory (1962) and the transaction cost work of Williamson (1985, 1975, 1979) to create a model that argues that transaction specific assets create partner dependence. Dependence theory suggests specific responses to partner dependence. The major relationships of

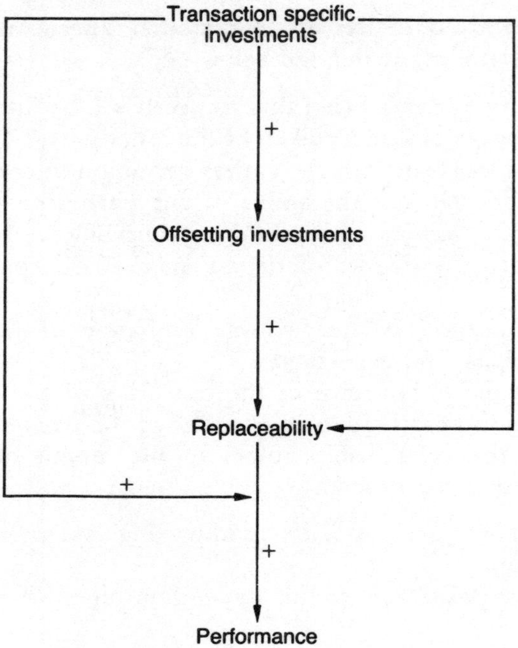

Figure 5.5 Major relationships in model
Source: Heide and John (1988)

the model are presented in figure 5.5. Heide and John suggest that small channel members protect themselves from exploitation by their manufacturing partner by making offseting investments in customer relationships that balance their dependency upon the manufacturer. The key constructs of their model which are presented below, have been set into a broader perspective than defined in their paper:

- specific investments in manufacturer relationships are those investments made by the channel member to maintain the relationship with the manufacturer,
- offsetting investments are those investments that a channel member makes to develop close bonds with its customers. These investments are intended to create switching cost for the manufacturer;
- potential replacement of manufacturer is the opportunity to replace the income from selling the manufacturer's products.

It is a measure of the channel members' dependence upon the manufacturer;

- performance is a negatively-scaled measure, and is the ratio of selling costs for the product and the income from sales of the product line;
- other variables, such as the number of manufacturer lines carried, concentration of exchange (fraction of sales from the largest manufacturer), and market and product factors were included in the test of the model;
- the model was tested using manufacturers' agents as the subject population. The results provided support for the basic model. This model is much more narrow in scope than the two previous models, but it does focus attention on the issue of investments in relationships.

Overall, each of the channel relationship models have some degree of similarity, in that they have similar constructs although these constructs are operationalized in different ways. Nevertheless, all of these models are exciting steps towards a better understanding of the variables that need to be managed in channel relationships.

Buyer and seller models of relationships

Dwyer *et al.* (1987), Wilson and Mummalaneni (1986, 1988), Mummalaneni and Wilson (1988), and Frazier *et al.* (1990) have developed models of buyer and seller relationships. These models draw upon similar theoretical concepts as the models reviewed earlier in this chapter. A major difference is that the Dwyer *et al.* and the Wilson and Mummalaneni models suggest the process by which relationships develop. In the next section of the chapter, these models are reviewed as background to a synthesis of the state of our progress in modelling the buyer and seller relationship process.

The Dwyer *et al.* model is described in figure 5.6. Again, there is similarity of the constructs with the earlier models. The relationship develops through five general phases, within each several subprocesses operate. The subprocesses in this model are broadly defined but are not specified as constructs that can be operationalized and measured. This model is akin to the IMP

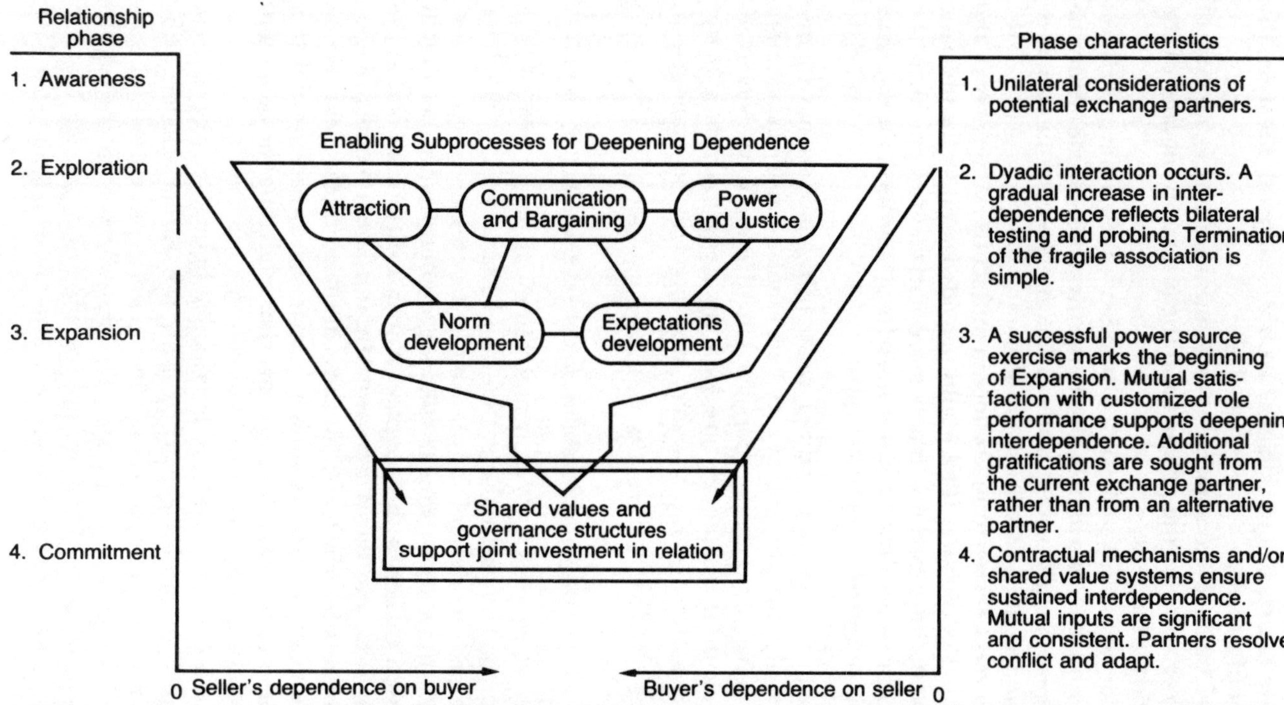

Figure 5.6 The Relationship Development Process
Source: Dwyer *et al.* (1987)

Group model, in that the main relationships are more loosely defined than the other models discussed in this chapter.

The first stage is awareness and the unilateral evaluation of the value of potential exchange partners. In the second stage, the attraction, communication, and bargaining, and power and justice subprocesses operate. Attraction is seen as 'the degree to which buyer and seller achieve – in their interaction with each other – a reward-cost outcome in excess of some minimum level (CL_{alt}) (p. 16)'. Dwyer *et al.* seemed to be unaware of the constructs developed by Anderson and Narus (1984, 1987) and Ford *et al.* (1986), as they would help structure their model.

Communication and bargaining are the processes by which the obligations, benefits, and burdens are shared between the buyer and seller. Power and justice as an attempt to relate the use of power by one party is seen as just and, hence, in their joint interests, or unjust and hence a selfish move that may lead to the dissolving of the relationship.

In the next phase, norm development creates a set of ground rules that will guide future relationship development. Expectations of behaviour that will guide the relationship develop during this phase. Trust is seen as an important concept by Dwyer *et al.*

In phase four, commitment, shared values and governance structures develop that will support joint investment in the relationship. Commitment is seen as having three measurable dimensions:

- inputs involves the exchange of communication, economic and possible emotional resources;
- durability relates to the length of the relationship, which is similar to the length of time for the relationship in the Anderson and Weitz model;
- consistency refers to a process that is predictable as to how resources will be input to maintain the relationship.

The final stage is dissolution, during which the relationship is terminated. This phase is not developed and will not be considered in this chapter.

The Dwyer *et al.* model introduces the development of relationships through several stages, which is an important step forward. The Wilson and Mummalaneni model (1988) evolves from their earlier model (1986) by more fully developing the concept of both structural and social bonding between buyers and sellers. Their model is described in figure 5.7.

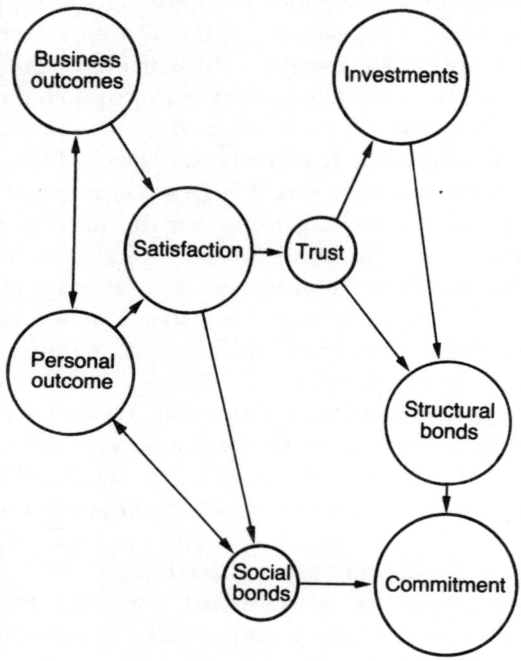

Figure 5.7 A bonding model of long-term relationships
Source: Wilson and Mummalaneni (1988)

This model is grounded in social exchange theory as is the Anderson and Narus model. In addition, Wilson and Mummalaneni draw upon the work of Johnson (1978, 1982), McCall (1970) and Rusbult (1980, 1983) in social relationships and Wilson (1975, 1978) process models of dyadic interactions between buyers and sellers.

The constructs of this model have strong similarities to previous models and are described below:

- commitment is determined by multiple factors and can be viewed as the dedication to the continuation of a relationship. It can be measured as the behavioural intention regarding continued participation in the relationship and the inverse probability of leaving the relationship;

- satisfaction is seen conceptually as the net of rewards minus cost of the relationship. Rewards and cost are both measured in terms of economic and social exchange. In a broad sense, satisfaction is the degree of positive effect associated with a relationship, and involves the positivity of feelings toward the relationship as well as the partner and the closeness of this relationship to the 'ideal' one;
- CL_{alt} is a measure of the best alternative relationship other than the current one in which the firm is involved. It can be measured using a multi-attribute model, where CL_{alt} is the difference in performance between the incumbent supplier and the best alternative over the attribute set;
- social bonds measure the strength of a personal relationship between the buyer and seller and may range from a business relationship to a close personal relationship. A personal relationship is distinguished from a business role relationship by the social bonds which eliminate the substitutability of individuals in a relationship. Also, a personal relationship is characterized by a greater degree of self-disclosure, concern for the welfare of the 'other' and liking for the other person. The various resources (material as well as immaterial) that are 'put into' and tied up with a particular relationship;
- structural bonds are the multiplicity of economic and social factors that develop during a relationship that tie the partners together. Structural bonds involve irretrievable investment, social pressures to maintain the relationship, ease of dissolving the relationship and contractual barriers to ending the relationship.

Each of these variables can be further specified and measured.

The social bonding model has been tested and provided encouraging results (Mummalaneni and Wilson 1988). Commitment is greater for strong social relationships than for pure business relationships. The model, as described in figure 5.8, received strong support from the data.

The final model to be reviewed has been developed by Fraser *et al.* (1990) to describe the development of just-in-time (JIT) as a special form of long term relationship. Drawing upon theory

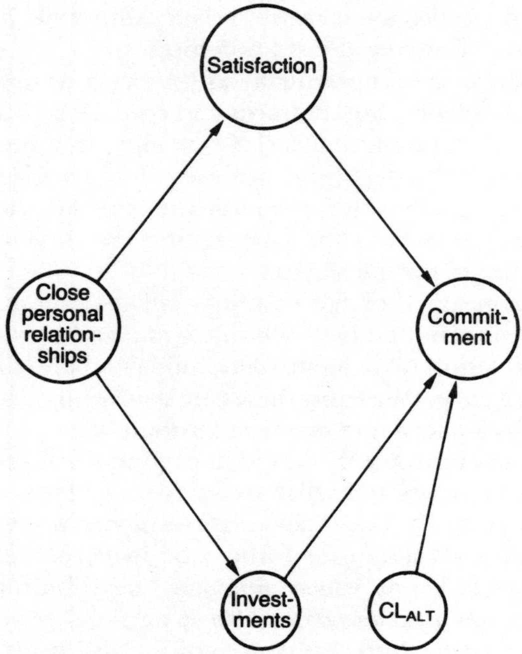

Figure 5.8 Hypothesized effects of close personal relationships
Source: Mummalaneni and Wilson (1988)

from channel research, transaction cost analysis, social exchange, and inter-organizational exchange, they suggest a four-stage model (interest, initiation-rejection, implementation, and review) to describe the managerial process for making a JIT decision, and the internal and external factors that influence the decision process. Their model is managerial in scope and is more focused on the process of making the decision. Although the model is not tested and the constructs are not operationalized, it does address a special case of long-term relationships, and is an interesting model.

TOWARDS A MODEL OF BUYER AND SELLER RELATIONSHIPS

It is obvious from the models described above that there are a number of approaches to describing buyer and seller relationships. The good news is that many talented people are addressing the problem, while the bad news is that they do not share common construct definitions, so that there is no way to build directly upon the work of others. The relational paradigm is new and, hopefully, we will begin to move towards some agreement on the basic constructs of interest. Although the authors use the same words to label a construct, how it is defined and operationalized varies by researcher. There is a trade-off between the freedom of the researcher to choose how he (she) will do the research and the need to be able to build upon the work of others.

Table 5.1 is a summary of the constructs used in the models reviewed in this paper. In creating this table, we have taken some liberties in interpreting constructs, so as to keep the table to a workable length. In some cases, constructs are discussed in the text of the chapter but do not appear in the model and, as such, they are not listed in the table. What becomes apparent is the number of constructs that are shared in the different models; at the same time, the number of constructs that are not shared is large. It seems that we need to begin to refine our models of buyer–seller relationship to move towards a common view of the process. Although the field is new, there is a discouraging lack of cross-referencing work and building upon each others' research. Researchers on each side of the Atlantic seem to ignore the work from the other.

The work of the IMP Group has provided a solid beginning for model building in buyer–seller relationship development. European business market relationships reflected economic conditions that are only now beginning to energize North American buyer–seller relationships. Buyers are becoming pro-active in seeking new types of relationships from their suppliers which is accelerating the push for research on long term relationships. The work reviewed in this chapter is an excellent foundation for further theory development in buyer and seller relationships.

The next step is to develop a contingency model of buyer and seller relationships that draws upon the work reviewed in this chapter. Such a model should recognize the range of relationships from pure market transactions to long-term relationships marked by close personal relations between the buyers and sellers. The development of such a model is beyond the scope of

Table 5.1 Constructs and sources

Construct	*IMP*	*AN*	*AW*	*DWO*	*HJ*	*WM and MW*	*FSO*
Trust	x	x	x	x		x	
Power of buyer		x	x	x			
Power of seller		x	x	x			
Dependence on buyer	x	x		x			
Dependence on seller	x	x		x			
Stake			x				
Age of relationship	x		x			x	
Communication		x	x	x			
Outcome of value performance					x	x	x
Satisfaction		x			x	x	x
Transaction costs					x	x	x
Transaction specific investment or irretrievable investment				x	x	x	x
Social bonding affective relationships				x		x	
Co-operation	x	x					
Conflict	x	x					
CL		x					
CL_{ALT}						x	x
Replaceability					x		x
Functionality of conflict commitment		x					
Expectations	x			x			x
Social distance cultural similarity	x		x				
Organizational factors	x						x
Individual factors	x						
Environmental factors	x						x
Norm development				x			x
Governance structures				x			
Perceived continuity of relationship			x			x	
Negative reputation			x				
Support provided			x				
Perceived competence			x				
Goal congruence			x				
Social pressure to maintain relationship					x	x	
Ease of relationship termination						x	
Exchange						x	x

Key:

IMP	IMP Group 1987
AN	Anderson and Narus 1987
AW	Anderson and Weitz 1987
DWO	Dwyer *et al.* 1987
HJ	Heide and John 1988
WM and	Wilson and Mummalaneni 1988
MW	Mummalaneni and Wilson 1988
FSO	Fraser *et al.* 1990

this chapter, but the work reviewed here is a solid foundation on which to build a contingency model. There are many well-developed concepts and constructs that could serve as building blocks in such a model.

In summary, we are making good progress in beginning to understand how buyer–seller relationships develop into long-term relationships. We may all benefit from moving towards clarification of the key constructs and a general definition of these constructs to let us build on each others' work. There are exciting and challenging opportunities for research in this area, as it will become a more critical management decision area for firms competing the global business environment. The pace of research will increase and we need to build a common vision to guide our research.

REFERENCES

Anderson, E. and Weitz, B. (1987) 'Determinent of continuity in conventional industrial channel dyads', unpublished working paper, The Wharton School, The University of Pennsylvania.

Anderson, J. C. and Narus, J. A. (1984) 'A model of the distributor's perspective of distributor–manufacturer working relationships', *Journal of Marketing*, 48: 62–74.

Anderson, J. C. and Narus, J. A. (1987) 'A model of manufacturer and distributor working partnerships', unpublished working paper, the J. L. Kellogg School.

Arndt, J. (1979) 'Toward a concept of domesticated markets', *Journal of Marketing* 43: 69–75.

Beier, F. and Stern, L. W. (1969) 'Power in the channel of distribution', in L. W. Stern (ed.) *Distribution Channels: Behavioural Dimensions*, Boston, Houghton-Mifflin.

Dwyer, F. R., Schurr, P. H. and Oh, S. (1987) 'Developing buyer–seller relations', *Journal of Marketing* 51: 11–27.

Emerson, M. (1962) 'Power-dependence relations', *American Sociological Review* 27: 31–41.

Etgar, M. (1979) 'Sources and types of intrachannel conflict', *Journal of Retailing* 55: 76–8.

Ford, I. D., Hakansson, H. and Johansson, J. (1986) 'How do companies interact', *Industrial Marketing and Purchasing* 1: 26–41.

Frazier, G. L., Spekman, R. E. and O'Neil, C. R. (1990) 'Just-in-time exchange relationships in industrial markets', *Journal of Marketing* 54.

Hakansson, H. (ed.) (1982) *International Marketing and Purchasing of Industrial Goods*, Chichester: Wiley.

Haller, L., Johansson, J. and Mohamed, N. S. (1987) 'Relationship strength and stability in international and domestic industrial marketing', *Industrial Marketing and Purchasing* 2: 22–37.
Heide, J. B. and John, G. (1988) 'The role of dependence balancing in safeguarding transaction-specific assets in coventional channels', *Journal of Marketing* 52: 20–35.
Homans, G. G. (1958) 'Social behaviour as exchange', *American Journal of Sociology* 63: 597–606.
Johansson, J. and Mattsson, L. G. (1987) 'Interorganizational relations in industrial systems: a network approach compared with the transaction–cost approach', *International Studies of Management and Organizations* 17: 185–95.
Johnson, M. P. (1978) 'Personal and structural commitment: sources of consistency in the development of relationships', paper presented at National Council of Family Relations, Philadelphia.
Johnson, M. P. (1982) 'Social and cognitive features of the dissolution of commitment to relationships', in S. Duck (ed.) *Personal Relationships. 4: Dissolving Personal Relationships*, London: Academic Press, 51–73.
Kelley, H. H. (1983) 'The situational origins of human tendencies: a further reason for the formal analysis of structures, *Personality and Social Psychology Bulletin* 9: 8–30.
Kelley, H. H. and Thibault, J. W. (1978) *Interpersonal Relations: A Theory of Interdependence*, New York: Wiley.
McCall, G. J. (1970) 'The social organization of relationships', in G. J. McCall *et al.* (eds) *Social Relationships*, Chicago: Aldine, 3–34.
Mummalaneni, V. and Wilson, D. T. (1988) 'The influence of close personal relationships between a buyer and a seller on the continued stability of their role relationships', unpublished working paper, ISBM, Penn State University.
Pruitt, D. G. (1981) *Negotiation Behaviour*, New York: Academic Press.
Robicheaux, R. A. and El-Ansary, A. I. (1975) 'A general model for understanding channel member behaviour', *Journal of Retailing* 52: 13–30, 93–4.
Rusbult, C. E. (1980) 'Commitment and satisfaction in romantic associations: a test of the investment model', *Journal of Experimental Social Psychology* 16: 172–86.
Rusbult, C. E. (1983) 'A longitudinal test of the investment model: the development (and deterioration) of satisfaction commitment in heterosexual involvements', *Journal of Personality and Social Psychology*: 101–17.
Stern, L. W. and Reve, T. (1980) 'Distribution channels as political economies: a framework for comparative analysis', *Journal of Marketing*: 52–64.
Thibault, J. W. and Kelley, H. (1959) *The Social Psychology of Groups*, New York: Wiley.
Thorelli, H. B. (1984) 'Networks: between markets and hierarchies', *Strategic Management Journal* 7: 37–51.

Turnbull, P. W. and Valla, J. P. (eds) (1985) *Strategies for International Industrial Marketing*, London: Croom Helm.
Williamson, O. E. (1975) *Markets and Hierarchies: Analysis and Antitrust Implications*, New York: The Free Press.
Williamson, O. E. (1979) 'Transaction-cost econcomics: the governance of contractual relations', *Journal of Law and Economics* 22: 3–61.
Williamson, O. E. (1985) *The Economic Institutions of Capitalism*, New York: The Free Press.
Wilson, D. T. (1975) 'Dyadic interaction: an exchange process', in B. Anderson (ed.) *Advances in Consumer Research*, Cincinnati: ACR, 394–97.
Wilson, D. T. (1978) 'Dyadic interactions: some conceptualizations', in T. V. Bonoma and G. Zaltman (eds) *Organizational Buying Behaviour*, Chicago: AMA, 31–48.
Wilson, D. T. and Mummalaneni, V. (1986) 'Bonding and commitment in buyer–seller relationships: a preliminary conceptualization', *Industrial Marketing and Purchasing* 1: 3.
Wilson, D. T. and Mummalaneni, V. (1988) 'Modelling and measuring buyer–seller relationships', unpublished working paper, ISBM, Penn State University.

Chapter Six

RELATIONSHIP ATMOSPHERE IN INTERNATIONAL BUSINESS

LARS HALLÉN AND MADELENE SANDSTRÖM

Exchange processes between companies in industrial markets are often long-term and strengthened by adaptations that the parties have made to each other's requirements. In this way technical, logistical, and other more or less physical links are established between the firms. To obtain this, information must be exchanged between the firms. The more specific the requirements of the customers and the more diverse the offerings of the suppliers, i.e., the more heterogeneous the markets, the less these communication needs can be satisfied by anonymous market contacts. Personal interaction is required. This both causes difficulties and opens up possibilities, as it increases the role of human differences, similarities, antipathies, sympathies etc. In international industrial business this becomes still more pronounced, as it involves personal interaction between people with different cultural backgrounds and different expectations and interpretations of performance, behaviour, practices, rules etc. In the terminology of Hofstede (1980), different cultures imply different mental programming, which governs activities, motivations, and values. Thus, in international business personal interaction becomes still more important and also more sensitive, as personal interaction is necessary to neutralize possible cultural barriers to business exchange.

When thus the focus is shifted from standardized and anonymous market relations to specific customer–supplier relationships, it is obvious that the interaction between business people does not take place in an emotional vacuum. This setting of the business interaction can be termed atmosphere (Williamson 1975). In introducing the concept of atmosphere, Williamson uses expressions such as transactions being modified by not taking place in 'attitudinally neutral' settings. 'Satisfying exchange relations' corresponding to a specific atmosphere (obviously an agreeable one) are seen to influence the relationships. Opportunism is assumed to be checked, for example, by courtesy, considerations for future business, and effects on the firm's reputation.

The purpose of this chapter is to examine the atmosphere concept by exploring its function in business relationships and by describing its constituting components as a set of descriptive dimensions. These are used to arrive at a typology of atmospheres.

THE FUNCTION OF ATMOSPHERE IN BUSINESS RELATIONSHIPS

Business relationships both in the domestic and in foreign markets are initiated, developed, and strengthened through interaction. The interaction *per se* means that the interacting parties – supplier and customer – invest resources in the relationship, that cannot be put to use elsewhere. These investments can take the form of informal information channels. Furthermore, technical and logistical adaptations are often made, and these are frequently often of an irretrievable character too.

Through social exchange the parties gradually may build up trust in each other by demonstrating a capacity to keep promises and showing commitment to the relationship (Blau 1964). This influences the subsequent interaction both with regard to actual business exchange and social exchange. Structural conditions have also been found to influence the interaction process, for example, technology (Hallén *et al.* 1987) or distance – geographic or cultural – between the parties (Hallén 1982).

The business exchange is influenced by more or less implicit rules, that have emerged as a result both of previous interaction and of environmental conditions. These rules can be seen as related to exchange in the same way as language is related to communication. These rules are formed, reinforced, and modified through exchange at the same time as they constitute the framework of subsequent exchange (Giddens 1975). A basic assumption is that those rules imply a mutual orientation, for example, in the form of a mutual trust, and a reciprocal interest awareness (Johanson 1989). An implication of this is that exchange may be irregular but the relationship is still existing although dormant.

The rules are specific to every relationship, which implies that expectations and evaluations of performance are made with respect to the specific counterpart, and not with regard to expectations and demands in a general sense. Every relationship has a pattern or 'language' of its own. The fact that these rules are unwritten do not make them less important; instead violations of the unwritten rules may produce much stronger responses and counteractions than the corresponding action may produce in a relationship based purely on formal agreements in a market setting.

The common rules and the rules about how to interpret the actions performed by the other party are not necessarily developed with the agreement of both parties. For instance, perceptions of the power balance in the relationship may shift as one of the parties sees possibilities to advance its positions – as in a game of chess. Still, such actions must be contained within the total framework of the relationship so as not to jeopardize it.

The idea of such rules or 'language' according to which the exchange is mediated is a concept with strong similarities to the atmosphere concept introduced above. The influence of structural conditions on actions can be seen as mediated through this atmosphere or according to these common rules of exchange (figure 6.1). The categories at the bottom section of the figure depict factors related to the individuals: actions performed by the actors (action profile) and the actors' feelings in the interaction process (atmosphere). The atmosphere is thus seen as a sum of the feelings, intentions, will, and interest of both parties. The atmosphere is thus not necessarily in balance, and when it is unbalanced it will probably change, if the latitude of choice allows this. This 'latitude of choice' in the upper section of the figure indicates activities and structures, and in this category connections between activities are included.

The latitude of choice is related to the structure in which the supplier–customer relationship is embedded. It determines what can or must be done by the actors. Structural conditions

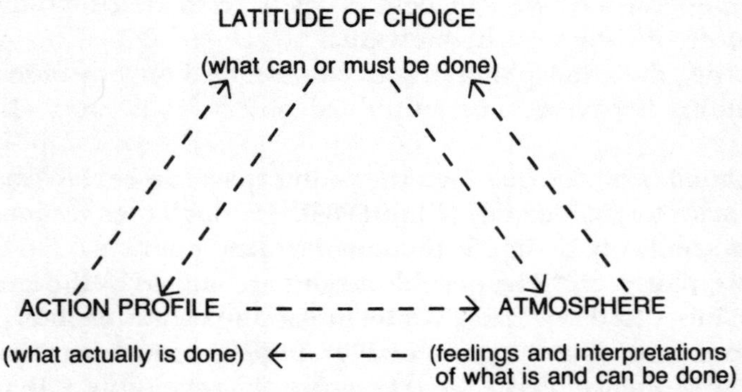

Figure 6.1 The function of atmosphere in business relationships

which influence the latitude of choice are access to alternatives (cf., Wilson and Mummalaneni 1986), the integration and interconnectedness within the network, for example, in terms of the directness and specificity of couplings (Johanson 1989), and the strength of the direct dyadic relationships, for example, in terms of adaptations, information channels, and other investments which cannot easily be recovered in another context.

The structural conditions can be further specified in terms of external, relationship-specific, or internal factors. The factors mentioned above belong to the external and relationship-specific groups. In addition to this amongst the internal factors one may point to competence, resources of one's own, authority structure within the organization, and individual predispositions due to culture.

The possibilities for action can be perceived, interpreted, and evaluated differently by the parties. For instance, the interdependence between the parties may be of a certain strength due to structural conditions, but a certain actor may feel that he or she is much more dependent on this specific counterpart than warranted by these conditions, for instance because he or she is imbued with a culturally-determined predisposition to interpret relations, for example, in a hierarchical way. Thus, the actions of a party are both directly influenced by structural conditions and indirectly via the atmosphere. Furthermore, there may be a difference between the general attitude held towards another firm and the attitude held by an individual. In this latter case, the general attitude can be seen as a restriction limiting the latitude of choice of the individual.

Thus, the atmosphere cannot be described only by observing manifest behaviour but attitudinal observations must also be made.

Actual behaviour *vis-à-vis* the counterpart can be described as the actor's action profile (Klint 1985). Through these actions the actor explicitly or implicitly demonstrates intentions, attitudes, plans, values, etc. The possible actions are limited by the latitude of choice, and the actor's interpretations of the counterpart's actions and of the actor's own latitude to manoeuvre have a major influence on the feelings within the relationship. In other words, through the action profile an actor intentionally or unintentionally demonstrates certain atmosphere dimensions. The possibilities that are present in the latitude of choice also influence the atmosphere, although these only potentially have a bearing on the atmosphere as latent threats or possibilities. Furthermore, there is an interaction between the different aspects of the atmosphere. They may strengthen, balance, or neutralize each other. The same balancing also characterizes the action profile and the latitude of choice.

The centrality of the atmosphere in the relationship is related to the degree of constraints put on activities by the structural conditions. The less latitude of choice for the individuals handling the relationship, the less important is the influence of the atmosphere. Its function is probably more important in situations of restructuring, for example, initiation, intensification, or change of a relationship.

It may well happen, that the atmosphere in terms of perceived feelings does not coincide with actual behaviour or actual structural conditions. For instance, two parties may very well be highly dependent on each other, as expressed by criteria such as share of sales or purchases accounted for by the counterpart, and still feel independent, as none of the parties exploits this situation or as a result of a different interpretation of the situation against the background of cultural or professional attitudes. Thus, atmospheres may combine seemingly incompatible characteristics, for example, simultaneous closeness and distance. The incompatibility is resolved when the contradictions are referred to different levels in the model, for example, feelings of closeness and understanding (atmosphere), together with structural distance (for example, cultural differences).

THE ATMOSPHERE CONCEPT

Above the atmosphere of a business relationship is tentatively equated with the rules that govern the relationship. More specifically, it is here defined as the emotional setting, in which business is conducted. It constitutes the working environment for the individuals in their interaction with each other. An atmosphere, which is perceived as positive by the parties, can be assumed to facilitate business. The characteristics of the atmosphere are however largely determined by factors outside of the individuals, but it nevertheless has its direct effects on the individuals, and it is also created through the individuals, as it is a perceptual phenomenon. As such, it is more or less differently perceived by all the involved actors. In particular, it can be differently perceived by people from the various organisations involved in the interaction processes. This partially creates a basis for their behaviour.

As seen from one of the parties, the atmosphere can be defined as constituted by the perceptions which one party holds about the other party and the perceptions the same party believes that the other party holds regarding oneself (cf., Hallén and Wiedersheim-Paul 1981). In other words, it is a matter of your own feelings *vis-à-vis* your counterpart and the feelings you perceive that the counterpart holds of you.

To some extent, the atmosphere in a business relationship can be discussed in the same terms as the attitudes in the behaviour of an individual. The emotional setting, the atmosphere, may thus be more or less intensively perceived. In a general sense, an atmosphere can be characterized as positive or negative, that is dominated by strong feelings, or else as undetermined, that is emotions play a smaller role and have less impact on the relationship. Furthermore, the atmosphere may be more or less central in the relationship in the sense that successful personal interaction as influenced by it may be more or less important for conducting the business. This may be related to the degree of institutionalization of the relationship.

These two dimensions can be expected to be related to each

other in the sense that the atmosphere is less pronounced in relationships which are of minor importance to the parties. They may also be quite different in unbalanced relationships, for example, when there is unilateral dependence between the parties. Still, by combining the two dimensions four relevant categories are obtained as shown in figure 6.2.

		Strength	
		High	*Low*
Centrality	*High*	pivot	potential
	Low	barrier	side issue

Figure 6.2 The function of atmosphere in business relationships

A clearly perceived atomsphere in a business relationship, where personal interaction, interpretations of hidden meanings, etc., are important, and where strategic issues are at stake due to the outcome of the personal contacts, gives the emotional setting of the interaction processes a pivotal function in the relationship. This may occur, for example, in the beginning of a relationship, where the parties have not yet committed themselves, but where the evaluation of the other party's intentions may determine whether the relationship will be discontinued or deepened. At this stage the function of the atmosphere is central. If the atmosphere is 'charged' either positively or negatively, the emotional setting at the outset may have a determining influence on the continuation of the relationship.

In a similar situation, where the future of the relationship is not determined and where the development may take many paths due to decisions that have to be made on grounds that are difficult to evaluate, but where no clear feelings have yet crystallized, the atmosphere plays the role of a potentialy important concept. This may be the case when there are possibilities to develop co-operation, but when no deep insights into the situation of the other party has been obtained, for example, after a joint-venture agreement has been signed. Creating a positive emotional setting – or at least not destroying its embryonic elements – in such situations may be proved very fruitful.

The atmosphere may also be strongly and clearly perceived or 'charged' without being a central element in the relationship. In cases where the relationship is well established and where the parties are connected by considerable irretrievable investments in the technological or logistical areas, the future of the relationship may be less due to conditions related to the individuals engaged in the relationship and more to the momentum of the direct business exchange processes. Still, there may be a distinct atmosphere, characterized, for example, by firmly established personal relations, friendly contacts, perhaps even cosiness, that may act as a barrier towards possible new entrants into the relationship. The atmosphere, although not central, may also be strongly negatively charged, which then may act as a barrier towards deepening the relationship although it does not threaten its continuation as a routinized relationship.

In the last combination in figure 6.2, where the atmosphere is neither strongly perceived nor central in the relationship, it is considered a side issue. The relationship is routinized, it builds mainly upon other bonds than personal ones, and there are no important vestiges from earlier, more personalized stages of the relationship that would either unite or separate the individuals involved in handling the business. However, also when the atmosphere is a side issue, it holds the potential of developing into a barrier either against newcomers or against further development of the relationship.

Thus, the atmosphere may or may not be important for the development and handling of the relationship due to its development stage and technological or market-related factors. In particular, it is expected to have an important impact on the establishment or restructuring of a relationship as far as there is a latitude for choice. It is also an important element in situations when much is at stake in the relationship, for example, due to investments made.

DIMENSIONS OF THE ATMOSPHERE

The selected dimensions

As defined above, atmosphere is seen as a perceptual construct describing the emotions of the parties towards each other and towards the relationship between them. Emotions can of course be held towards any aspect of a buyer–seller relationship. However, some should be selected as descriptors. To qualify, these should relate to aspects that are central to the possibilities of the individuals to act within the relationship, that is, they should refer to different types of behaviour, both personal (for example, negotiation style) and commercial (for example, use of business resources). They should also be related to the communication interface between the actors, i.e., the descriptive dimensions should focus the connectedness between them. And, as pointed out above, they should be formulated in terms of feelings rather than actual conditions, and as seen from a specific party, these feelings have two objects: what 'we' feel about 'them', and what 'we' believe 'they' feel about 'us'. In this the feelings that are directed towards the specific relationship in itself are also included.

As a result of the IMP Project (Hakansson 1982) five atmosphere dimensions are suggested. These are closeness/distance, co-operation/conflict, power/dependence, trustworthiness, and expectations. To make these compatible with the requirements specified above regarding descriptions of the atmosphere concept, some of them need to be redefined or replaced. Firstly, the expectations dimension represents another type of concept. All aspects of the atmosphere in a sense refer to expectations of behaviour or actions. Expectations are created by the previous actions of the parties and form an element of the institutionalization of long-term relationships. In this sense, expectations contribute to create the boundaries of the latitude of choice of the parties. Over time, the atmosphere and the latitude of choice can be seen as determinants of the actual activities, which in turn determine the new atmosphere. This new atmosphere reshapes the latitude of choice, and the new atmosphere and the new latitude of choice will determine subsequent actions, etc.

Secondly, some other concepts are formulated more as actual behaviour than feelings towards the counterpart with respect to certain behavioural dimensions. Therefore, co-operation is here replaced with co-operativeness (that is, willingness to co-operate), and trustworthiness is replaced with trust.

Thirdly, there are also other dimensions which seem relevant to include. Klint (1985) defines 'action profile', that is, the impressions relayed to the counterpart by the actions made by the protagonist, in terms of power, trust, understanding, and long-term orientation. Although he gives the atmosphere concept a somewhat different role in his terminology, it is still clear, that the dimensions of his 'action profile' are very closely related to the atmosphere concept as defined here. Power and trust are in common in the two listings of dimensions. Understanding is a concept which is closely related to closeness but still not quite the same. It basically refers to empathy, the ability to see each other's point. Klint specifies as important aspects of understanding the commonality in language and in tradition (Fhanér 1978). However, understanding may be reached also without this commonality. Therefore, understanding and closeness are both included as separate dimensions. Closeness then refers specifically to interpersonal closeness, informal, friendly relations, etc. These might be absent in cultures where formality is the norm without precluding understanding between the actors.

Fourthly, Klint's remaining dimension, long-term orientation, should however be added to the list. In a way it compensates for the exclusion of expectations as a separate dimension, a concept which is also oriented towards the future. However, it is here redefined as commitment, that is, a willingness to invest unrecoverable resources in the relationship. This concept plays a central role both in models of internationalization (Johanson and Vahlne 1977) and industrial bonding (Wilson and Mummalaneni 1986).

Finally, the power/dependence concept is redefined not to reflect the assumed total sum of power or dependence in the relationship but rather the balance of power or dependence. It is suggested that it is more important for the atmosphere whether one of the parties perceives that they hold the upper hand or conversely are the underdog in a relationship than if the parties in any absolute sense see themselves as basically independent or interdependent. A certain minimum degree of interdependence is anyhow always present in business relationships.

Strength and centrality, as discussed above, are not defined as atmosphere dimensions *per se*. Instead, these concepts reflect the total character and role of the atmosphere in relationship.

A summary of the descriptive dimensions of the atmosphere and examples of actions and structural conditions (that is, determinants of the latitude of choice), which impinge on the different dimensions of the atmosphere, is provided in table 6.1. After this more detailed comments are given regarding the different atmosphere dimensions.

Table 6.1 Atmosphere dimensions and related actions and structures

Atmosphere dimensions	*Action profile*	*Latitude of choice*
(one's own feelings and perceived feelings of the counterpart)	(examples of behaviour)	(examples of structural limitations)
power/dependence balance	negotiations	resource positions; alternatives
co-operativeness/ competitiveness	information sharing	resource position; strategy
trust/opportunism	adaptations; crises	market structure; technology
understanding	communication	nationality, culture
closeness/distance	non-task contacts	business culture
commitment	adaptations; exploitation	technology; business cycle; industry

Power balance

The relationship between two parties to industrial exchange may be characterized as balanced or imbalanced with regard to power or dependence. Imbalance in the relation may be indicated by unmatched dependences. Other possibilities to imbalances may be found in the resource position of one of the parties as compared to the position of the other party. Imbalanced power/ dependence relations do not imply that there must be conflicts between the parties, as it is not necessary that the more powerful one of the parties demonstrates his power or even makes it explicit. The power/dependence relation may therefore be perceived as balanced although the parties control their power bases to a different extent. Thus, the power/dependence balance is – as all the atmosphere dimensions – a perceptual construct, which may differ from the actual power/dependence due to resource control etc. One of the parties may play the cards so as to produce an impression either of power or of interdependence, thus creating an atmosphere which cannot be explained by external factors.

Neither balance or imbalance *per se* is expected to lead to harmonic or disharmonic relationships. A balance of power, where both parties command strong positions in relation to each other, may lead to power struggles where one of the parties tries to get the upper hand. When there is imbalanced dependences the weaker party may accept that position and thus neutralize the imbalance as far as it has an impact on the atmosphere. Adaptations may also be used as a tool to influence the power/ dependence position. However, strong imbalances may produce feelings of powerlessness and listlessness in the weaker party and indifference or overweening confidence in the stronger one.

A stronger power position does not necessarily imply larger relative size. The smaller firm may be quite irreplaceable for the larger firm because of its market position, technical competence, contacts etc. It may also attain this position due to adaptations made within the relationship, for example, with regard to technology, distribution systems, etc., which may render it virtually impossible for the counterpart to replace its partner.

Power – or prestige – may also appear at a purely personal level based on admiration of competence, strength, courage etc. A resourceful personality may thus dominate a relationship although other structural conditions would not indicate any basis for dominance for that organization

Co-operativeness/competitiveness

Co-operativeness indicates an attitude towards work in common, which in more advanced cases may be represented by R&D in common. However, it may also be less grandiose and take its form in collaboration on a 'tit-for-tat' basis, that is, a co-operation that at one stage gives advantages to one of the parties in expectation of corresponding assistance at a later stage.

The co-operative attitude may influence actions in the fields of technology, but also in marketing and purchasing, as well as regarding general support. The co-operativeness is also reflected in a willingness to understand the difficulties the other party may have combined with a preparedness to come to assistance rather than viewing the relationship basically as an arena for competing for the same limited resources.

The concepts of co-operativeness and its opposite competitiveness are related to the perceptions of goals being basically compatible or not. Competitiveness may or may not further efficiency in more widely defined systems, but within the relationship it is here seen as a lack of will to co-operate towards joint goals. In extreme cases, it can take the form of ill will or hostility.

Trust/opportunism

Trust refers to a long-term attitude of relying upon the other party in the relationship, where negative incidents can be tolerated provided long-term expectations of positive developments. Opportunism, that is, the other extreme pole of the dimension, applies a short-term perspective, where opportunities are exploited without consideration for the interests of the other party. However, opportunism should not be equated to dishonesty or discord. Opportunism may be present with both parties and also explicit in the relationship, that is, it may be clear that neither party strives for a long-term orientation. For instance, resources may be lacking for the development of a long-term relationship, and then opportunism may dominate the exchange.

Understanding

Understanding refers to the willingness to understand the situation and conditions of the other party. It is a matter of wanting to acquire information about organization, other relationships, technology, tactical and strategic considerations, and other factors that influence the action possibilities of the other party. Reasons for the other party's behaviour are sought, and attempts are made to forecast future actions. The other party's point of view is explored and used for clarifying his actions. Thus, understanding requires a mutual interest in each other as well as openness towards each other. In situations characterized by understanding, the parties are inclined to accept each other's idiosyncracies and have forbearance with occasional failures or problems. The other extreme pole, where these qualities are missing, is quite simply termed non-understanding.

Understanding may emerge between individuals in business also when there is a considerable cultural gap between them. Thus, understanding may bridge rather than eliminate cultural and educational gaps. Conversely, understanding may be absent in spite of cultural and educational affinity.

Understanding is a mutual phenomenon in the sense that both parties must hold this attitude in order to create a relationship atmosphere of understanding. If only one of parties possesses this capacity of empathy, the relationship will be characterized by non-understanding.

Closeness/distance

The closeness/distance dimension is here employed to denote the degree of familiarity with regard to cultural and social aspects. As pointed above, this concept differs from understanding, and understanding may be present in spite of distance and vice versa. Values, business practices, the influence of and attitude towards authorities and social bodies may be quite different, but still there may be personal alignment and efforts to see each other's points. Without being reduced, distance can thus be bridged by willingness to understand, which eliminates distance as an obstacle. Although differences remain, these are not considered as disturbances.

Some of the expectations and the demands that the parties have on each other are also influenced by the closeness/distance dimension. The impact of differences between national business cultures as well as between levels of technical development can be referred to this dimension. The international experience of firms and its normally reducing effects on perceived distance should also be noted.

Commitment

Co-operative adaptations can be viewed either as yielding to the other party's requirements or undertakings for a common goal. Commitment to these common activities represents a long-term undertaking. It is related to trust, but it particularly reflects the long-term orientation to obtain common results. It indicates a willingness to accept bonding and restrictions on the possibilities to switch counterparts and fields of activity. Non-commitment implies that the relationship is loosely bonded and that the exchange is based on current resources and structures rather than on future expectations. The parties are not oriented towards long-term exchange.

However, low commitment does not imply a negative or disinterested attitude towards the relationship. Other circumstances may motivate a lack of future-oriented adaptations, for example, small exchange volumes or standardized needs.

ATMOSPHERE TYPOLOGIES

Combining the descriptive dimensions suggested above, many partial typologies of atmospheres can be obtained. Below one of all the possible combinations is discussed. Power balance is selected as a major classification variable as it is of a different character than the other ones (Klint 1985). It is matched with trust/opportunism. The obtained types are tentatively designated as shown in figure 6.3.

	Trust	*Opportunism*
Power Balance	peers	competitors
Power Imbalance	paternalism	bully/underdog

Figure 6.3 Atmospheres classified by power balance and trust

In the situation with balanced power the parties feel equal to each other, that is, they are either both reasonably independent of each other or else they have both invested in a relationship to make themselves mutually dependent. A trustful atmosphere in this context makes the parties peers in the sense that they can negotiate on co-operation issues from a give-and-take perspective, which can be expected to be mutually rewarding. The parties have a mutual orientation towards each other, and the atmosphere can be expected to provide a good working environment for the individuals. This atmosphere can be expected to be associated with a high degree of understanding, but whether there will be much or little of co-operativeness or commitment is probably related to whether the relationship is in balance at a high or low level of interdependence. The closeness/distance dimension could take any value due to the cultural affinity between the parties.

If trust is absent in balanced relationships, the parties can be expected to interact in an atmosphere of competition, that is, lower values are expected for cooperativeness, understanding and commitment. As before, closeness/distance could assume any value.

An imbalanced, trustful relationship is typical for certain subcontractor relationships. This situation resembles largely the 'peers' situation with the exception of the power balance. However, imbalances can always be exploited, in which case trust is transmogrified into opportunism, creating the 'bully/underdog' atmosphere. This is probably the least productive emotional working environment, sharing many of the features of the competition-orientated atmosphere but without its drive towards efficiency.

CONCLUSION AND IMPLICATIONS

In the interaction approach, for example, as presented in Hakansson (1982), the atmosphere in a business relationship is viewed as an intervening variable used to explain discrepancies in the expected relations between the major constituting elements of the interaction model, that is, the interacting parties, the interaction processes, and the interaction environment. Here the atmosphere is redefined as the emotional setting in which the interaction takes place, which means that it is considered as a phenomenon which can be studied in itself.

The research implications of this approach relate both to model building and to empirical work. The outline of a model presented in this paper focuses on the role of the atmosphere in business relationships, the dimensions used to describe it and the combinations of these into typologies. The empirical work requires operationalization of these dimensions, which is done by formulating attitudinal statements measured by Likert scales.

Preliminary results, based on a factor analysis of the first thirty-two interviews made in Swedish supplier companies in the autumn of 1988, indicate that the respondents hold consistent attitudes to the items used to build up the dimensions. However, it also seems as if the dimensions can be subdivided further. Thus, the power balance dimension can be divided into power and dependence as two separate constructs, trust is made up of trust *per se* and perceived fair play, distance can be divided into national and organisational factors etc.

The suitability of the suggested typologies is to some extent also an empirical question. The patterns obtained through analyses of the descriptive dimensions will give further basis for the determination of relevant categories. These will be related to the variables which compromise the interaction model and the integration of these processes in networks.

Management implications can be drawn in at least two respects. First, conclusions can be drawn regarding the amount of attention that should be given to handling atmosphere-related issues in different situations. Second, more specific conclusions can be drawn regarding how to handle these issues in various cultures, technologies, at different stages of relationship development, and in different types of markets and networks.

REFERENCES

Blau, P. (1964) *Exchange and Power in Social Life*, New York: Wiley.

Fhanér, S. (1978) *Psykologi som förklaring, förståelse och kritik* (Psychology as explanation, understanding, and criticism), Stockholm: Bonniers.

Giddens, A. (1975) *New Rules in Sociological Method*, Colchester: Anchor Press.

Hakansson, H. (ed), 1982, *International Marketing and Purchasing of Industrial Goods: An Interaction Approach*, Chichester: Wiley.

Hallén, L. (1982) *International Industrial Purchasing: Channels, Interaction, and Governance Structures*, Acta Universitatis Upsaliensis, Studia Oeconomiae Negotiorum 13, Stockholm: Almqvist & Wiksell.

Hallén, L., Johanson, J. and Seyed–Mohamed, N. (1987) 'Relationship strength and stability in international and domestic industrial marketing', *Industrial Marketing and Purchasing* 2: 22–37.

Hallén, L. and Wiedersheim-Paul, F. (1981) 'Psychic distance in international marketing: an interaction approach', paper presented at the AIB/EIBA Conference, Barcelona.

Hofstede, G., (1980) *Culture's Consequences: International Differences in Work-Related Values*, Beverly Hills/London: Sage.

Johanson, J. (1989) 'Business relationships and industrial networks', in O. E. Williamson, S.–E. Sjöstrand and J. Johanson (1989) *Perspectives on the Economics of Organization*, Lund: Lund University Press: 65–80.

Johanson, J. and Vahlne, J.–E. (1977) 'The internationalization process of the firm: a model of knowledge development and increasing

foreign market commitments, *Journal of International Business Studies* 8: 23–32.
Klint, M. (1985) *Mot en konjunkturanpassad kundstrategi: om den sociala relationens roll vid marknadsföring av massa och papper* (Towards a customer strategy allied to the business cycle: on the role of the social relationship in the marketing of pulp and paper), Uppsala University, Department of Business Studies.
Williamson, O. E. (1975) *Markets and Hierarchies: Analysis and Antitrust Implications*, New York: Macmillan/The Free Press.
Wilson, D., and Mummalaneni, V. (1986) 'Bonding and commitment in buyer–seller relationships: a preliminary conceptualization', *Industrial Marketing and Purchasing* 1: 44–58.

Chapter Seven

RELATIONS BETWEEN THE CONCEPT OF DISTANCE AND INTERNATIONAL INDUSTRIAL MARKETING

JAN-ÅKE TÖRNROOS

> Through satellite communications we see people and events in far-off lands with an immediacy belying their distance. Yet, the devices designed to facilitate the process of communication do not always lead to better understanding among men. Communication is, after all, a human function, the essence of the human 'encounter'. [Crondon and Saito 1974]

The theme under analysis is treated in a brief and interdisciplinary fashion in order to find ways of dealing with distance in international marketing. My aim is to look at the interplay between industrial marketing on the international scene and distance variables defined and conceptualized in different ways. To date most of the research in the area has been concerned with the structure of the process of industrial buying and selling. The process itself is very complicated, and the term 'distance' is used here to give one dimension to the marketing process. This is done in order to examine the role of distances in an international setting.

Direct physical barriers exist between buyer and seller in all industrial business situations. In the international context this aspect of distance becomes more significant. The location of the firms involved in the transactions always has an impact on the process of marketing.

How the interacting parties look and deal with the process of buying and selling is another case in point. According to this, the term 'distance' can be interpreted in many different shades or senses, as we can also consider the various 'distances' between cultures, values, norms, and habits of the selling and buying firms and the individuals, especially those working within negotiations and marketing.[1] This is the most difficult way of conceptualizing distance and its influence on international business relations. Therefore in this chapter I will offer only brief suggestions of how this may be treated in broad terms.

Geographers, psychologists, and sociologists, as well as management scientists can all offer perspectives which may be relevant in finding important contributions to the study of the distance concept in international marketing. In the next section I will try to describe some ideas put forward in the project 'Finland as an international industrial market ' carried out at the Åbo Akademi. At the same time I will try to conceptualize distance and some of its different meanings. These aspects of the term are considered in the following approach:

- physical distance barriers;
- cultural features and distance;
- cognitive and psychological features;
- different levels internationally and distance.

Some other aspects of the term may also occur when dealing with these four 'groups' of distance. All these conceptualizations are dealt with in turn, and a model is suggested upon the premises. At this point it must be stressed that this is a first outline, and much is yet to be done before we can draw any far-reaching conclusions about the relations between distance and the interaction processes between international buying and selling firms.

PHYSICAL FEATURES

The concept of physical distance is, of course, closely related to the Euclidean sense of space as a measurable, more or less exact, conception of distance. We can measure the physical and/or temporal distance of communicating and distributing goods physically between firms in different countries trading with one another. Distance in the physical sense remains a concrete and problematic obstacle for efficient transactions between industrial firms. As the internationalization process of a firm proceeds, physical distances can form a critical obstacle for the marketing process between buying and selling firms. In particular, this affects physical distribution management and logistics, as well as time management and reliance on external firms in relation to the buying–selling interaction (shippers, fowarders, customs officials, port authorities, and others). Consequently, this means that physical distance and interaction across borders create an 'internal network' concerning the dyadic, triadic, or other directly interacting parties in an industrial network. Additionally, we can identify an 'external network', consisting of all other institutions, firms, and authorities directly or indirectly involved in the process of distributing goods between firms in different countries.

In physical terms industrial businesses often spend large amounts of time, money, and personnel on creating efficient logistics systems between the firms concerned, and especially for the firms individually. The seller is often obliged to concentrate on the role of transportation and physical distribution to find ways of creating systems which satisfies the buyer. Physical distance creates a need for management to find 'time and place utility' to this area. For many firms the reliance on external sources is quite important. This means that the interaction process is not influenced only by the selling and buying firms, but also other influences.

A country like Finland has a specifically heavy burden in carrying out these activities because of its relatively remote location within Europe and its severe winters.

Physical distance can also create cultural, communication, and other problems in carrying out interaction activities between firms in an industrial network. The problem of establishing and maintaining personal contacts is a critical variable in industrial marketing. In this respect multinational and large global companies are in a better position than smaller firms. Similarly, small remote countries face this 'locational' problem in overcoming physical distance.

To some extent, physical distance has become a lesser obstacle than previously due to the technology of transportation, communication technology, and the higher level of skills of firms operating on more international markets. Still, it seems that physical distance parameters are of significant importance in explaining industrial and other international buying–selling patterns.

CULTURAL CHARACTERISTICS AND DISTANCE

Physical distance and its relation to the process of buying and selling is more straightforward than the concept of *cultural* distance. The term cultural distance is preferred in this text, even though there are many similar concepts which refer to this same notion.[2] 'Culture' is not an easily defined concept. Culture may contain personal ideas, beliefs, and learnt meanings. Culture can be seen broadly as an integrated concept of everyday life and practices which are constituted in different areas and locations in complex and differentiated ways. In this respect we can also define subcultures and cultures of different activities, such as politics, arts, sports, business, religion, and so on. To grasp the whole seems impossible. Instead we can try to delimit a subculture called 'business culture', which can be characterized as the ways and habits which guide the way of doing business in a specific culture with which a firm may closely be identified. In recent years, for example, we have seen the publication of a large amount of books about Japanese management techniques and Japanese business culture.

In my view, business culture within a specific firm must be the outcome of the historical process of how the management of the firm has been carried out, and how employees of the firm perceive and behave in relation to how the firm strives to reach its objectives. The firm's culture is an integrated whole of the different cultures through its personnel, and especially its leading personnel. In addition, business culture is affected by the surrounding cultural habits, which are constituted in the national and subnational cultures where the firm operates.

The multinational corporation is of course a specific 'cultural' mixture, and as such has through its activities in many cultures a specific position. Therefore it can be difficult to find 'pure' Swedish, Finnish, German, or Italian companies, due to the international ownership and personnel of many firms.

It is possible to find business cultures on different levels of appearance in relation to culture 'in general' in a country or a region of a country, and further within business culture it may be possible to find specific forms of cultures or habits and personal and/or firm-specific as well as industry-specific cultures, as for instance industrial marketing in the paper business.

Cultural behaviour in the context of industrial marketing and buying behaviour should be seen as a process of dealing with these complex patterns in a specific context. First, the individuals who interact are members of an organization (buying or selling firm(s)). Secondly, as noted in the literature of industrial marketing, the process is carried out by professionals. This will affect their cultural behaviour. Thirdly, the individuals represent different cultures both in respect of business culture and national culture in the international setting. The notion of professionalism and industrial selling and buying behaviour leads to more rational behaviour in the industrial buying process, whereas the other notions can give rise to more unpredictable and problematic dimensions. Cyert and March (1963), in their notion of organizational learning, retain an important impact on the stabilization and long-term nature of relations between many industrial selling and buying firms.

However, the distance parameters are hard to estimate for example by quantitative methods. This stems from the dualistic concept of culture. This dualism derives from the notion of culture as *form* and as *meaning*. The form here means the way we express ourselves and the meaning is the message we want to transmit (Laine-Sveiby 1987).

Culture is bound to a specific group or sub-group of people who share similar cultural and/or geographical and historical backgrounds. This has to do with the internal cohesion within a cultural group. It means also that culture is dynamic and varies over time.

The self-reference criterion can be taken as a starting point when we try to look at other cultures. Our own cultural background is the starting point when we look at other cultures or interact with other people and/or organisations. This will bias our ways of perceiving each other across cultural borders.

Cultural barriers also create cultural distance in the setting of industrial marketing. Distance parameters are not easily defineable. In management research, Gertsen (1986) has defined three areas where cultural studies have been carried out:

- the study of communication and of how cultural aspects affect them;

- the study of the behaviour of people from different cultures meeting each other;
- the study of transcultural management.

The context of industrial marketing and cultural values and behaviour is closely related to the first topic of these approaches. Intercultural communication theory and the role of negotiation in international marketing are two distinct areas of study which should be of significance when researching problems of cultural distance and international industrial marketing.

This poses new challenges and problems to the approach. Sarbauch and Asuncion-Lande (1983: 46) examined eight distinct theoretical perspectives at a seminar concerning intercultural communication theory. These were codes and code systems, constructivism, different philosophical perspectives, mathematical models, relationship development, rhetorical theory, rules perspective, and systems theory. This gives a hint, perhaps, of the scale of the problem we are dealing with when studying intercultural questions, which is, to a great extent, interdisciplinary, and requires the consideration of many different perspectives. I believe this applies also to the complex of problems in industrial marketing. However, there can also be such similar business cultures as there can be similar tastes and preferences among consumers.

In the context of looking at the images that foreign firms have about Finland as an international market, the aim of the Åbo Akademi project is to find, through personal interviews, aspects that refer to the beliefs and personal experiences that marketing managers in five European countries have perceived when having business contacts with Finland. The aim is not to find an 'exact' picture which may be measured quantitatively. Both the methodology and the cultural parameters considered here are sufficient obstacles enough. Instead, a more action-oriented, case study research is carried out.

PSYCHOLOGICAL AND COGNITIVE ASPECTS

These are defined as the intra-personal aspects of having contacts with people from other cultures. In industrial marketing such personal skills and behaviour have an important impact on how business performance and negotiation are carried out. The significance of personal skills cannot be overemphasized. In inter-cultural meetings the coding and decoding mechanisms can be of great importance, for example, when sales persons from western cultures meet people from eastern cultures in business matters (high and low-context cultures). Personal distance may be a very important factor in coping with situations in business negotiations. In traditional business literature this factor has been lightly ignored by the use of notions such as 'economic man'. Today, it is more or less accepted that the manager is far from 'rational' in her or his decisions. This must also hold for professional industrial marketing and purchasing managers.

Cultural and personal characteristics are closely interrelated. Personal values stem more or less directly from cultural values. Culture is, however, a more group determined form of behaviour. The person, again, is always an individual and will act accordingly. In certain cultures it is more accepted to behave individually than in others (US versus Japan for example).[3]

Moreover, individual behaviour and its relation to the cultural factors as listed above can be problematic in the negotiation process. Personal skills in the command of language and other cultural assets, in the marketing process between negotiating partners, may well be as important as skills in technological know-how and organizational skills.

In research situations one may encounter difficulties in studying the impact of such personal factors. Data about specific personal assets and problems in international marketing should be obtained through personal and intensive contacts, and though participation in the process of industrial selling. This, in turn, is certainly a difficult task.

GEOGRAPHICAL CONSIDERATIONS

In this section, I will briefly discuss some concepts of distance and levels of study in international business which have been put forward by geographers in their studies of mainly multi-national corporations (MNCs).[4] These works introduce some spatial considerations in the analysis of MNCs. In doing this I will leave aside distance in the sense of direct physical space.

The distinction space/geography and the concept of distance are closely related with each other. An international firm uses space/distance on a much wider scale than a purely national or regionally-oriented firm. The internationally-oriented firm has to take into consideration all geographical levels in its activities (the firm, the local area surrounding its affiliates, the regional, national, and international scales). All these geographical levels interact with each other and have to be considered in tactical and strategic decisions.

Relations exist between the process level of the firm's activities and its spatial relations. Location of its markets and its competitors is one factor of relevance. Strategic choices of when and how to solve exchange of technologies or products relate closely to problems of overcoming spatial disparity between buying and selling firms. This holds for physical barriers (cultural as well as technological) and also for such 'indirect' distance parameters as tariff and non-tariff barriers between countries.

The process of industrial buying is an aspect that creates intra and interorganizational distance and/or delimits it and shortens the distance through organizational learning and exchange processes. The execution of business and business strategies in the international setting can be seen as a process of overcoming distances in intelligent competition between firms. A simple model derived from the preceding discussion may look like figure 7.1 shows below. The figure considers the term image instead of distance which is the topic of this chapter.

This is motivated by the fact that the Åbo Akademi project studies Finland as an international industrial market, and in this context, we are interested in knowing how industrial firms abroad perceive Finland as a market for their products. What are their images of Finland? This is in turn related to how the project group itself perceives Finland and its market for industrial products. Answers to these two questions are related to each other, and our aim is to see if the perceptions of the respondent firms and the project group's differ, and, if so, why such specific differnces exist? Figure 7.2 relates directly to the interaction process and the international dimension.

The figure is grossly simplified in order to make the point that spatial levels matter. In the international marketing process both

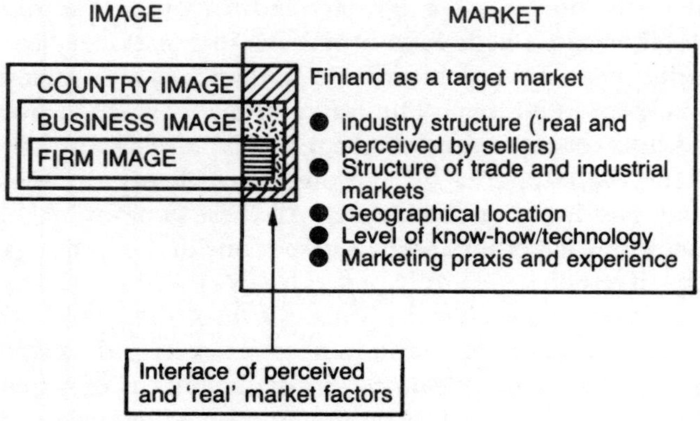

Figure 7.1 Relations between 'images' on different levels and the Finnish industrial market

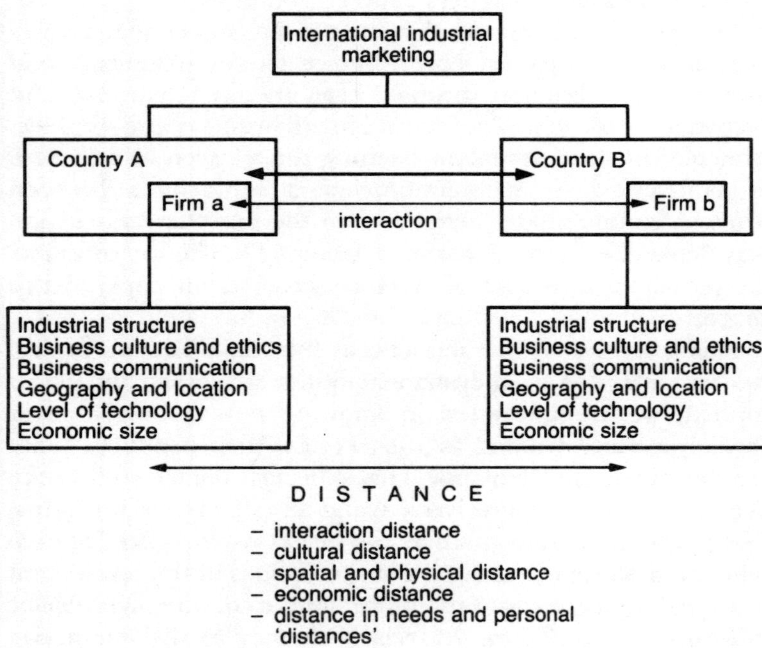

Figure 7.2 Relations between industrial marketing and distance factors in an international perspective. The figure is simplified in terms of both country and firm interaction

country-specific factors and firm-specific factors are relevant. Country-culture and habits, as well as organizational cultures, interact. On the other hand intra-national cultures and variations, as well as intra-organizational differences and variations, may distort interaction and make the interaction proces long and complicated.

The next section introduces the main outlines of the project.

STRUCTURE OF THE PROJECT

In order to ascertain the 'images' and the experiences of the Finnish market among marketing managers, five countries were selected for empirical research. The countries selected were Denmark, West Germany, France, Great Britain, and Italy. The aim was to choose countries that are not nearest neighbours to Finland. In this first phase the purpose is to look at firms who have business contacts with Finland and Finnish industrial buyers.

Hitherto many research projects carried out have been related to exports or direct investments abroad. Our import-oriented research differs in this respect. It seems to be a country-specific 'characteristic' of the research to look at exports and on its possibilities on the international market rather than of equally important import exchange. Imports can also create exports and other business relations in the future.

The home-based research is mainly carried out through secondary sources. This is a rather serious limitation, but is due to restricted resources. The country is taken as one spatial research area, and the industry as another. In addition, economic–geographic and cultural aspects, as well as directly economic data, are taken into account in the intra-Finland study.

Empirical research abroad is carried out by personal interviews. Because of the limited number of students doing the research, case studies are preferred, and it remains to be seen how many interviews can be carried out per country. This means that the specificity of each firm's experiences about doing business with Finnish counterparts is examined, rather than 'general laws' concerning international industrial marketing.

In accordance with the preceding description, the problems are related to the following categories:

1 questions of how Finland is perceived as a potential market, for example, in the light of economic growth, level of income, technological skills and level, and industry structure, as well as politics;
2 questions related to how relations with Finnish buyers have started, and which entry form has been selected;
3 questions about the impact of cultural differences (business ethics, ways of negotiating, and ways of doing business);
4 questions of spatio-geographic differences and location: does this affect business, and what is really known about Finland?

In this sense our project is divided into three distinct parts which will be compared in the final stage of the project. The first part relates to the 'image' of Finland in the light of the results of the interviews, and two related projects about the theme in question.[5] The second relates to the image the project itself has about Finland as an industrial market. The third part in turn looks at the firms perspectives on the same topic in the five countries.

The project is still at a very early stage: only three interviews have been carried out (in Denmark, Germany, and Italy). The questionnaire was seen to work well in the interviews, and has been only slightly modified.

The project looks, in a sense, at different kinds of distances between Finland and the countries that are important in the light of Finnish exports and imports.

A model of the distance parameters can be represented by figure 7.3. The relations between different distances have to be taken into account in studying industrial marketing – especially in the international arena. This is also a suggestion for further research areas and possibilities.

CONCLUSIONS

One possible approach in studying international industrial marketing is to study the interacting companies by using the concept of distance. There are also many ways of conducting empirical work from this point of view. The concept can be dualized into physical distance and cultural distance in a broad sense. But if we look more closely at the concept we must add

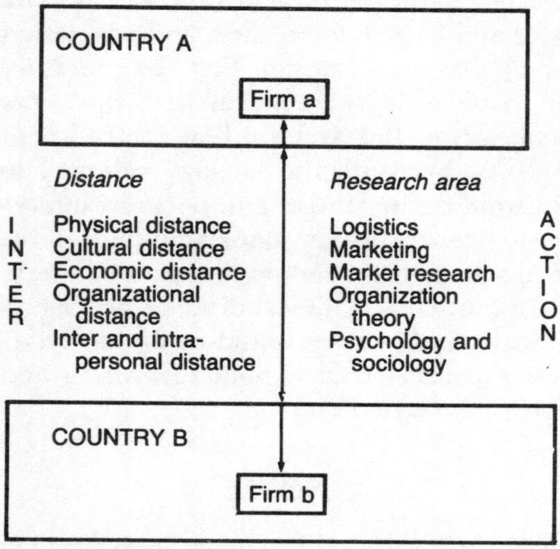

Figure 7.3 A simple model of some distance factors and their main research areas

also the role of cognitive distance and the role of spatial levels in the international setting. The first of these relates to the *personal* level and group behaviour in interaction contacts and communication situations, especially in face-to-face communication and negotiations. The second deals mainly with the *macro-level* and the relationship between the network of firms and the external environment, that is, social, political, and institutional surroundings.

If we can define and delimit those distance variables that are considered important in a firm's specific interactive environment, there may be possibilities of using this as a marketing planning tool in international industrial marketing. This approach could also be used as a model for interaction between buying and selling firms in a network. This chapter has concentrated on distance factors that are present especially on the international scene, but it has to be stressed that they seem to play an important role in all industrial business situations intranationally. The cultural distance variables may be outlined in terms of the problems in the interaction process and the atmosphere between the interacting parties. Physical problems of distance relate to the logistical field, as well as to the notion of relative space and its role in business and adaptation.

The empirical research design that the present project has adopted is mostly oriented towards case study research and qualitative measures. Research on how Finland is perceived in distance aspects, by using the analogy referred to above, is conducted through case studies and personal interviews.

In order to gain a deeper understanding of the different aspects of distance they should be studied in more detail separately. In particular, cultural distance and its role in international industrial marketing would be an important contribution. This is especially true if both theoretical and empirical research are to be carried out.

NOTES

1 cf. McCall and Warrington (1984) for an example of how important the negotiation function is considered in marketing.

2 The term 'psychic distance' is used by Carlson (1975), and this is also adopted by e.g. Hallén and Wiedersheim-Paul (1979) and Hallén *et al.* (1987).

3 Kato (1974) in his article shows how US and Japan look at each other (Condon and Saito 1974).

4 cf. Taylor and Thrift (1982), Clarke (1985), Taylor and Thrift (1986).

5 The first of these concentrates on 'image-mix' for the Finnish industry in international marketing, whilst the second deals with 'image from the perspective of Finnish industry'.

REFERENCES

Carlson, S. (1975) 'How foreign is foreign trade? A problem in business research', *Studiae Oeconomiae Negotiorum* 11: 11–26.

Clarke, I. M. (1985) *The Spatial Organization of Multinational Corporations*, London: Croom Helm.

Condon, J. C. and Saito, M. (1974) (eds) *Intercultural Encounters with Japan*, The Simul Press, Tokyo, 1974.

Cyert, R. M. and March J. G. (1963) *A Behavioral Theory of the Firm* Englewood Cliffs, NJ: Prentice Hall.

Gertsen M. (1986) *The Cultural Aspects of International Business: Initial Reflections in Connection with a Planned Study*, Working Paper, Copenhagen School of Economics, Institute for International Economics and Management.

Gudykunst, W. B. (ed.) (1983) *Intercultural Communication Theory:*

Current Perspectives, International and Intercultural Communication Annual Vol. VII, Beverly Hills: Sage.

Hallén, L. and Wiedersheim Paul, F. (1979) Psychic distance and buyer–seller interaction, *Organisasjon, Marked og Samfunn* 16: 308–24.

Hallén, L., Johanson, J. and Seyed Mohamed, N. (1987) Relationship strength and stability in international and domestic industrial marketing, *Industrial Marketing & Purchasing* 2: 22–37.

Keegan, W. J. (1984) *Multinational Marketing Management*, Englewood Cliffs, NJ: Prentice Hall.

Laine-Sveiby, K. (1987) *Kansallinen Kulttuuri Strategiana. Suomi ja ruotsi. Eroja ja yhtäläisyyksiä*, Stockholm: EVA.

McCall, J. B. and Warrington, M. B., (1984) *Marketing by Agreement: A Cross Cultural Approach to Business Negotiations*, Chichester: Wiley.

Rugman, A. M. *et al.* (1986) *International Business: Firm and Environment*, Singapore: McGraw Hill.

Sarbauch, L. E. and Asuncion Lande, N. (1983) Theory building in intercultural communication: synthesizing the action caucus, in W. B. Gudykunst (ed.) *Intercultural Communication Theory: Current Perspectives*, Beverly Hills: Sage, 45–60.

Taylor, M. and Thrift, N. (1982) *The Geography of Multinationals*, London: Croom Helm.

Taylor, M. and Thrift, N. (1986) *Multinationals and the Restructuring of the World Economy*, London: Croom Helm.

Chapter Eight

NEW PRODUCT DEVELOPMENT IN INDUSTRIALIZING COUNTRIES

A pilot study

HEIDI VERNON-WORTZEL AND LAWRENCE H. WORTZEL

The mature industrialized countries still account for the largest portion of the world's production, but the industrializing countries are rapidly increasing their share. In 1965, industrializing countries accounted for 14.5 per cent of the market economies' production; by 1985, their share had increased to 18.1 per cent. During the 1965–85 period production grew in the industrializing countries at almost twice the rate of the mature industrialized countries (7.2 vs. 3.8 per cent) (World Bank 1987).

The middle income industrializing countries, in which reside just one-third of the total industrializing countries' population, account for two-thirds of the industrializing countries' production. The larger middle income industrializing countries represent a substantial potential market for sellers of industrial goods, both components and capital equipment. To progress steadily in industrialization these countries will require a steady stream of new products. Each new product offers a potential market for new suppliers of both capital goods and components; new suppliers can enter without having to overcome barriers erected because of existing relationships.

Despite the growing importance of industrializing country markets and the extent of new product development in them, there is little empirical work on new product development in such countries. In fact, industrial buyer behaviour in industrializing countries is, itself, a little studied topic. Ford and Djeflat (1983) and Wortzel (1983) each identified and analyzed aspects of the buying process and the buying/selling relationships in developing countries; besides these two studies little additional empirical work exists.

Researchers have conducted innumerable studies of the new product development process in industrialized countries. The consensus is that new product development is among the most difficult activities a firm can undertake. A principal reason for the difficulty is often organizational inertia and an entrenched bureaucracy. To develop and commercialize a new product successfully, a new product developer must overcome these obstacles.

Because firms in the industrializing countries may be too young to have developed inertia and may be too thin in their managerial ranks to have become bureaucratic, new product development might appear to be a less difficult activity for such firms. But there is also another aspect of new product development that has to do with technical expertise. Successful new product development requires, at the minimum, both marketing and manufacturing skills. These are skills that are in short supply in every industrializing country. To be successful at new product development firms in these countries must find some way around the shortage.

In this chapter we report on an empirical study of new product development conducted in one industrializing country, Indonesia. Indonesia is the fifth largest country in the world, with a population of about 170 million. Despite a fivefold increase in value added in manufacturing between 1970 and 1984 (in constant terms), and an established manufacturing base, Indonesia ranks at the low end of the middle income countries; thus it has a very long way to go. Its size, which makes it an attractive market, coupled with its fast growth yet relatively early stage of industrialization, make it both managerially and intellectually interesting to study.

We analysed over forty new product development projects, some by means of personal interviews, others using a self-administered questionnaire. In both cases, we collected qualitative, rather than quantitative, data. The questionnaire and our personal interviews consisted of open-ended questions. In view of the early stage of inquiry about the topic, we set a modest objective for this study: to learn as much as possible in order to develop a basis for subsequent broader, and perhaps more quantitative, research.

Both interviewees and questionnaire respondents were senior

managers from firms located in or around Jakarta. Our sample was not a probability sample, but it did include a cross-section of industrial and consumer goods firms. In both the interview and the questionnaire we asked respondents about their most recent new product and probed the development of buyer–seller relationships for capital goods and components used to manufacture that product. In nearly every case, this was a product that had been on the market for two years or less. In order to secure co-operation from our respondents we had to assure them that their identities would be kept confidential. Therefore we will not identify by name any of the companies that participated in this study.

In the remainder of this paper, we first list the topics we covered and present our initial organizing hypothesis for each. We next present and discuss our findings. Finally, we discuss implications for further research and for managerial action.

TOPICS COVERED AND ORGANIZING HYPOTHESES

We focused our study on four topics, and entered with a simple organizing hypothesis about each. The individual topics, the organizing hypotheses, and a brief discussion of each hypothesis follows.

Market characteristics of new products developed

Principally these will be new-to-the-country or new-to-the-firm, rather than new-to-the-world. The industrializing countries, especially those of Asia (Indonesia included) seem to be adopting a Japanese/Western model of economic development, calling for factories and at least a modicum of capital equipment, rather than an appropriate technology or basic needs model (Dawson 1981). Much of what these countries produce is imitative of existing Japanese/Western manufactured goods.

We should expect that, because of scarce resources, industrializing country firms will be very much concerned with minimizing risk in making their new product development choices. Their preference, then, should be for products with predictable demand and easily determinable specifications. This means they will concentrate on products already available in the domestic market, either imported, or produced domestically by another firm. Of these two possibilities, the import substitution products should be the most attractive because of the possibility of restricting imports once local production begins. Similarly, products destined for the local market, or for indirect export should be less risky than products destined for export.

Stimulus to develop the new product

Stimuli for new products will result primarily from demand pull. A country at Indonesia's stage of development pursuing a Japanese/Western model of economic development will not have the resources or the incentive to invest in the kind of R&D that might lead to new products being developed as a result of technology push.

New product search processes

Firms will undertake little or no formal marketing research either to identify opportunities or to measure demand. Especially with respect to industrial products, search will consist of identifying existing products, and existing potential buyers for those products. Firms will then attempt to secure some commitment from the potential buyers before beginning production.

The product development process

In the industrialized countries, new product development usually includes two interlinked activities. One is designing the product, deciding on its appearance, specifications, content, and the like. The other activity is designing the process for manufacturing the product, including deciding on machinery and components. The new products firms in an industrializing country produce almost always exist somewhere in the world. In many cases, the new product design is a given, with all specifications set by the customer for the product. In the remaining cases, product design is a matter of copying, perhaps with a few simple modifications, a product that is already on the market somewhere.

The key issue, therefore, in developing new products in industrializing countries is manufacturing process design, with a heavy emphasis on procurement of production machinery. In an industrializing country, product development will be from the beginning much more supplier focused than is the case in an industrialized country. In the industrialized countries, of course, the major problem is to design the new product in such a way as to provide an advantage to customers over whatever has been available previously. Unless the product design requires new or arcane technology, the focus of successful development efforts is the product/customer match.

The search for suppliers does not really begin until at least a preliminary design is in hand. In the industrializing country, the product design is virtually a given, so the major problem is finding suppliers whose offerings will best satisfy the product's manufacturing requirements. New product developers will see potential suppliers as a key resource, not just for components or equipment, but for help and advice as well. The new product development process is very much a technology acquisition process, and product developers view suppliers as the most important potential sources of the needed technology.

The interaction model framework (Hakansson 1982) seems an appropriate way to organize the findings in this area. Although the interaction model was primarily designed to study existing, ongoing relationships, its framework appears highly appropriate for studying emerging relationships as well.

STUDY FINDINGS

In this section, we report our findings on each of the study topics. We then discuss the findings in terms of the organizing hypothesis just presented for that topic.

MARKET CHARACTERISTICS OF NEW PRODUCTS

Here, our findings support the organizing hypothesis. Figure 8.1 presents a new product classification matrix. The columns in the matrix classify new products by their prior domestic availability. There are three categories: new products already available locally and produced locally by others, available locally but imported, and products unavailable locally. The rows classify products by their destination: the domestic market; indirect export (as parts or components of exported products); or direct export.

	Prior domestic availability		
Destination	*Produced locally by others*	*Imported*	*Unavailable*
Domestic market	Candy Biscuits Cookies Shrimp feed Textiles Paving tiles Tiles Clothing	Stemware Petrochemicals Automotive batteries Automobile axles	
Indirect export	Textiles		
Direct export	Timber Plywood Athletic shoes Rattan furniture		

Figure 8.1 New product classification

We found only one new product in our sample that was previously unavailable in the domestic market, chocolate chip cookies. Given the non-probability nature of the sample, we cannot rule out the strong possibility that finding only one such product was an artefact of our sample. Not every new product is first introduced in industrializing countries via import. This is especially true of simple, easy-to-duplicate consumer goods.

On the other hand, this finding makes sense even for consumer goods. Indonesia has liberalized its import restrictions to the point at which a great variety of products can be imported, albeit in small quantities, and at high rates of duty. Since importing is less risky than manufacturing a product with unknown prospects, we would expect imports to occur before local production took place. Importing is a sensible way for a potential new product manufacturer to test product acceptance, and scanning successful imports is a good source of new product ideas.

Industrial goods firms believed that developing new products previously unavailable in Indonesia was considerably more risky than copying products already imported. They believed that demand for most industrial products was derived demand. The attitude of the majority was 'if the product isn't already imported, no one wants it'. Consumer goods firms, on the other hand, believed they could affect primary demand with a new product introduction.

We did find a few past new product development situations that came quite close to fitting in the domestically unavailable column. These were automobiles and television sets. In both cases, the Indonesian firm that manufactured (or assembled) the product entered the business as a joint venture partner with a foreign firm. In these earlier cases, the new product was a joint result of the efforts of the foreign firm to find a local partner, (as required by law), combined with a local firm looking for a new product to produce domestically.

As hypothesized, the bulk of the new products we studied fell into the prior domestically available columns. Industries such as automobiles and consumer electronics began in Indonesia, as in the other Asian countries, by assembling imported parts. As volume grew, and as the Government exerted pressure, local firms found opportunities to produce components and to replace imported parts with domestically produced parts. Many of the early entrants, in automobile parts especially, were joint ventures between Indonesian firms and the Japanese suppliers to the auto industry.

A significant proportion of the early more product entries were initiated by the foreign partner rather than by the Indonesian partner. In more recent ventures, it is the Indonesian firm that identifies the opportunity and initiates the new product development.

We were somewhat surprised by the number of respondents with new product entries into categories where there were existing local producers. In this classification, we found new product entries for both the domestic market and for direct export. These were markets in which the new product developers expected high growth. Just as in the industrialized countries, growth markets attract competitors. New entrants believed that growth prospects would enable them to prosper without going head-to-head against competitors; moreover, the competitors' offerings represented a target at which they could take specific aim.

Most of the new products in our sample bore some relationship to their firm's existing business. The majority of these new products were horizontally linked. All the new food products, for example, were developed by firms already in the food business. There were some instances of vertical integration as well, with raw rattan producers moving into furniture and loggers moving into plywood and semi-finished lumber. For some of the garment producers, clothing products represented a brand new business.

STIMULUS AND MOTIVATION FOR NEW PRODUCT DEVELOPMENT

As expected, all the new products we studied resulted from demand pull. But not all of the new products resulted from firms' entrepreneurial efforts in identifying growth or expansion opportunities. In some cases, the demand pull stimulus came from a specific potential customer's request. In other cases, the demand pull came indirectly, as a result of government regulations. Several new products, including automotive axles and batteries, and finished wood products, were developed at the behest of potential customers who required local sources to replace the imports they were using.

Two log exporters entered the plywood business, not because of entrepreneurial opportunities, but to protect their existing logging businesses. Both these firms were exporters of logs, and by integrating forward into plywood they were responding to a government regulation forbidding the further export of logs. The Indonesian government's desire was to increase the value added that the country received from exports of its fast dwindling timber reserves; it reasoned that prohibiting exports of logs would force the logging industry to integrate forward.

Government regulations were also the impetus for several firms to enter the manufacture of rattan furniture. These regulations prohibited the further export of raw rattan. But, in this case the entrants were not all former rattan producers. Several firms that had not previously had any connection with raw rattan production or export entered the rattan furniture business. Some rattan producers did not integrate forward. Instead they simply became suppliers to the new firms that entered the rattan furniture manufacturing business.

However, we identified one industry in Indonesia that has developed, at least in part, based on technology push, the batik design and printing industry. Certainly, there is demand for batiks in Indonesia and in other countries. But Indonesian artisans did not develop batiks because consumers were clamoring specifically for batiks. In a sense, the industry is still driven by technology push, in that there does not seem to be a specific focus on consumer-accepted design.

SEARCH PROCESSES

Most of the firms whose new products resulted from entrepreneurial search looked specifically for new products that would complement or fill out their present product lines. In a nutshell, their search process was one of 'find a product we think we can sell along with our existing line and duplicate it'.

Fewer firms looked for new unrelated businesses to enter. Those wanting to enter new businesses first tried to determine the industry's growth prospects, and then to search for a specific product example to duplicate. One entrepreneur, for example, discovered that commerical shrimp and prawn farming was a growth industry in Indonesia, and decided to go into business producing shrimp feed. Another, noticing a boom in home construction decided to enter the marble tile and bathroom fixture business. Each then identified an existing product to duplicate.

The entrepreneurial firms did not use systematic screening procedures. Rather, their search processes were informal, and based primarily on observation. As expected, we found little in the way of formal marketing research as part of the search process. Even among the packaged goods firms, we found no significant use of new product development techniques commonly employed in the USA or Western Europe, such as focus groups or problem inventory analysis, for example. However, we did find some firms using taste tests and conducting small studies of consumers' reactions to different packaging alternatives. Firms employed these techniques to tune the new product, rather than to develop the product from scratch.

In most cases, firms' new product scanning horizons included just the domestic Indonesian market. But food and garment manufacturers extended their searches outside Indonesia. One food manufacturer, searching for a cookie or cracker to add to his line, ended up inspecting and tasting chocolate chip cookies in the USA which he then adapted to the Indonesian market. A prospective clothing manufacturer who wanted to produce clothing for the domestic market visited Taiwan to see what clothing items he might duplicate in Indonesia. And the prospective entrant into shrimp and prawn food visited Thailand, where prawn farming was better established, in order to find shrimp and prawn food products to duplicate at home.

THE PRODUCT DEVELOPMENT PROCESS

In contrast to the situation facing many new product developers in the industrialized countries, the principal problem for Indonesian firms is not finding or designing a product that will sell. The new product development problem is to make correctly and profitably a product of fairly well-known design and at least somewhat certain sales. We identified two key dimensions that drive the product development process in Indonesia. Figure 8.2 shows these dimensions and maps a selection of the new products we studied.

The vertical dimension of figure 8.2 measures the degree of difficulty or complexity involved in manufacturing the new product as perceived by the firm developing it. Note that this is a perceptual measure. It would be possible to order various products according to their actual degree of difficulty to manufacture, using measures such as the amount of worker skill required, sophistication of machinery involved, and number of manufacturing operations. But such measures would provide only a rough guide to the behaviour of new product developers in a country such as Indonesia because the relationship between perceptions and reality may not be linear. It is the managers' perceptions that guide their actions, and what is important (and often different from reality) therefore is Indonesian managers' perceptions of the complexity or difficulty in manufacturing a product.

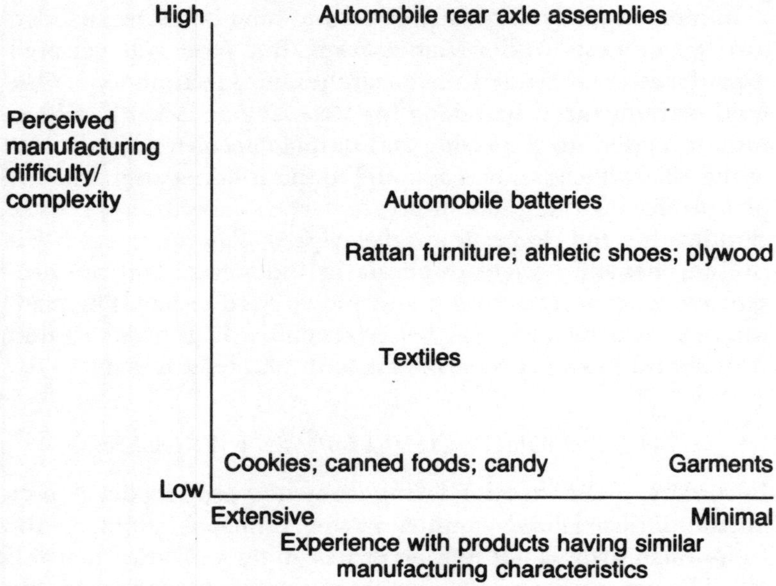

Figure 8.2 Classification of new product development projects

The horizontal dimension of figure 8.2 represents the firm's perceived experience in manufacturing products within similar production characteristics. This is, of course, a firm-specific as well as product-specific measure and it is again a perceptual measure. A firm's place on this dimension with respect to any specific product will depend on its perceived experience with similar products.

As shown on the map, our sample included firms representing new products that fell into various, but not all areas of the new product project classification map. There were no products in our sample that combined high perceived manufacturing difficulty/complexity and minimal perceived experience with similar products. Our impression, garnered from observation and informal discussion is that when an Indonesian firm introduces such products it usually does so as a licensee (or even more likely) a joint venture partner of a firm that is already established in such a business elsewhere.

As hypothesized, most of the new product development processes we studied were focused more on manufacturing process than on setting product specifications. The goal was to find suppliers that could ensure manufacturing success. The major concern expressed by potential new product developers was not to determine whether a particular new product would sell, but whether they could produce it competently, successfully, and efficiently. In essence, the new product development process was an instance of organizational buying behaviour that can be best understood in an organizational buying behaviour context.

The position a potential new product occupied on the new product classification map (figure 8.2) significantly influenced its development process. The environment, the atmosphere, and the interaction processes were significantly different for products with different characteristics. In sum, the major difference was that buyers of both capital equipment and components to produce new products were simply shoppers for products. These are located at the bottom left of figure 8.2. In these cases, the supplier had little involvement in developing the new product.

As one moves up the vertical axis, or to the right on figure 8.2, the purchase includes technology and technical assistance as well as product. Purchases are concentrated, and the suppliers are identified early and are highly involved in the new product development process. Buyers expect sellers to help define, organize, and debug the manufacturing process. This situation leads to a series of differences across other dimensions of the emerging buyer–seller relationship. The interaction model is a most useful framework for understanding the new product development process as it took place in Indonesia. We next look at each component of the interaction model individually.

ENVIRONMENT

Internationalization

In contrast with previous findings, those Indonesian buyers who relied on foreign suppliers typically had more involved supplier relationships than did buyers using domestic suppliers. The Indonesian firms requiring technical help almost always had to go to foreign suppliers in order to find it. Although we did not study individual differences systematically among foreign suppliers, our impression was that Japanese suppliers are significantly more adept at developing highly involved relationships with buyers than are European, or especially US suppliers. The Japanese evidently do this by providing both a great deal of technological assistance and, where possible, unique products that increase buyer dependency.

Market structure

With the exception of automobile axles, demand for the new products we studied was increasing rather rapidly, and further new entrants were expected in virtually every case. Thus, the number of potential buyers is growing; however the situation is less clear with respect to suppliers. Capital goods suppliers, virtually all of whom were headquartered outside Indonesia, formed a relatively stable group. But the number of components suppliers was steadily increasing, or at least changing, with local firms on the ascendance, replacing foreign suppliers. Component markets were considerably more dynamic than capital goods markets.

Markets for capital goods exhibited a degree of heterogeneity. In most cases, buyers believed there were significant differences among potential suppliers, if not in the physical product each offered, then in the service and technical assistance that accompanied the product. Components markets appeared homogeneous with respect to products, even between domestic and offshore suppliers. (The domestic producers offered copies of the imported component.) But they were heterogeneous with respect to the purchase transaction, differing on measures such as reliability, on-time delivery, and quality control.

The interaction process: relationships and episodes

In only one case, rear axle assemblies, was there an extensive previous relationship between a new product developer and supplier firms. This firm had extensive relationships with both machinery producers (for capital equipment) and with a steel producer. Its new product development process represented complex episodes in already extensive relationships. The buying firm's relationship with its machinery and steel suppliers was already at a long-term stage, and with good structural fit (as perceived by the buyers) between the parties. In this case, the new product merely deepened and widened an already good set of working relationships with suppliers.

In addition to steel and capital equipment, the axle manufacturer had to purchase a variety of components, so it also had to develop new relationships. The axle manufacturer's customer, an automobile producer, provided complete detailed specifications for the products it wanted to buy. The automobile producer dictated the choice of component suppliers, set the parts specifications and, we suspect, the price its suppliers would charge. The working relationships that developed with the new parts suppliers started as an extensive, rather than as a limited relationship; both sides knew that they would have to work together. These relationships really started at the development stage; buyers could do no evaluation of alternative sources. Nor did they have much power to negotiate price, delivery, or terms.

This situation is one that might commonly be found in the industrialized countries, where new products are often closely related to the existing line and/or manufacturing process and where many firms have wide existing networks. But it seems to be the exception in Indonesia, where many new products are not so closely related to the firm's existing line or to its existing manufacturing capabilities.

With respect to the other new products, we found significant differences in the importance given to supplier input as an ingredient in the new product development process. Working from the product development classification map in figure 8.2, there are differences in the depth and character of the emergent buyer–seller relationships. For products at the bottom left of figure 8.2 (low difficulty/extensive experience), in capital goods the relationship was limited and the episodes simple. The garment producers, for example had no difficulty in shopping for sewing machines and wanted just the product, not advice or help.

As we move up and to the right on figure 8.2, relationships for capital goods began with the understanding that they would be extensive, and the transactions complex. The plywood manufacturers, for example, recognized they would need continued assistance in using and maintaining the equipment they bought. The textile manufacturer wanted to introduce a higher quality, finer woven cloth. To do so, the company had to purchase a new, much more expensive type of Swiss-made machinery, rather than the Japanese-made machinery it had been using. The Swiss machinery was more difficult to set up and more complex to maintain. Trial runs with the new machinery made for some complex episodes early in the relationship.

Component purchasing did not follow the same pattern. A major concern for those firms using domestic sources was trying to ensure continuity of supply and uniformity of quality. A supplier firm that could provide both was a good candidate for an extensive relationship. In most cases, the episodes in such relationships tended to the simple. Here, clothing was an exception because of the need for different weaves and fabrics. The potential for developing extensive relationships, even for well-understood, repetitively purchased items is high, however, because of the limited number of reliable suppliers of such goods.

Power/dependence

Offshore suppliers especially had a great deal of power in both capital goods and components. For capital goods, the sources of power were the technical assistance they offered as well as the uniqueness of their machinery. Until the buying firm developed a thorough command of the manufacturing process, it was quite dependent on its capital goods suppliers. For components, offshore suppliers had considerable power when there were no domestic producers or when the buyer's customer specified a particular components supplier. In general, domestic components suppliers had less power because they usually came into the market after offshore suppliers were established. Here, the buyer could play off the domestic and offshore suppliers against each other.

Our impression is that offshore suppliers, especially the Japanese, tried very hard to keep buying firms as dependent on them as possible. This was very much resented by the buying firms, who were eager to find alternative sources that would allow them some independence. These power/dependency relationships represent a major potential source of buyer–seller conflict.

SUMMARY AND CONCLUSIONS

Because of the exploratory nature of its research, we must present our conclusions as working hypotheses rather than firm statements of fact. As working hypotheses, though, they can provide useful starting points both for further research and for managerial action. Our most important findings are as follows:

- The new product development process in industrializing countries seems quite different from the process observed in industrialized countries. In the industrialized countries, the uncertainties of new product development are on the demand side. Despite the widespread use of sophisticated marketing research techniques, estimating demand for the product and determining its exact specifications are major problems in the industrialized countries. In an industrializing country, the major problem is manufacturing, whether the firm can successfully produce the new product.
- The key reasons for this difference are that in the industrialized countries, a new product typically represents – at the very least – a significant modification of what is already available in the world; in an industrializing country, a new product is typically a copy of a product already available somewhere, and that industrializing country firms are significantly less skilled at manufacturing than are firms in the industrialized countries.
- The effects of internationalization were also different from those observed between industrialized country buyers and sellers. Relationships between Indonesian buyers and industrialized country sellers were more involved than purely domestic relationships.
- The supplier focus of new product development gives rise to both simple and complex episodes embedded in the limited and extended relationships. In Indonesia, both stable and dynamic market structures evolved. The interactive processes

we observed were different for capital goods and components. The interaction process framework proved to be a useful and applicable analytic tool.

- In general, suppliers are more powerful and buyers more dependent than is usually the case in an industrialized country. The reasons are a paucity of suppliers and a greater need for technical assistance.

IMPLICATIONS FOR RESEARCH AND MANAGEMENT ACTION

Studying new product development may be a very worthwhile way to learn how new buyer–seller relationships start and how they progress. The industrializing country appears to be a good arena in which to conduct such studies because there are so many new start-up relationships.

There is much of potential interest (and potential usefulness) to study. For example, we did not explore to any real extent, the processes and criteria by which new product developers identified and evaluated alternative supplier firms. Nor did we look at what made for effective marketing on the part of suppliers. Given the great importance of supplier firms in the new product development process, such studies could be extremely valuable.

Our study covered only the earliest stages of the buyer–seller relationship. It would be worthwhile to study how such beginning relationships, especially the more intense ones, developed over time. Manufacturing complexity/difficulty and manufacturing experience are key in determining the depth of the starting relationships. We might expect then, that some of the extensive relationships will become less extensive and episodes simpler as firms gain more experience in manufacturing the product.

It would also seem most worthwhile to explore the effects of power/dependency relationships, the factors that determine the persistence of such relationships and the factors that determine change. Maintaining power and dependence appears to be a key element in the marketing strategy employed by some sellers, especially the Japanese.

From the managerial perspective, new product development can be an important source of new business for potential supplier firms; a constant stream of new products provides many opportunities for new supplier entrants. However, to capture these new business opportunities, suppliers must be able to develop quickly the extensive relationships with buyers that capturing these opportunities requires. An intriguing possibility is that potential suppliers can speed the entry of industrializing country firms into new products by aggressively marketing their capabilities as suppliers. Given the characteristics of new products – predominantly, it seems, import substitutes – potential suppliers could identify potential target products and probably potential producers as well. Using a marketing approach of 'Let us put you into the ____ business' might be very effective.

REFERENCES

Dawson, L. M. (1981) 'Facing the new realities of international development', *Business* (Jan.–Feb.)

Ford, I. D. and Djeflat, K. (1983) 'Export marketing of industrial products: buyer–seller relationships between developed and developing countries', in M. R. Czinkota (ed.) *Export Promotion: The Public and Private Sector Interaction*, New York; Praeger.

Hakansson, H. (ed.) (1982) *International Marketing and Purchasing of Industrial Goods*, Chichester: Wiley.

World Bank (1987) *World Development Report*, New York: Oxford University Press.

Wortzel, L. H. (1983) 'Marketing to firms in developing Asian countries', *Industrial Marketing Management* 12: 113–23.

Part Two

MARKETING TO CHINA AND JAPAN: RESEARCH FINDINGS

Chapter Nine

MARKETING TO CHINA

A framework

AIDAN CRONIN

Since it opened to the outside world in 1979 China has spurred the imagination of businesspeople all over the world. Much has been written and projected about China as a future market. On the other hand, many companies have burnt their fingers and suffered substantial losses in the market. One problem with China is that the amount of material written and presented is not structured in a form which can be easily used by businesspeople. This chapter is intended to furnish the businessperson with a framework of the possible pitfalls he or she may encounter in China.

This chapter is the result of a thesis submitted by the author and Peder Iversen in December 1987, entitled 'A comparative evaluation of Danish and English companies marketing to the Chinese market with a view to creating a strategic plan as to how to sell to China'. The project was based on thirty-three company interviews in England, and thirty-four company interviews in Denmark. Results from the interviews undertaken were then coupled to existing desk research to form a modular marketing framework for China.

China as a market presents many problems for the individual company wishing to sell to it. The largest problem is where to start gathering information, and what information is decision-relevant to each given situation.

This chapter presents four flowcharts (figures 9.1–4) designed to give a businessperson guidance as to what is necessary to evaluate and penetrate the Chinese market. The flowcharts are, as such, not all-inclusive, but they provide valuable pointers derived from the successes and failures of others. The advantage of using flowcharts is that they give a simplified overview of a complicated area.

The flowcharts in question cover the following topics:

1 how a company should evaluate the Chinese market;
2 how a company should locate its marketing in relation to the Chinese market;
3 sales of traditional industrial goods on the Chinese market;
4 a company's marketing activities on the Chinese market.

The last section of this paper discusses what opportunities the Chinese market has to offer for the future. A discussion of the relevant flowcharts now follows.

FLOWCHART 1: HOW TO EVALUATE THE CHINESE MARKET

The first four questions are designed to make the company ask itself what it wants to do in China. It needs to put China in a perspective with regard to its resources and its products. Too many companies who have jumped on the bandwagon called 'China', were surprised at the cost and the time it took, and have suffered enormous losses, not to mention the Chinese irritation created when the companies suddenly pulled out of the market.

The first box in the flowchart (figure 9.1) is intended to make the company find out *why* it wants to sell in China. Does it expect China to provide cash for an expansion? Does it just want to sell because everybody else is on the market? Is it blinded by the fact that there are so many Chinese, and it equates them with Western consumers? The truth of the matter is that most companies producing consumer goods can forget China, at least in the short run.

The second box asks the company how long it is prepared to wait for a sale in China? Five years is not an unrealistic waiting time for a sale to China. Time is money, but not to the Chinese. They want to be sure that they don't make any mistakes. The Russian withdrawal of its experts in the 1960s and the ensuing chaos is a recent memory. Timewise, China is a life commitment. That also means that you need to be prepared to devote effort to the market.

Next, how much is the company to invest in order to reach its

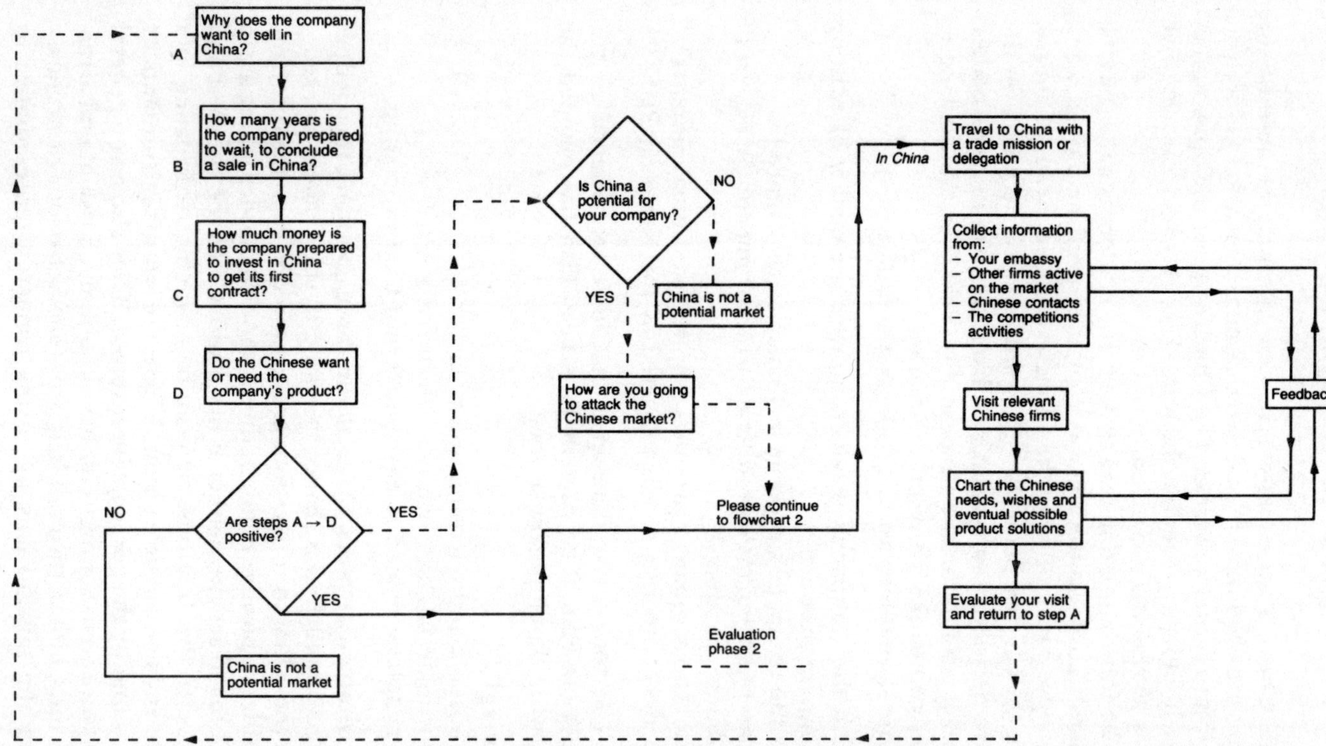

Figure 9.1 An evaluation of the Chinese market

goal? China is an expensive market, not only because of the many trips you have to make to that faraway market before you begin to register progress. The Chinese are of the opinion that you should pay to enter their market. Has the company five years of resources to invest in this market?

The fourth question may strike many readers as naïve, but the Chinese do not always know what they need or indeed want. When we speak of what the Chinese want we mean, of course, what the Chinese State wants. The information necessary for the above decisions can be obtained from consultants, state bodies, general reading on the Chinese Five Year Plan, and talking to other companies active on the market.

One should also ask the following questions:

1 Can the company's product improve the quality of existing Chinese products?
2 Is the company's product technologically advanced?
3 Can the company's product improve or initiate the export of Chinese products?
4 Can the company's products help reduce China's imports?
5 Is the company's product covered by the Five Year Plan?

All sectors to be developed in China are detailed in the Five Year Plan. The current Five Year Plan has mapped the following development sectors:

- energy;
- transport and telecommunications;
- raw materials and semi-manufactured goods;
- technology related to agriculture and food processing.

If a company answers 'No' to all the above questions, then it does not stand much of a chance in selling to the Chinese market.

If these first four questions are answered in what the company considers a positive manner, then it should consider taking a trip to China to see the market at first hand. Often the cheapest and most effective first time trip can be made by participating in a trade mission or delegation. These are normally substantially subsidized by the government involved. They also give a general introduction to Chinese culture without much risk of embarrassing the Chinese through inappropriate behaviour or actions.

On the mission it is up to the company representative to

absorb as much information as possible from his or her embassy, local firms active on the market, Chinese contacts, and Western competitors' activities.

A visit to some Chinese end-user factories provides the ideal background for the gathering of information. Having formed his or her own opinions, it can then be quite useful for the company representative to discuss possible solutions with those individuals in daily contact with the market. This should help obtain a realistic view of what China as a market can perhaps entail for the company.

The last step in the framework comprises of comparing the company's desired image of the market against the market as it is. The evaluation of the market is then best done by the company again asking itself, 'Has China potential?' If it has, then the company can begin to make preparations for its attack on the market. This should include, if possible, an analysis of the market structure. The next problem a company encounters is where to locate its marketing base and activities in relation to the market? The possible solutions to this problem are illustrated in flowchart 2 (figure 9.2).

A company who has decided that the Chinese market has potential, needs to locate its activities in relation to the market.

FLOWCHART 2: HOW A COMPANY IS TO LOCATE ITSELF IN RELATION TO THE CHINESE MARKET

Perhaps the ultimate is for a company first to try and sell directly to the market. The problem is that many firms are not of sufficient size or have insufficient resources to sell directly to the market. They have however the same choices as mapped out in flowchart 2 (figure 9.2).

As noted above, the best way of getting a feel for the market is to try and sell directly to it. If a company thinks that it does not have the necessary resources, then it can perhaps team up with another company, or give control to an independent organization. I have called the agent an independent organization, which may not be strictly true if it is a one-person operation. The agent or trading house, as it may be, can each have obvious advantages in different sectors for different goods. The level of control the company maintains is also dictated by its environment.

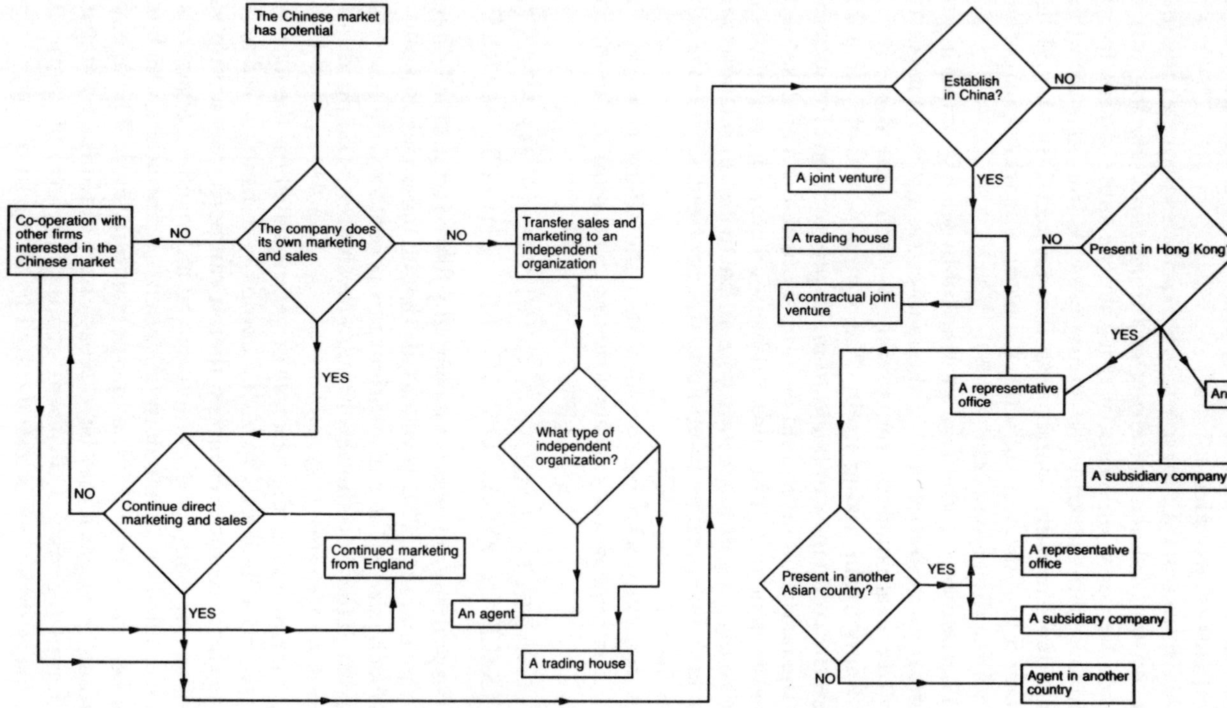

Figure 9.2 Locating the company in the Chinese market

Having tried to sell directly to the market, a company can then decide if it is going to continue to sell directly, or to establish itself in China. Being visible on the market is considered very positive by the Chinese, as it betrays a certain commitment to them.

A company can establish a joint venture with the Chinese, but as there have been cases involving quite harrowing experiences for many companies, it is advisable to proceed with caution. There have been high import taxes on raw materials, and problems in the quality of goods used in buy-back agreements. It is also almost impossible to repatriate profits from a joint venture in China.

Another possibility is to establish a contractual joint venture. This is basically an agreement for the Chinese and the foreign party involved to co-operate. It is not covered by the ever more complicated joint venture law. Many companies have used these agreements to set up Chinese service stations. The Chinese are happy, as training in repairs and maintenance automatically encompasses them learning a degree of technology. The Western company involved is happy, as it has access to the important people in its area.

A company can also place someone with an established trading company office in China. Trading companies are often accused of not being prepared to work hard enough for the companies they represent if left to themselves. This is a way around this problem.

A company can also establish an office. The problem is that the cost of an office can often be greater than the amount of business done. The cost of an office can also be prohibitive for a small company. The 48 Group in London have solved this problem by sharing an office between a number of firms.

If a company does not establish in China it can establish in Hong Kong instead. Nobody knows what will happen in Hong Kong in 1997. This is the biggest risk factor. Hong Kong has the advantage of having a modern society and infrastructure. A company employing a Hong Kong Chinese person has access to someone who understands both the Western and Chinese way of doing things. The problem is that the Hong Kong Chinese are treated with distrust in some areas of Mainland China.

A company can establish a representative office in Hong Kong, employ a full time agent or perhaps establish a subsidiary company. At the moment Hong Kong is not so much a gateway to China as a gateway to Asia. Whether it is allowed to hold this gateway open in the future is open to quite a lot of discussion.

A third and last possibility for a company is to use another Asian country as a base which could give a little less risk. With the extraordinary growth of Asian markets in the past few years and the huge potential Taiwan, Korea, and Singapore represent, it can be wise to position oneself in or near those markets. Location in one of Asia's stable growth economies will give a company minimal risk and less dependence on a fluctuating economy such as China.

FLOWCHART 3: THE PURCHASING PROCESS OF A CHINESE END-USER

A generalization of the Chinese end-user's purchasing process is presented in flowchart 3 (figure 9.3). This flowchart covers the situation where the end-user is not aware of the possible solutions which exist in relation to his or her problem. The end-user is then obliged to ask the relevant foreign trade corporation (FTC) to source the relevant solutions to his or her problem. The relevant FTC then puts the end-user's request through a decision process posing the following questions:

- Does the end-user really need the product?
- Is purchase of the product beneficial for China?
- Is there Chinese production of a comparable product?
- Will the authorities give permission to purchase?

If any of the above questions is answered with a 'No', then the FTC will normally refuse the end-user's request.

Should all answers be positive, then the FTC sends enquiries to the relevant foreign supplier companies. These in turn send in quotations. The FTC then normally arranges a trade delegation to visit the supplier companies concerned. Next the selected suppliers are invited to China, and after a time the FTC chooses two or three companies. These as such will be pitched against each other in negotiation.

Negotiations begin with the technical negotiations. During these the technical specifications of the machinery to be sold are

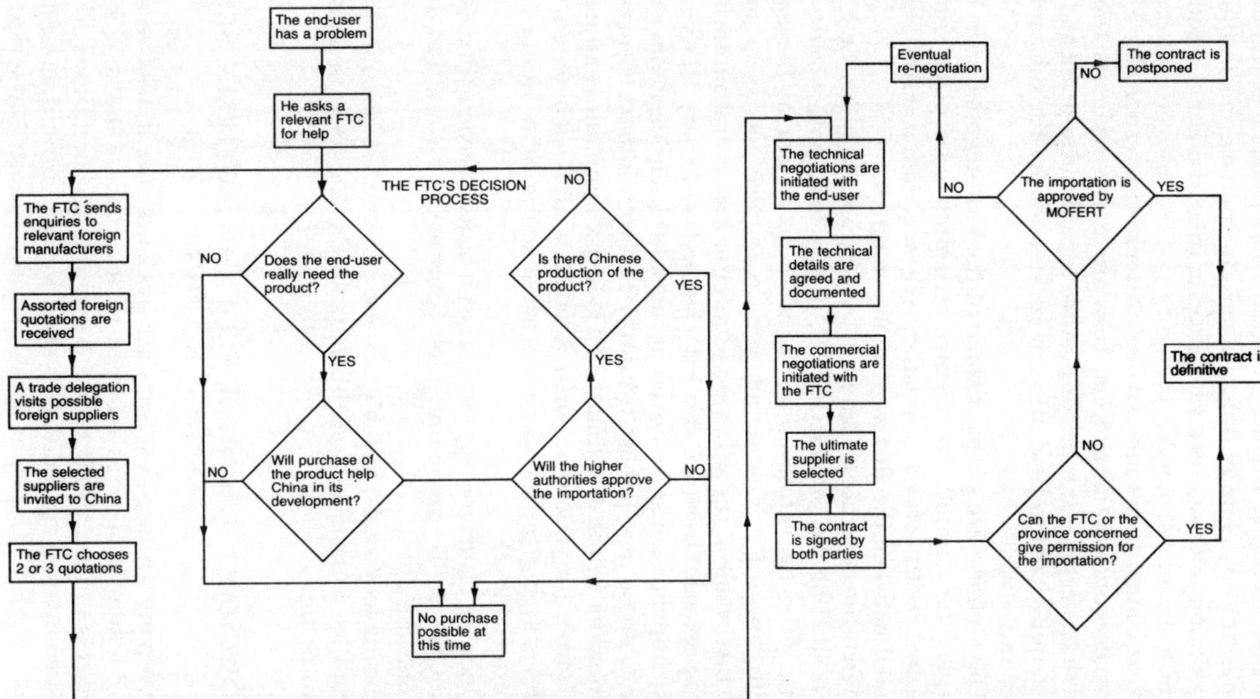

Figure 9.3 The purchasing process of a Chinese end-user

laid down. These, when agreed, are described in a technical memorandum. The end-user normally controls the technical negotiation and together with experts tries to tailor the equipment to his or her needs.

Next come the commercial negotiations. The responsible FTC normally controls this process. They are interested in one thing, and that is getting as much as possible for as little as possible. It is often quite hard to fend off their constant desire for substantial discounts.

The Chinese are perhaps some of the best negotiators in the world. The commercial negotiations often take place simultaneously with several companies, the negotiating teams being rotated between the different representatives.

When the contract is signed, it may be approved by the FTC concerned or the provincial FTC, if they have power to do so. During the decentralization of the trade system in the early 1980s, most FTCs were allowed to import goods up to a specified value without having to refer to the central authorities for approval. However, this has changed and many FTCs had their import licences removed in the subsequent tightening up. The Chinese now publish a list of FTCs with import licences.

Should it be the case that the FTC in question cannot approve the import in question, then it is MOFERT's job to do so. The really big project decisions are taken at State Council or ministerial level.

Once the contract is approved, then it usually becomes finalized. The Chinese like to honour their contracts to ensure that they do not lose face.

Having looked at a possible Chinese end-user's decision making system let us now look at things from the Western company's point of view.

FLOWCHART 4: HOW A FIRM CAN ACTIVELY SEEK SALES IN CHINA

A company wishing to actively sell in China once it has covered the decision process as outlined in flowchart 1 has to get in contact with the end-user. The question is how best this is done. Most companies agreed that the best way is to offer the relevant ministry or FTC responsible for your industry a series of

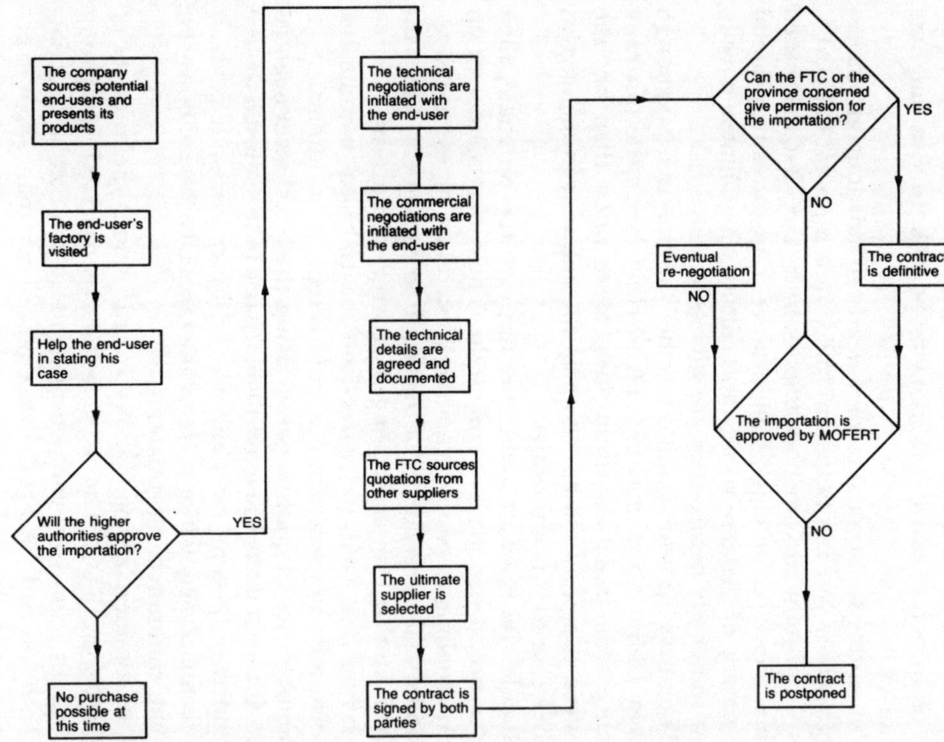

Figure 9.4 How a firm can actively seek sales in China

seminars on your technology. The Chinese are eager to support such seminars because of their educational function.

The Chinese themselves will ensure that the audience is full of relevant Chinese end-users. The question is, having got to them, how can one use this opportunity to maintain contact? The best way is to get as many invitations as possible to visit end-user factories.

On visiting them you can come nearer to individual problems, explain how you can help, and build up a rapport. Rapport is very important in China, so important in fact that it is called *guanxi*. Perhaps the biggest importance of *guanxi* is that due to the nature of Chinese society and culture, the Chinese have to trust somebody before they are willing to take a risk.

The next important point is whether the end-user has enough money to buy your machine and whether he or she can raise finance from the local authorities. More often than not the Western company will have to help the end-user in making his or her case to the authorities.

Should the relevant authorities approve the purchase, then the technical negotiations can begin. These negotiations often seem gruelling to people from the West. The Chinese are eager to understand every detail of the required equipment, and want to be sure that they are buying the correct equipment.

Having discussed and agreed on the technical parameters, a technical memorandum is completed. It is important to remember not to quote a price during these technical negotiations as the Chinese will expect you to stick to this, even if it were intended only as an estimate. The end-user normally controls the technical negotiations. He or she takes a back seat, however, for the commercial negotiations.

The commercial negotiations are run under the auspices of the relevant FTC. The FTC will have collected competing quotations from your competitors, and may in fact be negotiating with you and them at the same time. Their main aim is to get the price down to rock bottom, and they always want a discount (something you should always build into your prices). Never reduce price more than once, or they will consider you to be soft. To avoid a price reduction it is best to emphasize that 'a good deal is the only important thing between friends', a phrase they often use themselves.

When agreement is reached then both parties sign the contract. This is not, however, to say that the contract is definitive. The money required for the purchase has first to be approved. If it is possible to get approval at a provincial level of authority, then all well and good; if not then one has to wait for MOFERT's approval. MOFERT can say yes, or postpone the contract, which normally means a negative answer (the Chinese do not like to actually *say* no).

The contract may also be sent back for re-negotiation. Re-negotiation can be a very painful process, as the Chinese try to reduce the price substantially without reducing their level of purchase to the same degree.

CHINA: 'THE WORLD'S LARGEST MARKET'

China's future market potential must be seen as enormous, but one must remember that China as a market will grow slowly due to the economic constraints that are upon it.

One should bear in mind the following factors when considering business with China:

- China's lack of foreign exchange;
- the intended financing of an eventual sale;
- supply and reclamation conditions;
- problems in the installation, running, and maintenance of technologically-advanced products;
- the education of Chinese end-users;
- the decision competence/approval level of the Chinese negotiator;
- the control of market forces in the future;
- energy;
- transport and telecommunication;
- raw materials and semi-manufactured goods;
- technology related to agriculture and food processing.

To sell in China is a life's work in itself. It takes a lot of money, time, and preparation to enter the market. China will continue though to be a lucrative market for those companies with the correct product, preparation, time, and patience.

Chapter Ten

CONQUERING THE CHINESE MARKET

A study of Danish firms' experiences in the People's Republic of China

B. B. SCHLEGELMILCH, A. DIAMANTOPOULOS, AND M. PETERSEN

After Mao Zedong's death in September 1976 and the arrest of the Gang of Four one month later, the economy of the People's Republic of China (hereinafter referred to as China) began opening to the West. Initially, Hua Guofeng, who came to power after Premier Zhuo Enlai's death in January 1976, tried to initiate a large investment programme. This was related to Zhuo Enlai's 'Four Modernizations', that is, agriculture, industry, defence, and science and education. However, this ambitious programme of intensive technology import ran into problems in getting approval.

In 1977, after the end of the Cultural Revolution, Deng Xiaoping was rehabilitated and reinstated as Vice Premier. From this position, he gradually started taking over the power from Hua Guofeng, who lost his Premiership in 1980 to Zhao Ziyang and his Chairmanship to Hu Yaobang.[1] In September 1978, a modified reform programme was approved by the Communist Party's Central Committee and, in 1979, it was rubber-stamped by the National People's Congress. Parts of this reform programme are often referred to as the 'open door policy'.

This open door policy was primarily an opening to foreign direct investment, as a means of acquiring technology and know-how. Here, joint ventures with Chinese partners have been given absolute preference by the Chinese. Between 1979 and 1986, nearly 8,000 ventures in China involved direct

A shortened version of this paper was originally published in the *Journal of Global Marketing* (1990) 3: 47–71.

investment.[2] However, China did not only open to foreign direct investment, but also experienced a dramatic increase in both imports and exports. From a stable value of about US$7,500 million for both imports and exports between 1974 and 1977, by 1986, exports had increased to just over US$30,000 million and imports to US$42,000 million (United Nations 1984, Zhang 1987, a detailed review of the trade between China and the European Community is provided by Redmond 1987).

With the opening of the Chinese economy, an increasing body of literature about companies' experiences in China emerged. This literature has focused primarily on Chinese negotiation practices (Pye 1986, Frankenstein 1986, Kindel 1987) and on the problems faced by companies involved in dealing with China (Hendryx 1986a, 1986b, Crainer and Campbell 1986, Bertrand 1986, Nyaw and Lin 1986, Mayer *et al.* 1987, Henley and Nyaw 1988). The present study provides further evidence on the idiosyncracies of this market by analysing the experiences of Danish companies who have trading relationships with the People's Republic of China. Specifically, the study examines the motives underlying the decision to serve the market, the means used to establish initial market contact, the chosen mode(s) of entry, the bases of competitive advantage, the problems encountered in doing business with China, and the firm's perceptions of their success in this market.

BACKGROUND AND LITERATURE REVIEW

China is often referred to as the world's largest untapped market. Its one billion inhabitants have given foreign business dreams of selling 'just *one* mousetrap' to each of them! It is therefore hardly surprising that the motive of 'getting a foot in the door' prevails among many companies entering the Chinese market (Lassen and Lindberg 1987); equally, it comes as no surprise that it is particularly the larger companies which have entered the Chinese market relatively fast in the hope of penetrating it (Davies 1985, 1986). In this context, it is worth reflecting on the conditions in which early entry into a developing market is appropriate. Porter (1980: 232) observes that where 'image and reputation of the firm are important to the buyer, the firm can develop an enhanced reputation by being a pioneer . . . customer loyalty will be great, so that benefits will accrue to the firm that sells to the customer first'. In a country like China, where personal relationships are crucial (Stewart and Yeung Yun Choi 1987), these factors would appear to be of major importance.

Because of the numerous potential problems involved, companies should carefully examine their motives before entering the Chinese market (Delman 1987). Market entry should be part of a long-term development plan and internationally-inexperienced companies have been advised to try other markets before attempting to enter the Chinese (Mayer *et al.* 1987). However, once companies have decided to enter the Chinese market, they have to choose an appropriate method of involvement. This is one of the most important decisions to be taken in international marketing, as it pre-determines the firm's future strategic options (Terpstra 1987, Stahr 1979). When dealing with China in particular there are two major obstacles which limit the choices among possible methods of involvement: (i) the still under-developed distribution system which renders exports of industrial products through Chinese agents and distributors practically impossible; and (ii) the restricted currency situation, and with it the Chinese view that foreign ventures should help to generate foreign exchange, and not cause costs (Lassen and Lindberg 1987). As a result, many companies conduct their China business through Hong Kong; about 17 per cent of the Chinese imports and exports go through this route (Davies 1985). Hong Kong's placement is strategically important because it provides all the business support which China itself does not possess. Many large trading houses have been set up, with Denmark being the fifth largest investor in Hong Kong (Suk-Ching Ho 1984).

Companies considering various forms of exporting to China also need to bear in mind that the visits usually connected with exporting are very expensive. This holds in particular as it takes a long time to get through the negotiations and bureaucracy (Campbell 1987, Pye 1986). Thus setting up a branch office in China is often said to facilitate keeping contacts with both end-users and officials, thereby providing continuous information (Irvine *et al.* 1987, Brehm 1985). However, complications may arise as companies have to find a Chinese sponsor to support their application and there is no guarantee for approval (Arthur Andersen 1986, Ernst & Whinney 1985). Another route is to use foreign companies already established in China as agents. Danish companies are placed well in this respect as two of the major international trading houses dealing with China and Hong Kong are Danish (East Asiatic Company and Jebsen & Co.).

Because of the Chinese preference for joint ventures, many companies have been using different joint venture agreements to get involved into the Chinese market (Zhang 1987). Three types of such agreements can be distinguished: equity (EJV), contractual (CJV) and hybrid joint ventures (HJV). The EJV has the status of a limited liability company, while there is full liability in a CJV. EJV are governed by the state plans which gives them higher priority in the distribution of supplies. The tax imposed on EJVs is also lower than on CJVs. HJVs are a combination of the two others. As the Chinese contribution is regarded as equity, the limited liability status of such ventures means that they are taxed lower than CJVs (Lassen and Lindberg 1987).

Other alternatives to getting involved in the Chinese market are assembly and licensing. They require little or no finance from foreign companies, and the problems faced are generally fewer. However, as in joint ventures, it is still important to find the right Chinese partner and ensure, for example, that he has access to sufficient supplies (Ernst & Whinney 1985).

During the establishment phase, companies often face problems in finding out whom to contact (Furst 1986) because the Chinese bureaucracy is complicated and constantly changing (Von Lingelsheim-Seibicke 1987). Since the decentralization of decision power in relation to foreign trade, most companies initially contact the local trade corporations or the end-users. Depending on the size of the contract, different levels of bureaucracy are subsequently involved (Henley and Nyaw 1986, Simon and Rehn 1986). Although contacts with end-users are recognized to be of major importance (Saunders and Ton 1986, Stewart and Yeung Yun Choi 1987), it has been suggested that companies should establish personal connections at different levels (Grow 1986). Trade fairs, together with visits by trade delegations have been found to be a relatively cheap way of establishing such contacts and gaining access to the market (Touche Ross & Co. 1985).

Other problems experienced by companies setting up in China have been reported by Crainer and Campbell (1986). In their study of 115 companies with offices in Beijing, the lack of accommodation for foreign staff, the high prices for office accommodation, transport and communication problems, sudden price increases, and delays in negotiation were found to be of particular concern to the companies. Kristensen *et al.* (1987) estimated that the annual costs of a one-person operation in Beijing are around £150,000. The insufficient infrastructure has also been identified by others as a problem for foreign companies in China (Hendryx 1986a, Tung 1986, Bertrand 1986, Zhao 1987). Lack of foreign currency (Irvine *et al.* 1987), the Chinese culture (Kindel 1987, Jen *et al.* 1987), lack of co-ordination between different parts of the bureaucracy (Dennis 1982), insufficient protection in patent and trademark laws, demands for countertrade (Reisman *et al.* 1987) and the difficulties (faced especially by smaller companies) of obtaining finance for trading with China (Furst 1986) are additional areas of frustration.

Finally, as far as companies' performance in China is concerned, Copeland (1986) predicted that for every ten business people entering China, nine will return with big holes in their pockets. Although companies dealing with China are often said to have little success (Mayer *et al.* 1987, Pye 1986), few studies have attempted a systematic assessment of the success of foreign businesses dealing with China.

To summarize, while the potential of the Chinese market is undoubtedly very attractive for Western firms, there appear to be a number of distinct problems associated with dealing with China, which make the latter rather unique in terms of the constraints that have to be overcome in order to tap the market potential.

METHODOLOGY

Data

The data used to analyse the different aspects of business experience of Danish companies in China were gathered by means of a mail survey. Although conceptually the population was readily defined as all Danish companies having or in the process of establishing business links with China, considerable practical difficulties were encountered in the search for a suitable sampling frame. Danish government offices perceived information on which companies were dealing with China as confidential and none of the private China consultancy bureaux were willing to provide lists of their clients. Eventually, however, a sampling frame consisting of 121 companies was drawn up from a diversity of sources, including (i) a list of participants of a Danish trade fair held in China in June 1987 (ii) a brochure from the Aarhus Group;[3] (iii) the contracts section in various issues of the *China Business Review* (1982–7); and (iv) newspaper articles. A sample drawn from a frame of such diverse nature may not be truly representative of Danish companies trading with China, but some encouragement was drawn from a statement made by the Danish Ministry of Industry, putting the total number of Danish firms involved with China trade at around 150. Thus, the sampling frame appears to include over 80 per cent of these companies.

The questionnaire was initially designed in English, subsequently translated into Danish and then back-translated into English; this process helped ensure that the Danish translation was accurate, and was facilitated by the fact that one of the present authors is a native Danish speaker. Prior to developing the questionnaire, interviews were carried out with two industrial companies and three export agencies involved in trade with China. The questionnaire was also discussed with two consultants from the China Information Service. Finally, a company involved in trade with China completed the questionnaire and subsequently discussed its contents.

At the end of August 1987, the final version of the questionnaire was dispatched to all 121 companies previously identified, together with a covering letter personally addressed to the people responsible for dealing with China – where their names were known – or, in the other cases, to the export managers. Stamped return envelopes were enclosed and anonymity was promised. A total of seventy-two companies responded to the mailing, of which forty-nine returned a completed questionnaire, thus yielding an effective response rate of 40 per cent.

Variables

In accordance with the objectives of the study, the variables included in the questionnaire fall into six categories: (i) firm demographics; (ii) motivation for market entry; (iii) form of initial market contact; (iv) level of involvement; (v) competitive advantage; (vi) problems experienced in setting up/conducting business; and (vii) relative success of the companies.

Firm demographics include sales turnover (as an indicator of company size), the proportion of turnover attributed to foreign business and the proportion of turnover that came from doing business with China. As an indicator of international experience, respondents were also asked to indicate with what other international markets besides China they traded and when they first established contact with the Chinese market.

Motivation of market entry was examined through nine statements, agreement or disagreement to which was measured on a five-point Likert scale, ranging from 1= 'strongly agree' to 5= 'strongly disagree'. Companies were, for example, requested to indicate whether their motive for entering the Chinese market was based on 'getting there before competitors', 'a scarcity of business in other markets', or 'access to a large market'.

Initial market contact attempted to ascertain how important various approaches were in initiating business with China. These included participation in a trade fair in China, invitations of Chinese to Denmark, technical seminars in China, etc. Companies were also asked to state whom they approached for their first sales or co-operation offer and, where applicable, how long it took from establishing the first contact to obtaining the first order. To establish whether companies might favour possible joint marketing actions by Danish firms in the future, a five-point Likert scale, ranging from 1= 'strongly agree' to 5= 'strongly disagree', was employed to ascertain the extent of potential support.

Level of involvement posed a problem in that two types of companies were represented in the sample, notably those already established in China and those in the process of setting up business links. Thus, the relevant question was formulated as follows in order to cover both groups: 'How are you involved/or do you try to get involved in trade with China?' The possibilities given comprised importing, various forms of exporting, consulting engineering, licensing, assembly, three types of joint ventures, and the establishment of a wholly owned company. In addition, companies were requested to indicate with which Chinese industry they dealt, and whether they were involved in sales of products, sales of whole plants, transfer of technological know-how, or transfer of management know-how. For both questions, an 'other' category was provided to capture permutations possibly overlooked in the multiple choice formats.

Competitive advantage was described by means of fourteen items indicating different bases of competitive strength (such as 'quality', 'price', and 'negotiating skills'). A five-point Likert scale, ranging from 1= 'strongly agree' to 5= 'strongly disagree', was used to record the respondents' reaction to the statement: 'Our competitive strength in China is largely based on ...'.

Problems experienced were broken down into current problems and problems in the establishment phase. In the current problems section, respondents were requested to indicate their opinion on fourteen issues on a five-point bi-polar scale, ranging from 1= 'major problem' to 5= 'no problem'. The issues included, among others, 'change in legislation', 'ensuring currency risk', and 'price changes'. In addition, companies were also asked to estimate their establishment costs. As to the problems in the establishment phase, the same response format was applied to eleven issues, including 'language', 'reaching the right officials', 'cultural differences', etc. Since the preliminary interviews pointed towards finance as an important stumbling block in dealing with China, a question was included to establish what credit facilities were usually employed to finance the Chinese purchase.

Perceived success of the companies was measured on a seven-point bi-polar scale, ranging from 1= 'very successful' to 7= 'very unsuccessful'. Specifically, firms were requested to indicate how they viewed their success in trading with China in relation to their (i) international competitors; (ii) initial turnover expectations; (iii) initial profit expectations; and (iv) other export trade.

ANALYSIS

Firm demographics

In an international context, most of the responding companies are of small and intermediate size; 79 per cent have a sales turnover of less than £40 million and about half (49 per cent of the companies have a turnover of less than £10 million. In contrast, three of the analysed companies have a turnover larger than £100 million. As to the firms' business experience with China, nine companies have not yet signed their first contract with China and two have stopped trying. But even of the companies that already signed a contract, six had not as yet achieved any turnover. However, the companies actually trading with China managed to obtain, on average, 7.8 per cent of their turnover from this trade in the last financial year; a more detailed picture of the importance of the Chinese market to respondent firms is provided by Table 10.1.

Table 10.1 Proportion of turnover generated from business with China [$n=49$]

Proportion of turnover	*Number of firms*	*%*
No contribution	17	35
1– 2 per cent	11	22
3–10 per cent	13	27
11–20 per cent	3	6
More than 20 per cent	4	8
Information not disclosed	1	2

In general, the companies dealing with China are rather international in their orientation. The average percentage of foreign business is no less than 76 per cent of total sales, and about half (48 per cent) generate more than 90 per cent of their sales turnover from overseas business. The international orientation of the companies is also reflected in the spread of their business, with thirty-four (69 per cent) of the firms also conducting business with other countries in Asia, twenty-nine (59 per cent) conducting business with the USSR and other countries in Eastern Europe, and thirty-two (65 per cent) conducting business with Africa and South America. Finally, it is noticeable that the majority of companies are relatively new in the China business. Only fourteen (29 per cent) firms established their first contact with the Chinese market prior to 1982, whereas twelve (24 per cent) of the companies approached the market between 1982 and 1984, and another nineteen (38 per cent) since 1985; four companies did not provide any information on this question.

Motivation for market entry

Almost all companies have entered China motivated by expectations about the future development of the market and by the desire to gain access to a large market. It is clear that most companies take a long term stance with respect to entering the Chinese market. This is reflected in their attitudes towards long-term versus short-term profitability and their desire to obtain access before their competitors. Table 10.2 presents the importance attached to the various motives underlying market entry.

Table 10.2 Motives behind entering the Chinese market [*n*=49]

Motive	*Mean score*
Access to a market in development	1.28
Access to a large market	1.56
Long-term development plan of the company	2.07
Getting there before competitors	2.33
Long-term profit basis only	2.48
Try it and see basis	2.86
Getting short- and long-term profits	2.88
Getting short-term profits	3.60
Scarcity of business in other markets	4.38

Initial market contact

With respect to the means utilized by companies in their initial approach to the Chinese market, as table 10.3 indicates, direct personal contacts represent the most important method for establishing business links. Traditional sales letters, in contrast, are regarded as the least effective approach, comments such as 'it gets lost' are frequent. Participation in trade fairs is only perceived to be of major importance by about one-third of the analysed companies. However, one has to bear in mind that while trade fairs may be useful for making the first personal contact, companies should not necessarily expect to sell anything during this phase.

Table 10.3 Means of establishing initial market contact [*n*=49]

Approach	*Mean score*
Direct contact with Chinese end-users	1.42
Direct contact with Chinese officials	1.57
Technical seminars in China	1.59
Invitations of the Chinese to Denmark	1.83
Participation in group initiatives	2.31
Taking part in trade fair in China	2.32
Taking part in other trade fair	3.41
Sales letters	3.62

Respondents were also asked to state *whom* they approached for their first sales or co-operation offer. According to the results, nearly half of the companies concerned (49 per cent) approached the end-user directly, while the second and third most popular initial contacts were the local foreign trade corporation (FTC) (approached by 14 per cent of the respondents) and the national FTC (approached by 8 per cent). Furthermore, where applicable, companies were requested to state how much time passed between their first contact with China and the receipt of their first order. As can be seen from table 10.4, only

Table 10.4 Time between first contact and first order [*n*=33]*

Time span	*Number of companies*	*%*
Up to 6 months	9	27
7–12 months	8	24
13–24 months	9	27
25–36 months	3	9
37–48 months	3	9
49–60 months	0	0
More than 60 months	1	3

* *Nine companies did not receive an order, two companies decided not to continue their efforts, and five companies did not provide the requested information.*

about half the companies that did obtain an order from China achieved this in two years or less.

In the context of obtaining initial market contacts, companies were also asked to indicate their opinion on whether joint marketing approaches by Danish companies would be useful. Of the forty-one companies that expressed an opinion, sixteen (39 per cent) agreed and twelve (29 per cent) strongly agreed with this proposition. On the other hand, only four (10 per cent) companies disagreed and two (5 per cent) strongly disagreed, with the remaining seven companies (17 per cent) being neutral. The suggestions received regarding the form of such joint approaches emphasized that they should be within one industry, on a private commercial basis and organized as group visits to China. The setting up of joint representative offices with clear specifications of their role and responsibility was also mentioned.

Level of involvement

The analysed companies have chosen (or were about to choose) various forms of involvement in China. Table 10.5 demonstrates that exporting is the most popular mode of entry, with licensing and joint ventures coming second and third respectively; it should be noted that a few companies indicated the concurrent use of multiple entry modes.

Table 10.5 Chosen levels of involvement in the Chinese market

	Number of mentions	%
Import from China	1	2
Export – through agency in Denmark	21	43
Export – through Hong Kong	20	41
Export – direct from Denmark	26	53
Export – branch office in China	7	14
Consulting engineers	6	12
Agency to others	2	4
Licensing	9	18
Assembly	1	2
Joint venture – equity	4	8
Joint venture – contractual	3	6
Joint venture – hybrid	1	2
Wholly-owned subsidiary	0	0
No information provided	3	6

To expand the picture obtained on market entry modes, the respondent companies were also categorized according to the *highest* level of involvement they chose. For example, companies involved in exporting *and* joint ventures were grouped under joint ventures. The ranking of the various forms of export involvement from high to low is, of course, largely subjective and debatable. However, such a ranking provides an indication of the 'commitment' of the respondent companies to the Chinese market. Table 10.6 illustrates the highest levels of involvement (excluding imports and acting as an agency to others) chosen by the analysed companies.[4]

Table 10.6 Highest level of involvement in China [n=46]*

	Number of companies	%
Export – through agency in Denmark	15	33
Export – direct or via Hong Kong	12	26
Export – branch office in China	4	9
Licensing	7	15
Joint ventures	8	17

* *Three companies did not provide information.*

While it might be expected that the level of involvement will be largely determined by firm size (reflecting the resources at the firm's disposal), in the case of China this does not appear to be the case; a series of one-way analyses of variance of sales turnover against the involvement levels in table 10.6, failed to detect any significant differences.

With respect to the kind of industries the sample companies are dealing with in China, there is a dominance of agriculture and food processing, with twenty-two (45 per cent) of the analysed companies active in this area. Chinese infrastructure, with eight (16 per cent) companies and medical instruments with five (10 per cent) followed in importance, while the remaining firms were spread over a large variety of industries. As to the specific exchange relationship with the Chinese partner, companies are typically involved in more than one type of transaction. Specifically, twenty-eight mentions were received for sale of products, eighteen for sale of whole plant, twenty-three for transfer of technology, and six for transfer of management know-how.

Competitive advantage

As can be seen from table 10.7, product - and service-related factors are perceived by the respondents as the most important sources of competitive strength. Possession of superior technology and know-how translated into a high quality specialised product and backed by a high service level and direct contact with the end-user, appears to be the preferred combination in the Chinese market. In this context, the importance attached to service may reflect the Chinese's insufficient maintenance and/or repair capabilities, while the emphasis on direct end-user contact seems to highlight the fact that the Chinese are very loyal. Somewhat surprisingly, price is not considered as a particularly strong basis of competitive advantage (it ranks ninth overall), and neither is arranging finance for the Chinese purchase (ranking second last in importance).These findings are quite interesting both because the Chinese are often said to be hard negotiators with respect to price and because of China's rather problematic currency situation, notably the shortage of foreign exchange (Irvine *et al.* 1987). With regards to arranging finance, it should be remembered that the results may be biased by the fact that the respondents are small and medium-sized firms and, therefore, the Chinese purchases are likely to represent relatively moderate amounts; it should also be pointed out, that arranging finance – while not perceived to constitute a

Table 10.7 Bases of competitive advantage [n=49]

	Mean score
Quality	1.43
Specialized product	1.58
Know-how	1.76
Technology	1.98
Service	2.05
Contact with end-users	2.28
Delivery of a complete solution	2.46
Negotiating skills	2.61
Price	2.80
Contact with Chinese officials	2.85
Entry before competition	3.08
Contacts made by other Danish companies	3.18
Financing of Chinese purchase	3.44
Help to Chinese exports	3.68

basis of competitive advantage – is considered to be a major day-to-day problem in doing business with China (see next section).

Problems experienced

In an attempt to provide a comprehensive picture of the difficulties encountered by the respondent firms in their dealings with China, a distinction was drawn between problems in the establishment phase and those experienced in day-to-day operations. With regards to the former, companies perceive the Chinese bureaucracy, time delays in the negotiations and language as the major obstacles; on the other hand, researching the product's opportunities and cultural differences are perceived to be less problematic (table 10.8).

Table 10.8 Problems in establishing business with China [n=49]

Problem	*Mean score*
Chinese bureaucracy	2.46
Time delays in negotiations	2.61
Language	2.77
Reaching the right officials	2.89
Financing the Chinese purchase	3.18
Negotiating with the Chinese	3.24
Researching the product's opportunities	3.43
Cultural differences	3.53
Financing own project	3.59
Securing patents and trade marks	3.96
Securing exchange risk	4.23

For companies that have signed their first contract, the average establishment costs were £58,000, but 47 per cent of the companies reported establishment costs of no more than £20,000. However, when looking at problems subsequently experienced in the day-to-day operations of companies (table 10.9), costs were regarded as most problematic, followed by financing the Chinese purchase and dealing with the Chinese bureaucracy.

It might be argued that companies with trading experience in other countries with communist governments (USSR and Eastern Europe), experience in less developed countries (Africa

Table 10.9 Problems in day-to-day business with China [n=49]

Problem	*Mean score*
Costs	2.41
Financing the Chinese purchase	2.56
Chinese bureaucracy	2.88
Change in Chinese politics	2.90
Time delays in negotiations	2.91
Chinese infrastructure	3.06
Price changes in China	3.07
Language	3.12
Financing projects	3.33
Negotiating with the Chinese	3.45
Changes in legislation	3.65
Cultural differences	3.87
Securing exchange risk	3.93
Securing patents/trade marks	4.19

and South America), and/or experience in countries which have, in some respects, similar cultures (such as other parts of Asia) may experience fewer difficulties (both in the establishment phase and in the conduct of day-to-day business) than companies with no experience in any of these regions. To test this hypothesis, the Mann-Whitney-U test was employed to compare the companies with potentially relevant experience (thirty-nine in all) and those companies lacking such experience (ten firms) in terms of the intensity of the problems encountered.[5] Only two statistically significant differences were found, indicating that companies with relevant experience perceived fewer problems in negotiating ($p<0.05$) and in securing patents and trade marks ($p<0.07$) during the establishment phase. However, since no further significant differences between the two groups were detected in a total twenty-five comparisons, the two significant results could be dismissed as having occurred by chance. Thus, it would appear that, on the whole, previous experience is not particularly helpful in 'cushioning' the problems encountered in the Chinese market, which serves to emphasize the unique nature of the latter.

With 'financing the Chinese purchase' being second in the list of day-to-day problems listed in table 10.9, it is interesting to note that in 45 per cent of the cases, the Chinese customers arranged finance themselves. The second most widely used method of finance, representing 25 per cent of all mentioned, were Danish government loans, either on their own or in conjunction with a 60 per cent export credit. Other methods included World Bank loans as well as compensation-trade arrangements; however, none of these methods received more than 9 per cent of all mentions.

Relative success

As a final issue, respondents were asked to indicate how they regarded their performance in the China market to date. The overall attitude might be described as 'cautiously optimistic', as most companies place themselves either in the mid-point or just one point towards the success side of the seven-point scale utilized to measure success (see above). Looking at the individual standards of comparison, table 10.10 shows that companies regard their performance best when comparing it with that of their international competitors. The worst performance ratings are obtained when the comparison is made against other export trade. However, a correlation analysis showed that the four performance measures are highly intercorrelated (with zero-order correlations ranging from 0.44 to 0.91, all significant at the 1 per cent level or better). It is also worth noting that there are substantial variations in the performance self-ratings, as indicated by the size of the accompanying standard deviations.

Table 10.10 Perceived success in China [$n=49$]

Point of reference	*Mean*	*Standard deviation*
In comparison with ...		
(i) international competitors	3.08	1.70
(ii) first expectations of turnover	4.03	1.99
(iii) first expectations of profit	3.95	2.03
(iv) other export trade	4.14	1.94

In an attempt to assess the impact of the factors discussed in the above sections on company success, a regression model was developed and tested. The dependent variable utilized was an 'overall success' scale constructed by summing the success ratings on each of the four success dimensions in table 10.10; reflecting a high degree of face validity, the derived scale was also found to exhibit high internal consistency, as reflected in an alpha value of 0.83.

With respect to variables used as predictors, the multitude of individual variables describing company characteristics and aspects of operating in China had somehow to be reduced in order to enable a parsimonious specification of the model (given the limitations of sample size) and minimize potential multicollinearity problems. Three strategies were employed to this end, notably (*a*) dichotomization; (*b*) index construction; and (*c*) factor analysis.

The first strategy involved the transformation of nominal variables into dummies (0.1) to enable their inclusion in the regression equation. Two variables fall under this category, notably 'level of involvement' (representing a split between high- and low-involvement modes, as indicated by joint ventures and exporting/licensing respectively; see above and 'relevant past experience' (indicating experience in dealing with other communist countries, less developed countries, or culturally similar countries; see above).

Index construction was utilized in an attempt to develop composite measures of the overall degree of difficulties encountered in setting-up and conducting business with China. Two problem indices were constructed by summing the individual scores on the lists of problems faced in the establishment phase and in the day-to-day running of the business (see above); both indices displayed high internal consistencies as indicated by alpha values of 0.82 and 0.91 respectively.

Factor analysis was employed to derive orthogonal dimensions of initial market contact methods (see above) and bases of competitive advantage (see above). A total of three factors was extracted for the first set of variables, explaining 66.1 per cent of total variance, while the second analysis yielded six factors, together accounting for 70.9 per cent of the variance in the original variables. Tables 10.11 and 10.12 show the relevant factor loadings, following varimax rotation.

Factor 1 in table 10.11 accounts for 33.3 per cent of total variance and loads heavily on variables describing joint (that is, collaborative) efforts in establishing links with the Chinese market, hence the label 'collective approach'. Factor 2 represents the 'formal' (traditional) approach to initial market contact; it

Table 10.11 Factor matrix of initial market contact methods [n=49]

Variable	*FACTOR 1* *Collective approach*	*FACTOR 2* *Formal approach*	*FACTOR 3* *Direct approach*
Taking part in trade fair in China	0.86		
Taking part in other trade fair	0.78		
Technical seminars in China	0.85		
Participation in group initiatives	0.56		
Invitations of the Chinese to Denmark		0.80	
Direct contact with Chinese officials		0.74	
Sales letters		0.64	
Direct contact with Chinese end-users			0.90
EIGENVALUE	2.66	1.60	1.02

loads heavily on such variables as sales letters and invitations to visit the home country, and accounts for 20.0 per cent of total variance. Finally, factor 3 labelled 'direct approach' is self-explanatory, as indicated by the high loading on direct contact with the end-user and the absence of other variables.

As far as the sources of competitive strength are concerned (table 10.12), Factor 1 reflects the firm's 'technical expertise', loading highly on technology and know-how; 16.3 per cent of total variance is accounted for by this factor. Factors 2 and 5, accounting for 14.6 per cent and 9.2 per cent of total variance respectively, indicate 'transaction advantages' as they load on variables which would encourage/facilitate the exchange process between the Chinese buyer and the Danish supplier. With regards to the former factor, the provision of a specialized product at an attractive price coupled with a concern to assist with Chinese export efforts (for example, countertrade) would be expected to be conducive to selling to the Chinese market; similarly, the provision of a complete solution, the arranging of finance and the advantages of being an early entrant into the market would also facilitate the exchange relationship. Factor 3 can be viewed as representing the overall 'quality of supply', as indicated by the high loadings on quality and service; it accounts for 13.0 per cent of the variance. Finally, Factors 4 and 6 are labelled 'market contact' since all variables loading on these factors reflect the building of relationships with decision makers (for example, officials and end-users) in the

Table 10.12 Factor matrix of bases of competitive advantage [n=49]

	FACTOR 1	*FACTOR 2*	*FACTOR 3*	*FACTOR 4*	*FACTOR 5*	*FACTOR 6*
Variable	*Techn. expert.*	*Transact. advant. I*	*Supply quality*	*Market cont. I*	*Transact. advant. II*	*Market cont. II*
Know-how	0.91					
Technology	0.93					
Price		0.72				
Specialized product		0.80				
Help to Chinese exports		0.63	−0.50			
Quality			0.82			
Service			0.67			
Negotiating skills				0.80		
Contact with end-users				0.59		
Contact with Chinese officials				0.46		0.73
Delivery of a complete solution					0.45	
Financing of Chinese purchase					0.75	
Entry before competition					0.74	
Contacts made by other Danish firms						0.79
EIGENVALUE	2.28	2.05	1.81	1.40	1.28	1.10

market; they account for 10.0 per cent and 7.9 per cent of total variance respectively.

In addition to the thirteen variables obtained through the data reduction strategies employed (that is, the two dummy variables, two composite scales and nine factor scores), an additional two variables were also used as predictors in their original form (that is, untransformed); these were sales turnover (as an indicator of company size) and proportion of total turnover derived from international operations (as an indicator of international experience).

As a first step in the analysis, the tolerances[6] of all independent variables were calculated in order to assess the extent to which multicollinearity was going to pose a problem. While most of the variables exhibited high tolerances, the tolerances of four variables (notably 'initial problems', 'current problems', 'sales turnover', and 'relevant past experience') were rather low (below 0.50). As a result, and following an inspection of the zero-order intercorrelation matrix of the independent variables, it was decided to exclude three of the four problem variables in an attempt to reduce multicollinearity (the variable retained was the 'initial problems' index, because of its theoretical importance as an indicator of the 'hostility' of the environment; although the 'current problems' index would appear to be equally acceptable, the fact that most companies in the sample were new to the market created a preference for the former index).[7] Subsequently, the tolerances of the remaining variables were recalculated to check that no major changes in values had taken place as a result of the removal of the three variables. Next, the twelve variables comprising the final predictor set were entered in a stepwise multiple regression with the 'overall success' scale as the criterion variable. Table 10.13 summarizes the regression results.

Table 10.13 Regression results [n=46]

Independent variable	*Beta*	*t-value*	*Significance*
Transaction advantages II	0.31	2.26	$p = 0.029$
Direct approach	0.27	1.96	$p = 0.057$
Initial problems	−0.26	−1.98	$p = 0.054$
Market contact I	0.26	1.95	$p = 0.058$

Summary statistics

R	R^2 (adjusted)	F-value	(significance)
0.50	0.18	3.58	($p = 0.014$)

The final regression equation obtained through the stepwise procedure is significant and incorporates four predictor variables with significant coefficients; this implies that inclusion of further variables does not contribute to the explanatory power of the equation.[8] The significant predictors include two of the six factors representing dimensions of competitive advantage, one of the three factors reflecting initial market contact modes, and the composite scale indicating the severity of problems experienced during the establishment phase. The signs of the regression coefficients are consistent with expectations, in that all are positive with the exception of the problem index which has a negative impact on overall success; in addition it is worth noting that the absolute magnitudes of regression weights are approximately equal for three of the four predictors, indicating a similar contribution of 'direct approach', 'market contact I' and 'initial problems' to the equation.

Looking at the substantive content of the predictor variables which are positively related with company success, one cannot but notice that all of them describe aspects of the relationship between supplier and final user. Specifically, the 'direct approach' to initial market contact involves getting directly in touch with the end-user in order to establish trading links (table 10.11), while 'market contact I' and 'transaction advantages II' refer to dimensions of competitive advantage based on elements of relationship management (table 10.12). Thus the personal dimension appears to be very important, and companies which formulate their trading policy around it seem more likely to meet with success in the Chinese market.

With respect to the variables which were found *not* to be related to company success (that is, those which were excluded from the regression equation by the stepwise procedure), a number of points are worth making. First, according to the results, success in China appears to be independent of the particular mode of entry (that is, joint ventures versus exporting/licensing), which is somewhat surprising given the preferential treatment given to joint ventures by the Chinese authorities (see above). Second, initial market contact approaches, other than through direct personal contact with the end-user, have no impact on success; thus, given the choice, indirect routes (for example, through joint initiatives) should not be given preference to opportunities of final user contact. Third, the international experience of the firm (as represented by the proxy ratio international/total sales) also has no impact on success in the Chinese market, which provides complementary evidence in support of the contention made earlier that China is a rather unique market (see above); however, it should be remembered that practically all firms in the sample are internationally-oriented (see above), and, thus, the range of variation on this variable is rather constrained. Finally, certain bases of competitive advantage do not appear to be very effective in differentiating firms in terms of their relative success; this does not necessarily imply that, say, technical expertise or quality and service are unimportant, but may indicate that such elements are *prerequisites* for operating in the market, success in which depends on *other* elements and addition to and supplementing the former.

DISCUSSION AND CONCLUSIONS

The present study has attempted to draw a picture of Danish companies' experiences in the People's Republic of China and identify the factors likely to impinge on successful operation in this market. The findings of the study throw light on a number of issues of interest, particularly for small and medium-sized companies (since large companies are not well represented in the sample).

With regards to the motivations for entering this market, the results show quite conclusively that China is perceived as a 'long shot', that is, it is the long-run potential of the market that makes it attractive rather than any opportunity for short-term gain; in this context, proactive rather than reactive considerations underlie the decision to enter, in that China is not regraded simply as a solution to compensate for a decline in business elsewhere.

The fact that the majority of the firms surveyed had substantial international experience coupled with the fact that most firms are relatively new in the market, suggests that entry into China is a rather demanding exercise (Delman 1987, Mayer *et al.* 1987) and, once in, it takes time to do business; the latter point is partly illustrated by the time lag between market initial contact and receipt of an order, and partly by the repeated mentions of time delays in negotiations as a common problem (the latter has also been observed by Campbell 1987, Pye 1986 and Crainer and Campbell 1986).

With respect to the methods used to establish market contact and the problems faced at this stage, personal relations appear to be crucial. Specifically, direct personal contact with end users and officials is essential, however, reaching the latter is not perceived to be an easy task, not least because of language and bureaucracy problems. These findings closely reflect previous evidence on the difficulties associated with establishing a presence in the market (Saunders and Ton 1986, Stewart and Yeung Yun Choi 1987, Furst 1986, Von Lingelsheim-Seibicke 1987). However, a firm's problems are not over once initial contact has been established. The costs of doing business are considerable, financing the Chinese purchase is not always straightforward, and changes in the political arena (coupled with the perennial bureaucracy) are not conducive to speedy negotiations; the lack of infrastructure does not help either. Again, these findings are consistent with earlier investigations of the business environment in China (Bertrand 1986, Kristensen *et al.* 1987, Hendryx 1986a, Tung 1986, Zhao 1987, Dennis 1982). It is interesting to note that the Chinese culture *per se* is not perceived to constitute a major problem either during the establishment phase or after; according to the results, culture is the third *least* important obstacle, despite the importance attached to it in previous analyses (Kindel 1987, Jen *et al.* 1987). It is also worth noting that experience in other countries with similar characteristics (notably political regime, level of development and/or culture), does not appear to be particularly relevant in terms of lessening the intensity of problems encountered.

The chosen modes of entry to the market appear to reflect a combination of three factors, notably the preference of the Chinese for joint ventures, the strong Danish presence in Hong Kong (in the form of export trading houses) and the size of the firms concerned; exporting (in a variety of forms) is the most common mode of entry, with two-thirds of the firms in the sample using this option.

Competitive advantage is largely formulated along non-price factors, such as product quality/suitability and level of service. However, the crucial factors bearing on company success appear to be related much more to the social/communication capabilities of the firm rather than its technical excellence. Personal contact with decision-makers and effective negotiation skills seem to be the key elements underlying success, as is the provision of an entire 'package' (in terms of offering a complete solution and helping the buyer make the purchase). Nevertheless, one should always bear in mind the limitations of the success indicator employed, notably the fact that it is a perceptual measure based on self-assessment rather than on any objective criterion (such as actual sales growth or profitability).

Taken collectively, the findings of the present study are in line with previous evidence on the nature of the Chinese market as viewed from the perspective of a Western supplier and provide further insights on the factors likely to bear on a company's successful operation in this market. In addition, the study raises a number of questions which may constitute profitable avenues for further research. First and foremost among these is the role of personal relations in doing business with China; while attention to this issue has been drawn repeatedly in the past (see, for example, Pye 1986, Frankenstein 1986, Grow 1986, Kindel 1987, Stewart and Yeung Yun Choi 1987, Campbell 1987), a detailed investigation of the customer-service/communication mixes of Western firms operating in (or preparing to enter) China, would throw additional light on the role of personal relations as a determinant of successful market entry, effective operation and company performance. A second issue worthy of further investigation, concerns the identification of additional factors impinging upon company success in this market. In this context, the rather low proportion of variance explained by the regression equation, seems to imply that other influences remain undetected. Although it is difficult to speculate with any degree of confidence on what these influences may be (given that the set of predictors utilized in the present analysis already include a wide range of potential influences), there may be new dimensions highly specific to the Chinese market which need to be uncovered. Finally, a systematic assessment of company success in China utilizing objective measures of success, would provide a complementary perspective on the rewards accruing to firms operating in this demanding foreign market.

NOTES

1 Hu Yaobang became General Secretary, as the title Chairman was no longer to be used.

2 Zhang (1987) reported 3,210 equity joint ventures, 4,390 co-operative enterprises, and 138 wholly-foreign funded enterprises.

3 The Aarhus Group (China Information Service, Aarhus) is one of two organizations in Denmark that specializes in business advice to

companies dealing with China, the other one being the China Business Service, Copenhagen.

4 The ranking used to establish the highest level of involvement was as follows: (i) joint ventures; (ii) licensing and assembly; (iii) export with a branch office in China; (iv) direct export from Denmark; and (v) export through an agency. Consulting engineers have been grouped together with direct export if they did not use agencies; however, most of these companies did actually use agencies.

5 The Mann-Whitney-U test was used in place of the more powerful *t*-test for comparing differences between means, because of the small number of cases in the 'inexperienced' group.

6 The tolerance of an independent variable *j* is defined as $1\text{-}Rj^2$, where Rj^2 is the coefficient of determination obtained by regressing *j* on all other independent variables. Thus it is a measure of *residual* variance in that it indicates the proportion of variance in *j* left unexplained by its regression on the other predictors; the higher the tolerance, the less severe the multicollinearity problem. Calculation of tolerance values as a strategy for multicollinearity assessment is superior to sole reliance on the zero-order correlation matrix of the independent variables, because 'it is possible ... to find no large bivariate correlations, although one of the independent variables is a nearly perfect linear combination of the remaining independent variables' (Lewis-Beck 1980: 60).

7 The two problem indices are, in any case, highly intercorrelated, as indicated by a correlation coefficient of 0.65 ($p<0.001$).

8 Although a stepwise procedure to variable selection can be problematic if strong multicollinearity is present (Hebden 1981), in this instance, no such difficulties arose since steps were taken to deal with multicollinearity prior to employing the procedure.

REFERENCES

Arthur Andersen & Co (1986) *The People's Republic of China: Perspectives II*, London: Arthur Andersen.

Bertrand, K. (1986) 'China trade: more than joint ventures', *Business Marketing* (November): 20.

Brehm, C. L. (1985) 'Setting up shop in Shanghai', *The China Business Review* (November-December): 12–16.

Campbell, N. (1987) 'Negotiating with the Chinese: a commercial long march', *Journal of Marketing Management* 2: 219–23.

Copeland, L. (1986) 'China opportunity: amateurs need not apply', *Personnel Administrator* (July): 97–102.

Crainer, S. and Campbell, N. (1986) 'Only patience pays in China', *Management Today* (December): 68–9.

Davies, H. L. (1985) *Doing Business in the China of the Open Door*, Beijing: British Embassy.

Davies, H. L. (1986) *China: The Seventh Five-Year Plan: Opportunities and Obstacles*, Beijing: British Embassy.

Delman, J. (1987) 'Markedsforing i Kina', *Kina Information* 3: 27–30.
Dennis, R. D. (1982) 'The countertrade factor in China's modernization plan', *Columbia Journal of World Business* (Spring): 67–75.
Ernst & Whinney (1985) *General Information on Doing Business in China*, London: Ernst & Whinney.
Frankenstein, J. (1986) 'Trends in Chinese business practice: changes in the Beijing wind', *California Management Review* 29: 148–60.
Furst, A. (1986) 'China opens the door to US electronic firms', *Electronic Business* 15 March: 106–15.
Grow, R. F. (1986) 'Japanese and American firms in China: lessons of a new market', *Columbia Journal of World Business* (Spring): 49–56.
Hebden, J. (1981) *Statistics for Economists*, Oxford: Philip Allan.
Hendryx, S. R. (1986a) 'The China trade: making the deal work', *Harvard Business Review* (July-August): 75–84.
Hendryx, S. R. (1986b) 'Implementation of a technology transfer joint venture in the People's Republic of China: a management perspective', *Columbia Journal of World Business* (Spring): 57–66.
Henley, J. S. and Nyaw, M. K. (1986) 'Developments in managerial decision-making in Chinese industrial enterprises', working paper, Department of Business Studies, University of Edinburgh.
Henley, J. S. and Nyaw, M. K. (1988) 'The system of management and performance of joint ventures in China: some evidence from Shenzhen Special Economic Zone', working paper, Department of Business Studies, University of Edinburgh.
Irvine, J., Crokland, M. and Kelly, M. (1987) 'China: market in waiting', *Accountancy* (March): 67–75.
Jen, F. C., Lee, C. F. and Hsiao, F. S. T. (1987) 'Impact of culture, religion, and communist orthodoxy on Chinese management, paper presented at the International Conference on The China Enterprise, Manchester Business School, June.
Kindel, T. (1987) 'Understanding the Chinese cultural framework in the negotiating process, paper presented at the International Conference on The China Enterprise, Manchester Business School, June.
Kristensen, K. I., Williamsen, J. W. and Eisvang, G. (1987) 'Det koster 1.5 million kr. arligt at vaere i Kina', *Borsen* (12 February): 1.
Lassen, E. and Lindberg, P. (1987) 'Joint ventures i Kina', *Okonomisk Perspektiv* (April): 5–8.
Lewis-Beck, M. S. (1980) *Applied Regression*, London: Sage Publications.
Mayer, C. S., Jing Lun Han and Hui Fong Lim (1987) 'An evaluation of the performance of the joint venture companies in the People's Republic of China', paper presented at the International Conference on The China Enterprise, Manchester Business School, June.
Nyaw, M. K. and Lin, G. S. (1986) 'The organization structure of joint ventures in Shenzen, China: an empirical study', *Hong Kong Journal of Business Management* 4: 167–8.
Porter, M. (1980) *Competitive Strategy*, New York: The Free Press.
Pye, L. W. (1986) 'The China trade: making the deal', *Harvard Business Review* (July-August): 74–80.

Redmond, J. (1987) 'Trade between China and the European Community: a new relationship?' *National Westminster Bank Quarterly Review* (May): 31–46.
Reisman, A. Duu-Cheng Fuh and Gong Li (1987) 'Countertrade in China: some contributions of management science research, paper presented at the International Conference on The China Enterprise, Manchester Business School, June.
Saunders, J. and Ton Hong Chong (1986) 'Trade with China and Japan', *Management Decision* 24: 7–12.
Simon, D. F. and Rehn, B. (1986) 'Understanding the electronics industry at the national level and in Shanghai', *The China Business Review* (March-April).
Stahr, G. (1979) *Auslandsmarketing: Marktanalyse*, Stuttgart: Verlag Kohlhammer.
Stewart, S. and Yeung Yun Choi (1987) 'Chinese decision-making', paper presented at the International Conference on The China Enterprise, Manchester Business School, June.
Suk-Ching Ho (1984) 'Hong Kong: a bridge to China for foreign investors', *Management Decision* 22: 37–46.
Terpstra, V. (1987) *International Marketing*, Chicago: The Dryden Press.
Touche Ross & Co. (1985) *Tax & Investment Profile: The People's Republic of China*, London: Touche Ross & Co.
Tung, R. L. (1986) 'Corporate executives and their families in China: the need for cross-cultural understanding in business', *Columbia Journal of World Business* (Spring): 21–5.
United Nations (1984) *Statistical Yearbook for Asia and the Pacific*, New York: UN.
Von Lingelsheim-Seibicke, W. (1987) *Structure and Functioning Methods of the External Trade Operating System in the People's Republic of China*, report by the Bundesstelle fur Aussenhandelsinformation for the Commission of the European Communities, Köln.
Zhang, , H. (1987) 'Utilization of foreign funds in China', *New China Quarterly* (April).
Zhao, Jiahe (1987) 'The external environment of China's enterprises, paper presented at the International Conference on The China Enterprise, Manchester Business School, June.

Chapter Eleven

ALTERNATIVE APPROACH STRATEGIES FOR BUYER–SELLER RELATIONS WITH THE PEOPLE'S REPUBLIC OF CHINA

WESLEY J. JOHNSTON

Given the ambitious goals of the seventh Five-Year Plan, selling industrial exports to China should be an easy task. The Plan requires the following to be accomplished (Hong Kong 1987):

1 Under the premise of continuous increase of economic benefits, the total output of industrial and agricultural production in the five years ought to increase by 38 per cent; gross national product, by 44 per cent; and total investment in fixed assets in state-run enterprises by nearly 70 per cent over the previous Plan's five-year period.
2 Extension of foreign trade will be attempted. It is planned that the total business turnover from import and export in 1990 will be 40 per cent, more than 1985; and the scale of foreign loan utilization and introduction of advanced technology will also be enlarged.
3 Production development will be synchronized with the improvement of the consumption level of both urban and rural residents.

The only way to accomplish these goals is to open up the market for freer trade and to import technology at a fairly rapid pace. Despite all the confusion and inconsistencies in past policy, many analysts feel that opportunities for foreign companies are better now than they have ever been. The seventh Five-Year Plan dampens the free-for-all atmosphere that characterized the China market in the last half of the previous plan. More importantly, however, it promotes a stable pro-growth policy.

Import trends

The following represents a brief overview of the trends taking place with respect to industrial products being imported into China (Smith 1985).

China has developed a vertical pattern of trade, typical among developing nations. It exports mostly primary goods, such as grain, coal, and other raw materials and natural resources. In general, Chinese manufactured products are not competitive in the world market.

Plant technology

For several years, China has imported billions of dollars worth of plant and equipment, often included were complete turnkey operations. This rapid development of infrastructure is currently being blamed for foreign exchange shortages, and spending has been curtailed. It is unlikely that this sector will revive any time in the near future. However, replacement parts and maintenance, repair and operating (MRO) equipment will continue to be needed. A major exception to this will be energy production plants, since power shortages are the most critical of China's infrastructure problems.

High technology

Technology imports are shifting towards smaller items. Personal computer systems and related electronic equipment are targeted as growth areas. This area, in general, has always been of high buying importance to the Chinese. Export controls imposed for political reasons by western countries have limited the types of equipment that China can buy. China is still quite willing, however, to spend its foreign exchange currency to buy high technology products: so willing, in fact, it results in poor purchasing results. For instance, China has imported millions of dollars worth of computers, while lacking the knowledge to operate or service them. In their enthusiasm to buy, the Chinese have purchased thousands of machines they are currently unable to use.

Another error the Chinese have made in buying advanced

technology is always to prefer the most recent state-of-the-art technology. This was often too advanced to interface with their other existing technology, and difficult to operate or maintain. China still has an eagerness to purchase high technology, but a realization that merely possessing advanced technology is not enough is beginning to permeate. The emphasis on the level of technology is also beginning to shift from 'state-of-the-art' to technology that will fit in with existing operations.

Special buying priorities in the high technology area include: data processing, electronics, and fibre optic technology; another is high grade steel.

Infrastructure

Infrastructure improvement will be a critical area for buying products and technology for the foreseeable future. China is expected to add between 5 and 6 million kilowatts of energy generating capacity per year. Rail, sea, and air transportation capacity will also be expanded quickly. Aviation passenger capacity is to be doubled by 1990, and rail freight and passenger capacity by 2000.

ISSUES IN BUYER–SELLER RELATIONSHIPS

Approaching the market

Thus, while it appears that China is a very attractive market, it would be a mistake to think that penetrating the market would be easy. The Chinese traditionally have emphasized the importance of a developed business relationship. It is also important to establish this relationship by entering through the proper channels when making the initial approach to the market. While there are more direct methods of entry than struggling with the many layers of bureaucracy, using such an approach too early runs the risk of leaving out someone with veto power from the relationship. Taking the more complicated approach implies sincerity and commitment in dealing with a Chinese enterprise and the trade organizations that represent it.

It is also important to appear to have commitment to the market over the long term. This includes providing the necessary capital for what may be a lengthy period of minimal or nonexistent profits. Entering the China market is expensive, and the costs of maintaining an office in China are quite high. Presenting the image that a company is a large and well-established firm seeking a long-term relationship in China is an important aspect of being successful there.

The product of the company is also a critical variable. While most countries have restrictions on imports, the list in China is extremely long and detailed. Another problem occurs even with products within categories the Chinese want to import. Shortages in power supply and other infrastructure prevent the sale of some desired products. Product life cycles appear to have relatively long introductory stages with high learning curve requirements. Thus, even the strongest products can take a while before acceptance begins. The same loyalty that structures business relationships also applies to brand names. Heavy promotion can help overcome the lack of a previous presence in the market, however.

Understanding the bureaucratic structure

Perhaps the most difficult aspect of selling to China for many industrial marketers is understanding the numerous layers of bureaucratic structure and dealing effectively with them. The most important point to remember in selling to Chinese enterprises is that all are state owned. Thus, all enterprises have both professional management and government bureaucrats involved in decision making. In addition, various levels of government become involved in business decision making from local trade offices to the Ministry of Foreign Economic Relations and Trade (MOFERT).

Since 1980, when Premier Zhou Ziyang took office, central directives have aimed at increasing the co-ordination of policy between the regional trade offices. These regional trade offices present a unified foreign trade policy, and act as a regulatory liaison between the central authorities and the 'free-for-all' atmosphere of the local trade offices. In addition, import/export licensing requirements have been tightened, and the Customs Office has been separated into an independent body with augmented powers.

In addition to MOFERT, the central government agencies that administer and promote foreign trade are the foreign trade corporations (FTCs) under MOFERT, and related local and specialized trade offices. Less of a central link, but often crucial as a liaison between foreign business and the FTCs, is the China Council for the Promotion of International Trade (CCPIT).

The following represents a brief description of the key agencies and their responsibilities in regulating trade.

MOFERT

The Ministry of Foreign Economic Relations and Trade (MOFERT) is the principal co-ordinator of foreign trade. Its responsibilities include implementation of state-promulgated principles and policies on foreign economics and trade; importation of advanced technologies; and co-ordination of the activities of the regional and local foreign trade offices in accordance with its other responsibilities.

FTCs

China's foreign trade corporations (FTCs) were created to balance local and central authority. They are the primary link between foreign business and end-users. The FTCs also act as liaisons between foreign business and the central government. FTCs are divided along product lines into ten organizations. They are often the first point of contact for foreign firms trying to enter the China market. The duties of the FTCs include the implementation of the directives of MOFERT concerning the development of the import and export of their respective commodities; the signing of purchase and sales contracts with foreign enterprises and the arrangement of financial settlements; and monitoring of foreign exchange settlements. The central importance of the FTCs has been splintered in several ways. Ministerial and local trading corporations have begun to appear, and some individual enterprises have the authority to compete with the FTCs. FTC branch offices, located in the major industrial cities, act as mini-offices for trade promotion, issue some specialized import and export licenses, and conduct market research. The branches are under the control of the head office, but are supervized by local authorities. They are gradually becoming the centre of China's import business.

The CCPIT

The China Council for the Promotion of International Trade (CCPIT) is an independent organization under the jurisdiction of MOFERT. The duties of the CCPIT include promoting foreign economic and trade ties; concluding non-governmental trade agreements with foreign firms; and arbitrating economic, trade, and maritime disputes.

Others

Other political subdivisions of the local government are authorized to supervise auxiliary trade services. These offices handle transportation, shipping, packaging, advertising, and other issues. In addition, an increasing number of separate national agencies may provide trade assistance. Some, like the CCPIT, are under the jurisdiction of MOFERT. Others are independent, or related to other ministries. In special cases, large industrial enterprises and designated special projects may be authorized to conduct business within the boundaries of an approved plan, usually limited to a certain value. These exemptions may bypass the FTCs and local trade offices altogether.

Since China's formal trade structure is still evolving, it is not always clear whom the appropriate contact is, or whether contracts have been properly approved and signed by the correct legal and governmental agencies. The two best sources for contract decisions are the treaty and law department of MOFERT and the legal department of the CCPIT.

Conducting detailed business operations

In making an industrial sale, finding a buyer is probably not the most difficult aspect of the transaction. There are, however, several hurdles the industrial marketeer must negotiate after a potential buyer is located. First, an import licence must be secured. The end-user then must sign a contract, which is submitted to MOFERT for approval. Payment will depend upon the availability and approval of the expenditure of foreign exchange currency. Before shipping the goods, the industrial marketer needs to resolve a number of issues including trademark and patent protection, political insurance, and legal arbitrations should any problems develop.

Then the actual logistics issues have to be resolved. For instance, how to ship and deliver the goods, where to submit the imports for commodities inspection, and how much to set aside for customs duties. All of these details must be settled before delivery is attempted.

Negotiating through these levels of bureaucracy can be time consuming, confusing, and frustrating. It is a process which requires the proper sequence of procedures to be followed. Leaving out one step of the process or one of the administrative offices responsible for reviewing the contract or approaching end-user too early in the process can lead to problems that may be difficult, if not impossible, to resolve.

Summary

This section presents a summary of some of the problems industrial marketers have to solve in buyer–seller relationships with Chinese enterprises. The points come from the preceding background material and personal knowledge of marketing in China. The following problems or obstacles are often encountered in developing business relationships in China:

1 *Confusion caused by the overlapping bureaucratic organizations and enterprises*: The same transaction can be handled by different Chinese business sectors whether it be government level bureaucracy or local business. At this point, an inside-information provider is vital.
2 *Chinese process-oriented buying behaviour vs. Western action-oriented selling behaviour*: When a Western company does business with a government-owned business, or more accurately, a public bureaucracy, the Westerners find they have to sacrifice their action orientation for a process orientation, which is usually a trial of their patience. The Chinese process-oriented buying behaviour often involves hierarchical project evaluation, collective decision making on the approval of the

project, and other unusual delays, which are part of the reasons for low efficiency.

3 *Chinese indirect, non-verbal cues in negotiations versus Westerners' straightforward 'yes or no' style*: This is one of the biggest culture shocks in many business negotiations. The problem is worsened when more than one level of management from the Chinese side participate in the negotiations, and Westerners fail to read whose non-verbal cues play a decisive role and whose 'yes' carries no weight.

4 *Depending too much on a translator*: In most cases, depending extensively on a translator from a third party (such as Hong Kong) is unwise. First, s/he may not be completely trusted by the Chinese side. Second, s/he may not be familiar with the mainland situation and social or organizational norms. Third, s/he has no real commitment to either side. Therefore, a successful translator should be a person at least committed to and trusted by one side, while the other side can 'read' some information from the way the translator behaves. To judge the reliability of the information provided by the translator, the other side needs to see how well his/her advice and suggestions are accepted by the decision makers.

5 *Lack of skills in developing human relationships*: There are clusters of interpersonal relationships which are beyond the imagination of the Westerners, as well as the outsider Chinese. The Japanese are good at picking up various group dynamics occurring in the other negotiating team. When the Japanese do business with a Chinese enterprise, they like to meet the buyers in a social setting *before* conducting business. Westerners are often tempted to conduct business first, and then celebrate a successful negotiation. Presenting a 'gift' is the norm of Japanese (also a norm of the Chinese).

In a word, although cultural differences are a big issue in doing business with China, they are not the crucial ones. To understand Chinese buying behaviour, one has to learn how to cope with China's bureaucracy and red tape. Many companies are often trapped by bureaucracy and red tape. Presented in the next section are examples of three different approaches to cut through the Chinese bureaucracy and get around the red tape.

ALTERNATIVE APPROACH STRATEGIES

One way to approach the China market is directly. This involves selling to and/or through a local enterprise. This approach is described as the 'buying group' model, and requires great patience and significant skills on the part of the industrial marketing organization. A second approach, called the 'agency' model, is a case of using a local Chinese organization to represent the industrial marketer in a sales effort to enter the market. This approach requires some understanding of the official organizational bureaucracy, but relies on finding a key public sector organization and, more crucial, a very responsible individual within the organization to handle the marketer's case. The third approach, joint venture, requires both the industrial marketer and a domestic partner to contribute to, manage together, and derive profits from the marketing effort. In the joint venture, two different companies from two different environments are joined together in a business effort in which each may have its own objectives and priorities. Coordinating the two organizations' goals requires open and constant communication and endless compromise from both sides. In this section, each of these approach strategies for buyer–seller relations with the People's Republic of China are developed.

The 'buying group' model: doing business with China through an authorized buying bureaucracy

An example of selling directly to Chinese enterprises in the form of an authorized buying bureaucracy involves the Benxi Iron & Steel Complex Import & Export Corporation (see Appendix 1). BISCIEC (Benxi Iron and Steel Import & Export Corp.) is one of the four major iron and steel import/export corporations in China, and is a subordinate branch of the China Ministry of Metallurgical Industry of Beijing. Normally, any import transactions should be conducted through the Beijing bureaucracy; however, a local corporation, such as BISCIEC, has certain buying decision authority, depending on the total cost of the goods to be imported.

Buying and importing mining equipment through the ministry and locally

China, or more specifically, the Ministry of Metallurgical Industry of China, started buying mining equipment from America, Japan, and West Germany in 1977, a year before the Economic Reform. Import priority was given to heavy industrial technology and equipment. Unlike Taiwan or Japan, who depend totally on exporting, China is seriously limited by the budget of foreign currency, which is not the problem with any of the industrial sellers. Before a buying group can enter into any negotiation, a local corporation like BISCIEC is allocated a certain amount of foreign currency by the Beijing Ministry. It is very natural for the direct buyer to be extremely price-sensitive and focus on the limited budget – trying to get the most out of the least. Here is a case to illustrate what is meant.

In 1983, through the Beijing Ministry, a negotiation was being conducted for the Benxi Corporation on their hot-strip mill project. This equipment was urgently needed by the corporation to modify their hot-strip mill, which was constructed in the early 1970s. The plant had been constructed by the Chinese, but many technical problems could not be solved, which was why technicians strongly pleaded for the right to import foreign technology. Since the foreign currency allocation was made before the suppliers' bids were received and negotiations started, and the technicians had already set the criteria for the proposed product, the buying group was limited during the negotiation to meeting the technical specification with a 'no-higher-than' budget of $50 million appropriated for the project.

The first sellers who provided bids were three American enterprises. The president of one of the three came to China five times during two years for this bid, and conducted dozens of negotiations, but failed to win the bid. Instead, a West German business won the contract. Japanese businesses also provided bids, but Benxi Corporation did not even enter into negotiations with them. Several factors contributed to why the US firms missed out on the project. The Chinese wanted to do this transaction with the Americans because of their trustworthy reputation and business credit, as well as their open and straightforward negotiation. The Chinese, however, were unable to accept their price due to the fixed budget. At the same time, no one from the Chinese side could release the information about the $50 million appropriation. Therefore, negotiations became a matter of guesswork for the Americans. Also, the American side could not lower the price any further because of their more expensive labour costs. The American firms were without the sort of government subsidies provided to the Japanese and German businesses. This case shows how important it is for US industrial marketers to have 'inside information' while not violating the Chinese norms. The result was that the German business took the bid at $40 million, covering all the technical services that would be covered by the Americans.

The Chinese feel that negotiation is compromise. In this case there was less possibility of making a compromise between the American businesses and theirs. As the buyèr, they could not get any more money allocated from their government, although they had the decision right to choose from whom they could sign the contract. At the same time the American businesses were private ones and had their own problems in not being able to set their prices below the cost.

A local enterprise like Benxi does have the right to make some direct buying decisions. While the previous example examined buying from foreign countries through the head office – Ministry of Metallurgical Industry in Beijing – there are cases where Benxi Corporation made the buying decision independently.

One case is the import of a Direct-reading Spectrometer which cost $2 million. The reason to buy it was to improve technical equipment. Benxi technicians learned that other iron and steel enterprises had imported it, and they demanded that they should be allowed to also.

In a case like this, the importing procedures are much simpler and more efficient than the previous one described, which went through the Beijing bureaucracy.

Differences in buying through Beijing and locally

The first question is how much does the product cost. If it is less than $3 million for the project or the product, then a local enterprise is granted the buying and decision-making authority, provided there is appropriated foreign currency available at the beginning of every budgeting year. Every enterprise is appropriated a certain amount of foreign currency at the disposal of the user. If these enterprises do not find ways to spend the foreign currency, they have to turn in to the central government bank when the year ends.

For the Direct-reading Spectrometer product, the buying procedure was as follows:

1 The technicians of a subordinate factory of the corporation first fill in a report form describing the function of the product, the necessity of having it, some kind of feasibility study and other reports. Then they present their proposal to their factory's technology department. After being technically approved there, the technology department presents the proposal to the factory general manager who brings it to a collective decision-making session (composed of several top managers). Finally, the subordinate factory sends their request for the import to the import/export corporation.
2 The decision procedure in the import/export corporation is somewhat like that in the subordinate factory. The organizational chart in Appendix 1 only shows the import and export enterprise. But BISCIEC has 150,000 employees with dozens of subordinate mining branches and factories.

Upon receiving the report from the local factory, the corporation followed the following decision procedure. The equipment department managers held an extended meeting composed of the staffs from the planning department, the technology department, and the finance departments from both the subordinate factory and the corporation. At the meeting there was a technical defence of the proposed import project followed by a vote where the majority ruled. Finally, a formal document was developed. If by this time the corporation had foreign currency available, the corporation could directly start enquiries. If no money was available, the corporation would send the formal report to Beijing Ministry of Metallurgical Industry for allocation of foreign exchange currency.

If the corporation had a sum of appropriated foreign exchange currency, the general manager has the final decision-making power after the board of directors has made the decision. Benxi

Corporation has nine managers, but the general manager has the final say although in theory the decision should be made by majority rule.

The decision procedures are different for projects greater than $3 million. If started by a local enterprise, such as a subordinate factory, they would provide all the relevant technical data on the product wanted, to the import/export corporation. Then the import/export corporation presents it, after any necessary modification, to the Beijing Ministry of Metallurgical Industry. The Ministry then presents the project report to National Planning Committee for budget appropriation. After the National Committee has approved and allocated the amount of foreign currency, an inquiry will be conducted by another public sector in Beijing, called the China National Technology Import & Export Company (CNTI&EC is a national level public enterprise in charge of all the large transactions of technology and industrial equipment import). The CNTI&EC will invite bids from foreign countries through the Ministry of Metallurgical Industry. The Ministry will inform the local enterprise when the bid is taken. During the business negotiation which is conducted by CNTI&EC, the local enterprise or the ultimate user has the right to reject some contract terms or reject the whole contract or accept the transaction, although it is the CNTI&EC that signs the contract. Any transactions over $10 million have to go through the CNTI&EC.

Summary of the buying group model

Selling directly to China can be a difficult process. The larger the potential sale, the greater the levels of bureaucracy encountered. In the Buying Group model certain corporations are established as import/export enterprises, and are empowered to deal directly with the foreign industrial marketers. This power is contingent, however, upon a number of factors: technological feasibility studies, group consensus votes, availability of foreign exchange currency and other perhaps even unseen factors. The question quickly comes to mind as to whether the final profit is worth the effort.

The 'agency' model: doing business with China through a public bureaucracy

An example of selling to Chinese enterprises through an agency involves the Tianjin Scientific and Technical Exchange Center with Foreign Countries (see Appendix 2). TSTECFC is playing an increasing role in helping foreign businesses market their technology and products to Tianjin, one of the largest industrial cities in China.

In 1984, according to an agreement between Tianjin and Philadelphia, a three-member group from TSTECFC visited Philadelphia and some other cities in the US. When the group returned to Tianjin after their one-month trip, several business representatives from Philadelphia visited Tianjin, and were received by the Tianjin Centre, which arranged for them to meet with relevant manufacturers and businesses in Tianjin.

While the group from TSTECFC was in Philadelphia, its members visited the facilities of one industrial manufacturer, and were greatly impressed by the technology and services possessed by the factory. Also the highest ranking officials of the factory met with the group and presented them a catalogue of its products. On returning back to Tianjin, the Centre distributed the catalogues to appropriate factories in Tianjin in an attempt to locate potential buyers. The Centre then learned that this kind of product (special bearings) was needed by several customers, mostly electrical machinery plants producing different kinds of motor-driven products.

The Centre then held a city-wide information release conference to introduce the products of several US industrial manufacturers to other businesses. Present at the conference were representatives from Tianjin's industrial manufacturers, technology centres and concerned colleges. Thus, the special bearings manufacturer and other industrial manufacturers that the group from TSTECFC got to know during their month-long visit were introduced widely to the potential buyers in Tianjin.

Next the Centre presented its suggestions for further business co-operation between buyers and the special bearings manufacturer. The proposal included:

1 The Centre was to be responsible for advertising the manufacturer's technology and products in China. The benefit

for the manufacturer was that they would not have to send representatives or establish an office in China, which is very expensive. Also, the Centre had far more influence than the manufacturer's representatives could generate, because a public bureaucracy like the Centre has formal relationships with city bureaucracies such as the planning committee, different bureaux (like local departments or committees), and factories owned by the government. The Centre also is able to get accurate information regarding foreign currency appropriation, approvals from superior management, and other government information.

2 The products provided by the manufacturer were to be of advanced quality.
3 The seller was to provide catalogues and samples periodically to facilitate promotion.
4 The Centre was to be responsible for screening engineers to be representatives of the manufacturer. Two candidates were to be chosen with the final selection being made by the manufacturer.
5 The manufacturer was to be responsible for covering all of the expenses for the two representatives' thirty-day 'on-the-job' training in the US at the company's facilities.
6 The Centre was to provide the two representatives, upon their return from training in America, with an office and office facilities such as telex and other equipment.
7 The manufacturer was to pay $5,000 to the Centre for opening the agency, and $10,000 every year to the Centre for business activities.
8 The Centre was to be responsible for providing a written report to the manufacturer including: name lists of the customers visited; their interests in the manufacturer's products; the probability of potential transactions; and post-sale service and support required.

Based on these suggestions, the American side had an attorney prepare a formal 'technical sales representative agreement'. This agency representation was designed mainly made by the vice-manager of the Centre. The vice-manager is the person who is responsible for co-ordinating every one involved in the programme, and for the quarterly report to the manufacturer.

Identifying a reliable person, like this vice-manager, who is familiar with every procedure, responsible, and possesses a key position, is crucial for the establishment of an effective agency programme.

The required foreign currency must be approved by the national level bureaucracy. A relevant technical feasibility study is a prerequisite for the appropriation of the foreign currency. The Tianjin Science & Technology Committee is responsible for the feasibility study and approval, and the Centre is a direct subordinate sector of it. The implication here is the Centre has a much greater likelihood of having the appropriation granted than any other oganization.

Foreign trade corporations are responsible for signing the contract, and any foreign trade business has to be reported to the national level corporations. Due to the existing overlapping foreign trade corporations, sometimes it is confusing to decide which corporation one should go to, and competition sometimes occurs between the FTCs. For example, the import of bearings like this programme can be done through Machinery Import & Export Corporation, or by China Technology Import & Export Co., or by a foreign trade corporation and other related ministries. In a word, the higher the level of administration as the three mentioned, which all are in Beijing, the more red tape involved.

Chinese buying behaviour is so complicated that it is very difficult to list the specific procedures. Even with the listed steps at hand, it is still confusing with all the contingent approaches and the continuously changing situation. Going through a public agent like the Centre and having a very responsible subordinate manager may be a more efficient and effective way for industrial marketers to approach Chinese buyers.

The agency model helps to minimize some of the risk and uncertainty involved in marketing to China. The following techniques available through the agency model function positively in helping both sides in the buyer–seller dyad.

Long distance facilitation

If the seller is interested in a project including a joint-venture, technology transfer, or selling industrial equipment, s/he can send to the Centre his/her catalogue and other related materials.

The Centre will select some enterprises who may be interested in the programme, and transfer the materials to them. After that, the Centre will require a written report from the message receivers which should state: whether this programme can be developed; evaluation on the technology of the potential seller; what are the possibilities of establishing a co-operative relationship, and the relevant qualification of an enterprise; and their requirements for the programme.

After several letters or telecommunications, if both parties are interested in each other, the Centre will help send a letter of invitation and visas to have the potential sellers come to China to meet with the individual enterprise.

If both parties, having had a better understanding of each other after face-to-face communication, believe there are very good possibilities of co-operation with each other, the Centre will use its influence and push to promote and facilitate the business.

Direct interface support

Another approach to getting the sellers and buyers to know each other is to hold a technology exchange conference for the foreign businesses whose products are required by Chinese enterprises. This is a more efficient and effective way for some larger industrial marketers. The Centre will invite all the potential buyers from the entire country to the conference, which can not be achieved by the foreign businesses themselves, nor by their offices (if they have any) in China. Since the Centre has access to all kinds of home businesses and Chinese technicians and other experts, it gets more information and buyer reaction than would the foreigners themselves. The Centre decides the scale of the conference. The Chinese technicians are invited to the conference to evaluate the technology, the Centre may release the news to local or even national mass media. The foreign businesses pay an advertising fee and the administrative expenses for the advertising.

Summary of the agency model

The agency approach to marketing in China has several advantages for industrial marketers. It permits both direct and indirect representation for sellers with buyers. It also provides buyer- and seller-directed facilitation. The key question raised in the agency model is the ability of the agency and its representatives. In describing some of the issues the Tianjin Centre faced and solved, it becomes clear that the agency model can be a powerful tool for Western industrial marketers, if the Chinese representatives are effective business facilitators.

The joint venture model: full partnering with the Chinese to enter the market

Joint ventures have been a popular form of approaching the China market, and have been encouraged by the Chinese to increase direct investment in the market. Joint ventures are investments where both a foreign firm and a domestic partner contribute capital to, manage together, and derive profits from an enterprise. Two forms of joint ventures exist: contractual and equity-based.

Contractual joint ventures are typically service-oriented enterprises which last from five to twenty years. The foreign firm generally gives the technology and cash (foreign exchange currency) to get the project underway. The Chinese domestic partner provides the land, building, workers, materials, and natural resources. The foreign investor receives a predetermined rate of return and constant repayment of principle. After the obligation is fulfilled the domestic partner reaps the rewards of the continuing enterprise. In this form, the foreign investor is just slightly more involved than a typical lender.

Equity joint ventures require both the domestic and foreign partner to invest capital in the enterprise. Each partner provides at least 25 per cent of the capital. The two companies form a new limited liability corporation with themselves as shareholders. The profits are divided by a predetermined agreement which usually is reflected in the shares distribution. The rationale behind forming a limited liability company is so that debts, in the case of failure or adversity, cannot be carried back to the founding companies. In this form of joint venture, there is a finite liability and an infinite return possible to each partner.

Supraseas Corporation provides an excellent example of how a joint venture can be structured and implemented to penetrate the China market. The executive vice president of international operations for a large US industrial and consumer products firm became interested in developing a joint venture between his company and the People's Republic of China. The US corporation, however, was a subsidiary of a European conglomerate which was not interested in the China market. The executive was able to structure a compromise which effectively satisfied all parties – the Chinese, the parent corporation, and himself. The deal enacted between the executive and the parent corporation permitted the lease of corporate patents to the joint venture under an established agreement. The authorization to use the patents was for a five-year period at a nominal fee. By the end of the five-year period, the executive was required to have at least one of the joint venture's plants in China completed and ready to start production. After production began, the joint venture was to pay royalties on the venture's revenues. The executive had full authority to enact the joint venture in the People's Republic as he saw fit.

An international attorney who specializes in Chinese law was brought into the joint venture as a partner on the American side. The executive and this new partner determined that the risk factor of the venture should not be internalized. Instead, to divert personal risk to a legally-responsible entity, they formed a company to represent their interests and be the sole contact with the Chinese government. The formation of this company was the key strategic action that brought the deal together. By forming a separate company to be solely responsible for the risks involved in expansion into China, other companies that had previously thought the risk too high were lured into licensing arrangements with the new company. These companies were guaranteed that they had only their initial investment to lose.

The executive bought the rights to the company name, 'Supraseas' in Hong Kong and established the company there. Supraseas has three separate but interacting functional divisions. No previous joint venture had been structured in this manner. This structure was an important aspect in the company's success (see Appendix 3).

1 *Holding company*: The first division is that of the holding company. The holding company will hold the licenses of the

products which will be produced by the joint venture. The holding company will bear the legal and financial risks associated with introducing the already existing product lines into China. Having the holding company shoulder these risks, the parent companies would not have to formally enter the Chinese market. They could instead record the ventures as one-time profit transactions, a lease of their products to the holding company. According to the executive: 'They [the parent companies] can be unreasonable as they want about their licensing demands (costs), because we will say, "Fine, but we are just going to spread payment over a long period of time."' The executive intends to contact each company which presently holds the technology that is wanted by the joint venture and offer them a no-capital risk foothold in the Chinese market.

2 *Support company*: The second division is that of a support company. This support company is the line operations that supports the technology of the Hong Kong company. It will encompass all of the financial, manufacturing, marketing, administrative, and quality assurance departments. The support group will consist of the people who actually go to the joint ventures' operating location(s) to aid in day-to-day operations. They will be educating the Chinese staff in Western management approaches and production methods. They will represent the foreign firm to the actual plant/factory workers, just as the holding group will represent the foreign partner's interests to the Chinese negotiators.

The staff will consist solely of Hong Kong Chinese, with no expatriates. Hiring only Hong Kong Chinese offers two benefits. The joint venture will save on the $4,000/month apartments and other prohibitive expensive luxuries associated with American and Taiwanese professionals. The Hong Kong Chinese also have the benefit of both speaking and thinking Chinese, while also speaking and thinking English. Since they will be directly interfacing with the Chinese managers and labourers, fluency and understanding of Chinese culture is imperative. In addition, by being employees of Supraseas, they will not be simply third party negotiators/translators.

An executive board, consisting of the founding executive and other partners, will exist. This group will serve as a consulting group and directional leader to the support company.

3 *Development group*: The third and final division of the company is development. The development group is basically another support group, only it is the other side of the support group's activity. Whereas the support group manages and trouble-shoots the existing plants, the development group will plan, develop, and analyze future investment opportunities. They will be the team who will analyse the market/situation/environment in China and develop feasibility plans for both horizontal and vertical expansion. They will co-ordinate the functions of the basic operations.

The support and development division will be run on a cyclic schedule. The group members will be three weeks on location in China and one week out. Provisions for weekend trips to Hong Kong will also be considered.

The joint venture project follows an eight-phase itinerary for setting up operations in China. Each of these phases covers a different aspect of establishing the project. The eight phases do not follow in a chronologically-divided manner. More than one phase may be occurring at the same time. Appendix 4 shows the eight-phase itinerary and the steps involved in each phase.

Summary

At this stage of development, the joint venture looks like it will be successful. Each side is comfortable with the structure and potential profit schedule. The only problem the US partner is concerned about is the uncertainty of the situation. 'Are we really dealing with long-term stability here?' In developing a new business approach, no 'givens' exist. Every factor in the joint venture is an estimate or a guess, and nothing is certain. This is why so much time and effort was spent on the feasibility analysis. The venture was risky, but if everything works as planned, the reward should be tremendous. The founder's partner Lark, and the licensees will have established their claim to one of the world's fastest growing industrial markets.

CONCLUSION

China's industry is focusing on the future and buying new industrial products in addition to modification of existing and out-of-date industrial equipment and technology. If industrial marketers can realize this and develop products that can meet the present needs, China will be a large potential market for Western industrial products manufacturers.

Because of governmental bureaucracy and organizational systems which are not as efficient as those of other developed countries, there are a lot of frustrations and uncertainties in doing business with China. This chapter shows how complicated Chinese industrial buying can be, and presents three solutions to penetrating the China market – the buying group model, the agency model, and the joint venture. These three strategic approaches require different corporate skills and offer varying opportunities for developing buyer–seller relations with the People's Republic of China. Three specific organizational examples were detailed to indicate that each of these approaches is currently being used successfully in the China market.

REFERENCES

Hong, J. (1987) 'The development of the Chinese economy', in *Proceedings of the Third World Advertising Congress*, Beijing: Third World Advertising Congress, 17–18.

Smith, C. R. (1985) *Advertising and Marketing in China*, Hong Kong: The Asia Letter Ltd.

APPENDIX 1. THE 'BUYING GROUP' MODEL

BISCIEC handles the import of equipment, spare parts, instruments, meters and some special raw and semifinished materials for technical revamp and renewal of equipment to meet the needs for the production and scientific research of Benxi Iron & Steel Co.

It handles the negotiation and the signing of a contract concerning co-operative production, co-operative investment and management, compensatory trade and processing of imported materials.

It handles the export of the metallurgical products and

by-products produced by Benxi Iron & Steel Co. and also technical transfer.

ORGANIZATIONS OF BISCIEC

BOARD OF DIRECTORS

GENERAL MANAGER
VICE-GENERAL MANAGER

Export Dept: handling the export of products, equipment produced by Benxi Iron & Steel Co. and technical transfer;

Import Dept: handling the import of equipment, spare parts, instruments and qualified experts for Benxi Iron & Steel Co;

Dept of Foreign Economic Affairs: engaging in technical exchange, use of foreign investment, co-operative investment and management, processing of imported materials, compensatory trade, labour export, contracting foreign projects of Benxi Iron & Steel Co. and also handling the business in special economic and developing zones of China;

Comprehensive Planning Dept: engaging in the business of statistical tables and reports;

Finance Dept: responsible for the setting of foreign exchange and for the payment of foreign insurance, freight incidentals and internal current accounts;

Transport and Store Dept: responsible for the business of transport concerning the import and export of BISCIEC;

Market Conditions Dept: responsible for collecting international market conditions information.

APPENDIX 2. A BRIEF INTRODUCTION TO THE CHINA TIANJIN SCIENTIFIC AND TECHNICAL EXCHANGE CENTRE WITH FOREIGN COUNTRIES (TSTEC)

China Tianjin Scientific and Technical Exchange Centre with Foreign Countries is an organization for science and technology exchange and co-operation with foreign countries on a non-governmental level. It was established in 1980 with the aim to organize and promote exchange and co-operation between the scientific and technological circles in Tianjin and their counterparts in various countries on the basis of friendship, equality and mutual benefit so as to promote science and technology, economic and social developments and the mutual understanding and friendship between the Chinese people and peoples of all other countries.

The main activities of TSTEC are as follows:

1 building a bridge between scientific research institutes, academic societies, higher educational institutions, medical circles, factories, mines and other enterprises in Tianjin and various countries, so as to establish relations or exchange and co-operation in these fields;
2 exchanging scientific and technical personnel with foreign countries for joint research and technology development;
3 handling the business of technical co-operation, including joint design research and development, and handling the business of technical trade, including the transfer of techniques, know-how and patent licenses;
4 handling joint venture affairs, co-operative production, and compensatory trade;
5 inviting foreign specialists and scholars to give lectures and conduct technical symposiums in Tianjin;
6 organizing bilateral conduct, multilateral international science and technology conferences, and public lectures and seminars;
7 organizing specific or comprehensive international exhibitions for exchange of science and technology;
8 organizing overseas visits, study tours, short-term advanced studies, and other academic exchanges by scientific and technical personnel in Tianjin.
9 collecting and displaying catalogues and samples of new products from foreign countries;
10 promoting exchanges of scientific and technical information between science and technology institutions in Tianjin and their foreign counterparts;
11 receiving financial and material support provided by friendly individuals and science and technology communities in various

countries for personnel training and scientific and technical activities for Tianjin;

12 communicating and co-operating with China Science and Technology Exchange Centre and other organizations in scientific and technical exchange with foreign countries in various provinces and municipalities or China, and in carrying out scientific and technical activities.

APPENDIX 3. SUPRASEAS*

HOLDING COMPANY:	
holds licences for the processes which will be processed in China;	*Licences held*:
	Sarah Lee Leonides
carries all financial and legal risks which are associated with international expansion.	Smuckers Guernsey Dell Yoplait
SUPPORT COMPANY:	
aids Chinese factories in many areas of day-to-day operations;	*Support areas*
staff comprises Hong Kong Chinese.	Administrative Finance Manufacturing Marketing Quality assurance
DEVELOPMENT COMPANY:	
plans/develops investment opportunities, co-ordinates five functions of operations;	Administrative Finance Manufacturing Marketing
analyses market situations and environment; develops feasibility plans for	Quality assurance

both horizontal and vertical
expansion.

---

* Ownership: 20% Entrepreneur – International Attorney;
30% Entrepreneur – Executive Vice President;
50% Venture Capital Company.

APPENDIX 4. PROJECT ITINERARY

Phase I

Establish a joint venture agreement:
- licensing contracts;
- feasibility study (required by Chinese government);
- factory sight study.

Phase II

Develop factory plans and equipment layout:
- use US engineers for design;
- hire Hong Kong engineers to understand the layout (for repair and alteration convenience)
  (* inconsistent power flows are a major problem for the joint venture)

Establish Hong Kong financing:
- establish loan agreements (pay back schedule);
- establish bank accounts to operate with.

Phase III

Begin factory construction:
- supervise construction schedule;
- allow plans and construction format to be checked by Hong Kong engineers.

Phase IV

Furnish the factory:
- purchase, plan and layout equipment;
- recondition any equipment requiring assistance.
  (* Phase III and IV occur simultaneously)

Phase V

Employee training:
- bring the Chinese management to the US to learn the company culture and the US methods of management;

– send US management to the PRC to become acquainted with the area and culture.

Phase VI

Secure raw material supplies:

– secure domestic sources;
– secure foreign exchange ratios for foreign materials;
– bring in raw materials.

Phase VII

Shake down equipment:

– debug wiring and other potentially-faulty areas.

Phase VIII

Trial production:

– run for a while;
– prepare to launch marketing campaign.

Chapter Twelve

JAPANESE BUYER–SELLER RELATIONSHIPS

The use of the IMP interaction approach to elucidate the distinctively Japanese features

NIGEL J. HOLDEN

It is tempting to suggest that a significant, and possibly a major redefinition of marketing, is evolving. This development is related to the broad acceptance among marketers that (*a*) marketing is a *social*, just as much as an *economic*, activity; and (*b*) that it is exchange that forms the heart of marketing. But the main impetus is most clearly visible in terms of broad preoccupations in current marketing thinking. We can pinpoint the following examples:

1 dissatisfaction with the four Ps as operationally accurate and conceptually adequate descriptions of the marketing task;
2 awareness of the inapplicability, or, at least, limited applicability, of concepts derived from the consumer behaviour field to descriptions of industrial marketing;
3 misgivings over the status, as distinct from the undisputed importance, of international marketing;
4 increased interest in the historical evolution of marketing and its manifestations in pre-industrial societies;
5 growing extension of marketing principles and practices into 'non-business' areas, such as education, sport, the arts, and charity management;
6 awareness of the 'natural' linkage between marketing, seen as an all-pervasive organizational activity, and concepts (and the practice) of human resource development and total quality management;
7 the emergence of Japan as an international marketing force.

In this chapter we shall be concerned with the last of these factors, precisely because Japan has had such an enormous impact, both direct and indirect, on Western management thinking in general. But before developing the main theme of this contribution, a few words on the contextualization of Japanese marketing as a global phenomenon are appropriate.

A BRIEF CONTEXTUALIZATION OF WESTERN PERCEPTIONS OF JAPANESE MARKETING SINCE THE OIL CRISIS

Until Japan unleashed her massive energies in the 1970s as a direct result of the oil crisis, Japanese marketing practice, and even marketing success, were seen mainly to be associated with American (or American-style) methods. Even if in those 'early days' there were some who thought that the Japanese had merely copied their American business mentors, it rapidly became apparent that what was decisive about Japanese marketing was its *Japanese* character. But one of the problems facing interpreters of the Japanese phenomenon was that no one seemed to know exactly what was Japanese about Japanese marketing.

The West has now spent rather more than a decade writing about Japanese business and management, trying to distil 'the secret of Japanese success', an endeavour made all the more desperate for at least two reasons: first, the speed and ease with which Japan began to dominate the West's 'traditional' markets provoked a general disquiet, all the more so because the Japanese were competing with ominous brilliance 'at the cutting edge of management and technology' (Dower 1986: 316); second, Western theories were not proving themselves capable of explaining the specifically Japanese characteristics of Japanese business and management.

The resulting literature has been, not unreasonably, described as 'considerable, rapidly expanding, but ... of uneven quality' (Abegglen and Stalk 1985: 289). It is in the more unhelpful of these outpourings that we find naive allusions to 'Japan, Inc.' and to what might be termed 'the Samurai theory of Japanese marketing', both of which are largely silly diversions. In the meantime the Japanese have set up their factories in our midst and made Tokyo one of the world's key financial centres. All this has had the effect of putting the issue of Japanese culture even more squarely on the marketer's agenda.

However, the purpose of this chapter is not to discuss the intriguing topic of the impact of Japan on Western marketing thought. This chapter sets itself the task of throwing light on Japanese buyer–seller behaviour by focusing on those aspects which can be said to be distinctively Japanese. This, it is hoped, will be of some value both to marketing theorists and to practitioners, who for differing reasons may wish to come to terms with Japan as the least readily explicable major force in contemporary international business development.

The procedure adopted involves using the major elements and variables of the Interaction Approach and associated model (figure 12.1) as developed by the IMP Group (Hakansson 1982). The choice of the IMP interaction approach for elucidating the nature of Japanese buyer–seller interactions calls for brief explanation.

Preliminary observations on the use of the IMP interaction approach to describe Japanese buyer–seller behaviour

First, the interaction approach is flexible: that is to say, it has shown itself capable of accommodating and stimulating new perspectives on international buyer–seller relationship formation (see Turnbull and Paliwoda 1986). Second, some of the key elements of the interaction approach, such as 'organizational experience' and 'internationalization', involve, in the Japanese context, facets which are peculiar to Japan. A challenge, therefore, is to see to what extent the general approach can adapt itself to such unusual material. Third, this very tentative and experimental attempt to use the interaction approach may prove beneficial to marketers who wish to see it 'tested' in relation to the world's most dynamic, most puzzling, and, incidentally, most tranquil, industrial society. Fourth, one of the preoccupations of the IMP Group and its adherents has been to account for the phenomenon of *psychic* distance within the interaction approach.

It is impossible to study Japan, let alone do business with the Japanese anywhere on this planet, without being conscious of the heavy pall of psychic distance confusing mutual perceptions and interpretations of intentions. Accordingly, there is value in trying to establish the degree to which the IMP interaction

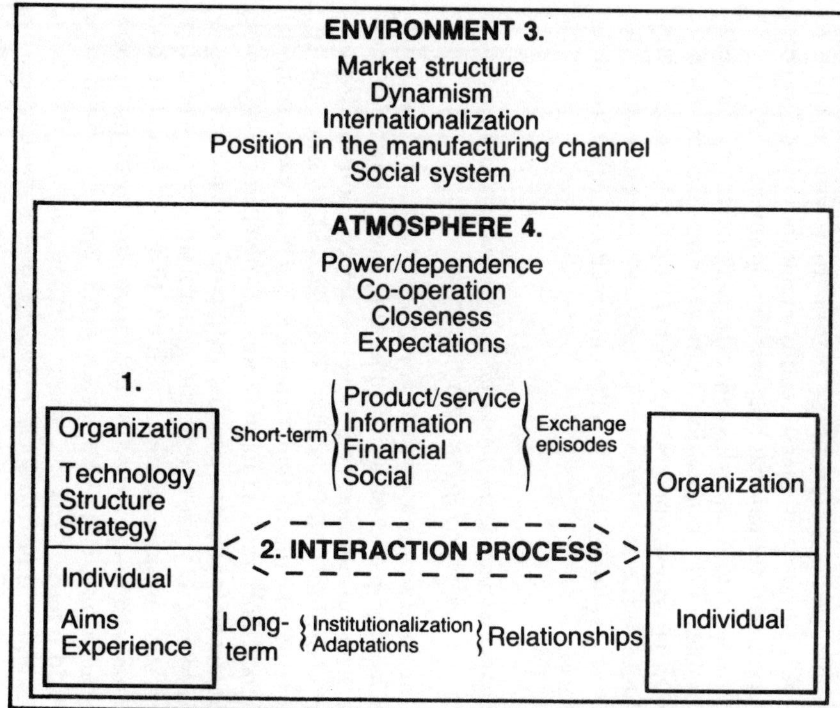

Figure 12.1 Illustration of the IMP interaction model
Source: Hakansson, 1982

approach can provide a framework for elucidating this most complex of issues.

APPLYING THE IMP INTERACTION APPROACH TO JAPAN

The interaction approach isolates groups of variables that influence the scope, scale, and duration of interactions between industrial buyers and sellers: (*a*) the process of interaction; (*b*) the interacting parties; (*c*) the environment; and (*d*) the atmosphere. With each of these variables there is a cluster of associated factors, as figure 12.1 makes clear. These factors will now be discussed in terms of their connotations in the Japanese socio-cultural context. The treatment will be largely thematic in an attempt to convey something of the 'logic of [Japanese] emotion' (Lazer *et al.* 1985), that most specific, yet least accessible aspect of Japanese business life.

Those with special knowledge of Japanese business organization will be only too aware that each of the four main variables mentioned above requires compendious treatment in the Japanese context. It is impossible, in the confines of this chapter, to do justice to all the issues involved; but the approach adopted here, with all its limitations, should make it abundantly clear that, in order to understand Japan, new perspectives *must* be explored.

The interaction process

The IMP approach sees interactions in terms of episodes, which involve exchange processes, and relationships, which pass through various stages until they can be termed 'institutionalized'.

These entire processes are seen as involving adaptations. These exchange processes incorporate four dimensions: product or service; information; financial; and social. This way of conceptualizing episodic interactions and relationship development is valid when applied to Japan, but it is essential to grasp the significance of exchange in the Japanese business context.

Perhaps the most striking feature of exchange in Japan is that it is invariably accompanied by *ceremony*. Witness ritual behaviour such as bowing or the (generally) gracious way in which businessmen exchange visiting cards; note the ornate forms of language which *must* be used in accordance with the hierarchical as well as social distance between people; think of the immense scale of business hospitality (eating in Japan is full of ritual and symbolism), and the lavishness of presents for business associates (Japan has two major gift seasons, which have, as it were, been appropriated zealously by companies for showing consideration to clients and other esteemed people); note too how a Japanese salesman, calling on a customer, would not dream of leaving a set of his brochures unless these were contained in a suitably sized envelope bearing his company name: it would be unthinkable to deposit his brochures in an otherwise unceremonious manner.

It is in fact by dint of ceremony and the associated felicitous language that order can be established and maintained in relationships in a mutually advantageous manner, and that mutual obligations can be harmonized and discharged with appropriate regard for all the niceties. We should note further that ceremony should be seen to be a *necessary* form of stylized behaviour for a people like the Japanese, who are ever at pains to avoid confrontation, and who need therefore to exhibit a polite and appropriately unperturbable exterior, even under adverse circumstances. It should therefore not surprise us that Japanese relationships are developed *on the basis of indirect control.* Furthermore, the mechanism for exercising control is obligation. The idea of control will be discussed under 'atmosphere' below, but a few words about obligation are in order.

In Japanese eyes a relationship without reciprocal obligation is a contradiction in terms; it stands to reason therefore that the longer a relationship, the greater the reciprocal obligation, and the greater the trust. This forms the basis of what has been termed 'relational contracting' (Dore 1986) and its correlate 'relational marketing' (Campbell 1987). Relationships of this type, according to Ronald Dore, 'ramify widely throughout the Japanese economy ... involving a degree of trust and moral obligation going well beyond the minimal requirements of honesty (non-adulteration and false description, no short-weighing, etc.) which apply to spot transactions in the market' (Dore 1986).

By this point it will be apparent that factors such as ceremony, obligation, and the preference for indirectness, give Japanese interaction processes a distinctive mood or quality. But we need to note one other very important element in these processes: it is what the Japanese call 'sincerity', and it is a problematic concept. In European studies of the IMP Group, the highest level of relationship is termed 'institutionalized'. Plainly there is among buyers and suppliers in Japan a drive to achieve this degree of closeness, and for much the same reasons as their European counterparts. But in Japan institutionalization should be seen as an outcome of the degree of sincerity invested mutually in a relationship (the choice of the verb 'invest' is deliberate).

An admirable explanation of 'sincerity' is given by Zimmerman (1985: 74) who writes:

> The Westerner is often puzzled by the Jàpanese use of the word 'sincerity' because to the Japanese sincerity is not open-hearted truthfulness, but a complex amalgam of ideas. The basic theme is that a 'sincere' person is one who fulfils all obligations no matter what and avoids giving offence unless he intends deliberate provocation, or, to put it another way, one who strives for harmony in all relationships and is always careful not to say or do anything without taking into account all the possible consequences of action.

Dore (1986: 77–8) gives an excellent example of sincerity in action: 'When there is a recession and Toyota starts suggesting that they [Toyota's suppliers] should be paid in ninety-day bills instead of sixty-day bills, or that it might begin to take into the home factory much of the work that is sub-contracted out, etc., the only thing that they can rely on is the relation of trust they have, partly with Toyota's purchasing manager as an individual, but more importantly in a corporate and impersonal way with the purchasing department'.

It is sincerity that 'forces' a large company to second its technical experts to small component suppliers to help sort out their quality problems. It is also sincerity which means that a company may purchase from an established supplier even when a cheaper source of equal quality is available. In such common instances sincerity can be said to be a key facilitator of mutually-adaptive corporate behaviour.

The interacting parties

Under 'interacting parties', the IMP Group is concerned with four major elements: (i) technology; (ii) organizational size, structure, and strategy; (iii) organizational experience; and (iv) individuals. As in the section above, the methodology will be to pinpoint the notably Japanese features of the interaction elements.

Technology

The IMP Group see technology as a key issue in the development of relationships between buyers and suppliers in industrial markets. They are interested in how the technological aspects of these relationships influence such matters as (*a*) the requirements for adaptations; (*b*) mutual trust; and (*c*) contact patterns. Applying these concepts to Japan, here is an extra dimension that must be taken into account, namely the Japanese attitude to technology.

With his customary succinctness, Ronald Dore (1986: 216) puts it like this:

> Japan is a society given over to the supreme virtues of science and technology to a greater extent, perhaps, than any society since pre-revolutionary Russia. In Britain we have recently become accustomed to hearing the pundits who seek to exhort the nation to greater competitiveness talking about 'the management of change'. This phrase is difficult to translate into Japanese. The Japanese assumption is that all good management is about change. The emphasis on continuous product and process development is striking.

This latter point coincides neatly with the trenchant observation made by Akio Morita, the founder of the Sony Corporation, that the job of an engineer in Japan is to convert scientific breakthroughs into marketable products (Morita 1987). This in turn fits in well with these comments in a monograph on Japanese innovation (Clark 1985):

> All sorts of surveys suggest that the Japanese enjoy novelty and admire technical invention. They seem prepared to emphasize the good that science can bring society, and to take an optimistic view that the evil consequences of science can be

> limited ... Above all they have *a marked awareness of the commercial significance of science*. [added emphasis]

Furthermore, technological advance is often co-operative in Japan. As Campbell (1987) explains:

> Japanese companies pursue innovation through relational activities with customers, suppliers and company members as well as through indirect relationships with government, research institutes, consultants and universities ... The close relationships with suppliers and customers frequently lead to joint developments. Technical knowledge is pooled to try to find a solution which will benefit both firms.

All of these points clearly suggest that the technological dimension is a major influence in industrial relationships in Japan, all the more so when one takes account of the sheer capacity of firms to (*a*) 'assimilate and deal with new technology' and (*b*) 'move products from development through production into the marketplace at a much more rapid rate than our Western client companies in competition with the kaisha [Japanese company] can' (Abegglen and Stalk 1985).

Organizational size, structure, and strategy

The size of organizations, the power they wield in the marketplace and the strategies they adopt to achieve their objectives all exert a major influence on their interactive behaviour (see also 'Market structure' below). This applies equally in Japan, but three organizational factors should be mentioned which give Japanese interactions a particular character: (*a*) the priority of social over economic goals; (*b*) decision-making; and (*c*) future orientation.

Although Japanese firms are committed to growth as their main economic goal, it is vital not to lose sight of the fact that they also have social goals. Indeed, with the universal insistence in Japanese business on 'human relationships', both internal ones and interorganizational ones, we must recognize that the Japanese operate on a simple principle that might be formulated as follows: 'Solve all the people problems and the economic benefits follow naturally'. This is, of course, in sharp contrast to Western business organizations, which as a rule emphasize the priority of economic goals over social ones (thereby providing a fine living to accountants, a non-profession in Japan).

The second factor relates to Japanese decision-making, one of the great unfathomable characteristics of Japanese firms. Once it is grasped that decisions are seen in Japanese eyes in social rather than economic terms, the logic is very straightforward. A decision cannot be anything else but an establishing of procedures by all concerned for the implementation of actions in which they are to be directly involved. Decisions of this kind take time, patience, and tact, because the objective is to secure harmonious agreement; but it does mean that practically every aspect of a proposed course of action is thoroughly and intensively discussed.

On now to the third distinctive element: future orientation. A striking, yet seemingly not widely appreciated characteristic of Japanese organizations is their preoccupation with the future. This manifests itself as 'a vision-led striving towards long-term business and social goals, whose achievement will not only ensure economic well-being, but also contribute to better harmony and understanding among the peoples of the world' (Holden 1988a: 115). This attribute should not be narrowly associated with the Japanese propensity for long-term planning, whose practical details and operational implementation may involve a relatively small number of people. Future orientation embraces *everyone*: it comes from the fact that in Japanese companies members are (*a*) bonded together through a powerful sense of shared fate and purposeful fellowship; and (*b*) find it easy to identify with the 'natural' fusion of social and economic goals.

Irrespective of the size of organization, these three factors can be seen to be key determinants of structure and highly influential in how firms shape and implement their strategies.

Organizational experience

If it is not too cynical, I would suggest that 'experience' in Western business parlance refers in effect to everything which an individual learns with any number of organizations, and which he or she can, in principle, transfer, often for reasons of self-advancement, to another employer. This is far removed from the Japanese understanding of experience. In Japanese firms experience is directly related to years of service with one's company. It derives from being fully knowledgeable about the entire company system – its visions, philosophies and objectives, on the one hand, and its human and technological capabilities, on the other, all in relation to the product range and to the markets served. In a large company it might take a man up to 15 years to master his company system (Holden 1988b).

This type of mastery is only possible in organizations where the members become widely socialized with *over several years* and identify easily with the company vision, and in which information is freely shared. Japanese companies, which emphasize very heavily the human factor, tend to fulfil these conditions. Thus Japanese companies do not just *have* experience; they cultivate it and mature in it. Furthermore, their experience is a major component not only of their product and service offerings, but also of their overall professional confidence.

Individuals

Whatever their position in a Japanese company, individuals are expected to be sincere in the sense described above. This requires them, among other things, to behave harmoniously in the groups and circles in which they move. This applies to internal as well as external activities.

In the context of buyer–seller relationships the individual plays a vitally important role: he does not just represent his company; he is a living symbol of it. He symbolizes not only the capability of his company, but also its *sincerity*. Because of this, Japanese companies choose with great care individuals charged with responsibility for handling relationships with particular customers. Social skills of the highest order (quite apart from the more obvious forms of functional competence) are called for, and companies will develop these in individuals showing promise and aptitude.

This emphasis on social skills is entirely logical because Japanese firms place great store not just on personal relationships, but also in the way in which they are conducted. It is important to grasp that any organization in Japan will be perceived, by insiders as well as outsiders, as 'a set of people rather than a set of roles' (Sasaki 1984). Thus it is that whenever

Japanese deal with each other in their company guise they are invariably on their best behaviour.

The interaction environment

The interaction environment has five key aspects: (i) market structure; (ii) dynamism; (iii) internationalization; (iv) position in the manufacturing channel; (v) the social system.

Market structure

It is customary to characterize the Japanese economy as having three key features. The first refers to the existence of major industrial groups (or rather groupings) which incorporate a trading company and a bank, all of whom are tightly inter-related through cross-holdings of shares and common directorships (Clark 1979).

The next feature relates to the so-called dual structure of the economy. In the words of Sasaki (1984: 31): 'A few big businesses with high productivity and high wages [co-exist with] numerous and small companies with low productivity and low wages. The latter have been left behind by the progress of the former, and have less advantages in the way of financial supplies and government assistance.' This commentator adds that this dual structure entails important control dimensions as smaller companies become highly dependent on large principals.

The third feature concerns so-called 'lifetime employment'. Although this is a benefit associated with employees of the large groups and companies, it is important to realize that the Japanese, when they join an organization, will tend to expect to remain with it for their working life. This is all part of the Japanese predisposition to identify very easily with any organization of which he or she is invited to become a member. It is, in my view, this capacity to identify which informs the well-known Japanese characteristic to be loyal *and remain loyal* to their company. The obvious structural implication of this is that firms, literally, organize themselves around this 'principle'.

This threefold characterization of the Japanese market structure is, of course, a vast simplification, but in it we can discern some distinctive constraints for inter-organizational relationship-building.

Dynamism

That the Japanese economy is highly dynamic scarcely needs saying. But accounting for its special brand of dynamism is both problematical and contentious. But (at least) two elements can be pinpointed.

The first of these concerns competition. This market factor has been most intense in the added-value and high-technology sectors of the economy, and especially where competitive advantage has focused heavily on quality control and after-sales service. That acute observer, Zimmerman (1985), is of the opinion that these two elements more than any others have been the driving force of Japanese economic growth; and this, in turn, may explain why Japanese firms 'are preoccupied with the activities of their competitors to a degree that is unusual by Western standards' (Abegglen and Stalk 1985: 8). It is as if no Japanese company is satisfied with keeping up with the competition; it wants to be permanently ahead.

This competitive attitude should, incidentally, be seen as part of the general Japanese tendency to see themselves as struggling against overwhelming odds (as represented at any one time by the *totality* of national or international competition). There is a further element of the Japanese attitude to competition, highlighted by Morita of the Sony Corporation (1987: 204): 'In business competition, as fierce as it is, the unwritten understanding of competition for a share of the market is not for a single company to greedily take everything.' Thus, in attempting to understand the dynamics of the Japanese market, we have to take account of the Japanese penchant for what has been strikingly termed 'collusive rivalry' (Johnson 1985) among otherwise directly competing companies.

The second important element of dynamism is to do with networks. The point is well grasped by Campbell (1987), in his discussion of Japanese relational marketing. Its success, he says, 'depends less on a succession of crisply executed programmes and more on the patient welding together of a group of firms who understand each other's requirements. To manage the multitude of links to the external network the firm must work as a team. An internal network must be created to serve and match the evolving external relationships'. For this reason, one of the major operational concerns of Japanese companies is to expand their networks, which serve both as the arteries and contact-making activities and the sensitive antennae of market intelligence.

Internationalization

One of the most striking features of Japanese firms has been their intense global activity. The scale, seeming success, and seeming invincibility of the Japanese tends to blur two inter-connected issues, of whose significance Western companies (and commentators) have limited awareness, and to which investigators of Japanese interactions with foreign markets must pay very careful attention. The Japanese have very complex attitudes to foreigners.

Foreigners, by definition, inhabit parts of the world which differ vastly from Japan, where everything is 'unique' (one gets very bored with references to the unique Japanese language, the unique Japanese management style, or [as I once read] the unique geographical setting of Japan). Two crucial considerations flow from this. First, foreigners, their tastes, their habits, must be very carefully studied: no foreign country can hold to be a mere extension of the 'unique' home market. All this helps explain why Japanese marketing research is so thorough. Second, the Japanese have great problems relating to foreigners, including their own expatriate employees. They suffer from a *communication malaise* (see Wilkinson 1983). No investigation of Japanese business can afford to minimize the impact of these influences.

Position in the manufacturing system

Under this heading the IMP Group is concerned with the status of relationships in the entire spectrum of interactions from primary producer to end-user. In the Japanese context these channel relationships are of key importance. At whatever point a company is along this spectrum, it will be concerned (though 'obsessed' might be a better word) with at least four main factors, all of which are discussed elsewhere in this paper: (*a*) the level and quality of sincerity; (*b*) quality; (*c*) service; and (*d*) innovation (in the widest sense of the word).

The social system

Under 'social system', the IMP Group is concerned with the wider environment surrounding particular relationships. The entire relationship between Japanese society and the business world is formidably complex. In this chapter it has only been possible to make fleeting allusions to important phenomena such as ceremony, obligation, and sincerity, etc. In the context of Japanese marketing interactions, two other social factors do appear to be of special relevance.

The first concerns the Japanese way of handling control in personal – and therefore corporate – relationships. This involves a capacity to exercise discretion *vis-à-vis* those who incur obligations. The Japanese call this capacity 'human feeling' or 'compassion'. It is well worth savouring the insightful words of the leading American scholar of Japanese society, Robert J. Smith (1985: 47), who has observed that this compassionate forbearance, if 'sensitively employed ... blurs abstract hierarcy, permits subtle adjustment and concession, and assures continuity of relationships mutually satisfactory to their participants in an ever-shifting universe of incalculable advantage and sacrifice'.

The second influential social factor with a great impact on the policies and operations of Japanese companies is the seemingly monolithic belief in the value of education. Specifically, education is seen in Japan as a major ingredient of business success. But we should note that in Japan one learns in order to behave in a conformist manner as well as to assimilate facts and figures. To a high degree many Japanese firms, through their training programmes, are merely perpetuating the Japanese tradition of endowing all forms of learning with a special aura.

We would do well to recognize that Japanese companies are normally strongly committed to 'educating' their staff and that staff for their part have a keen desire to learn and apply something new for the good of the company. These points reinforce the view that Japanese firms are 'learning machines' (Holden 1988b: 43–5).

The atmosphere

From the foregoing it will be evident that 'atmosphere' will be a vital condition of close business relationships in the Japanese context. We may assume that in Japan atmosphere derives from (at least) two main elements, which are notionally distinct, but operationally inseparable: sincerity and harmony. As the following short discussion should make clear, both of these elements blend in easily with the IMP attributes of atmosphere: (i) the economic dimension; and (ii) the control dimension.

The economic dimension

The first of these elements stresses that through close interaction various costs can be reduced covering a wide range of joint activities such as distribution, negotiation, as well as pooling technical resources and facilities. The investigations by Campbell (1987) and Dore (1986), alluded to in the section on the interaction process, make it crystal clear that Japanese firms frequently engage in a whole range of collaborative activity. Important as the social, technical and information exchanges are in these processes, Japanese firms will always be looking for economic benefits.

We should, however, note two important facets of this: first, firms will not normally expect short-term economic advantage; second, one firm in the relationship will normally be the active 'helper' of the other. This suggests that the concepts of power and dependence (which the IMP Group subsumes under 'the control dimension') should perhaps be seen more in terms of degree and type of help offered and accepted, with the added consideration that in the Japanese context help implies a complex fusion of preferred expertise and ethical imperatives.

The control dimension

The preceding sentence made clear how the concepts of power and dependence fit into the Japanese frame of reference. We do, however, need to note some other facets of 'control management' in Japanese interactions. The first is the Japanese tendency, mentioned briefly above, to engage in relationships on the basis of indirect control. Here we should bear in mind that *direct* control is seldom necessary between business partners who know, almost with mathematical precision, what their mutual obligations require them to do.

An extremely important facet of Japanese-style indirect control is a corresponding preference for dealing via intermediaries.

A striking example of this phenomenon is Japan's distribution system, which exists, it would seem, not merely to facilitate business in the usual way, but to satisfy the deep-seated Japanese need, manifested at the personal and corporate level, to engage actively in extending social networks for one's firm. The whole vastly complicated system thrives not just on intermediaries, but *on as many intermediaries as possible*; which helps to explain why there are twice as many wholesalers in Japan as in the USA, which has double the population of Japan; and why 'each retail sale made in Japan is preceded by more than twice as many wholesale transactions as is customary in America' (Christopher 1984: 253–4).

It has been pointed out that the Japanese distribution system exemplifies the most dramatic of all differences with Western business. Like every other facet of the Japanese economy, the distribution system must be seen first and foremost in terms of dynamic social interaction, underpinned by cultural and psychological motivations which lie outside normal Western experience of organizational interactions, whether as participants or investigators.

CONCLUSION

Using the main variables and elements of the interaction approach it has proved possible to elucidate facets of Japanese relational marketing behaviour; but what the above treatment suggests most strongly is that the interaction approach cannot be imposed on Japanese interactions without an appreciation of how its variables and associated elements must be reworked or 're-perceived' to take account of Japanese conditions.

This represents a major challenge to IMP Group adherents who might want to investigate buyer–seller relationships involving Japanese partners exclusively. It may indeed be impossible for any non-Japanese to know how much emphasis to place on factors like obligation or sincerity in such relationships, or to determine where the dividing line is to be drawn between economic exchange and social exchange. All in all we need studies of Japanese industrial interactions by *Japanese* scholars who are prepared to apply the IMP Group's approach to Japan.

There is, I would suggest, one area that is crying out for

investigation: networking, a topic which is becoming more and more important to IMP Group scholars (Johanson and Gunnar-Mattsson 1986). In Japan, as this chapter has suggested, networks have a special potency in multifarious internal and external interactions. I, therefore, strongly endorse Campbell's (1987) plea 'for a closer integration of marketing with the study of social networks to provide a powerful new stimulus for research'.

In so far as the material presented in this paper can claim reliability, it is perfectly clear that, when Japanese become involved with non-Japanese organizations, the scope for perceptual mismatch and mutual misinterpretations of intentions is enormous. Given their preference for ceremonious exchange relationships among themselves, it is easy to see why the Japanese tend to regard (some) foreign businessmen as blunt, unsophisticated, and only interested in short-term gain.

But what may not be obvious from the present treatment is that Japanese business behaviour with foreign organizations is strongly influenced by the locale of interaction, that is, whether this is in Japan or in another country. This is a very important complicating factor for *any* study of Japanese interactions with foreigners in general. All these points are to do with what is generally known as 'psychic distance', and it would seem that the interaction approach might be very beneficial in highlighting this factor as it affects industrial relationships with Japan. A team of European and Japanese scholars looking specifically at psychic distance might provide some valuable insights of direct value to European and Japanese firms alike.

At the very beginning of this chapter I referred to the fact that exchange is becoming seen increasingly as forming the heart of marketing. I subsequently suggested that one of the most noticeable features of Japanese marketing is that exchange is accompanied by ceremony. This particular facet of Japanese business behaviour is one that we might easily ignore or be indifferent to on the naive grounds that ceremony has such limited manifestation in Western marketing. But, if, as Kotler *et al.* (1985) say, the Japanese are world-class marketers, then we should surely be looking at the impact of exclusively Japanese marketing factors, such as exchange-ceremony, and attempting to assess their impact in and outside Japan.

As it happens, the IMP interaction approach, which emphasizes empirical, non-normative metholodogies, may well provide a satisfactorily flexible framework for studying Japanese buyer–seller behaviour. The first step must be to isolate the culture-specific elements of Japanese buyer–seller interactions from what might be termed universal elements. That indeed would appear to be a necessary preliminary phase prior to studying Japanese interactions involving non-Japanese participants.

REFERENCES

Abegglen, J. C. and Stalk, G. (1985) *Kaisha: The Japanese Corporation*, New York: Basic Books.

Campbell, N. C. G. (1987) 'Competitive advantage from relational marketing: the Japanese approach, paper presented at the First Conference of the British Academy of Management, University of Warwick, September.

Christopher, R. C. (1984) *The Japanese Mind*, London: Pan Books.

Clark, R. (1979) *The Japanese Company*, New Haven, CT: Yale University Press.

Clark, R. (1984) *Aspects of Japanese Commercial Innovation*, London: The Technical Change Centre.

Dore, R. P. (1986) *Flexible Rigidities: Industrial Policy and Structural Adjustment in the Japanese Economy 1970–80*, London: Athlone Press.

Dower, J. (1986) *War without Mercy: Race and Power in the Pacific War*, London: Faber & Faber.

Hakansson, H. (1982) *International Marketing and Purchasing of Industrial Goods*, Chichester: Wiley.

Holden, N. J. (1988a) *Visioning in Japanese Companies. Creativity and Innovation Handbook*, Manchester: Manchester Business School.

Holden, N. J. (1988b) 'Training Japanese-style', *Executive Development* 1.

Johanson, J. and Gunnar-Mattson, L. (1986) 'International marketing and internationalization process: a network approach', in P. W. Turnbull and S. J. Paliwoda (eds) *Research in International Marketing*, London: Croom Helm.

Kotler, P., Fahey, L. and Jatuspritiak, S. (1985) *The New Competition* Englewood Cliffs, NJ: Prentice Hall.

Lazer, W., Murata, S. and Kosaka, H. (1985) 'Japanese marketing: towards a better understanding', *Journal of Marketing* 49: 69–81.

Morita, A. (1987) *Made in Japan*, London: Collins.

Sasaki, N. (1984) *Management and Industrial Structure in Japan*, Oxford: Pergamon Press.

Smith, R. J. (1985) *Japanese Society: Tradition, Self and the Social Order*, Cambridge: Cambridge University Press.

Turnbull P. W. and Paliwoda, S. J. (1986) *Research in International Marketing*, London: Croom Helm.

Wilkinson, E. (1983) *Japan versus Europe: A History of Misunderstanding*, Harmondsworth: Pelican Books.
Zimmerman, M. (1985) *Dealing with the Japanese*, London: Allen & Unwin.

Part Three

EMPIRICAL STUDIES OF INTERNATIONAL MARKETING THAT ARE INDUSTRY-SPECIFIC

Chapter Thirteen

COMPETITIVENESS THROUGH NETWORKS OF RELATIONSHIPS IN INFORMATION TECHNOLOGY PRODUCT MARKETS

M. T. CUNNINGHAM AND K. CULLIGAN

The research from which this chapter derives has two dominant features. First, it takes as its focus competition and the competitive process within industrial markets. It seeks to answer the question 'How can firms both create and sustain a competitive advantage?' In taking this focus it runs counter to much existing research in the field of 'markets-as-networks'. Earlier studies have tended to highlight the co-operative as opposed to the competitive phenomena within industrial systems. Second, it is being undertaken in emerging information technology (IT) product markets – specifically markets for those interactive communication products known as value-added data services (VADS). From the point of view of 'markets-as-networks', what makes such product areas of particular interest is that some writers (e.g., Miles and Snow 1986) have argued that these are exactly the types of market in which the network form, as one of a range of alternative modes of organization, should be most visible. The argument advanced is that the sophistication of technology, the increasing rate of change of that technology, and the shifting patterns of international trade and competition have strained the ability to cope of traditional organizational forms. As a result, the network form has arisen as an alternative, and by implication a superior, mode of organization.

The objectives of this chapter follow directly from the above. First, it aims to report research into the existence and nature of network forms in IT product markets. Second, it aims to discuss

The authors acknowledge, with gratitude, the financial support provided by the ESRC under the 'Marketing Competitiveness' Initiative to what extent market players can identify and operationalize network concepts in their competitive environment and to what extent these are an influence on strategic action in the search for competitive advantage. Third, it aims to consider the competitive orientations revealed by a markets-as-networks analysis. Finally, it aims to investigate the various types of network and 'networking' opportunities that exist, and the market conditions under which they might be appropriate as unique sources of competitive advantage. In this sense, 'networking' is taken to be a composite of two abilities:

1 the ability to *create* a net of relationships with the potential for cohesive and mutually complementary action;
2 the ability to *harness* the synergistic potential of that net in pursuit of a competitive goal.

METHODOLOGY

The research has concentrated on two particular product types under the general heading of value-added data services. These are respectively, online information services (OIS) and electronic data interchange services (EDI).

For each product type, the research has identified small groups – pairs or trios – of major or representative companies whose orientation to the market-place appears to overlap in a significant way, for example, similar customer sector served, similar customer segment, or similar commercial competence. For firms within these groups, a comprehensive picture of competitive activity has been built up from interview data, secondary sources and expert comment. These company portraits have been supplemented by interview data from corresponding customer groups within the competitor's target markets. In this way, multiple perceptions of competition and the competitive process have been obtained for the product markets under investigation. The sample frame is outlined in Table 13.1.

NETWORKS AND FOCAL NETS

A network may be characterized as sets of two or more exchange relationships between individuals or organizations (Cook and

Table 13.1 Research sample frame

Activities of company	*Information type involved*	*Number of suppliers interviewed (n = 19)*	*Code for supplier firm*	*Number of customers interviewed (n = 16)*
Database provision	Scientific and general commercial	2	P_1, P_2	*
Data dissemination via computer ('hosting')	Scientific and general commercial	2	H_1, H_2	2
Database provision *and* data dissemination via computer	General commercial (market research, news, etc.)	3	PH_1, PH_2, PH_3	5 (for PH_1–PH_5)
	Company credit and financial data	2	PH_4, PH_5	
	Price, stock data etc., for financial services sector	4	PH_6, PH_7, PH_8, PH_9	3
General telecommunications	Not applicable	2	T_1, T_2	6 (for T_1–E_2)
Telecommunications and specific EDI services	Not applicable	4	E_1, E_2, E_3, PH_9	

* *Customers for these databases are indirect, since access is obtained via a 'host' system*

Emerson 1978). The components of exchange within the relationship can include the product or service, information, and financial and social elements, while the specific mix of these elements serves to characterize individual relationships. Consequently, the uniqueness of each network derives from a combination of two factors – the uniqueness of each relationship with its own specific history and dynamic, and the unique combination of several relationships into that network.

Research into networks can be linked with the work of the IMP Group (Hakansson 1982) whose prime focus was customer–supplier relationships in an international context. These vertical customer–supplier relationships were shown to be one important feature of industrial systems but other relational possibilities also exist. In particular, in more recent research Hakansson (1987) has investigated processes of technological co-operation, and has identified competitive and co-operative horizontal forms of relationships. The full range of vertical and horizontal relationships serve to define multiple patterns of interaction among various players within a market.

Clearly, under this interpretation, firms do not exist atomistically, nor act autonomously. Rather they have *direct* relationships with a range of partners – suppliers, customers, competitors, government and non-government agencies – and *indirect* relationships with a further level of partners with whom their direct partners have, in turn, direct relationships (Mattsson 1986).

Within this total network defined by interlinked layers of direct and indirect relationships can be identified one or more *focal nets*. A focal net consists of relations above a certain minimum degree of closeness to a focal or 'hub' firm. The focal net defines the set of most important relationships for that focal firm at any point in time. Membership of such focal nets can change over time as can the relative closeness of the portfolio of relationships within that net. The set of focal nets defines the total network, while the periodic interaction of such nets represents one manifestation of the phenomenon of competition.

The portfolio of relationships within the net represents investments over time for the focal firm (Turnbull and Wilson 1986). These investments can be both tangible, in the form of resources, time and energy or intangible in the form of social symbols (Levy 1957). The pattern of these relational investments serves to define the position of the firm within the net and ultimately within the total network (Mattsson 1985). Micropositions represent relationships with particular partners and macropositions represent the aggregation of individual micropositions. One basic function of the net is to supplement resources, competences and capabilities internal to the firm. Access to such resources, etc., will be conditioned by the structures of power and dependency overlaid upon the net. These structures identify the net as a 'political' concept and point to the contemporaneous existence of both competitive and co-operative elements within the net and within individual relationships. 'Networking' can then be construed as the attempt by the focal firm to create access channels to sources of resources, competence, and capabilities and to manage these access channels, once created. Networking is undertaken in pursuit of one or more competitive goals, and is subject to the constraints imposed by the structure of power and dependency existing within the net over a period of time.

Important to the current research is the belief that the literature concerning 'markets-as-networks' reveals two logically distinct orientations to the subject. The first orientation, largely *descriptive* in flavour, uses the notion of the network as a metaphor for commercial reality. While emphasis is placed on co-operative rather than competitive phenomena, the approach remains essentially an analytical convenience for the understanding of industrial systems. Indeed Thorelli (1986) has argued that in this respect 'network' and 'systems' metaphors are virtually interchangeable. The particular value of the approach, however, is that it allows the application of incisive network concepts – power, dependency, trust, exchange, etc. – to the analysis of corporate behaviour.

The second orientation, *prescriptive* in flavour, argues that the network concept is more than an academic tool. Rather it represents a new and evolving organizational form whose emergence is in direct response to changes in the competitive environment (Miles and Snow 1986). The implications of this orientation are both direct and operational. Specifically, that within particular industries we should expect to observe networks not only as analytical concepts, but also as purposeful organizational forms whose unique competences and capabilities should be consciously harnessed by practising managers.

THE NATURE OF VALUE-ADDED DATA SERVICES (VADS)

Over recent years, many firms have invested heavily in computerized information systems. Increasingly, it has come to be appreciated that information and information requirements are not confined to the boundaries of the organization. Instead, firms are constantly importing and exporting information across their organizational borders. VADS are the vehicles to facilitate this trans-border data flow in the age of computer technology.

What VADS do is allow the cost savings and increased efficiency achievable by the application of computer technology to internal processes to be replicated in the area of external processes. As a result, VADS are perceived to present both an opportunity and a threat to companies within sectoral markets and to national industry in aggregate.

The generic term 'value-added data services' subsumes a range of interactive communication products. In this context 'value-added' has a meaning specific to the communications industry. It implies that the products involve a capability over and above that of simple data conveyance between the two ends of a communication line. In the UK, as in most European countries, basic data conveyance is restricted to a small number of regulated companies. In contrast, the provision of VADS is a legitimate activity for any firm satisfying certain licensing conditions. The research is concerned with two particular product types.

Online information services (OIS)

These provide rapid access to information resident on a central computer which is usually located at some distance from the user's terminal. In the familiar case of travel agents, this information relates to holiday availability and prices. While the use of OIS is well established in particular business sectors – notably travel, financial services, and academic libraries – it has not penetrated deeply areas such as manufacturing or general commerce. Equally, outside the areas of travel and financial services, use of OIS is largely confined to a relatively small number of specialist information science job functions.

Technically, an OIS involves the distribution of information over a telecommunications link between a *host computer* and a user terminal. The user employs a *query language* to interrogate the database residing on the host computer and to retrieve the subset of that database pertinent to his/her information needs. In certain applications there is also a true interactive capability in the sense that the user is able to add to the central database (for example, make a holiday reservation).

Electronic data interchange services (EDI)

These involve the electronic linking of suppliers and customers in an industrial arena into a physical telecommunications network. The physical network is usually provided by a third party service provider, who also supplies computing, maintenance and management facilities to sustain the service's operation.

The service allows the electronic placing of orders and receipt of sales information, invoices, and the like. It both eliminates paper in the system and speeds up the business cycle. For example, a major food retailer might deal with a hundred or more suppliers. An EDI service eliminates the need for such a retailer company to have separate links with each of these suppliers. Rather, each company – suppliers and retailers – has a single electronic link to a central computer, configured as an electronic mailbox. Both the suppliers and the retailer can then address order related documents to the central mailbox. At an appropriate time, the addressee can then access his/her mailbox and retrieve the documents inside.

VADS MARKETS AS NETWORKS OF RELATIONSHIPS

Online information services (OIS)

The market for OIS lends itself very readily to conceptualization as nets of competence enhancing relationships. Four basic competences necessary for the provision of an OIS can be identified:

1 *Database supply*: Some organization must ultimately generate the information to which the user will have access. This supplier may be the primary source for that information (for example, a market research organization) or, more commonly, a secondary source (that is, a publisher or collator).
2 *Data processing*: For electronic dissemination, the database must be 'hosted' on a computer facility. Some facilities involve clusters of immensely powerful mainframe computers. Other commercially viable services rely on half a dozen or fewer, physically-networked personal computers.
3 *Software supply*: The hosted database must be capable of interrogation by the user, and this requires appropriate software. The software may be simple or may incorporate complex data analysis facilities.
4 *Telecommunications*: The host computer and users are linked via a telecommunications line. This may be phone lines

accessed through a modem, the data carrying packet switched network or a variety of private communication channels.

An analysis of commercial activity in the market reveals that different players do have markedly different roles to play. These roles are related to activity in one or more of the discrete competence areas outlined above. In offering an OIS to the market, companies with these discrete competences can be seen to link together in *networks of added value*. The typical pattern of this linked activity is shown in Figure 13.1. The critical points of overlap between competing focal nets are shown in the figure as being at the level of database suppliers and ultimate service users. Database suppliers tend not to have exclusive relationships with hosts, and thus it is common to find several hosts offering

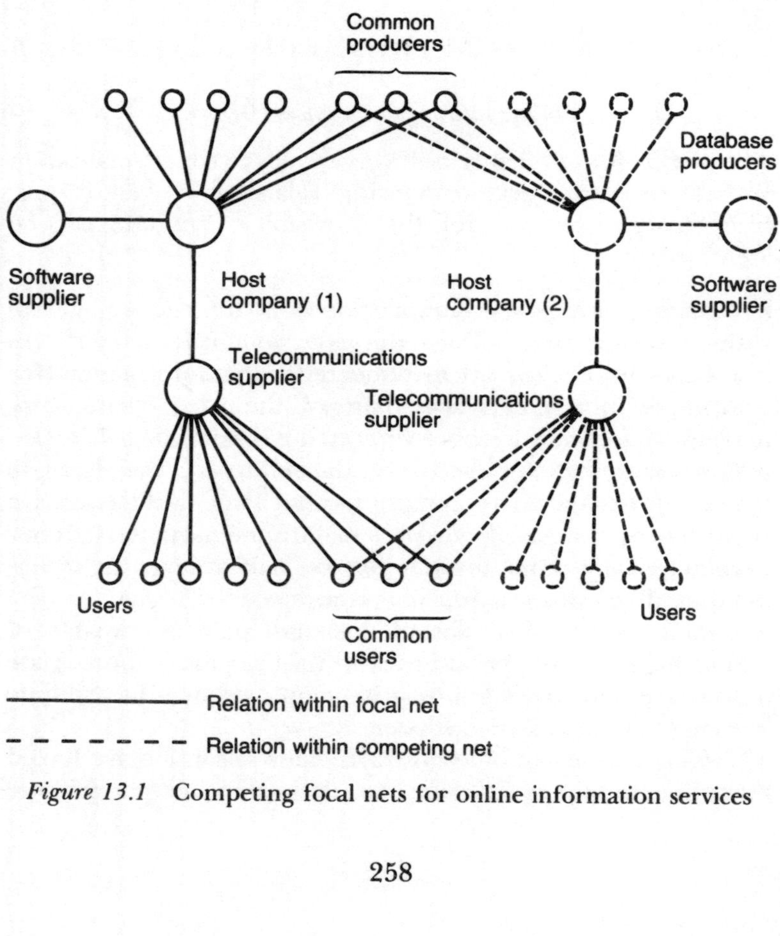

Figure 13.1 Competing focal nets for online information services

the same subset of databases within their total portfolio. At the other end of the net, it is important to appreciate that individual data services are not mutually exclusive in the eyes of the user. Indeed, it is normal to find a functional area within a corporate customer organization having access to several competing services.

The network as an operational concept

The research to date suggests that the network structure has more than analytical validity. While players do not generally use the term 'network' to characterize their competitive environment, they do use recognizable network concepts in such a characterization. Particularly, notions of *competence enhancement, technological co-operation* and *power and dependency structures* are commonly articulated.

Competence enhancement

This is the principal network concept recognized by players. The four competences outlined earlier (database supply, data processing, software, and telecommunications) represent investments in distinct and complex skills and capital resources. While there are players who possess several or all of these, many players concentrate on one or two core competences. Either they have made a conscious strategic choice as to their macroposition within one or more focal nets, or this position has resulted from historical and unplanned incremental adaptations. They then compete within a particular part of the value chain. The network is used as a facility for accessing the additional competences required to convey their output as a total OIS offering to the targetted customer segment. In particular, while there are a small number of large OIS players who have developed their own limited telecommunications networks, the very large investments and specialized competences required to run and manage telecommunications has meant that most players have simply tapped in to existing physical networks. The one major exception to this scheme is provided by prominent providers of real-time information to the financial community.

Table 13.1 shows how the research has stratified the sample to mirror the range of focal competences visible in the OIS market.

Generally, firms regard themselves as either information providers or as electronic disseminators of information. A number of firms possess competence in both areas, but these firms are usually information providers who treat electronic dissemination as one of a range of information publishing activities. Normally, such companies will also supply information to specialist host companies as a means of increasing revenue.

Technological co-operation

The history of the OIS industry reveals that the technology was spawned by project specific collaboration between a small number of major computer systems companies and industrial customers (for example, Lockheed and NASA; SDC and US National Library of Medicine). Now, a great deal of attention is being focused on the development of 'end-user' software. This is software held on the users' personal computer terminal to facilitate database interrogation or complex data analysis. The key skills required are in the areas of artificial intelligence and expert systems. There is evidence of several companies within the OIS industry, particularly those serving the financial services community, establishing relationships with software companies or academic bodies possessing these specialist skills. These relationships are often manifest as financial investments or joint ventures.

Power and dependency

The key to the dynamics of a network structure is the power and dependency structures overlaid upon it and the behaviour of firms to change or capitalize upon it. While the very existence of relationships implies some degree of co-operation, such co-operation does not subvert the competitive goals of the individual partners to that relationship. Thus, the orientation of relationships, the dominant direction of influence and the definition of the 'rules' of the relationship will be determined by the distribution of power dimensions between the partners. Such dimensions include finance, technology, expertise, trust, and legitimacy.

Within the OIS industry, players recognize the differential levels of financial investment and expertise required to develop a competence in each of the four areas outlined earlier. This differential is particularly important at the database supplier/

host interface. While the publishing and data collation skills of the suppliers are deemed to be unique and difficult to imitate, the core computing skills of the hosts are now in the realm of mainstream technology and relatively readily imitated by non-computer specialists. Thus, the balance of power is perceived to lie with the data suppliers and consquently the benefits of the relationship, in terms of the attainment of individual competitive goals, are perceived to accrue predominantly to these same suppliers. In many cases, this power imbalance appears to place a questionmark over the long term viability of host organizations, and highlights how the network itself is an evolving phenomenon.

Electronic data interchange services

The configuration of the *supply* side of the market for EDI is very different to that for OIS. Although it is possible to identify distinct competences which might logically be linked in patterns of added value by the network form, major competence enhancing focal nets (on the *supply* side) are, with one notable exception, not found. The reason for this may be linked to the scale of resources required to compete at any point in the relevant value chain. The companies who do compete are generally major national and multinational players with skills and resources in a diversity of value creating activities. The network concept is, however, still relevant, albeit in a somewhat different form, if we consider the relationship between the supplier and his/her target market.

The object of an EDI service is to map a physical telecommunications network onto the non-physical, relational network pre-existing within a business community. Players use terms such as 'honey-pot' or 'hub-and-spoke' marketing, since the core task is to identify focal nets which are tightly structured around powerful focal firms (Figure 13.2). As with other message carrying products (for example, telephone), commercial success of an EDI service relies upon the establishment of a *critical mass of users* – the very first user can gain no direct benefit from it. Hence for EDI suppliers, the primary application of network concepts relates to their target markets. They must actively search for business communities whose existing relational network structure is conducive to implementation of EDI. The

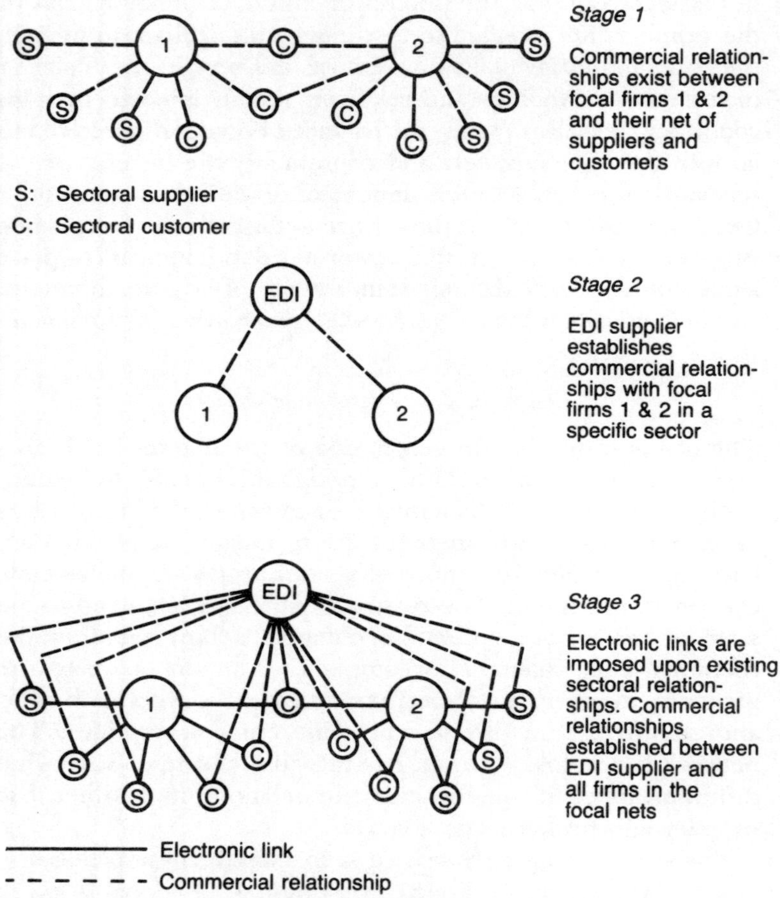

Figure 13.2 The development of the relational overlay net

'ideal' relational network structure within a target market is perceived to consist of a small number of powerful firms whose focal nets consist of a large number of dependent *customers* or *suppliers* – many of whom are *common to several focal nets.* This allows the EDI supplier to concentrate marketing effort on the focal firms and rely on *their* sectoral market power to bring the other net partners onto the service. These direct relationships which constitute indirect relationships to the EDI supplier become a key strategic contingency (Mattsson 1986).

The best example of the successful application of this technique has been in the UK retail sector. Here, a small number of high street retailers dominate relationships with a far larger number of suppliers. The successful conversion of the key retailers to the concept of EDI has thus resulted in the rapid and widespread adoption of the service by a large number of retail players. Of the two major retail users interviewed, one had set a strict deadline for adoption of the service by its own retail suppliers. After that date, suppliers would only be considered for contracts if they possessed an EDI capability.

ORIENTATIONS TO COMPETITION

Competition is a dynamic process involving purposeful rivalry over time. This rivalry may be within or between product markets and may be actual or potential (Littler 1987). Further, competitiveness, the capacity to engage in competition, is a relative term implying a comparative ability with respect to a specified source of rivalry. While network concepts focus on the co-operative features of industrial systems, it is important to bear in mind that competition remains an ultimate driver of corporate behaviour. The notion of the competence enhancement net, identified as a dominant feature of the OIS industry, allows some insights into this interplay between competition and network-based co-operation. In particular, a simple distinction can be made as to whether competition is orientated internally or externally to the net.

Intra-net competition

For a net to exist, there has to be some degree of complementarity between the competitive goals of the relational partners – what Thorelli (1986) has termed *domain consensus*. In general this consensus is unlikely to be complete so that relationships are always tensioned to some degree by the residual goal misalignment. This misalignment is manifest as intra-net competition.

In the OIS industry it has been seen how the distribution of power between the network partners conditions the competitive aspects of the relationships. Of course, social interactions can act as important mediating influences in controlling these competitive forces but are unable to remove them altogether. Given the existence of this competitive element within the net, part of the strategic choice set for the player emerges as the choice of the part of the value chain in which to compete (Jarillo 1988). Ultimately, this choice depends upon an assessment of the power of the focal organization with respect to its potential rivals and a comparative analysis of the competitive costs and benefits associated with one macroposition as opposed to others.

One area of the OIS market where intra-net competition is apparent is that of company credit and financial information provision. Here, six companies are major players, and while each of their offerings is unique to some extent, the core information is largely common. All six companies publish information in printed form. Two companies also host their information themselves, while the other four both host information themselves and provide it to third parties for hosting. Obviously, these six companies have chosen to occupy slightly differentiated macro positions within their focal nets.

Fundamentally, all four companies are to some extent in competition with the third party hosts to which they supply, because their printed products represent an alternative mode of information dissemination to that of the hosts. Moreover, at least one of the suppliers is offering a 'hosting' facility on which is available all the information supplied to the host in its focal net. Obviously such a situation can only be sustained if the business relationship between supplier and host is characterized by a great deal of trust and confidence on both sides. In the specific instance this trust is manifest in an unwritten agreement to segment the market in the terms: '... we know our customers and they [the host] know theirs'.

Extra-net competition

Jarillo (1988) has argued that two criteria must be met in order for the network form to be sustainable. One is an *effectiveness* criterion relating to the achievement of desired ends and the second is an *efficiency* criterion relating to 'satisfaction' achieved by players within the net to the potential satisfaction afforded by alternative organizational forms.

The network form affords the focal firm one mode of attainment of its competitive goals. Indeed, under certain circumstances this form may facilitate the achievement of goals unttainable by other means. Yet, the network also brings with it new modes of competition and may act as an inertial force constraining the deployment of the focal firm's resources in changed strategic directions or in response to transient strategic opportunities. The relevant choice for the market player of 'whether or not to network' depends upon a comparative cost benefit analysis of the merits of being in a particular net as opposed to being outside it. Moreover, this analysis has to be dynamic and future-orientated, recognizing the strategic costs and benefits over the planning time horizon.

In cases where the net is seen to be an appropriate organizational form, three types of externally orientated competition can be identified:

Competition between focal nets in the same product market is the most apparent type of rivalry. In its simplest form it will involve rivalry within an overlapping market segment and competitive advantage will accrue to that firm which has:

1 a focal net whose potential for synergy in respect to providing a relevant product offering is greatest;
2 the necessary 'networking' skills to harness and mobilize these network elements most appropriately.

A second manifestation of this inter-net rivalry is in terms of *competition for network partners*. Focal net membership is not static and a valid mode of competition involves the inducement of relational partners to break their existing ties and form new ties with a rival focal firm. The necessary inducement will involve a demonstration that the macro-positional benefits in the new net outweigh those in the old one. Competitive advantage in this situation can be seen to have both an active and passive element for the rival focal firm. First, it gains an active advantage through its new capacity to access the resources of the transferred partner. Second, it gains a passive advantage by denying access to the resource to its rival. The magnitude of this passive advantage will be dependent upon the extent to which the new relationship is *exclusive* (Bevan 1987).

In fact, the research evidence suggests that exclusive access to sources of database supply is very difficult to obtain. Not only do the specialist host companies, but also their suppliers acknowledge that exclusive access is, in general, desirable for the host organizations. However, to the suppliers the hosts represent simply an alternative distribution mechanism for their information, and so it is generally in their interest to supply the data as widely as possible. In consequence, while there are several examples of suppliers in one focal net being incorporated into a second focal net, this has not resulted in the supplier severing its original relationship. Rather, the supplier has become common to two (or more) focal nets.

Once again, this pattern of relational evolution is conditioned by the power structure of the industry. Since the database supplier is more important to the host than the host is to the database supplier, it is suppliers who largely determine those network structures which are viable. A third form of extra-net competition can also be identified. This involves a more indirect form of rivalry in which competitors are either potential entrants into the focal product market or are suppliers of substitute products. This *competition with external rivals* can often stimulate some form of concerted action not only among players in the same focal net, but also among players in different and otherwise competing nets. The necessary condition for this to occur is that the common external threat is perceived to be more dangerous than the patterns of individual rivalry. Understandably, such 'networks of focal nets' tend to be short-lived and goal specific, but in the case of cartel arrangements they may be persistent and have serious regulatory implications.

Outside the financial sector of the OIS industry there is a common perception that market demand needs to be expanded to include not only the relatively small number of information specialists within industry and commerce, but also the far larger number of managers and non-specialist 'end-users'. In this case the external rivals are print publishers and the 'threat' is the virtual collapse of the OIS industry. So strong and pervasive is this notion of the need to educate the end-user in the benefits of online information (as opposed to the printed substitute) that nineteen rival OIS players co-operated recently in a venture aimed at reaching this potential market. This venture involved a mailshot to 30,000 potential customers, the arrangement of advisory sessions given by independent experts, and the joint presentation of online products within the context of a trade exhibition.

FOCAL NETS AND COMPETITIVE GOALS

The discussion in this chapter has concentrated on the notion of a competence enhancement net as appropriate to the OIS industry. This focus was stimulated by the ready identification of the form by market players. Yet this is only one (albeit important) function of relational nets. Several other functions have been alluded to in the paper and still more can be inferred from analysis of behaviour in the industry. Whilst being a manifestation of inter-organizational co-operation, a focal net is a means for the achievement of a particular competitive goal. In common with other such means, in order for it to be sustainable, the net must satisfy both an effectiveness criterion in terms of being able to achieve a goal, and a relevant efficiency criterion in terms of being able to be a more economical way of achieving the goal than alternative arrangements.

The current research has identified several situations in which organizations appear to be involved in net forms and to employ networking concepts in pursuit of competitive goals. These are summarized in Figure 13.3. This array of network forms are not considered to be mutually exclusive. Rather firms may pursue several related competitive goals at one time and may equally belong simultaneously to more than one net.

Competence enhancement nets

This net form is one that is widely recognized by players interviewed and is the most visible to an external analyst. Competence enhancement is a major driver of the evolution of the network form. In certain markets, the patterns of organizations linked in chains of value-added may be stable and persistent. More often, intra-network tensions and changes in the external environment dictate that networks form, break, and reform in shifting patterns. In the OIS market, internal tensions at the host–supplier interface are causing a change in the existing network pattern. Some host–supplier bonds have been severely

Net goal	*Co-operating partners in net*	*Sample participants*
Competence enhancement	Complementary suppliers	All to varying degrees
Technological development	Establish customers and complementary suppliers	Many – notably E_3
Technological adaptation	Key customers	Many – notably P_2 E_1, E_2, E_3
Value adding	Complementary suppliers	H_1, H_2 E_1, E_2 PH_2, PH_4, PH_5, PH_6, PH_9
Relational overlay	Key customers and their relational partners	E_1, E_2, E_3
Market opening	Competitors and 'honest broker'	E_1, E_2, E_3, T_2
Technology monitoring	Complementary suppliers	PH_7, PH_8
Competitor appraisal	Personal contacts	All

Figure 13.3 Focal nets and competitive goals

strained – if not broken – while at least one major host is now considering the need to acquire data collation and publishing competences, despite the difficulties involved. A further important function of the competence enhancement net may be seen in relation to market entry. In the OIS industry company PH_9 was unique as being an integrated service supplier having competences in three core areas. Yet it cited a seventeen-year relationship with its hardware supplier as a foundation for its success. All PH_9's offerings are based on this one company's hardware and the benefits of the relationship are manifest in the lead which PH_9 has gained over its rivals in digital feed technology, affecting the speed of conveyance of 'real-time' information to users.

The three major competitive features of competence enhancement nets are in gaining first-move advantage, in achieving an internationalization of relationships and in joint venturing with other companies. Firm PH_4 was the first to develop a company information data base suitable for online access and so forged a relationship with the host firm H_1, which possesses the largest installed user base internationally. Firm PH_9 has established relationships with over 100 international trading exchanges to gather data, whilst firm PH_8 cites its recent negotiations to bring equity prices from the Thai Stock Exchange as a competitive coup.

In markets such as EDI, competitive entry costs in terms of resource investments are enormous. Hence, the dominant players are, on the whole, major multinational corporations. In this situation, the network form can provide an entry vehicle for companies unable or unwilling to commit such vast resources to a particular product market area. Within the EDI arena, there is one visible example of such a net, focused on a small 'facilitating' company. This company has links to one company which provides telecommunications expertise, one which provides computing and several which provide software capability. In addition, it has established relations with a major international telecommunications provider and an influential industry and standard-setting body.

Technological development nets

Here the primary focus of the net partners is the enhancement of individual R & D capabilities by access to external technological resources. This has been a notable theme of work by Hakansson (1987) among others.

The principal actors in such nets are likely to be the focal supplier along with innovative customers or suppliers of complementary technologies. Academic or government research bodies may also be important.

These nets may be particularly apparent at the initial stages of development of a new product market as in the case of OIS, where major systems suppliers and their customers collaborated to develop the new technology. At later stages these nets can serve to generate major process innovations, having a fundamental impact on the nature of the market. Many OIS companies are now keen to develop expert systems knowledge with a view to allowing end-users to search databases using 'natural language'. While the very large players have relevant expertise in-house, other players are tapping in to external resources. One example involves a database supplier and its related host co-operating with a research project involving the British Library and London University. The aim is to bring the results of the academic expert system research to commercial fruition.

Technological adaptation nets

While related to technological development, these nets are logically separate in the sense that they are concerned with initial deployment of product developments in the market place. In complex IT markets, even if initial development work does not arise within the context of network relationships, it is unlikely that products can be offered to the market without a period of testing and adaptation in an operational environment. This will involve suppliers working closely with a small number of key customers – often those with whom they have established relationships – in the process of implementation.

The first operational implementation of EDI in a retail environment, for example, involved collaboration between a major focal customer and a supplier for over a year. The supplier and customer had a long established relationship in respect of mainframe computers with the supplier having 'preferred' status.

Value-adding nets

Value-added is in this sense removed from the purely technical. It refers to the general ability of suppliers to link their products to add further commercial value to them. The nature of communications products is such that in many circumstances they can be interconnected relatively easily. Thus, suppliers of private network EDI and electronic mail services are able to link host computer systems to users as a simple value-adding adjunct to their existing value-added services. The hosts themselves benefit by tapping in to the established customer base for the existing network service.

A further example is provided by one of the specialist hosts interviewed. In order to augment its international capabilities it has established electronic links (gateways) with one major US and one major European host. This electronic gateway will allow users to access any of the three hosts directly through the computer system of the UK host. By providing these links, the UK host effectively increases the range of its database offerings, and, hence, adds value in the eyes of the customer. Obviously, such value-adding nets are likely to involve suppliers of complementary products.

Relational overlay net

The dominant feature of the EDI market as opposed to the OIS one is the requirement to overlay a physical communications network upon a pre-existing relational one. The relevant focal net then becomes one linking the EDI supplier to a series of corporate customers via a common major player in the target sector. Relative competitive advantage accrues to those players who can first identify a sectoral community within which the relational potential exists to overlay such a net, and second to those who can 'capture' the major players within the sector. As a means to capturing these key customers, evidence suggests that the role of industry bodies can be crucial.

In both the retail and automotive sectors of the UK, the development of an EDI network by a particular supplier has been catalysed by the recommendation to its members of a powerful industry body. This recommendation has taken the form of 'industry-approved' status for the relevant supplier. Naturally this status has been highly influential in developing the supplier's customer base, but interestingly from the point of view of general competition policy has elevated these suppliers to a position of quasi-monopoly within the particular sector.

Thus, an examination of the initial EDI implementation of the three suppliers E_1, E_2 and E_3 shows that E_1 developed a user base in the retail sector, E_2 in the automotive sector and E_3 in the financial services sector. In each case with the co-operation of a formal or informal trade association or standards body.

The 'capturing' of leading companies or industry bodies is a crucial strategic task for EDI suppliers. Yet ultimate success depends on the rate and extent of adoption of the service by the remaining majority of players. Two factors, the perceived credibility of the service supplier and the influence of organizational change agents appear to be significant determinants of the diffusion of this concept.

Market opening nets

In the early stages of market development, the orientation of competition is likely to be predominantly against substitute technologies. Often, this is a common objective which can be perceived by major players and which can provide a focus for joint action. The purpose of these nets is to stimulate latent demand in a general sense, and consequently they are often referred to as pre-competitive initiatives. Given the basic competitive orientation of the participants, there is often a role for an intermediary organization such as an industry or regulatory body to act as an 'honest broker'. In the VADS market the UK Department of Trade & Industry has taken this role and acted as a co-ordinating body for the VANGUARD initiative. This initiative has been sponsored by all the major VADS providers in an attempt to create awareness and knowledge of VADS in the market place.

Technology monitoring nets

In markets characterized by rapid and frequent technological change it may prove impossible for a focal company to keep abreast of all technological alternatives. Equally, it may prove risky to back one particular technology stream. A coping strategy under these conditions is to forge loose relationships with a variety of 'leading edge' technology companies. These relationships allow some priority access to the technology should it emerge as a dominant type but do not imply commitment on a large scale should the technology fail.

In the financial services sector of the OIS market there is intense competition among specialist software companies to provide analysis packages suitable to the needs of financial players. Software development is both costly and risky since only a small number of packages will subsequently be adopted by the industry on a large sale. While it is important for OIS players to incorporate leading software developments into their product offerings it is risky for them to fully commit themselves to one development in the early stages. Thus, several players have established loose relationships with a string of software companies (up to ninety being claimed by one player) with a view to adopting the dominant design as and when it is determined by market forces.

Competitor appraisal nets

This type of net is somewhat different to the others but is no less important, particularly in evolving or turbulent markets. One of the key tasks of strategic management is competitor appraisal, but authoritative market data is often scarce and published information from competitors uninformative. A key source of competitor information under these circumstances may prove to be the network of personal contacts of the managers involved (Cunningham and Turnbull 1982). These contacts exist over and above the corporate level relationships and act as a constantly updated transmitter of market information.

The role of the personal network in this respect is certainly recognized by the players involved in the VADS market – parts of which are renowned for their obsession with corporate secrecy. Equally important as the contacts on the supply side, are perceived to be personal contacts on the customer side. Since customers are in direct receipt of competitive tenders from a range of suppliers, in times of change and turbulence they are often perceived to be in possession of the most complete information as regards new product developments or strategic reorientations.

SUMMARY

This chapter has investigated the existence and relevance of networks and network concepts in the market for two related information technology services. It has found that in one, the online information services market, the competence enhancement net is a visible and effective organizational form. In the second, the electronic data interchange services market, the most apparent application of network concepts relates, by way of contrast, to the demand side of the market. Here the marketing imperative for suppliers is to identify and tap into a suitable relational net pre-existing within the chosen target sector. The task is then to overlay a physical communications net on to this relational net. While being of interest in its own right, this phenomenon also opens up a new avenue of approach for researchers in the area of industrial market segmentation.

The chapter has also argued that while network forms are necessarily manifest in terms of co-operative relationships, the underlying driver of these relationships is the search for competitive advantage. Consequently, while networking is a valid method of competition with elements outside the focal net, inevitably, competitive forces reside within that net and condition its operation and evolution.

In the light of these competitive orientations an attempt has also been made to set the competence enhancement net in the context of a wider typology of focal nets. Competing firms within the industry are involved in several nets simultaneously to achieve specific and complementary goals. This tentative typology gives an indication of the way in which certain relational behaviour can be interpreted in a goal directed and competitive sense. It is proposed that each net type may be particularly effective under certain market conditions and that each will be characterized by the involvement of particular dominant partners. Future research may refine this typology or widen its application to other product areas.

REFERENCES

Bevan, M. (1987) 'Harnessing the network', unpublished UMIST working paper.

Cook, K. S. and Emerson, R. H. (1978) 'Power, equity, and commitment in exchange networks', American Sociological Review 3: 721–39.

Cunningham, M. T. and Turnbull, P. W. (1982) 'Interorganizational personal contact patterns', in H. Hakansson (ed.) *International Marketing and Purchasing of Industrial Goods*, Chichester: Wiley.

Hakansson, H. (1982) *International Marketing and Purchasing of Industrial Goods*, Chichester: Wiley.

Hakansson, H. (1987) *Industrial Technological Development: A Network Approach*, London: Croom Helm.

Jarillo, J. C. (1988) 'On strategic networks', *Strategic Management Journal* 9: 31–41.

Levy, S. J. (1957) 'Symbols for sale', *Harvard Business Review* 37: 117–19.

Littler, D. A. (1987) 'An approach towards an understanding of the concept of competitiveness', unpublished UMIST working paper, Series A, No. 2.

Mattsson, L. G. (1985) 'An application of a network approach to marketing; changing and defending market position', in N. Dholakia and J. Arndt (eds) *Changing the Course of Marketing: Alternative Paradigms for Widening Marketing Theory: Research in Marketing Supplement 2*, New York: JAI Press.

Mattsson, L. G. (1986) 'Indirect relations in industrial networks: a conceptual analysis of their strategic significance', paper presented at the 3rd IMP Research Seminar on International Marketing, Lyon.

Miles, R. E. and Snow, C. C. (1986) 'Organizations: new concepts for new forms', *California Management Review* 28: 62–73.

Thorelli, H. B. (1986) 'Networks: between markets and hierarchies', *Strategic Management Journal* 7: 37–51.

Turnbull, P. W. and Wilson, D. T. (1986) 'Investing in relationships: strategic alternatives, paper presented at the 3rd IMP Research Seminar on International Marketing, Lyon.

Chapter Fourteen

MARKETING AND PURCHASING OF INDUSTRIAL GOODS

A study of the US commercial aircraft engine industry

CARL R. FREAR AND LYNN E. METCALF

Events over the past fifteen years have brought about a shift in the focus of marketing to the exchange relationship (Bagozzi 1975, Day and Wensley 1983, Hunt 1983). Concurrent with this shift in focus has been the growth in the number of studies conducted, particularly by European scholars, utilizing concepts and models that, collectively, have become known as the interaction approach to organizational buying and business marketing (Hakansson and Ostberg 1975, Hakansson 1982, Turnbull and Valla 1982).

Viewed as an exchange process, business marketing no longer implies a relationship between an active buyer and a passive seller (Spekeman and Stern 1979) nor a relationship between an active seller and a passive buyer (Ryans and Weinberg 1981). Instead, these studies have emphasized the interaction between two active counterparts (Hakansson and Ostberg 1975). With the recognition that both buyer and seller are *active participants* in the exchange process, it becomes possible to conceptualize the dynamic nature of the exchange process, and to identify the factors that lead to long-term relationships between buyers and sellers.

One might ask of what importance this new knowledge is to marketing professionals. Its significance lies in an increasingly competitive global environment. The competitive pressure felt by corporations today is intensifying; not only are they facing fierce competition from well-established firms in fully developed countries, but also from a myriad of 'tigers' located in the newly-industrialized countries. Managing this change in the competitive environment is a challenge of increasing importance to the top management of companies who wish to capitalize on the world market; thus, it is not surprising to see, as a management response to the new international competition, the development of new strategies. A vital part of these new strategies is the role that marketing and purchasing play. Top management, then, in addition to purchasing and marketing professionals, must understand these new roles as well as their impact on the firm's international competitiveness.

Two new strategies which have emerged in response to these market conditions, just-in-time inventory management systems and co-ventures, have tended to contribute to the intensity of the competitive environment by reducing the number of marketing opportunities available. As the costs of development of new products increase, firms, in growing numbers, are forming co-ventures with their suppliers in order to share the burden. Likewise, as manufacturers have reduced their inventory costs by shifting the responsibility back to their suppliers, the suppliers, in turn, have insisted on longer-term contracts as compensation for assuming the risk. There is evidence that both of these strategies have resulted in fewer requests for bids and a reduction in the number of suppliers with which manufacturers deal. According to Porter (1988), General Motors places special emphasis on 'partnership relations' with its suppliers. The traditional adversarial relationship between a buyer and its suppliers, with multiple sourcing and competitive bidding to keep the suppliers competitive, is giving way to one which is more co-operative and long term. Thus, not only must management understand the dynamics of the interaction process between buyer and seller but also they must develop management systems that will nurture long-term relationships.

The purpose of this article is threefold: first, we seek to examine the nature of the interaction process between buyers and sellers in the commercial aircraft engine industry in the United States; second, we will attempt to clarify and operationalize constructs relating to the interaction process; finally, we will present empirical findings that describe the relationships between buyers and sellers in this research setting.

REVIEW OF RELEVANT LITERATURE

Webster and Wind (1972), Sheth (1973), and Choffray and Lilien (1978), have developed models and frameworks within which the myriad of factors affecting organizational buying behaviour could be classified. These models, however, are implicitly unidirectional in focus, in that little attention is paid to the seller's influence on buyer behaviour, and run contrary to contemporary exchange theory and research (Sweeney 1972, Bagozzi 1975, Hakansson 1982, Day and Wensley 1983, Hunt 1983). As a result, there is a shift underway toward exchange models which focus on transactional relationships between buyers and sellers (Hakansson and Ostberg 1975, Bonoma and Wesley 1978, Hakansson 1982, Dwyer *et al.* 1987). Included in these models are elements relating specifically to the interactive process among buyer and seller. It was apparent to the developers of these models that an understanding of organizational buyer–seller relationships could be achieved only through the simultaneous analysis of both the buying and selling sides of the relationship.

Of the models comprising the interactive genre, the interaction model developed by the IMP Group is the most comprehensive (figure 14.1). Building upon the earlier work of Hakansson and Ostberg (1975), the interaction model provides a conceptual framework through which the purchasing–marketing interface may be examined as a whole. Specifically, the IMP interaction model is composed of four groups of variables which both define and influence the interaction between buying and selling organizations: (1) variables describing the organizations and individuals involved; (2) variables describing the elements and process of interaction; (3) variables describing the environment within which the interaction takes place; and (4) variables describing the atmosphere affecting and affected by the interaction.

Wilson and Mummalaneni (1986) note that the IMP interaction model seems to be the best equipped to deal with the various issues pertaining to buyer–seller interaction and relationships; however, they suggest that the constructs set forth in the model require further explication, and that they be operationalized in such a way that allows testing of the model. Furthermore, they suggest that the model be tested extensively,

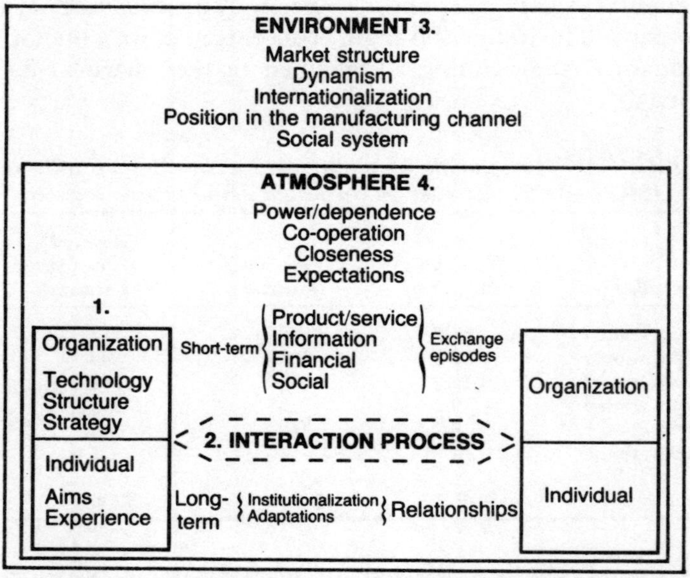

Figure 14.1 An illustration of the IMP interaction model
Source: Hakansson, 1982

especially in non-European settings. Following these suggestions, this article represents an effort to go one step further than previous studies by operationalizing the constructs and applying the IMP interaction model to the commercial aircraft engine industry in the United States.

RESEARCH DESIGN

The environment: the aircraft engine manufacturing industry

The scope of this study was limited to the analysis of manufacturers of commercial aircraft engines. Presently, there are six manufacturers of *commercial* aircraft engines in the United States; all six firms sell internationally. Each of the parent companies of the aircraft engine manufacturers rank among the top 200 in sales as listed in *Forbes* (Baldwin *et al.* 1987). Total sales of the parent companies in 1985 ranged from $4.7 billion to $84 billion (see table 14.1). Furthermore, sales of aircraft engines represent a significant portion of the total sales of each company. The industry is highly concentrated, with the top two companies commanding a combined market share of 85 per cent.

Table 14.1 The buying corporations, Aircraft Engine Industry (SIC Code 3724); sales by corporation and engine segment

Corporation	*Total sales ($ billions)*	*Engine sales ($ millions)*	*Important engine sales ($ millions)*
Corporation 1	83.9	800	100
Corporation 2	28.3	3835	199
Corporation 3	15.0	4560	168.8
Corporation 4	9.1	463	316
Corporation 5	5.7	100	40
Corporation 6	4.7	40	2.6
Totals	$146.7	$9798	$286.4

This industry was selected for several reasons. First, it was necessary to minimize the conceptual differences between firms in order to observe some general patterns of behaviour across similar purchasing or selling situations; each of the manufacturers is a second-tier supplier, selling their products to manufacturers of commercial aircraft. Second, it was necessary to minimize the impact of the external environment on the variables under consideration. This industry is investment intensive and is heavily regulated by the Federal Aviation Administration (FAA). Each manufacturer is subject to the same set of constraints; for example, product introductions, as well as the qualification of suppliers, are subject to FAA approval. In addition to FAA regulations, the present recession in the general aviation market serves as an effective barrier to entry to any potential market entrants. Furthermore, the cost of qualifying numerous sources is prohibitive. Thus, movement within the industry is slight. All of these factors point to an external environment which is extremely stable. As a result, the environmental variable may also be essentially eliminated from the analysis as well. Finally, given the industry coverage in this study, the data represent an enumeration rather than a sample. It was felt that a census would address somewhat the rather problematic characteristic of small sample size which is so common to this type of research.

Fieldwork

A field study was conducted, first, to discover what components were common in the manufacture of all aircraft engines so that the purchase of these products could be examined across all buying organizations and, second, to identify the attributes which were perceived by aircraft engine manufacturers as being important to the component offering. In addition, technical experts in the industry were interviewed as to the relevancy and adequacy of the measurement systems proposed for use in this research. Based on this fieldwork, it was determined that cast parts were purchased by all aircraft engine manufacturers in sufficient quantity and complexity variation to be representative of the different buy classes identified by Robinson and Faris (1967) – straight rebuy, modified rebuy or new task.

Fieldwork similar to that conducted in the aircraft engine manufacturing industry was undertaken in the cast parts industry. The fieldwork undertaken in both industries yielded a consensus that the following attributes were important to the casting offering: level of technical assistance; product quality; product service; product reliability; and timely delivery.

The environment: the cast parts industry

The selling side of the buyer–seller relationship was represented by nine casting manufacturers. Each of the manufacturers of cast parts included in the study must have done business with at least one of the commercial aircraft engine manufacturers. In the same manner as the aircraft engine industry, suppliers of cast parts to the aircraft engine industry are regulated heavily by the FAA. In addition, the Environmental Protection Agency (EPA) imposes strict air quality standards on this industry.

As can be seen in table 14.2, total sales of the parent

organizations of the nine manufacturers of castings ranged from $4.7 billion to $9 million; two of these organizations are included in the 'Forbes 500' (Baldwin *et al.* 1987). Like the aircraft engine manufacturing industry, the aircraft engine casting manufacturing industry is highly concentrated; 85 per cent of the market is held by the three leading manufacturers (all three sell internationally and one is French-owned). However, the industry is also very fragmented, in that there are many small owner-operated firms competing for the remaining share. For major suppliers of large, complex castings, the industry is investment intensive. While these casting manufacturers are third-tier suppliers to the commercial aircraft industry, they do have greater flexibility than the aircraft engine manufacturers since they serve other industries, such as the medical industry, requiring precision parts.

Table 14.2 The selling corporations, investment casting (SIC Code 3360, sand castings (SIC Code 3369) industries; sales by business unit

Corporation	*Total sales ($ millions)*	*Casting SBU sales ($ millions)*	*Casting sales this study ($ thousands)*
Corporation 1	4700	25	117
Corporation 2	2200		
SBU 2_a		50	517
SBU 2_b		55	521
Corporation 3	850	85	120
Corporation 4	140	140	663
Corporation 5	27	14	2
Corporation 6	22	22	657
Corporation 7	11	11	0.4
Corporation 8	9	9	9

Organizational frame

For each cast part specified, the purchasing firms were requested to identify two vendors. Some firms, however, single-sourced their casting requirements. In addition, several vendors were identified by two or more of the aircraft engine manufacturers. The organizational frame of this study, then, was composed of six purchasing organizations (aircraft engine manufacturers) and nine vendor organizations (cast parts manufacturers).

Respondents

The process of key informant selection was conducted as follows. First, contact was made with senior executives in each of the aircraft engine manufacturers. They were asked to designate a purchasing manager, involved with the purchase of castings for aircraft engines, who would be responsible for the co-ordination of the survey within the buying organizations. Second, these purchasing managers were asked to identify decision-makers from other functional areas involved with the purchase of castings. The judgement to interview the decision-makers within the buying centres of each of the six firms was made in accordance with Campbell's suggestion that key informants should occupy roles that make them knowledgeable about the issues being researched (John and Reve 1982). Third, the decision-makers comprising the buying centre of each aircraft engine manufacturer were interviewed on site. Nicosia and Wind (1971) note that understanding organizational buyer behaviour necessitates identifying purchasing activities wherever they are performed.

A similar procedure was followed in the cast parts industry. A senior executive in each of the casting companies identified by the buying organizations was asked to identify the marketing manager responsible for the sale of castings purchased by the buying firm. Then, the marketing managers were asked to identify additional decision makers from other functional areas involved in the sale. These decision-makers in the selling centres were interviewed on site.

Expansion of the interview process in this manner is referred to as snowball or circular interviewing. It is generally acknowledged that snowball interviewing is superior to alternative methods for this type of multiperson research (Wind and Thomas 1982). Sixty-eight members of the buying centres and forty-eight members of the selling centres were so identified. Participating functional areas in both the buying centres are shown in table 14.3. Respondents' experience with their firms, their experience with the purchase or sale of castings and their level of education are shown as well. The individual team members of both the buying and selling organizations have substantial experience and are well educated; however, it appears that the members of the buying centres are better educated than those in the selling centres.

THE INTERACTION PROCESS

Exchange episodes

The episodes which occur in an industrial market relationship involve exchange between buyers and sellers. According to the IMP Group (see Hakansson 1982), these exchange episodes are composed of four elements: (1) product or service exchange; (2) information exchange; (3) financial exchange; and (4) social exchange.

Table 14.3 A frequency distribution showing the respondents functional area of assignment by buyer and seller

	buyers			*sellers*		
Functional area	*No.*	*%*	*Cum. %*	*No.*	*%*	*Cum. %*
Engineering	16	23.5	23.5	13	27.1	27.1
Manufacturing	16	23.5	47.1	9	18.8	45.8
Quality assurance	16	23.5	70.6	12	25.0	70.8
Purchasing	20	29.4	100.0	0	0	70.8
Marketing	0	0	100.0	14	29.2	100.0
Total	**68**	**100.0**	**100.0**	**48**	**100.0**	**100.0**
Experience with company						
Less than one year	2	2.9	2.9	3	6.3	6.3
One to five years	4	5.9	8.8	6	12.5	18.8
Six to ten years	20	29.4	38.2	10	20.8	39.6
Eleven to twenty years	24	35.3	73.5	20	41.7	81.3
Over twenty years	18	26.5	100.0	9	18.8	100.0
Total	**68**	**100.0**	**100.0**	**48**	**100.0**	**100.0**
Experience purchasing castings						
Less than one year	2	2.9	2.9	6	12.5	12.5
One to five years	12	17.6	20.6	8	16.7	29.2
Six to ten years	10	14.7	35.3	8	16.7	45.8
Eleven to twenty years	24	35.3	70.6	11	22.9	68.8
Over twenty years	20	29.4	100.0	15	31.3	100.0
Total	**68**	**100.0**	**100.0**	**48**	**100.0**	**100.0**
Education						
High school graduate	2	2.9	2.9	7	14.6	14.6
Two years college	22	32.4	35.3	16	33.3	47.9
College graduate	18	26.5	61.8	20	41.7	89.6
Graduate degree	26	38.2	100.0	5	10.4	100.0
Total	**68**	**100.0**	**100.0**	**48**	**100.0**	**100.0**

Product and service exchange

Each of the purchasing organizations (aircraft engine manufacturers) were asked to identify two cast parts: one, which was complex in design and/or difficult to cast and that was specifically developed for incorporation into a major aircraft engine; and, another, which was simple in design and/or to cast and that was designed for incorporation into the same engine. The two cast parts selected by each of the aircraft engine manufacturers provided the product focus of this research. The cast parts selected by the purchasing organizations are shown in table 14.4. The price of these cast parts ranged from a low of $3 to a high of $2,012 per part; quantities purchased ranged from a low of 11 to a high of 6,000 units.

The exchange of the product or service is at the core of the exchange process; as a result, the product attributes are likely to have a significant effect on the relationship as a whole (Hakansson 1982). Therefore, the overall essentiality of the castings under consideration and the salient attributes identified by the technical experts in the field work were established as the product exchange variables. A measure of these product exchange variables was derived which mirrors closely the work of previous researchers (Czinkota and Ricks 1981, Johnston and Czinkota 1985). Respondents were asked to evaluate the essentiality of the casting and each of its attributes to the functioning of the aircraft engine on a four-point attribute rating scale as follows. In terms of the success of the engine under consideration in this study, this casting is:

1 neither important nor unimportant;
2 important;
3 very important;
4 absolutely essential.

The variables describing the essentiality of the castings and their attributes and the operationalization of these constructs are shown in table 14.5. In addition, the modal values of essentiality, as perceived by the buyers and sellers separately, are listed. It is apparent that both buyers and sellers perceive the castings to be essential, and that product quality and product reliability are the essential attributes. Buyers and sellers perceive

Table 14.4 A frequency distribution showing products by type, price, and quantity; investment or sand castings

Type	*Amount purchased ($ thousands)*	*Unit price ($)*	*Quantity*
Nozzle	503.0	2012	250
Compressor extension	448.3	2000	111
Casing		1500	335
Power turbine cover	225.0	1500	150
L.P. rotor	17.6	1036	17
Inlet case	117.0	746	150
Carrier assembly	229.0	557	225
			200
Main casing	3.8	337	11
Retainer casing	7.3	30	250
Shroud	516.0	18	5500
			6000
Oil sump cover	3.0	6	500
Cap tube	9.2	4	1840
Dowel plate	6.6	3	1000
			1200

that product service and timely delivery are very important attributes but disagree on the importance of the technical assistance furnished to the buying organization.

Information exchange

A second element exchanged by buying and selling organizations is information. This information exchange construct relates to each partner's perceptions regarding the responsiveness of its counterpart to requests for information as well as the adequacy of and confidence in the technical, delivery, and pricing information exchanged. The operationalization of the various dimensions of the information exchange construct may be seen in table 14.6 which contains the modal values of each variable as perceived by buyers and sellers separately. Without exception, the partners believe that the other is responsive, that the information provided by the other is adequate, and that they have confidence in the validity of the information furnished.

Monetary exchange

Another element exchanged by buying and selling organizations is money. Sales of six of the products under consideration in this

Table 14.5 Product exchange variables

Variable	*Operationalization*	*Buyer mode*	*Seller mode*
Product essentiality	In terms of the success of the engine under consideration in this study, how important do you consider this casting?	4	4
Product quality	In terms of the success of the engine under consideration in this study, how important do you consider the quality of this casting?	4	4
Product reliability	In terms of the success of the engine under consideration in this study, how important do you consider the reliability of this casting?	4	4
Technical assistance	In terms of the success of the engine under consideration in this study, how important do you consider the level of technical assistance furnished by the buyer/seller?	2	3
Product service	In terms of the success of the engine under consideration in this study, how important do you consider the level of product service furnished by the buyer/seller?	3	3
Timely delivery	In terms of the success of the engine under consideration in this study, how important do you consider the timely delivery of this casting?	3	3

Scale = 1: neither important nor unimportant, 2: important, 3: very important, 4: absolutely essential

study exceeded $100,000. It should be noted, however, that this is not the total value of the business between the parties (see table 14.2). As can be seen in table 14.7, operationalization of the monetary exchange construct encompassed the establishment of the price paid by the buying organizations as well as the exchange and adequacy of pricing information. Modal values of each variable as perceived by buyers and sellers are also presented in table 14.7. Buyers and sellers, alike, agree that pricing information is available and adequate and that the establishment of a price is not a problem.

Table 14.6 Information exchange construct and its operationalization

Variable	*Operationalization*	*Buyer mode*	*Seller mode*
Call frequency	Salespersons from buyers/sellers call frequently.	4	4
Request sales calls	Buyer/seller quickly responds to our request for one of their salespersons to call.	4	4
Late quote	Buyer/seller usually takes a long time to answer our request for a quotation.	2	2
Technical documentation	Buyer/seller usually provides technical documentation in substantial detail.	4	4
Technical information	The technical information supplied by the buyer/seller is often inadequate.	2	2
Delivery information	We have considerable difficulty in getting delivery information from the buyer/seller.	2	2
Poor understanding	Buyer/seller generally has a poor understanding of how our company operates.	4	4
Commitments in writing	The bulk of communication with the buyer/seller takes place via letters and written documents.	2	2
Confidence in information	We have full confidence in the information provided to us by the buyer/seller.	4	4

Scale = 1: strongly disagree, 2: disagree, 3: neither agree nor disagree, 4: agree, 5: strongly agree

Table 14.7 Monetary exchange construct and its operationalization

Variable	*Operationalization*	*Buyer mode*	*Seller mode*
Problem with terms	We find a lot of unnecessary problems in establishing terms of payment with the buyer/seller.	2	2
Pricing information	Necessary pricing information is readily available from the buyer/seller.	4	4
Pricing information confidence	The pricing information supplied by buyer/seller is often inadequate.	2	2

Scale = 1: strongly disagree, 2: disagree, 3: neither agree nor disagree, 4: agree, 5: strongly agree

Social exchange

The dimension of social exchange refers to the interpersonal relationships which exist between individual buyers and sellers involved in the exchange process. This social exchange construct relates to overall attitudes toward dealing with one another, whether or not open communication lines are maintained between individual buyers and sellers, as well as whether or not there is mutual understanding with regard to the differences in business practices and mutual trust in business dealings with one another. Table 14.8 contains the operationalization of the various dimensions of this construct and the modal values of buyers' and sellers' perceptions of the social exchange process. Again, buyers and sellers find their dealings with each other to be mutually agreeable.

Relationships: mutual adaptation

This dimension of the interaction process refers to the adaptations which either the buyer or the seller may make in either the elements exchanged or the process of exchange (Hakansson 1982). Of the nine variables comprising this construct, three relate to product adaptations, three relate to adaptations in delivery or inventory procedures, and three relate to adaptations in process. Table 14.9 contains the operationalization of these variables as well as the modal values of buyers' and sellers' perceptions with respect to each of the adaptation dimensions. Overall, the buyers perceived that their vendors were willing generally to change procedures in order to facilitate business with them, were able usually to adjust delivery schedules in order to accommodate their production plans, and were willing generally to make the product adaptations that they requested.

The selling companies, however, in general, did not perceive the buying organizations as being as willing to adapt to their needs as vendors. It appears that the sellers regularly accept that delivery schedules are based upon the buyer's production plans, and that buyers do not take into consideration their production problems in establishing those delivery schedules. In terms of those adaptations relating to process, the sellers perceive there to be little mutuality in the co-ordination of quality control procedures, production plans, or business procedures. Finally,

Table 14.8 Social exchange construct and its operationalization

Variable	*Operationalization*	*Buyer mode*	*Seller mode*
Business practices	Differences in corporate business practices often make it difficult for buyers/sellers to have a close relationship with sellers/buyers.	2	2
Delivery information	We have considerable difficulty in getting delivery information from the buyer/seller.	2	2
Fully informed	We can always trust the buyer/seller to keep us fully informed of any developments that may affect us.	4	4
Mutual trust	Business is usually based on mutual trust rather than legal agreements.	4	4
Understanding problems	The buyer/seller has a good understanding of our problems as seller/buyer.	4	4
Personal contacts	Marketing/purchasing activities by the seller/buyer are usually based upon personal contacts rather than written information.	4	4
Difficult to make friends	It is difficult to make personal friends with salespersons and technical people from the buyer/seller.	2	2
Poor understanding	Buyer/seller generally has a poor understanding of how our company operates.	2	2
Written communication	The bulk of communication with the buyer/seller takes place via letters and written documents.	2	2
Like dealing with them	We like dealing with the buyer/seller.	4	4
Personal contacts	We usually have personal contacts with people in the buyer/seller company.	4	4

Scale = 1: strongly disagree, 2: disagree, 3: neither agree nor disagree; 4: agree, 5: strongly agree

and perhaps, most importantly, we find that, overall, the selling organizations did not believe that the buying firms were willing to consider the product adaptations that they suggested, nor did they believe that the buyers were particularly willing to consider

Table 14.9 Adaptation construct and its operationalization

Variable	*Operationalization*	*Buyer mode*	*Seller mode*
Product adaptation	Buyer/seller is generally willing to make the product adaptations that we require.	4	2
Delivery plan	Buyer/seller readily accepts that deliveries are based on our production plans rather than theirs.	4	2
Local stock	Buyer/seller is usually willing to establish local stock near our plant.	2	2
Joint product development	Buyer/seller is often interested in joint product development activities.	3	2
Change quality control	Buyer/seller is generally ready to change quality control procedures in order to meet our requirements.	4	2
Their product	Buyer/seller is characterized by their persuading us to accept their product rather than analyzing our needs.	2	2
Co-ordinate production	Buyer/seller often suggests that we jointly co-ordinate our production plans.	3	2
Demand delivery	Buyer/seller is willing to respond to a demand-oriented delivery schedule.	4	4
Change procedures	Buyer/seller is generally ready to change procedures in order to facilitate business with us.	4	2

Scale = 1: strongly disagree, 2: disagree, 3: neither agree nor disagree, 4: agree, 5: strongly agree.

their analysis of product needs. A more detailed discussion of the adaptation process is contained in the 'Data analysis' section of this chapter.

The atmosphere

Co-operation/conflict

This construct refers to the extent to which each partner perceives there to be co-operation or conflict present in the exchange relationship. Of the thirteen variables comprising the operationalization of this construct, one is a global measurement of co-operation with the partner and the remaining twelve

Table 14.10 Co-operate/conflict construct and its operationalization

Variable	*Operationalization*	*Buyer mode*	*Seller mode*
Co-operate	It is impossible to co-operate closely with seller/buyer company.	2	1
Irritate	Seller/buyer seems to get irritated by complaints concerning minor weaknesses or problems.	2	2
Product use	Seller/buyer is particularly interested in following up on how its/our products are used.	4	4
Expedite	Seller/buyer usually responds promptly to our expediting efforts.	4	4
Technical solutions	Seller/buyer often wants to offer us new technical solutions.	4	4
Marketing co-operation	Marketing/purchasing people co-operate closely with us.	4	4
Quick complaints	Buyer/seller is quick to handle complaints.	4	4
Excuses	Buyer/seller often gives far-fetched excuses for not delivering on time.	2	2
Request salesperson	Seller/we quickly respond(s) to our/their request for one of their/our sales-persons to call.	4	4
Late quote	Seller/we usually take(s) a long time to answer our/their request for quotation.	2	2
Confidence in information	We have full confidence in the information provided to us by buyer/seller.	4	4
Business practice	Differences in corporate business practices often make it difficult for buyers/sellers to have a close relationship with sellers/buyers	2	2
Understanding problems	Buyer/selle has a good under-standing of our problems as sellers/buyers.	4	4

Scale = 1: strongly disagree, 2: disagree, 3: neither agree nor disagree, 4: agree, 5: strongly agree.

deal with the frequency with which technical and commercial problems arise, the partners' attitudes toward the solution of these problems and the speed of the response by the responsible partner. Table 14.10 contains the operationalization of each of the various dimensions of this construct as well as the modal values reflecting buyers' and sellers' perceptions of how their respective partners deal with these problems.

Power/dependence

The nature of the power/dependence relationship existing between partners was assessed through the examination of the interview transcripts. Discussion with each of the respondents regarding the critical issues surrounding the relationships revealed the existence of both reward and expert bases of power. We shall discuss the impact of the exercise of this power in the 'Data analysis' section following.

DATA ANALYSIS

The constructs developed to assess the exchange episodes, the relationship between buyers and sellers, and the nature of co-operation and/or conflict may be viewed solely in relative terms. As a result, the data were analysed using nonparametric methods as suggested by Siegel (1956). The Mann-Whitney test was used to assess the equality of the distributions for buyers and sellers with regard to product essentiality, monetary exchange, information exchange, social exchange, co-operation/conflict, and adaptation. According to Siegel (1956), the Mann-Whitney test is an excellent alternative to the t-test; the power efficiency approaches 95.5 per cent as n increases.

The characteristics of interacting buying and selling organizations and individuals comprising the buying and selling centres are measured quantitatively, while the market environment and power/dependence relationships are measured in qualitative terms.

Analysis of the interaction process

The exchange episodes

The results of the Mann-Whitney tests for the episode constructs are found in table 14.11. As can be seen, buyers' and sellers' opinions are similar. In addition, no significant differences exist between buyers' and sellers' perceptions regarding

Table 14.11 Results of Mann-Whitney U tests of buyers' and sellers' perceptions of the episode construct

Construct	*Mean rank Buyer n = 68*	*Mean rank Seller n = 48*	*U*	*p*
Product essentiality	56.65	61.13	1506.0	0.46[a]
Product quality	56.73	61.01	1511.5	0.46[a]
Product service	59.23	57.47	1582.5	0.77[a]
Product reliability	57.14	60.43	1539.5	0.56[a]
Timely delivery	59.68	56.83	1552.0	0.62[a]
Monetary exchange	61.73	53.93	1412.5	0.19[a]
Information exchange	58.38	58.67	1624.0	0.96[a]
Social exchange	59.66	56.85	1553.0	0.66[a]

[a] Since p values for these constructs are greater than 0.05, fail to reject H_o and conclude that there is no significant difference between buyers and sellers.

product essentiality or monetary, information, and social exchange.

Mutual adaptation

The results of the Mann-Whitney test for the adaptation construct are found in table 14.12. As indicated, a significant difference was found between the opinions of buyers and sellers. That sellers perceive the buyers to be the less adaptive party in the buyer-seller relationship is interesting to note. In order to gain further insight into the above findings, the mutual adaptation construct was decomposed, and each of the items comprising the scale was examined separately.

The Mann-Whitney test was used to assess the equality of the distributions for buyers and sellers with regard to each of the nine items comprising the adaptation construct; the results are

Table 14.12 Results of Mann-Whitney U tests of buyers' and sellers' perceptions of adaptations' relationship

Construct	*Mean rank Buyer n = 68*	*Seller n = 48*	*U*	*p*
Adaptations	67.96	45.10	989.0	0.00[b]

[b] Since p values for these constructs are less than 0.05, H_o is rejected and conclude that there is a significant difference between buyers' and sellers' perceptions

presented in table 14.13. Perceptions across buyers and sellers are inconsistent over all but two of the nine items. In other words, *mutual* adaptations were present in only two of the nine situations in which they might be expected to occur.

Table 14.13 Results of the Mann-Whitney U tests of buyers' and sellers' perception of variables comprising the mutual adaptation

Variable	*Mean rank* *Buyer* $n = 68$	*Seller* $n = 48$	*U*	*p*
Makes (considers) product adaptations	64.42	50.11	1229.5	0.01[b]
Deliveries based on our production plans	73.68	36.99	599.5	0.00[b]
Establishes (requires establishment of) local stock	66.44	47.25	1092.0	0.00[b]
Interested in joint product development	52.91	66.42	1252.0	0.03[b]
Ready to change quality procedures	64.93	49.39	1194.5	0.01[b]
Designs products based on our needs (willing to consider our analysis of our product needs)	58.91	57.92	1604.0	0.86[a]
Suggests production co-ordination	51.55	68.34	1159.5	0.01[b]
Demand-oriented delivery	57.88	59.39	1589.5	0.80[a]
Willing to change business procedures	67.73	45.43	1004.5	0.00[b]

[a] Since *p* values for these constructs are greater than 0.05, fail to reject H_0 and conclude that there is no significant differences between buyers and sellers.
[b] Since *p* values for these constructs are less than 0.05, H_0 is rejected and conclude that there is a significant difference between buyers and sellers perceptions.

A review of the qualitative data gathered during the interview process sheds additional light on these findings. Two intervening factors become apparent, the first of which is the obvious reward power wielded by the buying organizations. Certainly, the ability to provide monetary rewards for compliance, or, the ability to reward the vendor with the contract for the job, rested with the buying organizations. Furthermore, the very nature of the market structure in the aircraft engine industry adds to the reward power base of the buying organizations. The two largest buyers, in terms of engine sales, command an 85 per cent share of the market; in addition, both of these organizations are divisions of large, financially-sound parent organizations (see table 14.1). Thus, manufacturers of castings who sell to the aircraft engine industry are reliant on a few, very powerful buyers.

Additional interview data suggest that the second factor influencing the perceived level of mutual adaptation present in the buyer–seller relationship is the number and type of technical personnel comprising the buying centres. No only did all six of the buying centres include engineers who specialized in aircraft engine design, but also four of the buying centres included technical personnel who were casting specialists. The range of technological know-how present in the buying centres was far broader than that found in the selling centres; this indicates that the expert power resided, for the most part, with the buying organizations. In interviewing the members of the selling centres, we observed that the technical personnel exhibited an attitude of acquiescence; the perceived lack of adaptation on the part of the buying organizations may reflect this compliant attitude.

Co-operation/conflict

The results of the Mann-Whitney test of the co-operation/conflict construct are contained in table 14.14. No significant differences exist between buyers' and sellers' perceptions regarding the items making up this construct. It appears that there is uniform opinion that the atmosphere surrounding the interaction process among buyers and sellers in this industry is one of co-operation.

Table 14.14 Results of Mann-Whitney U tests of buyers' and sellers' perceptions of the *Atmosphere* constructs

Construct	*Mean rank* *Buyer* $n = 68$	*Seller* $n = 48$	*U*	*p*
Co-operation/conflict	59.94	56.46	1534	0.58[a]

[a] Since p values for these constructs are greater than 0.05, fail to reject H_0 and conclude that there is no significant difference between buyers and sellers.

CONCLUSIONS

The focus of this study has been on the interaction process between buyer and seller. The commercial aircraft engine industry provided the research setting; the organizational frame was composed of manufacturers of commercial aircraft engines and their casting suppliers.

Four areas of the IMP Interaction Model (Hakansson 1982) were defined and analysed: the interaction process, the interacting parties, the interaction environment, and the atmosphere. Operationalizations were developed for the constructs relating to the exchange-episode and long-term-relationship aspects of the interaction process as well as the atmosphere. Relationships between buyers and sellers were measured for these constructs by utilizing the Mann-Whitney test. With the exception of the mutual adaptation construct, both buyers and sellers perceived there to be no significant differences regarding:

1 the essentiality of the product;
2 the attributes of the product;
3 the exchange of monetary information and the establishment of price;
4 the exchange of information;
5 social exchange;
6 the degree of co-operation.

That the buyers' and sellers' perceptions of these constructs are consistent supports the stability and long-term nature of buyer–seller relationships that the IMP interaction model implies.

The lack of agreement in the buyers' and sellers' perceptions regarding mutual adaptations made in either the elements exchanged or the process of exchange may be attributed to two factors. First, the exercise of the expert and reward power by the aircraft engine manufacturing organizations resulted in their vendors perceiving that there was no mutuality in the adaptation process. Second, the adversarial buying practices or general attitude which prevails in purchasing management organizations in the United States may give rise to conflict which is resolved generally by the exercise of power; these practices and attitudes mediate the adaptation process.

Notwithstanding this impediment to close, complex buyer–seller relationships, other factors emerge from the data which support such relationships. Interdependencies found among buyers and sellers included in this study suggest a marketing system that, while complex, is somewhat stable. The very nature of the regulatory environment leads to the interchange of technology between buying and selling organizations and the joining of forces (although predominantly driven by the buying organization) in product development activities are producing long-term institutional integration. They share a mutual strategy of product success; failure of a casting, in some cases, could result in a disastrous engine failure. Hence, both parties invest substantial amounts in pressing the state-of-the-art in casting technology and processes. These findings support Williamson's (1979) notion that, with the presence of transaction-specific investments, buyers and sellers have a vested interest in designing a relationship that has good continuity properties.

Finally, as a measurement of the longevity of the relationship, it is important to note that these firms have been doing business with each other for an average of eighteen years. Without exception, the relationships between buying and selling organizations are long and enduring. The exchange episodes, particularly those dealing with technical information, are frequent and extensive.

IMPLICATIONS

The movement toward the institutionalization of relationships between buyers and sellers tends to restrict market entry and reduce the number of market opportunities available. These trends pose two problems for the marketing firm today. First, the marketing firm must identify its strengths and weaknesses *vis-à-vis* the competition and limit itself to being an efficient counterpart in relationships in which it has a differential advantage; it must bring all of its strenths – technology, know-how, and organization – to bear on serving the needs of those customers. The second problem relates to the identification of the customers with whom these special relationships should be developed and how the long-term issues of power-dependence and co-operation-conflict should be addressed (Hakansson 1982).

Kotler (1984) acknowledges this new role for the marketing organization and concurs with the need to identify key customers which merit relationship management. He recommends that a skilled relationship manager must be assigned to each customer and that the primary responsibility of the relationship manager must be to develop goals and objectives for each relationship. Ford (1981) suggests that, since the relationship manager's overall responsibility is the successful development of the buyer–seller relationship, that individual must be someone of sufficient status to co-ordinate all aspects of the marketing organization's relationships with major customers.

Finally, there are several implications which are important to purchasing and marketing managers. First, buying organizations should consider the product and/or process adaptations suggested by their vendors. In so doing, they may achieve positive gains by making full use of their vendors' unique competencies, facilities and resources. Second, the movement toward institutional integration has a tendency to restrict market opportunities. As a result, buying firms should reconsider their adversarial attitudes toward their suppliers, recognizing that partnerships or co-ventures are more likely to maximize the resources of both firms and, thereby, enable them to meet growing competitive pressures effectively. Third, marketing firms must dispose of their episodal approach to dealing with key customers and strive to develop and manage strong, long-term relationships. The resultant institutionalization of the links between the two organizations should ensure the marketing firm of a place in its chosen niche.

REFERENCES

Anderson, P. F. (1982) 'Marketing, strategic planning, and the theory of the firm, *Journal of Marketing* 46: 15–26.

Bagozzi, R. P. (1975) 'Marketing as exchange', *Journal of Marketing* 39: 32–9.

Baldwin, W. *et al.* (1987) 'The nation's largest companies ranked four ways', *Forbes* 139: 128–328.

Bonoma, T. V. and Wesley, J. J. (1978) 'The social psychology of industrial buying and selling', *Industrial Marketing Management* 17: 213–24.

Choffray, J. and Lilien, G. L. (1978) 'Assessing response to industrial marketing strategy', *Journal of Marketing* 42: 20–31.

Czinkota, M. R. and Ricks, D. A. (1981) 'Export assistance: are we supporting the best programs?', *Columbia Journal of World Business* (Summer): 73–8.

Day, G. S. and Wensley R. (1983) 'Marketing theory with a strategic orientation', *Journal of Marketing* 47: 79–89.

Dwyer, F. R., Schurr, P. H. and Oh, S. (1987) 'Developing buyer–seller relationships', *Journal of Marketing* 51: 11–25.

Ford, I. D. (1981) 'The development of buyer–seller relationships in industrial markets', *European Journal of Marketing* 14: 339–53.

Hakansson, H. and Ostberg, C. (1975) 'Industrial marketing: an organizational problem?', *Industrial Marketing Management* 4: 113–23.

Hakansson, H. (1982) *International Marketing and Purchasing of Industrial Goods*, New York: Wiley.

Hunt, S. D. (1983) 'General theories and the fundamental explanada of marketing', *Journal of Marketing* 47: 9–17.

John, G. and Reve, T. (1982) 'The reliability and validity of key informant data from dyadic relationships in marketing channels', *Journal of Marketing Research* (November): 517–24.

Johnston, W. J. and Czinkota, T. V. (1985) 'Export attitudes of industrial manufacturers', *Industrial Marketing Management* 14: 123–32.

Kotler, P. (1984) *Marketing Management*, Englewood Cliffs, NJ: Prentice-Hall.

Nicosia, F. M. and Wind, Y. (1971) 'Emerging models of organizational buying processes', *Industrial Marketing Management* 6: 353–69.

Porter, D. C. (1986) *Global Sourcing: The Bottom Line*, Glendale, AZ: American Graduate School of International Management.

Robinson, P. J. and Faris, C. W. (1967) *Industrial Buying and Creative Marketing*, Boston, MA: Allyn and Bacon.

Ryans, A. and Weinberg, C. (1981) 'Sales force management: integrating research advances', *California Management Review* 24: 75–89.

Sheth, J. N. (1973) 'A model of industrial buyer behaviour', *Journal of Marketing* 37: 50–6.

Siegel, S. (1956) *Nonparametric Statistics for the Behavioral Sciences*, New York: McGraw-Hill.

Spekman, R. and Stern, L. W. (1979) 'Environmental uncertainty and buying group structure: an empirical investigation', *Journal of Marketing* 43: 52–64.

Sweeney, D. J. (1972) 'Marketing: management technology or social process?', *Journal of Marketing* 36: 3–10.

Turnbull, P. W. and Valla, J. P. (1982) *Strategies for International Industrial Marketing*, London: Croom Helm.

Webster, F. E. and Wind, Y. (1972) 'A general model for understanding organizational buying behaviour', *Journal of Marketing* 36: 12–19.

Williamson, O. E. (1979) 'Transactional cost economics: the government of contractual relations', *Journal of Law and Economics* 22: 232–62.

Wilson, D. T. and Mummalaneni, Y. (1986) 'Bonding and commitment in buyer–seller relationships: a preliminary conceptualization', *Industrial Marketing and Purchasing* 1: 44–58.

Wind, Y. and Thomas, R. J. (1982) 'Conceptual and methodological issues in organizational buying behaviour', *European Journal of Marketing* 14: 239–63.

Chapter Fifteen

MARKETING STRATEGY AND THE METEORIC RISE OF CAPTIVE IMPORTS AMONG THE US BIG THREE AUTOMOTIVE MANUFACTURERS

MARC N. SCHEINMAN

From the perspective of marketing strategy it is clear that the most recent motor vehicle boom in the United States, begun in 1984, has been characterized by an intensification of competition between the US Big Three (Ford, General Motors (GM), and Chrysler) and foreign manufacturers. This competition has not been limited to a simple confrontation between those cars produced domestically by Ford, GM and Chrysler, as opposed to those manufactured in Japan and exported to the United States. On the contrary, the new stage of competition is truly international. For example, American producers have increasingly looked overseas to low-cost producing countries like Mexico and South Korea to furnish them with small, relatively inexpensive subcompact and compact cars, as well as for major automotive parts and components. These 'captive' imports, from their overseas subsidiaries and affiliates, have provided them with critical price advantages against the Japanese, while simultaneously allowing them to focus their American marketing plans on the production of vehicles with much higher profit margins, in more upscale segments such as luxury, intermediate size, and sports cars, as well as minivans and sports utility vehicles. While the Big Three have increased their captive imports since 1984, the Japanese have pursued the very different strategy of establishing new production facilities in the United States to complement their export sales strategy – the so-called 'transplants'. To further complicate matters, there has been a growing number of joint ventures between American and Japanese companies. Finally, there has been a proliferation of new foreign-produced cars like the Hyundai (South Korea), Yugo (Yugoslavia), and Fox (Brazil) that have also increased price competition, among entry-level vehicles.

Contemporary auto analysts have emphasized the growing threat to the Big Three represented by the transplants, and by the enormity of the price pressure, at the low end of the market, exemplified by the recent arrivals from South Korea and Brazil. However, they have ignored the explosive growth in captive imports and auto parts, too, especially from Mexico and South Korea. The significance of these captive imports can hardly be overemphasized, for during the 1984–7 period, when the Japanese aggressively sold more than one million vehicles produced by their transplants, the captive sales of the Big Three *matched* these transplant sales.

Although Ford, GM and Chrysler have been importing vehicles from their Japanese affiliates for two decades, the unprecedented growth in imports from Mexico did not begin until 1984, while those from South Korea started only in 1987. Therefore, one reason that auto analysts have ignored these developments is because they are a relative novelty. We simply have not grown accustomed to identifying lesser developed countries (LDCs) as export platforms for such capital-intensive, high technology products as fully assembled vehicles. A second reason, in the case of Mexico, is that statistical information has proved somewhat difficult to obtain. Whatever the justification, the unparalleled growth of US Big Three retail car sales of Mexican assembled cars – 3,494 per cent, (from 2,575 to 92,540 units) during the 1984–7 period, and more recently, burgeoning imports from South Korea, make it impossible to ignore the increasingly important role of these two LDCs any longer.

The major purposes of this chapter are to examine the import strategies of Chrysler, Ford, and GM since 1984, both from the vantage point of the individual companies and in the aggregate. Although domestically sponsored imports from Japan and South Korea are analysed, too, this article focuses more on the imports of passenger cars from Mexico, the country that has emerged as the fastest growing export platform for the US automakers in the 1984–7 era. In addition, imports of automotive parts will be examined.

DEFINITIONS

Before actually analysing the substantive issues it would be useful to review briefly some definitions of key terms and the reasons why the 1984–7 period was selected for study. The central definition is what precisely captive imports are, and how they are differentiated from the Big Three's imports of cars from their wholly owned foreign subsidiaries.

Technically-speaking, captive, or domestically sponsored, imports are vehicles that American manufacturers import from their foreign affiliates, companies in which they are minority partners in joint ventures. A case in point, is the Chrysler–Mitsubishi relationship, in which Chrysler owns 24 per cent of the Japanese company from which it imports cars exclusively for sale in the US market. However, after importing these Japanese-produced cars from Mitsubishi, Chrysler markets the vehicles under its own nameplates, such as Dodge Colt, Dodge Vista, Plymouth Colt, Plymouth Vista, and Chrysler Conquest.

The badging of these cars with American names serves a critical psychological purpose for the American manufacturers, since it allows them to take advantage of the growing consumer satisfaction with Japanese manufactured vehicles, which it emphasizes in their promotion and advertising campaigns. Yet, although the sale of such cars are recorded among Big Three sales, they are categorized as imports of a special kind – captive or domestically-sponsored – because they are produced specifically at the request of and for the benefit of American companies. And clearly this type of import can be distinguished from those traditional imports that we so readily identify with foreign companies like Honda, in which the US companies have no equity position and, therefore, no influence on Honda's production and marketing programmes as Chrysler has with Mitsubishi's.

On the other hand, conceptually, at least, US retail sales of vehicles assembled in and imported from the Big Three's 100 per cent wholly-owned subsidiaries in Mexico are registered as domestic American sales and not as imports. The primary distinction is based ultimately on the ownership issue, since cars produced at the Canadian subsidiaries of the American manufacturers, but sold in the US market, are also considered domestic sales. If we put the Canadian case aside, because it has been governed by unique bilateral agreements for more than twenty years, then there are compelling analytical reasons to include the sales of cars imported from the American companies' Mexican subsidiaries with their captive imports. This new, more inclusive definition of captive imports enables us to illustrate more precisely and dramatically the startling rate at which US automakers have begun to import cars since 1984, from LDCs like Mexico. However, in the charts below conventional captive import sales are distinguished from those of Mexican subsidiaries, but these two sets of figures are also combined into the larger captive category. Whenever the new captive definition is used *captives* will be italicized in order to avoid confusion.

The selection of the 1984–7 period is predicated on the assumption that 1984 marked a watershed year in which the American auto companies embarked on their new, bold *captive* import strategies, with their Mexican subsidiaries and Japanese affiliates, while it was also the same year in which Honda, Toyota, and Nissan began to establish their transplants in the United States. In addition, given the fact that both of these strategies have accelerated throughout the period and into 1988 it is clear that the *captive* import strategy will increase in importance in the immediate future as the most effective marketing strategy by which to neutralize further Japanese penetration of the US market, particularly in the small car segments that are highly price sensitive.

THE INTENSIFICATION OF FOREIGN COMPETITION IN THE US CAR MARKET

The Japanese and voluntary restraint agreements

From 1979 to 1982 the Big Three recognized unmistakably that American consumers had changed their car tastes and preferences in response to spiralling gasoline prices and deep recession. While Chrysler, Ford, and GM constructed new platforms to down-size their cars, they lost considerable market share to the Japanese, largely as a result of a $1,000–1,500 cost advantage in producing small vehicles, and the growing perception among US car buyers that Japanese products were superior to those manufactured in the United States.

At the beginning of the Second Oil Shock in 1978–9, imports comprised only 17.7 per cent of US retail car sales, but four years later that figure soared to 27.9 per cent, as more than four out of every five foreign cars sold here were manufactured in Japan, being small and fuel-efficient vehicles. During Detroit's three worst years (1980–2) the Big Three lost a combined total of $6.2 billion; total retail sales (domestic plus imports) averaged only 8.5 million cars annually, as opposed to the much higher 10.8 million level that prevailed during the preceding four years.

In response to the rapidly increasing Japanese penetration of the US market, exclusively through exports, top American government officials lobbied vigorously with their Japanese counterparts, on behalf of the Big Three. The most immediate and far-reaching consequence of these negotiations was the acceptance of Voluntary Restraint Agreements (VRAs), under which the Japanese agreed to limit their car exports to the United States for four years, 1981–4; each manufacturer was allotted a specified quota that could not be exceeded. While the quotas were in force it was hoped that the American automakers could narrow, if not eliminate, the Japanese cost advantage.

In spite of the expiration of the original VRAs, and the decision by the Reagan Administration in March 1985 not to request their renewal, the Japanese have continued to limit their exports voluntarily to the United States. The rationale for sustaining these quotas has been based on the fear that a rising protectionist sentiment in the US Congress could produce even stricter legislation, in the absence of such self-imposed restraints. Whatever the intent, at least one result of the quotas is unequivocal – they have reduced significantly the growth rate of US car imports from Japan. For example, from 1981–7 imports from Japan only increased 3 per cent annually, from 1.9 to 2.2 million cars. Yet, if the number of captives imported by the Big Three were factored out, then the growth rate would be still lower, at 1.6 per cent. By contrast, during the previous six years

(1974–80), the rate of growth was a startling 51.3 per cent – before the establishment of the VRAs. Even if the captive imports were eliminated, the growth rate was an impressive 36.7 per cent per year, or approximately twenty-three times faster than in the subsequent period covered by quotas. In order to compensate for these export restrictions, the Japanese manufacturers have responded by greatly increasing the value of the cars that they export to the United States through providing additional componentry and new, up-scale models, such as the Acura. Also, it is obvious that the launching of an aggressive transplant strategy was designed to increase Japanese market share, while simultaneously avoiding the political turmoil associated with imports.

Detroit's reponse 1984–7: captive imports

1983 was the first year of Detroit's remarkable recovery from the Second Oil Shock and severe Japanese import penetration; in this year the Big Three returned to profitability, as GM, Ford, and Chrysler earned a combined total of almost $6.3 billion. In addition, car sales in the United States grew an impressive 15 per cent over 1982's figures. The recovery persists today, in its sixth year, but the rate of growth slowed somewhat in 1987.

From 1984 to 1987 new car sales averaged near-record levels for a four-year period – 10.8 million cars, annually, a solid 27.1 per cent increase over the depressed 1980–2 levels. However, this growth was distributed very unevenly between domestically-produced and imported vehicles. For instance, while overall sales increased more than 10 per cent between 1984 and 1986, before declining in 1987, domestic car sales plummeted 11 per cent throughout the 1984–7 period. On the other hand, imported car sales increased by 31 per cent, but those from Japan grew by only 15 per cent – six times slower than imports from other countries. Nevertheless, in spite of this slower growth, relative to other countries, imports from Japan accounted for almost three out of every four imported car sales, from 1984 to 1987.

Before examining the recent explosive growth in American *captive* imports from Mexico and South Korea, in particular, it is crucial to analyse the nature of the Japanese imports, further, because it is clear that most of the recent increases in these imports stem from captives of the US Big Three *not* from the imports of Japanese nameplates, such as Honda, Nissan. As table 15.1 below indicates captive import sales of Chrysler and GM increased at the unprecedented rate of 148.1 per cent for the 1984–7 period – twenty times faster than those cars imported under Japanese nameplates, which increased by only 7.3 per cent.

Table 15.1 US retail sales of cars imported from Japan 1984–7 (thousands of units)

Year	*US captives*	*Japanese nameplates*	*Total Japanese imports*
1987	258	1934	2192
1986	296	2087	2383
1985	190	2028	2218
1984	104	1803	1906

This tremendous growth in captive imports from Japan was accounted for by only two of the Big Three – Chrysler and GM, both of whom imported relatively small cars from their joint venture affiliates. Chrysler, the smallest American automaker, was the pioneer in the captive strategy. As early as 1984 Chrysler imported 90,882 Conquests, Vistas, and Colts from Mitsubishi, and by 1987 had increased this figure by 32.4 per cent, to 120,337 vehicles.

By contrast, GM was much slower in launching similar arrangements with its two Japanese affiliates, Isuzu and Suzuki, from which it imports Spectrums and Sprints, respectively. However, GM's captive programme has grown much faster than Chrysler's, and currently has surpassed it. In 1984 GM imported and sold only 13,000 cars from Isuzu and Suzuki, but by the end of 1987 this number had increased to 137,211 cars, a growth rate of an astounding 955.1 per cent.

To date, Ford imports no captives from Japan and has no immediate plans to establish such a programme. The keys to Chrysler and GM's captive import strategies are rooted in the existence of the VRA quotas. Since Honda, Toyota, and Nissan, the largest and most powerful Japanese companies have tended to dominate the quota allotments and have eschewed foreign participation, the American companies have been able to achieve captive programmes only with less powerful firms like Mitsubishi, Isuzu and Suzuki. And it is important to emphasize the fact that the captive imports of Chrysler and GM utilize about 12 per cent of their Japanese partners' export quotas for the US market.

If these captives from Japan appear to have spurred the pervasive import penetration in the US market during the 1984–7 period, a closer examination reveals that the fastest growing sources of imports were Mexico and South Korea, but these two countries got belated starts. For example, in 1984 Japan accounted for almost 86 per cent of total American *captives*, or approximately 104,000 cars, while imports from Mexico totalled only about 4,000. In 1984 American automakers did not import a single car from South Korea. Three years later, however, at the end of 1987, Japan's share of US *captives* dropped almost 30 per cent, to 58 per cent of the 440,694 total. By comparison, imports from Mexico now represent almost 23 per cent, and, after only one year, South Korea gained a 14 per cent share.

MEXICO'S EMERGENCE AS AN EXPORT PLATFORM FOR THE BIG THREE

Sales in the Mexican auto industry: from local to export markets

The emergence of Mexico as a significant export platform for the US Big Three car manufacturers began modestly in 1983–4, before Chrysler, Ford and GM had time to implement the bold programmes that are now in place. The role as an exporter was entirely new for Mexico, since the auto industry had always been domestically driven. During the end of the last decade, six of the world's leading car manufacturers – Volkswagen, Nissan, Renault/American Motors, Chrysler, Ford, and General Motors – all rapidly increased their Mexican marketing and manufacturing operations in order to meet the growing local demand.

From 1978 to 1981 Mexico's average yearly growth in gross domestic product (GDP) was 8.4 per cent, the fastest among Latin American's major industrializing countries, and this boom, largely the result of increasing international prices for its leading export, oil, was reflected in higher living standards and enormous gains in new car purchases. During this period, Mexican sales zoomed 50 per cent, from 226,587 to 340,363 vehicles. At the conclusion of 1981, the peak year, domestic sales accounted for almost 97 per cent of all cars sold, while the remaining 3 per cent, or 9,296 vehicles were sold abroad. Of the six manufacturers, only Volkswagen had a strong programme that produced 99 per cent of these Mexican exports. In 1981 no US manufacturer exported a single car; on the contrary, all of the Big Three's autos were consumed in the domestic market.

Six years later, at the end of 1987, the situation changed drastically. Sustained economic growth was transformed into deep recession, as yearly inflation averaged more than 100 per cent; and during four of the six years the economy experienced negative growth. Not unexpectedly, this severe contraction caused car sales to hit decade lows. However, the depression in domestic auto sales also created the very conditions that have resulted in an unprecedented export boom. Yet, as Donald Peterson, the Ford Chairman, observed, the major automakers in Mexico lost a combined total of $1.5 billion during the first five years of the crisis, 1982–6.

If the Mexican car industry in the late 1970s and early 1980s was driven by an expansive economy in which exports were virtually non-existent, then the recession reversed this scenario. By 1987, exports accounted for 45 per cent of total sales, or 123,955 vehicles, an extraordinary increase of 2234 per cent over 1981's figures. In sharp contrast, domestic sales declined by 55 per cent throughout the same period (from 340,363 to 154,152).

The transformation of the Mexican auto industry into one spurred by exports has been led by the American manfucturers, the three of whom dominated approximately 92 per cent of all cars exported from Mexico in 1987. Almost all of these vehicles were shipped to and sold in the United States. Volkswagen, the 1981 export leader, not only relinquished that position, but placed last in exports among the leading car manufacturers operating in Mexico in 1987. For the year, Ford was the leader with 41.8 per cent of export sales, Chrysler placed second with 33.1 per cent and GM third with 16.7 per cent. Volkswagen's export sales represented less than 1 per cent of the market that it had literally monopolized until 1985.

As recently as three years earlier, in 1984, only Chrysler exported autos, although GM did export pick-up trucks to the United States. However, in 1984 Chrysler held a 29.7 per cent share of the export car market, good for second place, behind the perennial leader Volkswagen's commanding 67.2 per cent share. Yet, perhaps the most astounding turnaround for the US Big Three in 1987 was the fact that for every ten cars sold, about seven were exported. Only three years earlier eight of ten were sold in the domestic market, while in 1981 all ten were consumed locally.

From the perspective of the dollar value of the Mexican exports, as opposed to units, 1987 was the Big Three's best year too, as car exports totalled about $1.2 billion to the United States alone; two years before, in 1985, with only Chrysler exporting cars, this figure was just $110 million. As significant as this achievement appears it is magnified further if it is examined in terms of the volatile changes in the Mexican economy during the 1984–7 period, and the radical restructuring of the sales/marketing and production strategies that these changes forced the Big Three to make quickly.

Table 15.2 illustrates how Chrysler, Ford and General Motors completely reorganized their sales efforts in favour of exports to overcome the depression in the domestic market and enable them to sell 22 per cent more cars than ever before, which is to say that combined 1987 export and domestic sales exceeded the Big Three's unit sales in 1981, the previous peak year, which was based entirely on domestic consumption in a booming economy.

Data through the first six months of 1988 indicate that the Mexican export boom is continuing to accelerate – by 18 per cent over the same period in 1987 for the Big Three (63,858 cars vs 54,058, respectively).

In retrospect, these changes in strategy transformed the Big Three's Mexican subsidiaries into the fastest growing foreign suppliers of US retail car sales for Ford, Chrysler, and General Motors (*captive* imports). In 1987, 82 per cent of the 113,520 cars exported from their Mexican operations – 92,540 – were sold in the American market; and during the 1984–7 period US retail sales of these Mexican *captives* increased an astronomical

Table 15.2 Total US Big Three Mexican car 2 sales (domestic and export), 1981, 1984, 1987

Company	*1987*	*Percentage of sales*	*1984*	*Percentage of sales*	*1981*	
Ford						
Export	51,773	75.8	0	0	0	0
Domestic	16,524	24.2	28,861	100	53,365	100
TOTAL	68,297	100.0	28,861	100	53,365	100
Chrysler						
Export	41,037	63.6	6,686	17.7	0	0
Domestic	23,464	36.4	31,102	82.3	57,730	100
TOTAL	64,501	100.0	37,788	100.0	57,730	100
GM						
Export	20,710	58.9	0	0	26,345	100
Domestic	14,444	41.1	18,470	100	26,345	100
TOTAL	35,154	100.0	18,470	100	26,345	100
Total Big Three						
Export	113,520	67.6	6,686	8.0	0	0
Domestic	54,432	32.4	76,608	92.0	137,440	100
TOTAL	167,952	100.0	83,294	100.0	137,440	100

3,494 per cent! Expressed in unit terms, retail sales of these cars amounted to only 2,575 in 1984 – and all were K-cars from Chrysler.

This meteoric rise in exports has produced similar results in the US sales of Mexican *captive* cars. In 1984, these sales amounted to only 2,575, but at the end of 1987 they totalled 92,540 cars. Expressed differently, in 1984 Mexican-assembled cars represented 2.2 per cent of the US Big Three's *captive* sales. Yet in 1987, this figure skyrocketed to 21 per cent, while those from South Korea added another 14 per cent. Preliminary 1988 figures indicate that the combined *captive* sales from both Mexico (23.1 per cent) and South Korea (26.0 per cent) have surpassed those from Japan, for the first time (47.9 per cent). By contrast, in 1984, sales from the Big Three's Japanese affiliates accounted for 85.5 per cent of all *captive* sales. Clearly, Mexico and South Korea, two LDCs, are surging to the forefront of the American captive marketing strategy. By the end of 1988, *captive* sales in the US amounted to 511,650 – an increase of 328 per cent over 1984 sales.

The surge in car imports from Mexico and South Korea has also been accompanied by rapid growth in auto parts, particularly from Mexico. From 1982 to 1986, these imports from Mexico increased from less than $480 million to almost $2 billion, and represented 60 per cent of all such imports in the United States.

THE POLITICS AND ECONOMICS OF CHANGE

Today, this reorganization of the Big Three's marketing strategies, from being entirely oriented toward the Mexican consumer to now aimed primarily at the US export market, appears natural and logical, but the circumstances under which these decisions were taken have been difficult and unexpected. Though Mexico's abrupt declaration in August 1982 that it was suspending, temporarily, interest payments on its approximately $86 billion foreign debt had several causes, the most important was the steep decline in international oil prices that produced an acute foreign exchange shortage. Subsequently, loans were restricted and FDI slowed to a trickle, which further exacerbated the foreign exchange crisis. The economic situation worsened in 1983 as inflation accelerated and GDP contracted by 5.3 per cent.

In addition to imposing foreign exchange controls, the Mexican Government publicly announced the 1983 Auto Decree to reduce the enormous balance of trade deficit in the auto industry, a deficit that burgeoned to almost $3 billion with the United States, during 1981 and 1982.

The key provision in the decree was the requirement that foreign automakers balance their foreign budgets, that is, match $1 of exports for every $1 of imports.

While this decree made the Mexican Government's intention unwaveringly clear, it actually took the coincidence of two other critical developments before Chrysler, Ford and GM committed themselves to the vigorous export programmes that have demanded annual investments of about $100 million from each. These two developments were the intensification of Japanese competition in the American car market, at the low end – relatively inexpensive sub-compacts and compacts – owing to the Japanese cost advantage; and the accompanying challenge to the Big Three to identify new, foreign sources of cheap labour that were capable of meeting the increasingly exacting quality standards of the American market. Throughout the 1970s and 1980s Mexican labour had been comparatively high-priced among LDCs, but from 1982 to 1986 the hourly compensation of Mexican auto-workers declined 42 per cent to $1.48 or 32 per cent lower than the Korean rate of $2.12. This substantial lowering of wages made Mexico very competitive, on a cost basis, and encouraged Chrysler, Ford, and GM to invest heavily in new, export operations. Yet, even after the key decisions were in favour of Mexico it took almost four years before all three began exporting cars in 1987.

US CAPTIVE IMPORTS FROM MEXICO, 1984–PRESENT

Since the implementation of the Auto Decree the Big Three have utilized their Mexican subsidiaries as increasingly important suppliers of *captive* imports for the US market. However, each of the automakers has developed very different programmes in an attempt to serve their specific marketing objectives and niches.

Ford Motor Company

Ford is the most recent entrant. 1987 marked the first year that the company exported cars from Mexico. These *captive* small, fuel-efficient sub-compacts sold for approximately $6,000 in the United States and were marketed as Mercury Tracers by the Lincoln-Mercury Division. About 60 per cent of the car's components were Japanese, and were sourced from Ford's foreign partner, Mazda. Ford's Mexican subsidiary has been the only supplier of the Tracer, which is not produced in the United States; it is also the only car that Ford currently produces in Mexico for the export market.

From the perspective of Ford's total US retail car sales in 1987, the 51,233 Tracers represented only 2.5 per cent, but from the vantage point of the Lincoln-Mercury Division they accounted for 8 per cent of sales. Given the recent announcement by Ford that it intends to source both the successor to its best-selling Escort and current Tracer from Hermosillo plant, it is clear that Mexico will figure more prominently in Ford's future. At present, the new model, slated for launch in 1990, is code-named CT-20; it will have a two-door version marketed under the Mercury nameplate, as the Tracer is today; and a four-door selection, the substitute for the Escort. This dovetailing of the Tracer/Escort plans is likely to extend the Mexican plant to its full capacity – 130,000 cars, while the remainder are supplied from the Wayne, Michigan plant.

After only one year, Ford's imports from Mexico represented 55.5 per cent of its US *captive* import sales in 1987; similar imports from its South Korean partner, Kia Motors, accounted for 29 per cent of such sales. These small sub-compacts were marketed as Ford Festivas and sold for slighty more than $5,000. In unit terms, 26,750 Festivas were sold or about half the number of Tracers. 1987 was also the initial year in which captives were imported from South Korea. In contrast to the other American manufacturers Ford continued to import captives from West Germany, the up-scale Merkur and Scorpio from Adam Opel, but these models totalled only 15.5 per cent of Ford's *captive* sales in the US. For 1987 Ford's total *captive* sales from Mexico, South Korea, and West Germany comprises 4.5 per cent of its US sales, compared with 0.7 per cent in 1986.

Chrysler Motors

If Ford was the last to adopt a captive import strategy, then Chrysler established this new trend, both in Mexico and Japan. Among the Big Three, Chrysler has produced the greatest variety of models for export. Unlike Ford and General Motors, Chrysler began exporting pick-up trucks, Dodge Ram Chargers, as early as 1985, in addition to cars. These truck exports have totalled more than 21,000 in each of the last two years, although their significance is declining, while car exports are growing increasingly prominent.

In 1984, Chrysler initiated its export programme in Mexico by producing Plymouth Reliants and Dodge Aries – K-cars – for the American market; in that year the company sold 2,575 of these cars as *captive* imports in the United States. Three years later this number increased by 1,092 per cent to 30,696 cars, which now included Chrysler LeBaron Coupes, as well as the K-cars; 46.4 per cent of Chrysler's Mexican captive sales in 1987 were LeBarons, while the rest were K-cars. These Mexican-made LeBarons comprised 14.0 per cent of all LeBaron Coupe sales in the United States. On the other hand, sales of similar Mexican captives, Plymouth Reliants and Dodge Aries, amounted to 8.0 per cent and 6.8 per cent, respectively, of total model sales in the United States in 1987. On a company basis the cars imported from Mexico represented 2.8 per cent of Chrysler's American sales.

The true significance of Mexico to Chrysler's overall *captive* important strategy can be understood better if these Mexican developments are compared with those that Chrysler has experienced with its Japanese partner, Mitsubishi. In 1984 Mexican car imports were about 2.8 per cent of the number imported from Japan; three years later, in 1987, cars imported from Mexico amounted to 26 per cent of approximately 120,000 captives imported from Japan. When the sale of these imports from Mexico and Japan are combined, then it is immediately apparent that *captive* imports constituted 13.8 per cent of Chrysler's American retail car sales in 1987, an increase of 61.6 per cent over three years – from 95,457 vehicles in 1984 to 151,033 in 1987. This dependence on *captives* is by far the strongest among the American automakers.

General Motors

For all intents and purposes, GM, America's largest car manufacturer, has been, along with Ford, the most recent exporter of passenger cars from its Mexican subsidiary. Although the firm actually began exporting small pick-ups (the unique El Caminos and Caballeros), these vehicles were recorded as US truck sales. On the contrary, the Mexicans recorded them as passenger car sales. In 1987, these vehicles were phased out and in their place GM initiated an export programme for Chevrolet Celebrities. For the year it sold 10,611 of these Mexican-made cars in the United States, which amounted to less than 1.3 per cent of its entire American car sales, but 3.35 per cent of all Celebrity sales. Although Mexico may appear as a tiny source of General Motors' total *captive* strategy, the recent reorganization of the Mexican operations under the Chevrolet Pontiac/Canada Division, and the accompanying announcement that as many as

100–200,000 Celebrities are likely to be exported to the United States by 1989–90 should dispel such an assumption.

GM increased its Japanese captives, from its affiliates, Isuzu and Suzuki, by 995 per cent from 1984–1987, a rate of growth that was more than ten times as fast as Chrysler's. These captive sales in the United States increased from 13,004 to 137,211 cars during the three-year period. In addition, General Motors began to import the Pontiac LeMans from its South Korea affiliate, Daewoo Motors, in 1987. For the year it sold 35,564 of these sub-compact captives in the United States after only seven months' production. South Korea is the sole source of the LeMans.

Taken together General Motor's total *captive* sales of imported cars for 1987 – Mexico, Japan, and South Korea – were 183,386 and represented about 5 per cent of the company's American car sales. Given the latest developments in 1987, it is certain that the captive strategy will become still more important to General Motors.

CONCLUSION

Three powerful conclusions have already resulted from the initiation of the US Big Three *captive* strategy in 1984.

Chrysler, Ford and GM have increasingly turned to Mexico and South Korea, as opposed to Japan, as primary sources of captive imports. In 1984 Japan accounted for almost 86 per cent of US *captive* sales, while those from Mexico barely accounted for 2 per cent, there were none from South Korea. By the end of 1988, it appears that Mexico (23.1 per cent) and South Korea (26 per cent), combined, have overtaken Japan (47.9 per cent). Clearly, the new energy in *captive* imports is located in the two LDCs with comparatively cheap labour costs.

The shift towards LDCs as low-cost producers of small relatively inexpensive cars has put enormous price pressure on foreign competitors like the Japanese and Germans who have traditionally competed in this segment. Volkswagen has already stopped manufacturing in the United States – it has failed – and will begin producing Golfs for the American market in Mexico. Yugo even more recently has gone bankrupt. The Japanese have responded by going up-scale instead of competing in this most volatile market segment (small sub-compacts).

Mexico and South Korea's continuing success has and will continue to increase the US trade deficit with those countries, but this negative effect may be ameliorated somewhat by decreasing Japanese exports, as a result of increasing transplant production, the high cost of the yen, and the existence of the VRAs.

To date, the *captive* import strategy has been very successful: it is likely to become even more important in the immediate future.

NOTES

This article is an attempt to systematize a vast body of statistical and auto industry information in order to clarify the growing importance of *captive* imports as a Big Three marketing strategy.

Although several books have been published during the past few years on the US auto industry, *none* has focused on *captive* imports or more particularly on the recent surge in Big Three imports from Mexico and South Korea. As a result, the researcher is dependent on collecting and evaluating industry statistics and developments for himself. Five major industry sources in the United States and Mexico have been used for their auto statistics as well as interviews with industry analysts and executives. The US sources are Motor Vehicle Manufacturers' Association of the United States, Inc. (MVMA); *Ward's Automotive Reports*; *Automotive News*; and United States International Trade Commission (USITC). The chief Mexican source is Asociacion mexicana de la industria automotriz (AMIA). While *Ward's Automotive Reports* and *Automotive News* are not formally cited, they were very important to the writing of this article.

REFERENCES

AMIA (1988) *La Industria Automotriz Terminal en 1987* (11 January).

MVMA (1988a) 'Passenger car sales in the US, reported by US manufacturers', RS-1 (11 January).

MVMA (1988b) *4th Quarter 1987, Economic Indicators: The Motor Vehicle's Role in the US Economy* (9 February) 14.

Chapter Sixteen

THE ROLE OF NETWORKING IN THE DEVELOPMENT OF SUCCESSFUL INNOVATIONS BY SMALL- AND MEDIUM-SIZED FIRMS IN THE UK MEDICAL EQUIPMENT INDUSTRIES

BRIAN SHAW

The increasing rate of products, markets and technical change, the impact of the development of a critical mass in technology in some developing countries, such as South Korea, enabling them to become potential technological competitors for the advanced countries and the increased complexity and cost of advancing technology are creating an increasing interdependence throughout the innovation cycle.

As Haklisch (1986) stated, the upward spiral of stakes and thus risks, in semiconductor technology and markets has reduced the ability of all companies, even the largest, to be self-sufficient in the total range of areas necessary for this growth in competitiveness. This development has resulted in organizations linking together to widen their base of scientific and/or technological resource to gain access to markets, especially Ohmae's Triad (1985) and to increase their flexibility and adaptiveness.

Rothwell's (1986) analysis of some of the literature on user–producer links supported his proposition 'that in many industrial sectors, user–need specification and product development involve more than simply a passive role for the user, and innovatory success is associated with active user involvement in product specification, design and development. Users also have an important role to play in the process of re-innovation. Moreover, it is users who are themselves technically progressive and innovation demanding who have the greatest potential in this respect.'

The development of these user–producer links parallels the development of Hammarkvist's (1984) network theory for the description and analysis of industrial markets. Here the firm is described in terms of network concepts, instead of traditional market concepts. An example of the networking model is illustrated by Tornqvist *et al.* (1985) when they describe CART (computer-aided radio therapy) as an interdisciplinary Nordic R & D programme based on active participation from users, science (medical and technological), and industry. The purpose of CART is to be a co-operative programme between nationally-financed projects and local activities in companies and institutes. The objective of CART is to design an integrated information system in radiotherapy for the next generation of technical systems. This programme's participants are medical product companies, other high-technology OEM companies, Nordfisk, Department of Oncology, Lunds Lasarett, Uppsala University Datacentre, Medical Computer Physics, Department of Radiation Physics, Malmo, all in Sweden and the Technical Research Centre of Finland, Medical Engineer Lab., Tampere, Finland, plus the Oncological Department of the University Hospital in Iceland. This formalization and funding of the networking system of centres of excellence seems to be a development, based upon a common cultural and geographic interdependence similar to the UK model developed below.

THE UK MEDICAL EQUIPMENT INDUSTRY

There has been a great deal of structural change in this industry, resulting in increasing dominance of the multinationals. There has also been a restructuring to form a band of companies with turnovers of about £5 million between the multinationals and the bulk in number of small companies who employ less than 200 people.

MEDICAL EQUIPMENT INNOVATION

The author's detailed research project into user–producer–intermediary interactions in the medical equipment industry (Shaw 1986b) fully supports Rothwell's proposition, but extends the work by introducing into the interactions the 'intermediaries' and the 'inside and outside product champions'. The analysis of the very effective formal and informal networking system used to develop medical equipment innovations substantiates Hammerkvist's networking theory in terms of industrial markets, but also extends it by applying it to the innovation process in the medical equipment industry. Also Von Hippel (1982) utilized the concept of the appropriability of innovations as the predictor of the functional locus of innovation. Whilst, as Rothwell says, this is a crucial factor, a second factor which was found to be vital in the research examined here, which should be added is the locus of state of the art expertise, that is, the locus being with the medical researchers/practitioners in their clinical and/or diagnostic expertise.

USER–INTERMEDIARY–PRODUCER INTERACTIONS

The sample of innovations, studied in the research examined here, was of thirty four medical equipment innovations developed and marketed by eleven small and medium-sized enterprises (SMEs), companies in collaboration with users and intermediaries. An example is The Cardiff Infusion System MK 3.

The Cardiff Infusion System

Oxytocin Infusion System (No. 18 in sample list) was developed by Graseby Dynamics (Pye) Ltd, in collaboration with Turnbull and Anderson of the Anaesthetics and Medical Physics Department of the Welsh National School of Medicine. It consists of a pump which is loaded by the insertion of an administration set. The pump is driven by an electric frequency controlled 'stepper' motor. The dose rate can be adjusted manually or automatically. A sensitive pressure transducer is coupled to the patient by an open ended fluid-filled catheter inserted into the amniotic fluid. The transducer output is amplified by a feedback controller amplifier and displayed on a meter. The output from the amplifier is also connected to circuits providing the necessary signals for operating the alert and dose rate control functions.

Functional utility

> A most successful substance (according to Turnbull and Anderson 1968) to induce labour in pregnant women is oxytocin. Because patients require widely differing rates of infusion to induce labour successfully, infusion starts at a low rate and the dose is increased every ten minutes until labour is established. This is achieved by means of measuring the frequency and strength of the patient's contractions, to regulate the oxytocin dose to the patient's needs.

Twenty-four of the innovations were developed such that they created a new product for the company addressed to their present market (the UK National Health Service [NHS]) using present technology. Another two innovations used new technology to develop new products for the NHS market. Three innovations used the companies' present technology to reposition the present products in their present markets. Five innovations created new products, using present technology for new markets.

The prime characteristic identified by the study of the medical equipment innovation process is that there are multiple and continuous interactions between the users, intermediaries, and producers throughout the process. In the sample of thiry-four innovations, twenty-six (76 per cent) were developed through continuous user–intermediary–producer interactions, resulting in twenty-two (65 per cent) being successful, one too early to judge and three being failures. The failures were due to unsatisfactory technical performance. A successful innovation was one that achieved the technical and commercial objects set for it.

The nature and frequency of this multiple and continuous user–intermediary–producer interaction is displayed in table 16.1. As table 16.1 indicated, the interaction consisted not only of joint prototype development, testing, product evaluation, and marketing, but also joint prototype development and product marketing and joint product specification and marketing. In seventeen (94 per cent) of the eighteen user-dominated (Von Hippel 1976) innovations, after the transfer of the user innovations to the producer, the users continued joint prototype development, testing, evaluation and marketing of their products with the manufacturer. In thirteen cases, the user specified the final product with the manufacturer. In eight of

Table 16.1 Frequency of multiple and continuous user–manufacturer interaction by classification of innovation

Classification of innovations	*No.*	*%*	*Multiple user–manufacturer interaction*					
			Joint prototype testing and product evaluation		*Joint prototype development and product marketing*		*Joint product specification and marketing*	
			No.	*%*	*No.*	*%*	*No.*	*%*
Basic equipment innovation	10	29	10	100	8	80	8	80
Major improvement innovation	8	24	8	100	6	75	4	50
Minor improvement innovation	10	29	5	50	3	30	1	10
Failures	6	18	2	33	2	33	0	0
Total	34	100	25	74	19	56	13	38

Source: *Shaw* (1985)

the 'manufacturer-dominated' (Von Hippel 1976) innovations, the user tested and evaluated the manufacturer's prototypes and helped market the final product. One user helped develop the prototype, test, evaluate, and market it, and one helped develop the manufacturer's prototype and market the final product. An example of the interaction between users, intermediaries and the SMEs is the development of the Sealed-Fluids Autoclave by Surgical Equipment Supplies Ltd.

SEALED-FLUIDS AUTOCLAVE

Surgical Equipment Supplies Ltd was founded in 1932 to develop and manufacture boiled water sterilisers. They developed two such models and also manufactured glass syringes and disposable needles. In 1964 the then Managing Director saw the potential for the greater development of the company outside the group which now owned it and effected a management buy-out. A major asset was its excellent standing with the NHS regarding the safety and reliability of its equipment.

The UK Department of Health and Social Security (DHSS) received various requests from its Area Health Authorities for a small autoclave suitable for sterilising sealed fluids. The Medical

Research Council (MRC) had a large autoclave which sterilized sealed fluids, but it was too large and cumbersome. There were manufacturers who built these enormous autoclaves with capacities of one to two hundred litres. One of these companies was a customer of Surgical Equipment for its smaller equipment. Because of the autoclave expertise in Surgical, the DHSS approached them to develop a small, safe, and effective autoclave for sealed fluids. The MRC advised them of the performance specifications required, based on their large autoclave, and Surgical worked closely with the manufacturer of the MRC autoclave, in developing a new small autoclave which could sterilise 5ml bottles. When the patent was taken out by Surgical on the sealed fluids autoclave, the large company, under licence, used the techniques developed in the patents to advance the performance of their own machine. The basis of the development by Surgical was against a specific order from the DHSS and with full co-operation from MRC, other DHSS experts, and full access to hospitals for clinical trials. The company developed and successfully patented a 'load simulator' for the equipment. The prototype was built and then tested for twelve months in-house because this testing was very dangerous. Having satisfied themselves, they tested a pre-production model for a further three months in a hospital. Although this new model was based substantially on previous autoclave modules, the build cost of the new hardware incorporated in the autoclave and the cost of the patented 'load simulator', coupled with the excellent design and performance of this equipment enabled the company not only to have a registered design for it, but also the need and ability to charge four times the price of their other autoclaves. The sealed fluids autoclave enabled this company to move into the private sector health care market by supplying autoclaves to small pharmacies, laboratories, and opticians, thus reducing their dependence on the public sector market.

THE USER

The user identified in this sample was the consultant clinician/physician whose prime objective is to develop state-of-the-art diagnostic techniques and/or therapies. These consultants work in the UK 'centres of excellence' (the fifteen undergraduate, six postgraduate teaching and research hospitals and twenty universities with hospital schools) with technicians, scientists and engineers. These teams work together to find new, more effective means of achieving better patient care through equipment innovations. The clinician/physician specifies a need, for example, for a means of monitoring the flow of blood in babies. The physicist, engineers, technicians, and nurses then work together with the consultant in an attempt to test out the conceptual basis of their solution to the need, usually in the form of a rough 'handmade' prototype.

NETWORKING

Activities are made known to the informal and formal networking system through personal contacts, through publication and presentation of papers at international conferences, articles in journals, and the writing of books: for instance, when G. D. Searle and Co. Ltd collaborated in the development of the Neonatal Oxygen Monitoring System with Dr Parker of London's University College Hospital (UCH), the university team had worldwide contacts with the ten major 'centres of excellence' concerned with this area of development. Parker gave papers at international conferences detailing the clinical results using the Searle probe, and the professor in charge of the neonatal unit at UCH, where the probe clinical trials were done, acted as a 'reference point' for expert advice to other potential users on the most effective way of using the probe. In addition, another member of this network was an 'Intermediary', the Medical Research Council (MRC), who seconded scientists and engineers to UCH's team and/or funded some of the staffing and prototype development costs. The professor in the neonatal unit used his international reputation to influence the MRC's actual involvement in the project. Because of this close networking of fellow researchers, the university team was introduced to a new use for the oxygen probe – the continuous monitoring of venous oxygen in adults. This was in turn developed by Searle in collaboration with the researches in the UCH team, resulting in another successful innovation, the Venous Oxygen Probe. The advances made in developing this product were taken into account in the re-innovation stage of the innovation cycle of the original neonatal system resulting in a significant increase in functional utility.

As identified in the Neonatal Probe case study, the results of the clinical trials are only available to the physicians and clinicians who do the trials and, therefore, some means of dissemination of data to other potential users and producers has to be effected. The three principal means of communication found were: (1) personal contract (41 per cent); (2) the presentation of papers at international conferences, professional meetings, and industrial liasion groups (21 per cent); (3) publication of articles in professional journals (21 per cent). Credibility is given to the equipment through the personal networking system and publications because a 'peer group' buyer behaviour pattern exists in the purchase of medical equipment. The strong linkages to sources of information external to the centres of excellence is a major source of the consultants' power in these centres. The dominance of the consultant in the process of effective use and purchase of medical equipment results from their perception of the effectiveness of the equipment in improving diagnostic skills of enhancing therapeutic ability. The prime base for these judgements is the clinical results achieved by using the equipment. The acceptance of these results is a function of who carried out the clinical trials and their degree of personal contact in the network. This 'peer group' buyer behaviour relayed very specific signals to the medical technology decision makers, the Area Health Authorities, and were fully accepted. Evidence was present in twenty-seven of the innovations of peer group buyer behaviour. This 'peer group' buyer behaviour mirrored that found by Coleman *et al.* (1966) in the diffusion of the drug Gammanym. He found that doctors relied on the experience of their peers, conveyed in interpersonal networks for evaluative information about the innovation. Similarly, Greer (1984) found that the collegium deferred to the judgement and preferences of a requesting physician.

The firms studied therefore locked into this complementary asset (Teece 1986) of peer group behaviour through their interaction with users and intermediaries.

INTERMEDIARIES

The intermediaries are the MRC scientists and/or engineers; the DHSS, which has a consultant in every medical discipline who links into the networking system: the Department of Industry (DOI) which gives pre-production orders to equipment; and the British Technology Group (BTG), previously the NRDC. The importance of these intermediaries can be seen in that the MRC acted as intermediary for twelve innovations, the BTG for eleven, the DHSS for four, and the DOI for one (Shaw 1985). The principal interaction mechanisms which these intermediaries bring to the innovation process are: (1) patenting; (2) the funding of user and manufacturer research; (3) provision of engineering and the scientific skills to users and manufacturers by the MRC and DHSS and the development by them and the MRC of their own innovations with chosen users and manufacturers; (4) purchase of prototypes, pre-production and production models.

1 The BTG patenting of eleven innovations, ten of which were successful, was seen by the small companies as the major benefit of this form of interaction.
2 In 1981–2 the DHSS funded 101 R & D and 84 evaluation projects. The industry funding by the DHSS tends to be initially for feasibility studies. If the new idea or product appears feasible, further funding will be made available for all stages up to prototype development at a normal level of funding of up to 50 per cent of the cost. The DHSS also has a pump-priming budget for the seeding of new products.
3 The MRC second scientists/engineers to units who do not have the necessary expertise and also develop their own innovations with users and producers. The MRC supplied experts for the innovations.
4 The DOI, under their pre-production order scheme purchased six of the pre-production models of Innotron's 'Hydragamma 16' for £6,000, on the understanding that this money would be refunded on the commercial sale of the instruments for £9,500.

'INSIDE AND OUTSIDE' PRODUCT CHAMPIONS

The MRC experts mentioned above worked as 'outside' product champions with the manufacturers to develop, test, and evaluate the prototypes and pre-production models.

These 'outside' product champions, in co-operating with the inside product champions, determined the role and the nature of the product development and the final form of the resultant innovation. These outside product champions were coupled with inside product champions in thirty-one of the innovations. The evidence of the research suggested that the status of the majority of the outside product champions in their own organisation, especially where there was more than one product champion, was matched by the status of the inside product champion, and these outside champions were positive driving forces in ensuring that user needs were reflected fully in the final design. Previous research on product champions has not identified the existence of these outside product champions, but in the innovation process analysed here they had a significant role to play. If these public sector actors in the innovation process can be effective in facilitating successful innovations, this mechanism should be encouraged and developed as part of public health care policy, especially if focused on SMEs in the industry.

FUNCTIONAL LOCUS OF INNOVATION

Von Hippel (1982) hypothesized that the differences in the 'functional locus' of the innovation were dependent upon the differing abilities of innovators holding these different functional relationships to a given innovation to appropriate benefits from the innovations. This applied in the development of these innovations, in that the user was able to appropriate output-embodied benefits from the innovation which neither the supplier, producer, nor the intermediary were able to obtain. The output-embodied benefits are those gained through the existence and use of the medical equipment. For instance, the medical equipment developed is capable of enabling a particular clinical objective to be achieved, that is, the functional utility of the Cardiff Infusion System. The achievement of the clinical objective gives the clinician a greater understanding of bodily functions, greater diagnostic ability, and the basis for further research. The experience of testing and evaluating the equipment before it becomes commercially available gives the clinician a significant advantage both in terms of research expertise and practice in the implementation of the therapy or diagnosis developed. In addition, the world-wide diffusion of knowledge, best practice and social benefits through the 'Invisible College' (Crane 1972) increases the status of the consultant in this college.

This increased status may bring extra financial rewards and/or licence fees and/or profits from the ownership of the companies producing and marketing the equipment.

Three of the eleven companies studied were set up by entrepreneur users to develop further and to market products which they considered warranted the risk of starting their own business – Innotron Ltd, P. K. Morgan Ltd, and Oxford Medical Systems. Two other companies, Rigel Research Ltd and Surgical Equipment Supplies Ltd were also set up by entrepreneurs who worked in the medical equipment industry, Rigel being set up from scratch and Surgical being a management buy-out by their managing director. They identified gaps in the marketplace through being part of the networking system.

Innotron was started by Professor Chard of London's St Bartholomew's Hospital to develop a multiple Detector Head Gamma Counter for Radioimmunoassy. Chard was an expert in and a founder member of the study of radioimmunoassy. The first multi-detector system was developed by Searle Analytic, but was superceded by the sixteen head directional counter, the NE 1600, developed by Nuclear Enterprises Ltd. This counter reduced the total counting time from 85.3 min to 3.3 min (1979). Chard was Nuclear's consultant on Radioimmunoassay and it was as a result of a brainstorming system which he led that the concept of the NE 1600 was born. Because of its quite dramatic impact on the productivity of the routine RIA laboratory, especially his own at Bath, Professor Chard decided to set up his own company to develop a solid state gamma counter using sophisticated software so as to engineer around Nuclear Enterprises patents. He was successful after two and a half years' development and evaluation in hospitals' laboratories, and, by August 1981, fifteen months from launch, had sold 160 units of the Hydragamma 16 at a price of approximately £9,600 each.

Where users had a high probability of deriving these

'output-embodied' benefits, the more involved they would want to be and they would become the functional focus of the innovation. Where these benefits were not perceived to be present, they would try not to become involved. The closer these benefits are perceived to be to enhancing state-of-the-art knowledge, the greater will be the user involvement. Where state-of-the-art knowledge resides in the user in terms of clinical diagnosis and/or therapy, the fashioning and interpretation of clinical trials and the dissemination of their results, the functional locus of innovation must reside principally with the user. It is therefore important that the SMEs develop equipment which will help enhance the state of the art knowledge thereby ensuring close involvement of the user in the successful development of such equipment.

The intermediary benefits, for example, MRC, from an efficient use of its funding and personnel and acting as an effective medium for the transfer of technology: the DHSS from the diffusion of technology throughout the service and effective use of clinical, scientific and engineering personnel; the BTG from licensing income; and the DOI from effective use of its funds in stimulating the international competitiveness of the industry. In addition, the intermediaries facilitate the transfer of private and social benefits to both the user and the producer, but also retain some social benefits themselves.

The producers' output-embodied benefit is reflected in the profit and sales achieved and the positive image generated from producing socially responsible products. These profits are gained through establishing a quasi-monopoly through the use of patents, trade secrets and 'response time'. With all of the innovations that benefited primarily from the presence of trade secrets, the response-time benefit was also present. Because of these inter-relationships, it is difficult to quantify exactly the significance of any of these mechanisms individually (Shaw 1986b).

DISCUSSION

Thus the innovating firms have enhanced their private returns and transferred some of the social benefits to themselves by developing close interactions between users, intermediaries and themselves. It would seem that improving the mechanisms of these interactions or even making companies have a more proactive stance with regard to interaction would ensure increased capture of private innovation benefits.

Similarly, by stimulating effective interactions the manufacturing sector could become increasingly competitive. As Rothwell and Zegveld (1985) stated, since much of the state of the art research in many fields in many countries is performed in universities, government laboratories and other public sector institutions, clearly the above results have implications for public policy.

With the increasing need for multi-disciplinary teams to cover the spread of skills necessary to develop commercially effective technological innovations, linkages and networking will become more and more important.

It is therefore essential that SMEs effect strategies which enable them to become members of or enhance the networking systems of users, producers and intermediaries in the innovation process.

REFERENCES

Coleman, J. S., Katz, E. and Menzel, H. (1966) *Medical Innovation: A Diffusion Study*, Philadelphia: Bobbs Merill.

Crane, D. (1972) *Invisible Colleges: Diffusion of Knowledge in the Scientific Communities*, Chicago: The University of Chicago Press.

Greer, A. L. (1984) 'Medical conservatism and technological acquisitiveness: the paradox of hospital technology adoptions, in New York'. *The Social Impact of Medical Technology:* 4: *Research in the Sociology of Health Care*, New York: JAI Press.

Haklisch, C. S. (1986) 'International technical alliances agreements in the semiconductor industry: company-to-company agreements', paper presented at the Lucca Conference on Technical Co-operation and International Competitiveness.

Hammarkvist, K. O. (1984) 'Markets as networks', paper presented at the MEG Conference.

Ohmae, K. (1985) *Triad Power: The Coming Shape of Global Competition*, New York: Free Press.

Rothwell, R. (1986) 'Innovation and re-innovation a role for the user', *Journal of Marketing Management* 2: 109–23.

Rothwell, R. and Zegveld, W. (1985) *Reindustrialization and Technology*, London: Longman.

Shaw, B. (1985) 'The role of the interaction between the user and the manufacturer in medical equipment innovation', *R & D Management* 15/4: 283–92.

Shaw, B. (1986a) 'Appropriation and transfer of innovation benefit in the UK medical equipment industry', *Technovation* 4: 45–65.

Shaw, B. (1986b) 'The role of the interaction between the manufacturer and the user in the technological innovation process', D. Phil. thesis, Science Policy Research Unit, University of Sussex.

Teece, D. J. (1986) 'Profiting from technological innovation: implications for integration, collaboration, licensing, and public policy', *Research Policy* 15: 285–305.

Tornqvist, J., Moller, J., Vitanen, J., Dahlin, H., Nilsson, M., and Myrdel, G. (1985) 'CART: computer-aided radio therapy', *Proceedings of the XIV International Conference on Medical and Biological Engineering and VI International Conference on Medical Physics*, Espoo, Finland.

Turnbull, A. C. and Anderson, A. B. M. (1968) 'Induction of Labour', *Journal Obstet. Gynaec. Brit. Cwlth* 75: 24–31.

Von Hippel, E. (1976) 'The dominant role of users in the scientific instruments innovation process', *Research Policy* 5: 213–39.

Von Hippel, E. (1982) 'Appropriability of innovation benefit as a predictor of the source of innovation', *Research Policy* 11: 95–115.

Chapter Seventeen

COMPETITIVE DISTRIBUTION NETWORKS

The Finnish magazine paper industry in the UK

BO FORSSTRÖM

This study[1] relates mainly to foreign market entry by the Finnish paper industry into important European industrial markets (UK, West Germany, France, etc.) for highly-differentiated paper grades in the 1980s. In this case it is not the question of entering new markets, but rather of penetrating a market where firms already have positions in the distributing networks.

Since the 1950s the UK market has established itself as the most important single market area for Finnish paper products. During the 1960s and 1970s newsprint was the most important single bulk product, but in the 1980s more differentiated products – especially magazine paper – SC, MF woodfree, and LWC grades – have also been rapidly increasing in volume. In short, the fastest growing market has been the magazine paper segment, where the annual increase has been between 15–25 per cent since 1985.

Since 1947 Lamco Papers Sales Ltd have been the main British supplier of Finnish paper through the sales organization Finnpap.[2] Finnpap is the sales and exporting organization of the Finnish paper mills to foreign markets and behind Finnpap were eleven paper companies in 1988. They represented twenty-one paper mills, with a capacity of 5.9 million tonnes, and their share of total Finnish paper export was about 75 per cent. This means that other Finnish producers also have access to the British market outside the distribution channels of Finnpap-Lamco. But together they have established a very strong position in the British market certainly since the 1950s, and even from the prewar period. Tailor-made qualities for British customers together with the high technical capabilities of Finnish paper mills have developed and maintained excellent customer relations.

In the 1980s the single distribution chain scene started to change. Several Finnish companies who specialized in more differentiated products and grades broke out of Finnpap to set up a new direct network for supplier–customer relations.[3] There are several strategic reasons for establishing direct market and distribution channels, for example, the possibility of establishing independent product profiles and grades under brand names, but also achieving access to direct market information and closer producer–user relationships.

Consequently parallel market and distribution networks now exist for Finnish paper in the UK and the aim of this chapter is to describe these competitive distribution networks by analysing the buying behaviour process for magazine papers. The main research problem here is the impact of interaction between Finnish producers and distributors to British buyers in the UK market. A set of variables that describe different aspects of the interaction between suppliers and buyers in the distribution network will highlight possible differences in the perceived distance between the two parts in the network. The focus is thus in an information-related exchange. The approach will be the Swedish 'market as networks' approach, where changing micro- and macro-positions describe the firm's relationships with specific counterparts and the relations to a network as a whole.

THEORETICAL FRAMEWORK

A traditional model for distribution of board and paper

The international paper and board market varies greatly depending on grades, quantities and markets. Although the paper industry is considered a mature industry, trading with different countries does not confirm any straight-line pattern. Based on empirical foundings, marketing is, however, mainly in accordance with the model shown in Figure 17.1 for sales channels.

Many paper mills have their own sales organization, with agents throughout the world, and mills with complementary product ranges co-ordinate their marketing by joint selling, for example through a central sales organization. This is very much

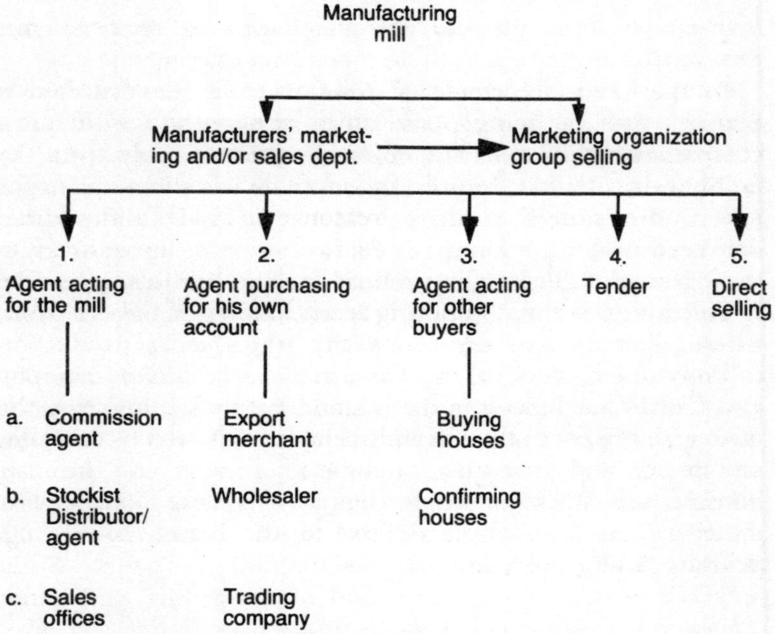

Figure 17.1 Paper and board sales channels
Source: Prodec, s.50

the case for Finland through Finnpap, although some firms have changed the distribution chain scene so that both indirect and direct distribution channels form a competitive distribution network.

Finnpap-Lamco distribution channel

Finnish paper products have traditionally been exported through Finnpap, and this is rather unique. Finnpap is owned by its member companies, and its main task is to sell the entire volume produced by the member mills. Beside marketing and product planning, Finnpap looks after their entire export procedure (land transport, shipping, pricing, financing, and documentation). In the UK market Finnpap is represented by Lamco Paper Sales Ltd.[4] The sales company (former agents) Lamco concentrates upon operational tasks. This co-ordinated approach should ensure that the producing mills are fully aware of market developments and changing customer requirements, thus ensuring the best possible service to customers.

Finnpap can be seen as a *focal* actor in the distribution network with far more power in its relationships with forest companies in Finland than might be assumed, only from the point of distribution. Indirect influence on investment plans for new product ranges and direct influence on grades and volumes delivered underline Finnpap's focal position in the network to the UK market. From a single firm's perspective this, according to Finnish marketing literature, is an example of *indirect export*, where Finnpap can decide on the single mill's production capacity due to sales volume from the year before. So Finnpap and Lamco are links in a distribution network connecting the mills with buyers in the UK industrial market, which comprises newspaper and magazine publishers; printers and printing houses; and stockists, wholesalers and trading houses. The industrial market is here defined as the British converting, printing, and graphic industry.

Direct distribution channels

Due to structural changes in the Finnish forest industry, that is, a clear tendency to larger company formation through mergers and joint ventures, there is a strong trend towards highly specialized and diversified products. With more resources and assets in house several companies have invested in internal market networks, thus creating *direct distribution channels* to the UK to gain from closer co-operation with their major buyers in the industrial market. For example, the Finnish state-owned Enso Oy is now represented through Enso Publication Papers plc (a subsidiary company) and distributes *direct*, thus competing with Finnpap. Kymmene Oy – one of the largest forest companies in Finland – has, through foreign investment, set up a production unit in Scotland, Caledonian Paper plc, and will distribute directly to UK customers via internal channels. Both Enso and Kymmene/Caledonian represent direct distribution channels through wholly-owned subsidiaries in the UK. These are two examples of different business strategies, one representing direct export and market investments in the UK through an extended marketing network (Enso Oy); and the other representing downstream (to raw materials) and forward integration through market investments in extended marketing and extended production capacity (Kymmene Oy).

Both examples combine some of the strategic elements in Porter's (1980) model for analysing the competitive forces of industrial structure and the main empirical findings from the buying behaviour study will finally be given a strategic evaluation following the Porter line.

The competitive distribution network

The two distribution channels described above form a distribution network where different actors positioned in the network are related in a supplier–buyer relationship through *bonds* in exchange with a strong two-way interaction regarding technical service and product development (information-related exchange). Due to the products and grades in question, the suppliers have close relations with their major industrial buyers. The fact that sales departments have specialized knowledge of customers' needs, and of the coated and uncoated grades supplied, guarantees expert technical support for buyers. Very strict quality control at the mills in Finland should ensure a consistent quality and the technical service departments monitor the performance of different qualities supplied in order to provide further checks in printing performance. So *functional quality* is very much the core question in the interaction between suppliers and buyers.

Technical support from the mill level and the sales organization level is also applied to *new product development*. The printing and paper converting industries are characterized by the changing needs of their customers, through the introduction of new technology and improved processes. So investment in improved and new grades and modifications to existing ones match the changing demands of the industrial market for papers. The single distribution chain perspective has changed into a parallel distribution network, combining direct and indirect distribution links from suppliers to industrial buyers. The balance is thus changing from only dyadic relationships to *triadic* relationships, emphasizing a competitive distribution scene with several directed to buyers using supplier portfolio strategies.

The industrial market perspective

Aware of the long historical industrial and business tradition (see Fidler 1987) behind Finland's position as a main supplying country (see Appendix 1) of paper and board for the UK market, the industrial marketing focus should not be on products or on markets but on buyer–supplier relationships (Webster 1979). It is also obvious that a simple 'top-down' strategic approach (Turnbull and Valla 1986) cannot easily be applied in an industrial market, where the products are tailor-made for major industrial buyers, and where the products meet very strict *functional* and *technical* qualifications. In this chapter these products are SC, MF, and LWC grades for offset and gravure printing processes (see Appendix 2). Following the terminology in the network approach this means that the products and grades can be classified as *heterogenous*.

Market entry strategic decisions are not initiated on a corporate level among top management as an entirely internal process. Recent developments in industrial marketing theory with their focus on the interaction approach (Turnbull and Cunningham 1981, Hakansson 1982) stress the interaction between buying and supplying companies, as well as the management of single main supplier-customer relationships (Johanson and Mattsson 1987). Also studies analysing technological processes in an industrial marketing perspective emphasize technical exchange between different actors, and innovations and product development can be seen as a result of an interplay between several actors networking together (Hakansson 1987).

Markets as networks

The Swedish 'markets as networks' approach (Johanson and Mattsson 1987) stresses exchange relationships with customers co-ordinating interaction between the actors. One aspect of those relationships, *bonds* of various kinds, are developed between firms, for example technical, knowledge, social and legal bonds. The network is characterized by complementarity and there are of course important competitive relations and possibilities. The relationships imply that there are specific interfirm dependence relations which differ from the relations in the traditional market model.

When a network is set up – in a new market or when a change in distribution channels is implemented – old, existing relationships are broken up, or new ones are added to existing ones. Initiatives can be taken from both ends of the network.

This approach underlines the firm's activities as cumulative learning processes where relationships are established, maintained, developed, and broken in order to give a satisfactory, short-term economic return, and to create positions in the network securing the long term survival and development of the firm. From a strategic point of view this market position in the network is an important concept.

The *micro-* and *macro-positions* in the network stress the importance of the firm's relationships with specific single counterparts and the relations to a network as a whole. Thus the macro-position is not an aggregation of all micro-positions. All in all, marketing activities in networks serve to establish, maintain, develop and break relations and to handle the actual exchange. Since activities are cumulative, one important marketing problem is related to investments.

Market investments in networks

Investment processes are related to the creation and acquisition of both tangible and intangible assets for the future. The basic assumption in the 'market as networks' approach is that a firm with specific internal assets is dependent on external resources controlled by other firms. Positions in the network can give the firm access to these external resources and, over time and with effort the firm's 'market assets', generate revenues for the firm via other internal assets.

The firm can develop its position by establishing relationships with counterparts in national nets, new to the firm; this is an *international extension*. The firm can *penetrate* by increasing resource commitments in a net where the firm already has positions. The third possibility is *international integration* through increasing co-ordination between positions in different national nets.

Hammarkvist (1983) identifies five general situations relating the company to the market network. These categories are:

- the company is outside a network that it wishes to enter;
- the company is in a network but feels threatened;
- the company wishes to change its position in a more drastic way than by merely adapting to the evolution of the network;
- the company has a stable position but must adapt technologically to changes in the network;
- withdrawal from a network.

This network approach sees marketing as a border function balancing between the *internal resources* of the company and assets and demands of the customers in the network. The implication of this approach (Paliwoda and Druce 1987) is an institutional perspective focusing between micro- and macro-marketing where tasks can be directed not only to the market but also to strategic commitments and supplier-customer relationships. This means that the focus is on the intermediate case between *markets* (external relationships) and *hierarchies* (internal relationships) whereby marketing problems become closely linked with investments and organisations.

The basic idea in this paper is the evolution of the patterns of interorganisational contacts (information-related exchange) between supplier and customer in the distribution networks. By using the two alternative distribution channels available, the perceived distance (proximity) can be described between supplier and customer, and a chosen number of variables will highlight the indirect and the direct distribution scene over all and in detail to find structured behaviour.

THE EMPIRICAL BACKGROUND

A recent study[5] highlighting the buying behaviour for magazine papers and the importance of technical information in the paper market in the UK gives some interesting results regarding the positions and qualifications of the actors in the distribution network. This study consists of interviews with a sample of important publishers and printers using magazine grades in the UK. The main focus was on interaction in the buying process and the variables that describe the supplying/buying company, the customers, the competition, demand–price–supply questions, the British publishing and printing industry and a future scenario. The small sample allows only qualitative analysis but the carefully chosen sample represents the main customers in the UK market for magazine papers.

Main empirical findings

Although the strategic setting – very limited in this study – from a theoretical point of view varies between the distribution channel alternatives, everyday behaviour in the UK industrial market for magazine papers was very similar – even if the intrinsic possibilities of Caledonian Paper plc are taken into consideration. Due to the use of specific paper grades some *differences* in behaviour were obvious between publishers and printers, the latter having more purely technological interests whereas publishers were more interested in the whole product and in lay-out and other visual aspects of the paper grades. Printing techniques (offset and rotogravure) divided customer interest into specific categories. SC grades are suitable for rotogravure, but LWC grades are suitable for offset printing methods; MF grades are not suitable for LWC printing machines etc. Ninety per cent of SC grades go to publishers of magazines (50 per cent of this to Sunday supplements), and 10 per cent to printers and stockists. LWC grades are shared 50:50 between publishers and printers/stockists.

Some *general characteristics* could be seen in the industrial market for magazine papers:

- extremely strong and personal bonds between supplier and customer, which means an intense need to discuss innovative capabilities, technical qualities, price-setting, and aftersales services;
- in both distribution channels the supplier-customer relationship ranged over periods of over forty years;
- major customers use supplier portfolios: for SC grades publishers use 1–2 other suppliers; for LWC grades 2–3 other suppliers with printers using 2–11 suppliers in general;
- all three firms have an almost entirely British sales and marketing staff;
- annual contacts between mill and customers, visits to Finland or visits to the UK;
- sales organization–customer contacts personal: major customers visited twice a month and minor customers every second month;

- although long-standing relations with customers, with printers every deal is a new deal (volumes, grades, prices, deliveries);
- a fairly long-term span to achieve orders from new customers between 6–12 months;
- the supplier portfolio strategies used by major UK customers underline the competitiveness of German and Dutch suppliers with as advanced innovative capacity and product planning, thus demanding offensive distribution and production strategies.

Some firm-specific profiles are shown in table 17.1.

Table 17.1 Profiles of Lamco, Enso, and Kymmene/Caledonian

Lamco
Competition: German, Dutch, (Finnish)
Each sales person: 18–25 customers
Multiproduct company
Mill profile of grades to publishers and brandname of grades to stockists and converting industry
Market leader in LWC (50 per cent) and SC (70 per cent)
Volumes and pricing from Finland
Customer portfolio; all market/customer strategy
Sales staff education: technical qualifications import
Main supplier orientation: five publishers buy 35 per cent of LWC grades and five printers buy 27 per cent of uncoated grades
Enso
Competition: Finnish
Each sales person: forty to forty-five customers
Middle range product comp. (with additional products from Finland)
Always brandname to all customers
Equal shares with two other Finnish producers of MF
Volumes from Finland but pricing in UK
Mixed customer strategy: 50 per cent national magazines and 50 per cent regional magazines
Sales staff education: technical qualifications important
Main supplier orientation: on MFP grades
Kymmene/Caledonian
Competition: Finnish, German, Dutch
Each sales person: fifty to sixty customers (?)
One-product company
Brandname (name still a matter of confidence)
Target market share 20 per cent in LWC
Volumes and pricing in UK
Customer portfolio; all British customer categories
Sales-staff education: user side oriented, especially towards publishers
Main and minor supplier orientation

Conclusions from the empirical study

The main empirical findings and the firm-specific profiles of buying behaviour in this study cannot confirm any clear differences in perceived distance behind the theoretical distribution alternatives as such. Anyway some results from the empirical study indicate that the brandname possibility and the intensive need for technological information exchange takes the buyer closer to the supplier. Still, in my view it is more a question of single priorities and nuances from single individuals and actors in the network.

On the other hand, one should notice that Enso's new micro-position in the distribution network is of a very recent date and might still alter in quality, while Caledonian's marketing activities still relate to the 'pre-selling' stage.

Thus both printers and publishers strongly stress the need for close relationships with the supplier. Both suppliers have had longlasting relationships with their customers and Enso simply took over 'old' customers for specific grades from Finnpap. Therefore one cannot stress too much the argument of learning/ experience as the single logic behind the internalization of networks.

Although tempted, I will not stress the value of some kind of 'stage model' behaviour in this chapter, simply because reverse behaviour is not even possible in this particular case. Instead the strategic setting, bonding the customers, is a much more thrilling theoretical question here. So I end up with the quite trivial notion that this study raises as many questions as it tries to answer. But before going over to empirical conclusions in a strategic perspective, a few general remarks on the qualifications of the actors in the distribution network. With two new entrants in the UK market for magazine papers, *the network has opened up, both in micro- and macro-positions*. Enso has now penetrated the UK market by stronger commitments – internal market investments – outside the Finnpap-Lamco distribution chain. Enso's internal distribution network is definitely a challenge to Finnpap-Lamco and certainly Caledonian's even more so. These two are entrants (Porter 1980) forcing Finnpap-Lamco into a defensive position, in relation to paper grades and supplier choices. Enso's micro-position is now closer to the customer in the network (brandname, differentiated tailor-made grades) and the macro-position of the network will be changed when Caledonian reaches the market position, in terms of production and distribution. So offensive market investments in extended market assets bond customers closer to the producer, in the case of both Enso and Kymmene. Changing positions in a competitive distribution network can lead into changes in inter-organisational behaviour and as a consequence that might influence the intraorganisational structure in firms. These aspects are outside this study.

To sum up, from a Finnish–British perspective the competitive scene is changing fast in the short term through a *new* micro-position balance in the network and a *stronger* macro-position for the Finnish–British network overall. But overall distribution network positions are of course also influenced by other foreign actors and institutional factors.

The strategic perspective and the distribution network

But also other foreign competitors (for example German Feldmuhle, and Haindl, Dutch KNP) have basically the same opportunities as the Finnish companies. When to this is added forthcoming British home production, the whole competitive network for global distribution and marketing takes on its full scope.

Although the market for magazine grades in UK is constantly increasing, the Caledonian output in 1989 will threaten Finnpap-Lamco severely, not only in UK with a 20 per cent target share in LWC grades, but possibly also in the EC market. So old users of Kaukas/Kymmene grades will probably accept the new Irvine/Kymmene grades, thus forcing Finnpap to direct former UK export volumes to other foreign markets. Enso will broaden their narrow MF assortment with additional grades achieved through changes in owner structure at mill level in Finland (the Varkaus mill).

All in all, it is obvious that Finnpap-Lamco will have to be prepared for substantial losses in market shares with these changes in the micro- and macro-positions of the competitive distribution network in the UK.

With new foreign direct investment strategies within the EC market the Finnish paper industry will further weaken

Finnpap's position as a major supplier by setting up internal direct distribution networks. After 1992 and with the tendency to increased protectionism globally, joint sales organizations such as Finnpap may be viewed as cartels. In this situation UK-produced (and also elsewhere-produced) volumes will gain from closeness to raw materials, shorter distribution chains, local brand names, etc. In this perspective Irvine/Kymmene will gain a very strong strategic position and its increased production capacity (to be doubled from the initial 170,000 tonnes) can be directed to other attractive markets inside the EC.

The final notion underlines the importance of integrating all global actors and institutional forces analysing the competitiveness or distribution networks or how a firm's activities in one country affect or are affected by what is going on in other countries (Porter 1986). Integrating Porter's value chain way of reasoning could be useful for an understanding of how firms keep their core competence in house, but for example, externalize their productive tasks. The case of Irvine/Kymmene comes close to this setting. Here it meant sharing the high investment costs of £215 million with British investors and incorporating an externally-financed leased paper machine, thus producing in the UK but keeping the key technological core skills in house in Finland.

So, combining the Porter line of strategic analysis with the Swedish market as networks approach, adding the locational flexibility framework (Christensen 1988) could be a fruitful way of analysing the global industrial market scope. Studies of micro- and macro-position balance in distribution networks is only one way of highlighting aspects of competitiveness stressing perceived dimensions of the network. The overall strategic setting must be applied if the aim is to analyse global competitiveness and this requires a locational flexibility framework to deal more explicitly with the frictions of space.

NOTES

1 This study is a part of a dissertation project 'Technological strategies in the Finnish paper industry: a network approach', where different market networks and innovation and technological networks are analysed in a strategic context.

2 Finnpap was founded in 1918 as The Finnish Papers Mills Association

in order to promote and market *Finnish* paper on a world-wide basis as a joint marketing organization. Finnpap is the largest paper exporting company in the world, with a network of subsidiaries and agents in fifty countries and customers in 125 countries.

3 These companies are Kymmene Oy 1976, Lohjan Paperi Oy 1984, Enso-Gutzeit Oy and Tervakoski 1987 and A. Ahlström Oy 1988.

4 A sister company, Varma Services Ltd, handles storage and physical distribution to support Lamco's sales activities in the UK.

5 This study is a part of the dissertation project 'Technological strategies in the Finnish paper industry'. The empirical part of the study is based on interviews with seven major magazine publishers and printers and with sales and marketing directors for Lamco, Enso, and Caledonian Plc in the UK. The study was completed in the summer of 1988 and was undertaken by Outi Oinonen, MSc (Econ.) from Åbo Akademi in Finland.

REFERENCES

Christensen, P. R. (1988) 'Enterprise flexibility and regional networks', paper for the 28th Regional Science Association Conference, Stockholm.

Fidler, I. (1987) *The History of LAMCO*, London: Outline Creative Limited.

Finnmap World, (1988), Helsinki.

Hakansson, H. (1982) *International Marketing and Purchasing of Industrial Goods: An Interaction Approach*, Chichester: Wiley.

Hakansson, H. (1987) *Industrial Technological Development: A Network Approach*, London: Croom Helm.

Hammarkvist, K. O. (1983) 'Markets as networks', Marketing Education Group Conference Proceedings, Cranfield Institute of Technology, Bedford, England, July, pp. 567–581.

Johanson, J. and Mattsson, L. G. (1988) 'Internationalisation in industrial systems – a network approach' in N. Hood and J.-E. Vahlne, *Strategies in Global Competition*, London: Croom Helm.

Oinonen, O. (1988) 'Den finländska pappersindustrins marknadsföring av journalpapperskvaliteter till Storbrittanien', unpublished MA thesis in international marketing, Faculty of Economics and Social Sciences, Åbo Akademi.

Paliwoda, S. J. (1986) *International Marketing*, London: Heinemann.

Paliwoda, S. J. and Druce, P. (1987)*Industrial Marketing and Purchasing* vol. 2, 1 pp. 3–25.

Porter, M. E. (1980) *Competitive Strategy*, New York: Free Press.

Porter, M. E. (1986) 'Changing patterns of international competition', *California Management Review* vol. 28: Winter 1986 pp. 9–40.

Prodec/Handbook on Procurement of Paper & Board, Helsinki (1987).

Turnbull, P. and Cunningham, M. T. (1981) *International Marketing and Purchasing: A Survey Among Marketing and Purchasing Executive in Five European Countries*, Basingstoke: Macmillan.

Turnbull, P. and Valla, J-P. (1986) *Strategies for International Industrial Marketing*, London: Croom Helm.

Webster, F. E. (1979) Industrial Marketing Strategy, New York: Wiley.

Appendix 17.1a Finnpap's main markets in 1987

	'000 tonnes	%
UK	1142	23.2
Germany	536	10.9
USA and Canada	544	11.1
Finland	418	8.5
USSR	317	6.4
France	343	7.0
Japan	137	2.8
Netherlands	149	3.0
Denmark	160	3.3
Australia	106	2.2
Other countries	1069	21.6
Total Finnpap sales	4921	100.0

Appendix 17.1b UK consumption of paper and board 1987

Main supplying countries	*'000 tonnes*
Finland	1559
Sweden	1238
Norway	300
Canada	389
West Germany	436
Netherlands	296
France	254
Austria	111
USA	218
Others	481

Appendix 17.1c UK consumption by grade 1987

	'000 tonnes
Newsprint	1605
Printings and writings	2677
Tissues	520
Packaging board	2754
Packaging paper	454
Industrial and speciality	723
Total	8733

Appendix 17.1d Lamco sales

	1987 '000 tonnes	*Share of each market %*	*1988 forecast '000 tonnes*
Newsprint	364.5	23	316
Specialities	17.5	27	14.5
TD, lightweights	60	83	57
SC	221	71	236.5
Coated mech reels	192	46	220
Bulky book papers	35.5	55	35.5
Other mechanicals	14.5	26	14
Uncoated woodfrees	104	10	101
Coated woodfree	2		11
Coated mech sheets	13.5	22	17.5
Wallpaper base	34.5	34	33
Kraft papers	33	8	33
Other specialities	25	4	28
Total sales	1117	13	1117

Appendix 17.2 Magazine paper grades in 1988

MF SPECIALITY

A paper grade to be used when relatively high bulk and low basis weight are needed. Moderate information capacity and good stiffness at a competitive price. The grade is especially designed to be printed in cold set offset or letterpress, but can be printed in HSWO if ink-tacks are reduced.

SC ROTOGRAVURE

The most economical magazine paper grade when 4-colour printed by rotogravure. Due to low roughness and ink absorbency and good brightness and gloss, the information capacity is relatively high. Paper volume is low, making the grade especially suitable for publications with high pagination.

SC OFFSET

The grade is also well known under the trade names WSOP, RR-Offset and Jetset etc. The grade has the SC rotogravure grade's character with little two sidedness and high density. The grade is designed for TV magazines, supplements, direct mail advertising materials, etc. where good information capacity is needed. As the grade name indicates, the paper is best used in the HSWO process with inks of medium tackiness.

SURFACE TREATED OFFSET PAPER (STP)

SC offset production, begun in 1979–80, is now followed by a new generation offset grade. The new grade is also a supercalendered paper where special attention has been given to the surface strength and printed gloss potential. Because of its low ink absorbency, good surface strength and optical properties, the grade is recommended for use in mass circulation magazines and similar products printed in HSWO.

MF PIGMENTED (MFP)

A coated paper with high volume, opacity, stiffness and good readability properties. The grade is designed for use in special interest magazines where good readability and high quality illustrations are needed. The high brightness, semimatt surface and good opacity give the end product a distinguished appearance. The grade is recommended to be printed in HSWO process only.

LIGHTWEIGHT COATED (LWC)

The paper to be used when high information capacity is required. High smoothness, brightness and gloss give the printer brilliance and contrast. The higher basis weights (65. . .80 g/m) are successfully used by special interest magazines, where high quality advertising is a must. The low basis weight papers are best used in high paginated magazines and catalogues. The grade is available for both HSWO and gravure. The matt finished version is only manufactured for HWSO.

MEDIUM WEIGHT COATED (MWC)

This grade is also known as a double coated grade. The second coating creates a homogeneous surface suitable for the most demanding print quality. The high basis weight makes the paper most useful as a cover stock and as a grade for special interest magazines.

Chapter Eighteen

CHANGES IN INDUSTRIAL NETWORKS AS FLOW-THROUGH NODES

GEOFF EASTON AND ANDERS LUNDGREN

A network actor has a number of options available when faced with a change initiated by another network actor. In this paper the characteristics of these options are described. In terms of change sequences actors may reflect, absorb, adapt, transmit, or transform the change. They may also change its amplitude, either increasing or reducing it. Finally they can disperse or concentrate the impact. These options are exemplified using a case study of the development of the Swedish computer imaging industry. Analysis of the application also provides a framework for analysing change sequences in terms of the competitive/co-operative context and the relationship of the change to a nodal actors core activity. Finally the characteristics of whole networks comprising pure and mixed change sequences are described.

Change in industrial networks is a continuous process. Some changes are relatively discontinuous, others occur in the evolutionary fashion. It is arguable that changes of the former type reveal more about the structure and processes of networks and that is the reason that they have been studied more intensively than changes of the latter kind (Hakansson 1986). Recently attention has been drawn to the processes which may drive change in networks (Hakansson 1990). As befits a network view these studies look at networks as a whole. However, networks can also be viewed from a less elevated viewpoint. Analysis of the midrange (Easton and Smith 1986) or small group analysis (Laage-Hellman 1988) not only provides insights into the operation of networks at a microlevel. It also offers an aggregative alternative to the usual top down disaggregative perspective. In summary, if we understand the workings of small components of a network there is, at least in theory, a chance that we can predict network processes as a whole. Thus in this paper a midrange approach to network change is described and used to make predictions about network processes. The approach is illustrated by means of a short case study of the development of the Swedish computer imaging industry.

The basic concept during the analysis that follows is what might be called flow-through nodes. Actors in a network may be regarded, for purposes of theoretical analysis, as nodes connecting flows. In this case the flows are the two-way resource exchange processes which can be said to form the backbone of networks. In this way the complexities of networks are simplified to allow for easier theoretical analysis and to allow the use of physical analogies from the physical sciences to be employed. The ultimate usefulness of this process lies in the insights which it generates and not in the surface similarities or dissimilarities between physical and social/technical/economic systems.

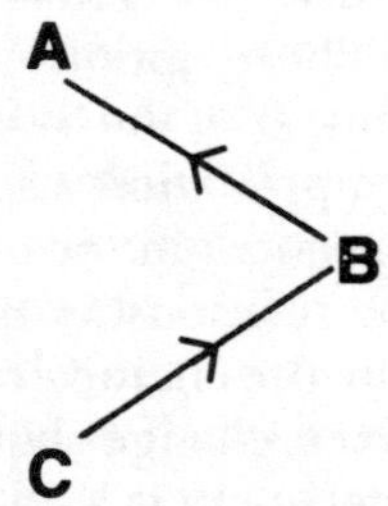

Figure 18.1 Network triad

Figure 18.1 illustrates a simple small group triad which will form the basic unit for the analysis that follows.

In the figure, three actors or nodes are connected by two exchange relations. This might be, for example, three manufacturing firms in a typical manufacturing channel. Organization B is the node through which flows will be analysed and it will be assumed that changes are transmitted from the organization C. Such changes may themselves have been 'passed on' from organizations with which C has exchange relationships or may have been initiated within C itself. Network theory would suggest, however, that in the latter case the spontaneous ocurrence of change within an actor is largely illusory. Such changes almost inevitably occur, it is argued, in the space between organizations. However, in this type of small group analysis the boundaries are tightly drawn around the group concerned and thus whatever the processes of initiation, the change may be regarded as originating in organization C.

The change to be modelled is one which may alter the form, structure or content of an exchange relationship, temporarily or permanently, in any of the dimensions used to characterize such relationships, that is, economic, social, technical, legal, or informational. For some well regulated, stable, homogeneous relationships, changes of the type defined above may be quite rare and easily distinguished from the baseline activity. For other relationships, each new exchange episode, whether because of the implicit heterogeneity of the exchanges or the time between them, may contain novel features compared with the last. What is important here is how the nodes act upon changes rather than the context in which they take place.

Changes as dealt with in this paper also include situations where new exchange relationships either of the type A–B or B–C are formed. Clearly the two situations are rather different. Changes within existing relationships might well be termed network working/adaptation; those involving the formulation of new relationships might be called network change/restructuring. In principle the differences may not be so important. It is the flow-through node process which is being examined here and the change which initiates the process may well be in the form of the establishment of a new relationship. The network effects of such a change are the crucial parameters.

As examples of the types of changes, one might include alterations in product specification, payment terms, delivery times, quality levels, contractual terms, staffing and personnel reporting, and co-ordinating procedures and joint activities. It is also useful to distinguish between requested and executed changes. Clearly one actor in the network can demand a change of another, but it is not certain that the demand will be met. Some changes can, of course, be made unilaterally, but will have a major impact on the relationship.

It is perhaps necessary to acknowledge that the changes described here are likely, in practice, to be affected by the context, particularly the network context, in which it takes place.

By characterizing the change as independent of context we may be in danger of oversimplifying in order to theorize. Some analysis of change by context is provided later in the chapter.

CHARACTERIZING FLOW-THROUGH NODES

There are a number of dimensions which can be used to describe the possible processes by means of which changes such as those already described may be transmitted through a network. The first of these dimensions can be labelled change sequences and five sequences are identified and described below.

The first sequence is described as *reflection*. In this sequence C requests or initiates a change in the exchange relationship with B, which B either rejects or nullifies, that is, B reflects the change back to the initiator. Rejection is meant to imply refusal of a request; nullification describes a situation where a unilateral action is reversed, for example, a consignment of a redesigned product is returned. Why should reflection occur? The most fundamental reason is that the nodal actor cannot, or perceives it cannot, comply with the request. The inability to perform may lie not only with the nodal actor but also wholly or in part with the net of other actors to which they are connected. Thus the nodal actor may, in one sense, be replying on behalf of that net. 'We can machine the material if it is on this form, but we cannot purchase that kind of material.' The roles of perception and network awareness become important at this juncture. The request for change is not passed on; the nodal actor assumes it knows what is feasible for the appropriate net. The nodal actor acts as a gatekeeper, and in sparsely connected nets there may be no means by which C can assess the validity of B's claim.

The second reason for reflection is that the nodal actor chooses not to accept the change. In this situation it must be the case that it feels that the change is in some sense detrimental. The detriment may be manifest in the relationship itself, for example, a request for a price reduction. It may also be seen as adversely affecting the position of the nodal actor in the network, for example, a request by a customer to a supplier to use a specified component in the manufacture of the supplied product. Whether the reflection can be made to stick depends on the relative power of the actors, the availability of alternatives and their desires and objectives. In any case the initiating actor is left to make the necessary adjustments or accept the stuatus quo.

The second sequence may be termed *adaptation*. In this case the change is managed between the organizations rather than by one or the other. It may be that the requested change is modified in negotiations between the organizations such that the objectives of the change are met but the means by which it is achieved are different from those first envisaged. For example a component specification change may be shown to be unnecessary if the product it is being incorporated in is manufactured in a slightly different way. Alternatively a compromise may be reached such that the impact of the change is shared, in some sense, by both organizations. In any case the change is localized within the dyad and does not substantially affect the rest of the network, at least via the nodal actor.

The third sequence is *absorption*. In this instance the nodal actor B accepts the change and absorbs the impact within the boundaries of the organization. For example the phrase 'absorbing a price increase' is common parlance in industry.

Again it is probably helpful to distinguish two situations in terms of the matter of choice. A nodal actor may be unable to pass on the effects of the change since the activities concerned are solely within its own control and no network solution is apparent. This could occur where the change involves a manufacturing process which requires particular skills and no subcontractors are available. A second situation arises when an actor chooses to absorb the change. Such may occur in technological development where an actor chooses not to involve other network members since in doing so they might be letting valued information and skills outside their control.

The fourth sequence, and the one which is largely assumed to be modal in discussions of industrial networks, is *transmission*. In this sequence the nodal actor B simply transmits the effects of the change or proposed change to one or more other members of the network (A) with minimal change in the form or interpretation. 'Passing price increases on' is a phrase which describes this process quite well. Even where rather complex changes are required, transmission implies that all such changes should be handled by the network and not the nodal actor. In other words the nodal actor wishes to minimize the impact of the change upon itself. This is not necessarily a sensible strategy since in doing so they may well be improving the network position of other actors at their own expense. Organizations which are essentially assemblers or assorters may, however, have little recourse except to transmit change in a rather transparent way. They act as a conduit and may simply be unable to even interpret the change to others. Or, as in other cases, they may choose not to get involved but rely on the competence of the net of which they are a part to cope with the change.

The final sequence is *transformation*. Transformation occurs when a nodal actor accepts the demand for a change but is both willing and able to change both the production and exchange activities it undertakes. One would, for example, imagine a situation in which the production activities change little but the network is asked to change quite considerably. The more usual situation is where both must change. The transformation sequence is clearly the most difficult to describe since the envelope of possibilities is very large. For example a request for shorter delivery times might lead to redesign of the product and demands for a new set of raw materials and components (albeit from the same actors).

There are two other nodal characteristics which are likely to have an impact upon network operation. The first might be called amplitude modification. It captures the extent to which the size rather than the character of the change presented to the node is modified. Size as defined here is not always an easy variable to capture. At its simplest it might represent the way in which a nodal actor passes on changes in demand from its customers to the rest of its supply net. Forrester (1961), in his study of industrial dynamics, modelled the processes by which distributors responded to demand changes. In some cases predicted shortages of supply in the fact of increased demand were met by increasing the demands upon suppliers by a factor greatly in excess of what was actually required. This was done in the hope and expectation that something like the required amount would be forthcoming via some sort of scarcity allocation mechanism. The effect was, of course, to amplify the change at each stage of the distribution/manufacturing channel and present the ultimate suppliers with an entirely false picture of the demand for their products. Such demand quickly collapses when the actual demand is met and downstream actors cancel their excess orders. The resulting system is eminently unstable. However by introducing appropriate levels of stockholding into the channel the demand changes can actually be reduced rather than amplified, stabilising the system, albeit at extra cost.

One can imagine other changes the impact of which can be amplified by a nodal actor. Improvements in delivery times required of suppliers can be exaggerated. Customer product quality changes can be used as a lever, by a nodal actor, to get even better quality components from suppliers. Price reductions demanded by the ultimate customer can be used by a nodal actor to improve their own margins. Clearly the nodal actor may also reduce the amplitude of the initiated change.

If transformation describes the qualitative ways in which actors alter the demands placed upon them, then amplitude modification is concerned with the quantitative ways in which those same changes are handled by a nodal actor. Central to this process is the extent to which the nodal actor is prepared to absorb change or pass it on to the rest of the network. If a nodal actor amplifies the change, this is tantamount to passing on the impact of the change to the rest of the network and even, perhaps, attempting to improve their position as a result. Whether or not this strategy is successful depends upon a number of factors already identified earlier in the paper. However this represents a fundamental decision for any nodal actor. Do they use internal resources, change internal activities to cope or do they attempt to use their relationships with other actors to help them out? The former strategy may consume resources and reduce their perceived efficiency, for example, not passing on price reduction requests to suppliers. It may also increase their long-run effectiveness and strengthen their network position, for example, by developing new lower cost ways of carrying out the same activities. The whole process of absorption versus transmission and amplification versus reduction is not only crucial to the success of the individual firm but also to the *modus operandi* of the network of which it is a part.

The third and last nodal characteristic is termed dissemination. It is however closer to a network characteristic since it concerns the number of other actors involved in the change. When a change is required of a nodal actor which in turn requires the network to support that change, the nodal actor has the choice of involving many or few other network actors in the process. For example if a product specification has to change, it is possible to work with just one supplier to solve the problem or to do so by involving several, either competitively or co-operatively. The former strategy has the advantage when it is simply a case of re-arranging existing resources and activities. However, if the response requires combinations of resources or activities not already dedicated to the existing activity set then the second strategy has the advantage. This would be particularly true where the change requires information flows different from those already in existence. Such a process could be described as *dispersal* (see figure 18.2).

By contrast, particular nodal actors may *concentrate* rather than disperse the impacts of a change. This is particularly likely where a number of actors connected to the nodal actor demand the same or complementary changes. In this case the nodal actor may be able to identify one or a small number of actors with whom they have relationships capable of meeting the change. Distributors, par excellence, have this capacity to aggregate demands for change and see it concentrated upon a small section of the net of which they are a part.

Also possible in the concentration process is the existence of a trigger/threshold effect. The change may be reflected by the

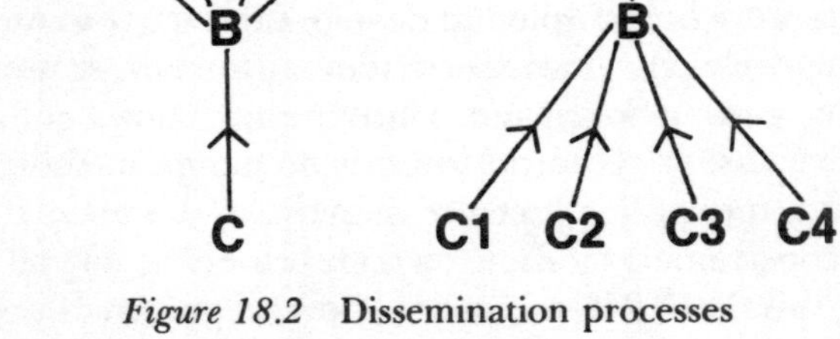

Figure 18.2 Dissemination processes

nodal actor until a critical number or weight of initiating change triggers off the flow through the node.

AN ILLUSTRATIVE CASE STUDY: THE DEVELOPMENT OF THE SWEDISH COMPUTER IMAGING INDUSTRY

In the mid-1960s a young, ingenious Swedish researcher, Nils Aslund, and his group, hereafter called Physics IV, developed an image reading instrument system (IRIS). Through this system it was possible to transfer data extracted from certain images automatically to computers. The system replaced previously manual and semi-mechanical methods of spectroscopy. IRIS was one of the first image processing computers developed in Sweden. It was presented at a local exhibition and a Saab–Scania division showed great interest in the system. Saab–Scania had previously initiated the development of two other scientific instrument systems, and they perceived IRIS as complementary to their approach. The two actors came to an agreement and Physics IV sent the blueprints to Saab–Scania who developed, internally, commercial versions of IRIS and the other two systems. When the three systems were completed, Saab–Scania marketed them as their approach to imaging. Saab–Scania were however unsuccessful in their attempts to interest their customers in the systems. The only IRIS produced was sold back to Physics IV in 1972, where it still was in use in 1987.

The initial sequence between Physics IV and Saab–Scania was one of absorption. Because Saab–Scania had already developed two instruments of a similar nature to IRIS, they were able to develop commercial versions without too much recourse to other network members; that is, without asking them to do things they were not already doing. Conversely the sequence between Saab–Scania and its customers was clearly reflection. Customers were being asked to change their current methods of operation, replacing manual or semi-automatic scanning by a completely automatic system. Clearly they chose not to do so perhaps because it required too much change in their internal systems for too little perceived benefit or because they were network constrained by their own customers or suppliers.

During this time IRIS was used by several groups of researchers from different scientific fields. This usage of the instrument showed that most of the problems could be solved with less sophisticated image processing computers. Physics IV therefore developed a small-sized processing computer, OSIRIS, based on a previously developed scanner. At this time, 1979, the Swedish Board of Technological Development launched a programme for their product development in the emerging Swedish image processing industry. OSIRIS became a part of this effort to support a high technology industry. To convert the scientific achievements of OSIRIS to a commercially successful product, Physics IV once again approached Saab–Scania. By this time Saab–Scania had, however, changed their direction towards industrial automation and therefore they were not interested in the development of OSIRIS. Instead they suggested that Physics IV should contact another division of Saab–Scania, here called by their present name Saab Space.

Saab Space showed a great interest in the development and production of OSIRIS. The production technology in the space industry and at Saab Space can be characterized as highly flexible at a high technological level and thus well suited for projects such as OSIRIS. Saab Space believed, though, that they lacked sufficient resources for the marketing of OSIRIS. They contacted Hasselblad, a well known Swedish camera producer highly reputed also within the space industry, and asked them if they would be interested in the marketing of OSIRIS. To Hasselblad, unfamiliar with electronics, OSIRIS seemed to be an interesting complement to their production of cameras. Through their existing marketing channels Hasselblad had access to a market. Furthermore OSIRIS promised to introduce Hasselblad to opto-electronics, an area of the highest importance in the development of the camera of the future. To support the project the Swedish Board of Technological Development demanded that an interested potential user should be involved in the project. The group approached the Swedish Space Corporation and asked them their potential uses for OSIRIS. The Space Corporation's main interests in image processing were in the field of remote sensing. By taking part in the development of OSIRIS they hoped to avoid having to develop image processing systems internally.

The sequence illustrated in figure 18.3 is a rather extended form of transmission. Physics IV did not have the resources to launch a successful image scanner. Saab Space passed on their need for a customer base to Hasselblad, and all of them required of the Swedish Space Corporation that they act as a development customer. Only some of the required changes were transmitted, others were absorbed.

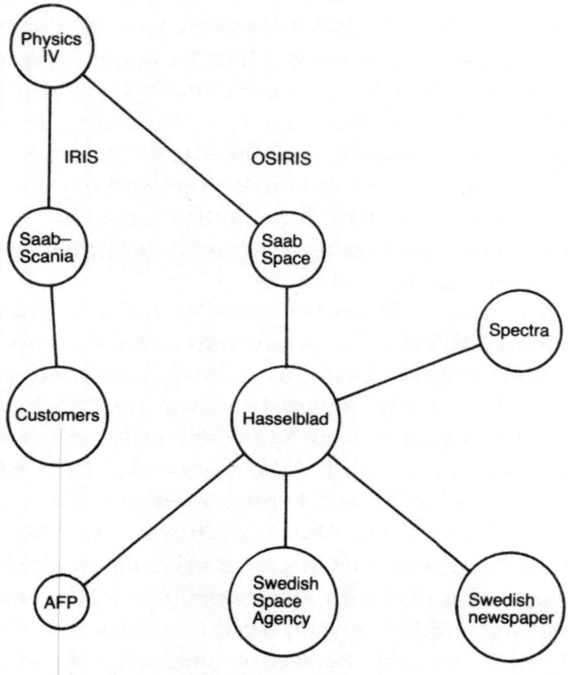

Figure 18.3 Diagram of part of the Swedish imaging network

The OSIRIS project was not a technical success. Hasselblad left the project, though they did not abandon opto-electronics. In 1982 it was obvious that opto-electronics had the potential to dominate the future of photography, and Hasselblad decided to prepare themselves for this technology. Through their relationships with the international press, Hasselblad formed a new project, aiming at the development of a digital image transmitter, Dixel. The basic technology used in the development of Dixel was similar to the technology used in OSIRIS, but Dixel was more appropriate considering Hasselblad's main business. In the pursuing of the Dixel project Hasselblad appointed several persons experienced in micro-electronics. For the development of the image transmitting parts of Dixel, Hasselblad contacted a newly established Swedish firm, Sectra, one of the leading actors in this area. Hasselblad also persuaded a Swedish newspaper to adapt the traditional analog receiver to the new digital technology. The first prototypes of Dixel were presented and used, by the Swedish newspaper, during the summer Olympic Games in Los Angeles in 1984. The existence of a new digital image transmitter, produced by Hasselblad echoed through the press world.

Here we have an example of transformation. The original request by the OSIRIS group to deliver a customer network has been transformed, by Hasselblad. Employing similar technology they convince a supplier and a customer to get involved in the development of a new product, Dixel.

In the further development of Dixel, Hasselblad came in contact with AFP (Agence France Presse). AFP were developing a total and fully digitized system for the handling of pictures at newspapers. In this system a digital image transmitter was needed. AFP and Hasselblad came to an agreement that Hasselblad should adapt the transmitter to the AFP system. Together with AFP and some other actors the second generation of the digital image transmitter was specified. One specification that posed some internal problems was that the system would not be able to transmit images taken with the Hasselblad camera. In 1985 Hasselblad initiated the development of the second generation of Dixel. In the development and production of Dixel, Hasselblad were able to use some internal resources. Some resources were also developed internally, but mainly sources outside Hasselblad were tapped, the most important one being Sectra. Sectra were well established in a network for the development and production of electronic systems and to manage the changes suggested by the new specification. Through their relationship with Sectra Hasselblad were able, not only to meet the specification, but to go beyond it. Sectra were responsible for the production of specific parts of Dixel. They also developed more general systems for image compression and transmission, which they supplied to other image processing actors. In 1986 the second generation of Dixel was completed and more than twenty systems delivered to AFP. Hasselblad also delivered Dixel to some Swedish newspapers.

This sequence offers examples of transmission and transformation. It also exemplifies adaptation. Hasselblad and AFP worked together to adapt Dixel to the current AFP system, even though in doing so Hasselblad had to accept, in the early stages, that the resulting system would not use their camera. The respecification was transmitted to Sectra who not only drew on their own network, but also established a broader market by transforming the request to accomodate more general systems.

What is evident from this analysis is that while the sequences can be distinguished, events are often rather more complex than a simple categorization can handle. This is only to be expected. It seems particularly problematic that changes involving new relationships offer a greater variety of responses than those which do not. The next empirical step should be to concentrate on changes in existing networks, that is, adaptation/working. It is also clear that, as with many other aspects of network operation, phenomena are mixed in nature. Thus it was clear that parts of some changes are absorbed, parts are transmitted and parts are transformed. Knowing this it then becomes important to look at the components of change to see which are more likely to follow through which sequence. However even this analysis suggests some rather general results and these are discussed in the next section.

FACTORS AFFECTING CHANGE SEQUENCES

Why do different actors behave differently towards the same type of change? From the case study two sets of variables seem to emerge; the relationship of the change to core activity and the competitive/co-operative context of the network.

The change required of an actor may be more or less peripheral to its core activity. Core activity describes both the existing production activities undertaken by the actor as well as the value placed upon them. Clearly if an actor is asked fundamentally to change the nature of what is being done, then the chances of that happening are slight. Even where the actors would be prepared to accept new and different activities it is not certain that they would be successful in organizing themselves to do so.

Relationships between actors will usually be a combination of the competitive and the co-operative. Where the activities undertaken are highly substitutable the relationship will tend to the competitive; where they are complementary they will be rather more co-operative. Axelrod however reminds us that neither of these statements should be taken wholly for granted.

If we take just these two variables each comprising, for the sake of simplicity, two categories then a matrix of contexts for change behaviour can be described, as in figure 18.4.

		Core activity	
		Change is external to core activity	Change is internal to core activity
Competitive context	Competitive	Reflection	Absorption
	Co-operative	Transmission	Transformation

Figure 18.4 Relationship between contexts and change sequences

Reflection occurs where relationships are competitive and the nodal actor is being asked to perform outside its core activity. Where the change is within existing core activity, competition persuades the actor to absorb change either to protect resources or because other competitors would simply reflect the change.

Conversely, in a co-operative network, change which is external to core activity is simply transmitted. Co-operation demands some form of assistance but since the activity required is peripheral, the most the nodal actor can do is to pass the request on. Where the change is internal to the core activity co-operation demands that the nodal actor does what is possible then sends transformed changes to other actors to access their co-operation.

Adaptation, under these assumptions lies at the centre of the matrix. The change requires activity midway towards the core so that absorption or transformation are not fully possible. Similarly reflection would be too harsh an alternative at the co-operative/competitive midpoint and transmission would be less than a modicum of co-operation would demand.

NETWORK EXTENSIONS

Having examined the characteristics of flow through nodes and how they are likely to be influenced by contextual and nodal characteristics, it will be useful to attempt to work through the implications of patterns of flows for network processes as a whole. Networks which comprise actors with different patterns of nodal characteristics must be expected to operate rather differently. In the first part of this section networks comprising only one type of node are described and the implications for network operation described. In the second part of the section some networks with actors having different nodal characteristics are described.

A network comprising actors operating in a reflecting mode, it could be argued, is most likely to simulate the ideal of an economist's atomistic market. Clearly strong relationships would not prosper in a situation where all changes are denied. The most obvious question is how the network, if such it can be called, operates at all. The answer lies in the ability of any actor to change exchange relationships at will and with low transaction costs. Thus the network would have patterns of rapidly changing exchange relationships, none of them particularly strong, and relatively stable, inflexible actors who are more likely to disappear under the wheels of evolution than adapt.

A network of adapting nodes would be more like the traditional view of a network with one significant difference. Since changes are localized to a dyad the pattern might be said to epitomize the difference between the interaction and network approaches. Such a network could only exist where co-ordinating activities within the actor are not especially important compared with the ability of the boundary functions to solve problems without having recourse to other resources/activities within the actor. An example of such a situation is where a firm produces a portfolio of relatively unrelated products/services serving, and served by, rather different networks. Heavily divisionalized organizations provide another example. Both of these examples, however, call into question the notion of actors and their boundaries.

A network comprising absorbing nodes is likely to have somewhat similar characteristics, that is, local aggregations of intense dyadic relationships with little in the way of network effects. However, the nodal actors would be differently organized. An absorbing node needs to be highly flexible, well resourced and well integrated in order to be able to take upon itself the onus of meeting the changes without recourse to the rest of the network. A network comprising actors of this type would be rather 'dead' in the sense that network activity would be confined to localized interactions. One can imagine such a network in a localized, self-sufficient community comprising rather small organizations with highly flexible technologies.

Transmitting nodes introduce network effects proper. In theory if all nodes simply transmit the change then any change affects the whole network. The network is completely linked and, in one sense, transparent. It would also be remarkably sensitive to changes and, as a result, rather unstable. Distribution is one type of activity where transmission of change is likely to occur rather quickly and without modification, since the form of the product remains unchanged by the 'productive process'. However, the size of each change is likely to be rather small in this situation, resulting in continual small adaptations rather than daily revolution.

Transformation is different from transmission in that the nodal actor may interpret or transform the change for the rest of the network. In this situation the network remains sensitive to change and transparent but the form of the change is highly unpredictable in advance. If, in a network of transmitting nodes the change initiated is one which demands faster delivery then all the actors in the network have to deliver more quickly. However, in transformation based network this change may result in many different types of changes throughout the network. Such a network corresponds most closely to a typical manufacturing based network.

Networks are most likely to comprise mixtures of the different types of nodes and indeed the same actor acting as different types of node at the same time. What is of interest is not whether pure types of network exist but what the mixture is at any point in time and what impact that has upon network operation. For example it is clear that transmitting and transforming nodes must be damped by the existence of adaptive and absorbing nodes otherwise the networks would be too sensitive to change. Absorbing and reflecting nodes might provide the practical boundaries to a network. Transforming nodes could provide the leavening and creativity which tranform the whole network even if only one or two of them exist.

CONCLUSION

It is always dangerous to take notions from the physical sciences and attempt to employ them to describe social systems. The nodes and flows ideas described here are, in part, adapted from electronics. However, it is to be hoped that the provenance of an idea does not weigh heavily in its evaluation. The characterization of flow-through nodes, as yet in a rather crude analytical form, does, we argue, offer real insights into network operation. It provides, albeit at a microlevel, a feel for the dynamics of network processes. It offers a new direction from which to attack the complexity that makes network analysis both frustrating and exciting.

REFERENCES

Easton, G. and Smith, P. C. (1986) 'Network relationships: a longitudinal study', *Proceedings of the Third IMP Seminar*, Lyon.

Forrester, J. (1961) *Industrial Dynamics*, Cambridge, MA: MIT Press.

Hakansson, H. (1986) *Industrial Technological Development: A Network Approach*, London: Croom Helm.

Hakansson, H. (forthcoming) 'Evolution processes in industrial networks', in G. Easton and B. Axelsson, *Industrial Networks*, London: Routlege.

Laage-Hellman, J. (1988) 'Industrial networks: a small group analysis', unpublished doctoral dissertation, Uppsala University.

INDEX